The Last Templar

The tragedy of Jacques de Molay
last Grand Master of the Temple

ALAIN DEMURGER is an honorary lecturer in medieval history at the University of Paris. He has written and published extensively on the military religious orders which grew out of the crusades, including a history of the Templars and a general work on the 'soldiers of Christ'.

ANTONIA NEVILL is an accomplished translator of French history into English. Her translations include François Furet's *The French Revolution*, Maurice Agulhon's *The French Republic*, Serge Lancel's *Carthage: A* .... *he Roman Conquest of* .... many others.

D1078250

The Last Templar

The tragedy of Jacques de Molay
last Grand Master of the Temple

Alain Demurger

translated by

Antonia Nevill

P

PROFILE BOOKS

This paperback edition published in 2005
First published in Great Britain in 2004 by
PROFILE BOOKS LTD
58A Hatton Garden
London EC1N 8LX
www.profilebooks.co.uk

First published in France in 2002 as *Jacques de Molay* by Éditions Payot & Rivages

1 3 5 7 9 10 8 6 4 2

Typeset in Fournier by MacGuru
info@macguru.org.uk

Printed and bound in Great Britain by
Bookmarque Ltd, Croydon, Surrey

A CIP catalogue record for this book is available from the British Library.

ISBN 1 86197 553 8

Published with the kind assistance of the French Ministry of Culture

Liberté • Égalité • Fraternité
RÉPUBLIQUE FRANÇAISE

CONTENTS

Maps viii

Picture Acknowledgements ix

Preface xiii

1 1250 – Molay's Youth 1

2 1265 – Jacques de Molay, Rank-and-file Templar 20

3 1273 – Thomas Bérard and Guillaume de Beaujeu. Two Masters, Two Policies for the Temple? 34

4 1292 – Grand Master of the Order of the Temple 53

5 1293 – Journey to the West 73

6 1300 – The Isle of Ruad 95

7 1303 – Cyprus 111

8 1306 – Plans and Problems 139

9 1307 – In the Snares of the King of France 154

10 1309 – Escaping the Trap 173

11 1314 – Burnt at the Stake 193

12 Conclusion. A Portrait of Jacques de Molay 206

Notes 223

Contemporary Popes 257

Genealogies 258

Chronology 262

Bibliography 268

Index 277

'Quar nous navons volu ne volons le Temple mettre en aucune servitute se non tant come il hy affiert.'

(For we did not and do not wish the Temple to be placed in any servitude except that which is fitting.)

MAPS

1   The Mediterranean at the time of Saint Louis' Crusade (1248–54)   x

2   The Templar fortresses and the end of the Latin States of the East (1260–91)   54

3   Mongols, Mamluks and Templars around 1300   94

PICTURE ACKNOWLEDGEMENTS

1, 2: Paris, BnF, © Roger-Viollet; 3: Avignon, Musée Calvet, photo André Guerrand; 4: château de Malmaison et de Bois-Préa, © RMN-Arnaudet; 5: Dijon, Musée Magnin, © RMN-R.G. Ojeda; 6, 7, 8: London, British Library/Bridgeman Art Library; 9: Paris, Bibliothèque Nationale/Bridgeman Art Library

While every effort has been made to contact copyright-holders of illustrations, the author and publishers would be grateful for information about any illustrations where they have been unable to trace them, and would be glad to make amendments in further editions.

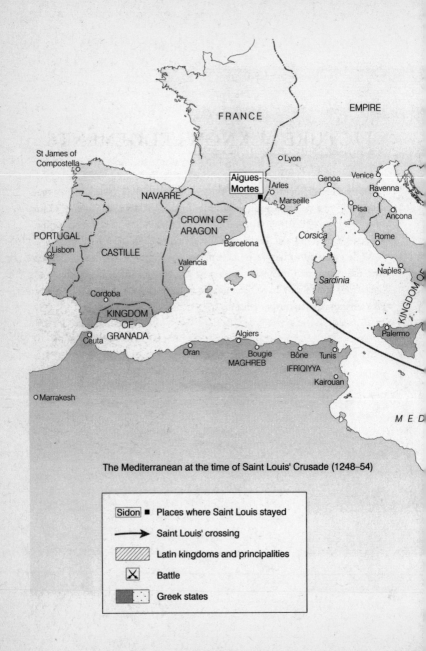

The Mediterranean at the time of Saint Louis' Crusade (1248–54)

Sidon ■	Places where Saint Louis stayed
→	Saint Louis' crossing
▨	Latin kingdoms and principalities
☒	Battle
▒	Greek states

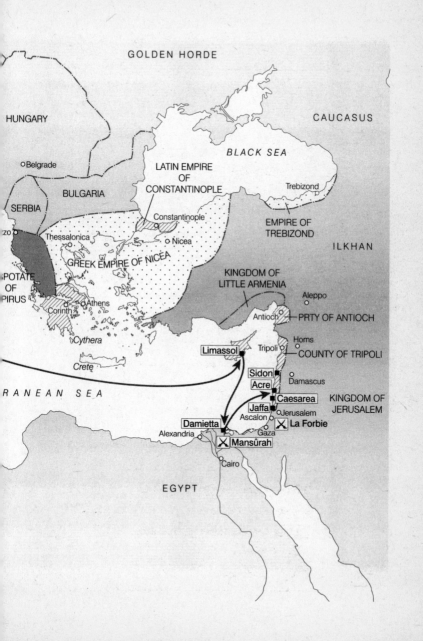

PREFACE

What is known about Jacques de Molay, last Master of the Order of the Temple and its twenty-third since the foundation of the Order by Hugues of Payns in 1120? Very little in total and virtually nothing about two-thirds of his life.

The Order of the Temple was the first military-religious order in western Christendom. It was an order which men entered by taking vows, in which they lived following a Rule, celebrated Mass and recited the hours. But instead of devoting themselves to meditation and God's work (*opus Dei*), as in the Benedictine and Cistercian orders, they practised a military profession in the service of God and His Church. The term 'soldier of Christ' (*miles Christi*), which had a long history, was eventually completely appropriated to this new form of religious life.

The Order began during the crusades, initially as defenders of pilgrims visiting a Jerusalem that had recently been delivered from the Infidel – as Muslims were described at the time – then as part of the military defence of the Latin States in the East, founded during the first crusade in 1098–9.

Installed at first in the outbuildings of the al-Aqsa mosque on Mount Moriah (or Temple Mount), Jerusalem, the new Order called itself the 'Poor Fellow-Soldiers of Christ, Knights of the Temple of Solomon'. Having received alms from both the East and the West, it was able to set up a network of commanderies across Christendom, grouped in bailiwicks, then provinces, all placed under the authority of a Master and dignitaries based first in Jerusalem then, when that was lost in the thirteenth century, at Acre. Other orders came to imitate the Temple: in the East, the Hospital and Teutonic; in Spain, the Calatrava, Santiago, etc.; and in the Baltic region, the Teutonics, who took over from minor orders such as the Dobrin, or Sword-bearers.

Born around 1245–50, Jacques de Molay entered the Temple in 1265, and became its Grand Master in 1292. The Franks had just been driven out of the Holy Land for good; and the year before – 1291 – Acre and the last crusaders' fortresses had fallen into the hands of the Mamluk sultans of Egypt and Syria. Grand Master Jacques de Molay's headquarters were in Cyprus, until the fatal day when, having come to France to confer with the pope, he and his fellow knights fell victim to the king of France, Philip the Fair. The Templars were arrested in 1307, the Order was dissolved in 1312 and Jacques de Molay was burnt at the stake on 18 March 1314.

Though little is known about Molay, documents and pieces of information exist, which are often terse, imprecise and indirect and allow a not-too-cursory biography of the man himself to be constructed. In the period when the destiny of the Temple lay in his hands, we can pick out the broad outlines of his deeds; without too much questioning of sources or exaggeration, it is possible to detect Jacques de Molay's hand in the conduct and government of the Templar Order in the last twenty years of its existence.

Contemporary chronicles offer accounts of the events in which the Temple and its leaders were involved. The chronicle of the Templar of Tyre, who although not a Templar himself had been secretary to the Grand Master Guillaume de Beaujeu, is a key work for understanding the period. It was later taken up by Amadi, then Florio Bustron, who added a few details. Western chronicles – those of Guillaume de Nangis and his successors in France and of towns in Italy, that of Villani and the monastic chronicles in England or imperial countries – also contribute invaluable information.

To those may be added items of correspondence. The Archives of the Crown of Aragon, in Barcelona, contain a wealth of letters which provide completely new pieces of information, though they must be treated with caution as they are often second-hand. Writings by Molay himself are to be found among these documents: two memoranda written by the Grand Master at the request of Pope Clement V, one on the crusade, the other on plans for uniting the Orders, accompanied by a small packet of letters, in Latin and French, of which I have drawn up a provisional corpus in an appendix (see pp. 260–7). There are also, if not replies to these exact letters, at least letters addressed to Molay which supplement our information. These exchanges of letters sometimes take a personal turn, which render them invaluable when trying to grasp the Grand Master's personality. The papal archives, accessible by means of the Register of papal letters formed under the aegis of the École française of Rome, also contain much information that must be complemented by referring to the original.

Lastly, there are the interrogations of the Templars at the time of their trial: those of Jacques de Molay first (there are five), but chiefly those in which he is mentioned or sometimes implicated. These are a fundamental source, but difficult to handle: imagine if history were founded solely on police reports, legal case preparations or documentary sources based entirely on memory. The case against the Temple was all of these simultaneously; it was a politico-police machination. If we put any trust in chief accuser Guillaume de Nogaret, then we are also prepared to trust Prosecutor Vyshinsky or Senator McCarthy. Those interrogations were carried out by torturers and then inquisitors for whom the only verdict was guilty. In any case, the testimonies of all those who were questioned owed a vast part to memory; how many facts emerged that were twisted, misplaced or wrongly dated? They certainly had some basis of truth, but what basis and what truth?

How to extract from that over-abundant dross the many nuggets of truth it contains? Every historian who has taken an interest in the history of the Temple and its tragic end has been aware of this problem; but all of them (and I include myself) have approached it in schematic fashion: were the Templars guilty or not guilty? If the answer was 'yes', the trial was reliable; if 'no', then it was not. A new trend currently surfacing among historians is to concentrate on the texts and pick out their contradictions, shortcomings and many errors, but also their share of truth; to dissect the procedures followed against the Templars and there, too, extract the divergent interests and objectives. The pope and his judges (the papal commissioners) did not approach the question of the Temple's misdeeds in the same way as the royal judges and their allies of the Inquisition, since they did not share the same objective. The first wished to reform the abuses within the Order; the second wanted to eliminate an Order seen as heretical, idolatrous, immoral, useless, etc. As for the Templars who were being questioned, they wanted to save their skins. In these conditions, it would be naïve to place any faith in their testimony; yet those testimonies exist.

Reading Barbara Frale's, *L'ultima battaglia dei Templari* (2001), which came to my notice while I was working on this book, finally decided me to take account of all those documents which are 'suspect' because based on memory – and a tortured memory, at that – on hearsay and rumour, on the evidence of someone who saw someone who knew ... Why reject the testimony of many observers, the ambassadors, special informants, semi- or totally anonymous correspondents present in Paris or Poitiers who corresponded with the king of Aragon, with the Templars or other religious men in his states, and who provide information that is obviously unverifiable from other sources, yet accept at face value the testimony of a Templar undergoing trial (which is similarly unverifiable, because unique)?

I use the words 'take account of', but that does not mean 'accept'; however, at least between taking account and accepting or rejecting, the testimony will be examined, whatever it may be. I have therefore sometimes made a few rather lengthy digressions in order to resolve the matter, and it is possible that occasionally I may have made the wrong choice.

Nor has Jacques de Molay made my task any easier. I am grateful to him for his few letters, mostly preserved in Barcelona, which reveal a man rather different from the weak person who is ordinarily presented to us. But having made some very short statements at the outset of his trial, he chose to remain silent during the rest of it. On reading the interrogations of the Templars carried out by the papal commissioners in 1310–11, one cannot help but think that, even though they should not be taken too literally, Jacques de Molay could have taught us much about his Order and about himself. He would have been selective, of course, and it is a shame that he made the wrong choice of system of defence.

One of the major obstacles I encountered in writing this biography was that of chronology. At the risk of wearying the reader, I have gone to some lengths to establish facts and date them correctly – not always with success. Most of the letters written by Molay are not dated, nor are those which were exchanged between Templars, or Templars and other correspondents of the Crown of Aragon. It is usually possible to come up with an acceptable date through context, but countless times fine reasonings have had to be consigned to the wastebin when a new date has been found for the documents that gave rise to them. The demagogues of history with no date (and soon with no memory) must be fully aware: without reliable chronology, history is built on sand.

Without students or teachers, colleagues or conferences, meetings or exchanges of ideas, this imperfect book would have been still more imperfect. It gives me great pleasure to thank all those who, by a suggestion, a piece of information or research into a collection of archives, have kindly passed on to me what they know: Pierre-Vincent Claverie and Damien Carraz; Claude Mutafian in France, Frédérique Lachaud and Helen Nicholson in England; Simonetta Cerrini, Barbara Frale, Dominique Valerian and Yves le Pogam in Rome; and in Spain, Philippe Josserand in Madrid, and Alan Forey, whose work on the Templars of the Crown of Aragon has been so useful to me, and who has provided me with many items of information extracted from the Archives of Barcelona, which he knows so well; my friends Joan and Carme Fuguet, who enabled me to make two visits to Barcelona, and helped me gain access to the Archives of the Crown of Aragon, where I have always received the warmest welcome, both from the secretary and the staff and readers. (Did not Françoise Bériac decipher one of those letters for me – from Jacques de Molay or some other – faded, holed, stained, in short illegible, but so precious?)

Cergy, 13 February 2002

1250

MOLAY'S YOUTH

To the judges interrogating him in Paris on 24 October 1307, Jacques de Molay said that he had been received into the Order at Beaune forty-two years earlier by Humbert de Pairaud, a knight.[1] Unlike with most of the Templars questioned in Paris in October and November 1307, there is no indication in the trial transcript of the Grand Master's age. Thus armed with a single numerical pointer, we must try to establish the year of his birth. If he had been with the Temple for forty-two years in 1307, then he would have been received in 1265. Is this the first certain reference point? But when questioned by the pope's envoys at Chinon in August of the following year, he again said he had been received forty-two years earlier, which would mean 1266. Or maybe he was mechanically repeating his former statement.[2]

Theoretically, one entered the Order as an adult:

> Although the Rule of the Holy Fathers (Rule of Saint Benedict) allows children
> to be received into a religious order, we do not advise you to take them on …
> For anyone who wishes to give his child for life to the religious knighthood
> must maintain him until he is of an age to bear arms vigorously, and root out the
> enemies of Jesus Christ … and it is better that he should not take vows as a child,
> but when he is old enough …[3]

Molay was a noble who was received into the Temple as a knight, but that does not mean that he had already been dubbed. Men were generally knighted at the age of twenty. Supposing that to be the case, his date of birth could be put at 1245 or 1244.[4] But a certain number of Templars interrogated in 1307 had entered the Temple at around sixteen or seventeen years old. One of them,

Guy Dauphin, son of Count Robert II of Clermont, Dauphin of Auvergne, was even as young as eleven, although he had certainly not been knighted.[5]

Take the group of the 138 Templars questioned in Paris: the age of 123 of them is given; and for the same group, with the exception of two, we know the date of their entry to the Temple, according to the same data as those relating to Jacques de Molay ('I was received … years ago'). The average age in 1307 was 41 years 8 months, and the average age on entering the Temple was 27 years 9 months; 28 had entered the Temple at 20 years old or younger (12 between the ages of 11 and 16), and 25 between the ages of 20 and 25.[6] At Chinon, where four other dignitaries of the Temple were being interrogated alongside Molay, two of them gave their age upon entering the Order: Raimbaud de Caron said he had entered 43 years ago (1265?) and had been 17 years old when he 'was made a knight and received into the Order of the Temple';[7] Geoffroy de Charney, too, had been 17 when he had been received into the Order, 40 years earlier (1268?),[8] also as a knight. Supposing that Jacques de Molay had been received at about 16 or 17 years of age, that would place his date of birth at around 1248/9 or 1249/50.[9] One clue points to the latter supposition: in another interrogation, in 1309, speaking of the period from 1273 when Guillaume de Beaujeu had been Grand Master, Jacques de Molay describes himself as belonging to a group of 'young knights'. It must be remembered, however, that in the perception of the period youth could last quite a long time.[10] So no conclusive decision can be reached, and we must stay in the realm of approximations, confining ourselves to placing Molay's date of birth somewhere around 1244/5–1248/9, even perhaps 1240–50.

Molay was a small child at the time of Louis IX's first crusade. Announced in 1244, in preparation from 1245 to 1248, accomplished between 1248 and 1250, and prolonged by Louis' stay in the Holy Land from 1250 to 1254, this crusade, which thus occupied a decade in the life of both the king and his realm, must have left its mark on the infant Jacques de Molay. Stories about the misfortunes, the courage and unshakeable faith of the future saint king, the warlike adventures and exploits, but also the harshness of the famine, sickness, even captivity, related by those who had travelled to the East, the memory of those who had not returned – all these cannot but have affected Molay's knightly forebears.

But where was he born? There are four French communes which bear the name Molay; they are situated in the *départements* of Calvados, Yonne, Haute-Saône and Jura.[11] Information on hamlets and localities must also be added. It is known that Molay was a Burgundian; but the Yonne locality, though home to a Templar (or possibly Hospital) Order, must be eliminated, as Jacques de Molay belonged to a noble family of the county of Burgundy which today is in Franche-Comté. 'Burgundian of the diocese of Besançon', wrote Pierre Dupuy[12] in the seventeenth century. That leaves two lineages and two localities from which to make a choice.

Molay in Haute-Saône, canton of Vitrey, belonged at the time to the parish of Laître. This parish did not come under the control of the diocese of Langres, as is sometimes maintained, but under that of Besançon,[13] because of its connections with the deanery of Traves. It is known that a family of minor nobility had been there since 1138, when an agreement had been made between the Cistercian abbey of La Charité and one Aimé or Aymon, lord of Molay, and his three sons concerning the benefices from the churches of Frétigney and l'Étrelles, near Gy.[14] Jacques is assumed to have been his descendant, the son of a Gérard de Molay, recorded in 1233.[15] This identification is supported by the fact that two Templars of Jacques de Molay's 'household' once he had become Grand Master originated from around Molay, Haute-Saône. One of them, Jacques de la Rochelle (de Rupella), born at La Rochelle, a village very near to Molay,[16] and a sergeant 'of the diocese of Besançon' cited as 'being in the Master's service', was received into the Order at Limassol, Cyprus, in 1304. The other, Guillaume de Gy, 'of the diocese of Besançon ... of the household and *familia* of the Grand Master of the Temple, provost of equipment and his animals', who was received into the Order in 1303,[17] originated from Gy, some twenty kilometres from Molay. Lastly, according to the testimony of a Templar questioned at Poitiers in 1308 during the proceedings brought against the Order, the Grand Master (that is, Molay) had a brother who was dean of Langres, and Langres is not far from Molay.[18]

Molay in the Jura, canton of Chemin, is a village which was in the feudal dependency of the nearby château of Rahon,[19] situated some 10 kilometres south of Dole. Jean de Longwy, known as de Chaussin (both neighbouring localities), had married the daughter of Mahé (or Mathieu), lord of Rahon, and Alix. Several children were born of their union, including Jacques (sometimes called Jean), the youngest son.[20] Cited in support of this identification is Jean de Longwy's will, made in 1310, under the terms of which he bequeathed possessions to his son Jacques. According to J. Labbey de Billy,[21] the will was recorded at the ecclesiastical court of Besançon; but this document, if it ever existed, has disappeared (the testaments of the court of Besançon having been dispersed and partly destroyed). It is possible it never existed, since there is no mention of it in the (complete) catalogue of Dom Berthod.[22] The links that might have been maintained by the lords of Rahon with other families in the county, such as that of Oiselay (Monte Avium), or Oiselier or even Oseler (which supplied a Marshal of the Temple during the Masterships of both Molay and Grandson), even supposing that family connections existed, are neither proven nor convincing.[23] To return to the will, the date of 1310 (though some writers say 1302) is most curious, chiefly in that Jacques de Molay should be cited at all; for Jean de Longwy must surely have known what had happened to his son at that date. To bequeath one's goods to the Master of the Temple, a prisoner, tried and almost condemned, was to leave them to the ruler, in this instance the Count of Burgundy, as the Temple's possessions had been confiscated since 1307. And so, although there is more to be said about this very important point, there are sound reasons for opting for Molay, Haute-Saône.

Jacques de Molay was received into the Order by two dignitaries of the highest level: Humbert de Pairaud, Visitor General of the Order in France and England, and Amaury de la Roche, Master of the province of France. Both came from fine noble families which may possibly indicate that Jacques too belonged to a notable family, of middle nobility rather than landed gentry,[24] as connections between the middle stratum of nobility and the military orders and the crusades were well established in this Burgundian region.[25]

So, Jacques de Molay may have come from a notable Burgundian lineage and he was born somewhere between 1240 and 1250. This spatial and temporal context is important. The county of Burgundy was imperial territory; it did not belong to the kingdom of France and so Molay was not a subject of the king of France. However, he was born and grew up in a time when the king of the neighbouring kingdom was Louis IX; he entered the Temple in 1265, two years before the king took up the cross for the second time. It is therefore inconceivable that he had not heard about him, the more so because both Burgundies (the county belonging to the Empire, and the duchy belonging to the kingdom), like nearby Champagne, had provided a number of crusaders since the start of the movement. Yet the only mention of Louis IX to be found in Molay's writings is rather muddled, since he speaks of the king's presence at the second Council of Lyon in 1274, when the holy monarch had already been dead for four years: 'I remember that when Pope Gregory [Gregory X] was at the Council with Saint

Louis ... Brother Guillaume de Beaujeu, then Master of the Temple, was there too ...'[26] A curious slip of memory, perhaps, since Molay had been a Templar for nine years when the Council took place.

Although Louis IX's crusade had been well prepared, it was not embarked upon under the best conditions, even if the events that had shattered the Holy Land in the decade 1240–50 must have brought about a massive mobilisation of western Christendom. The West was doubtless more preoccupied by the terrible Mongol invasion which struck Poland and Hungary at its eastern-central margins in 1240–42. By now, the Mongols had retreated, but with a promise that they would return. Above all, western Christendom was torn apart, paralysed by the conflict – of ideology and power – between its two heads, the pope and the emperor.[27]

All appeared peaceful in the kingdom of France when Louis IX left it in 1248, the upsets of the first part of his reign having been overcome. Since Louis had been twelve years old, that is, a minor, when he came to the throne in 1226, his mother, Blanche of Castile, had assumed the regency. The opposition of certain barons (the Poitevins, the Count of Brittany) had provoked revolts which the regent, and then the young king, had managed to quell. The *Grandes Chroniques de France* – the official history of Capetian royalty – tell of these troublesome episodes, but also remark on long periods of calm: in 1231, 'it happened that the king governed his kingdom for four whole years without any adversity'; in 1237, 'the king saw that God had granted him peace in his kingdom for the space of four years or more'.[28]

Internal disturbances resumed, however, in 1240–2, aggravated by the attempt by Henry III of England, with the help of some of the local nobility, to reconquer Poitou and, if possible, Normandy, Maine, Anjou, etc., that is, all the territories that had been lost in the time of the French king Philip Augustus. Henry III landed at Royan on 20 May 1242, but was defeated at Taillebourg, near Saintes, on 24 July. The Poitevin rebels submitted, and truces were agreed with the English king the following year.

To leave a kingdom in peace also meant putting an end to the abuses and injustices perpetrated by the royal administration, which was then thriving. The preparations for the crusade and the difficulties in funding it revealed to the king the magnitude of the injustices committed against his subjects and the corruption of his agents. Having ordered inquiries throughout the realm in 1247, he took the reins of administration firmly in hand again. This had the dual result of

soothing the discontent of his subjects and improving the government's returns
– above all, financially. When he set off in the summer of 1248, Louis IX left
behind a kingdom in good order; his mother, Blanche, was to assume the role of
regent with a council in whom the king had complete confidence.[29]

Louis IX also wanted to leave behind him a western Christendom that was
united and at peace. However, the West at that time was being ripped apart by
the conflict between pope and emperor; the former, confident of his supremacy
on the spiritual plane, aspired also to control temporal powers and subject the
first among them, the imperial power, to his authority. Emperor Frederick II of
Hohenstaufen, who was also hereditary king of Sicily, did not share his view.
The struggle went through some violent phases, as is revealed in the tone of
the letters exchanged between the two protagonists. Excommunicated by Pope
Gregory IX for the second time in 1239, Frederick II and his allies of the Pisan
maritime republic went so far as to make a military strike. On 3 May 1241, a
Pisan fleet seized a Genoese vessel which was carrying a number of bishops,
who were responding to a summons from the pope to Rome, among them some
French bishops whom Frederick took captive. Louis IX protested vigorously:
'The kingdom of France,' he wrote to Frederick II, 'is not so enfeebled that it
lets itself be dominated or trampled under your spurs.'[30]

Louis IX was all the more bitter since the French monarchy had maintained
cordial relations with the Staufens since the time of Philip Augustus. The row
did not die down, however, with the election of Innocent IV to the papacy on
25 June 1243; quite the opposite. Just as Louis IX pledged his crusade, Innocent
IV assigned somewhat different objectives to the ecumenical council which he
convened at Lyon (where he had taken refuge, for fear of the emperor's threats
in Rome), among them the deposition of the emperor.

In this conflict, Louis IX did not adopt a neutral attitude; while disapproving
of the deposition, he forbade Frederick any act of aggression against the pope.
Above all, he tried to reconcile the two rivals; Christendom should unite for the
sake of the Holy Land. The French king's attempts, however, proved futile,[31] thus
handicapping the crusade for which he was preparing. Henceforth he could rely
on the human and material resources of his kingdom alone, and on a few gestures
of goodwill here and there. He had failed to make the crusade 'the business of the
entire West'.[32] Frederick II was deposed by the Council of Lyon on 16 July 1245,
but he resisted and the papacy did not manage to oust him from his kingdom of
Sicily. The struggle was to continue beyond the emperor's death in 1250.

The manner in which Louis IX decided to leave on crusade is noteworthy. The Lateran IV Council of 1215 had prevented the formulation of a 'true right' to crusade; specifically, it had given the pope alone the initiative to launch one. However, this isn't what is happening here, since Louis decided to take up the cross by himself. In December 1244, Louis was staying at Pontoise, where he fell so gravely ill that for a while it was feared he would die. Having been restored to health, he decided to leave on crusade.[33] Shortly afterwards, the West learned of the dire events – the loss of Jerusalem, defeat at La Forbie – that had taken place in the Holy Land in the preceding months; these were enough to unleash strong emotions and bring about the mobilisation of Christians.

Previously Emperor Frederick II, who had been excommunicated in 1228, had also gone on crusade. Lacking the means to make any real impact, he had astutely negotiated with the sultan of Egypt, al-Kamil, for the partial restitution of Jerusalem to the Christians. In 1241, playing on the traditional rivalries between the sultan of Cairo and the emirs of Syria (Aleppo, Damascus) – who nevertheless were all members of Saladin's family, the Ayyubids – the Christians had gained several additional advantages. Thus, from 1229 Jerusalem had once more found itself in Christian hands, as in the twelfth century, and the Holy Sepulchre had again become easily accessible to pilgrims. But in 1244 the ravages committed in Syria by the Khwarezmians led to the loss of the Holy City.

Formerly settled in substantial numbers on the Iranian plateau, this people had been completely destabilised by the Mongol offensive; driven out of Persia, they wandered into Mesopotamia, Syria and then Palestine, looting and massacring both Christians and Muslims as they went. One of their raids brought them to Jerusalem, which they pillaged before capturing it, driving out the Christians on 23 August 1244. Subsequently, the Khwarezmians entered the pay of the sultan of Egypt, Salih Ayyub, to help fight the coalition formed by the emirs of Aleppo and Damascus, who were themselves allied with the Franks. All together, the Frankish forces of the Latin States, knights from Jerusalem, Tripoli, Antioch and Cyprus, the military Orders (Temple, Hospital, Teutonic and the leper knights of Saint Lazarus) engaged in a gory battle at La Forbie in which they were defeated on 17 October 1244. The Frankish army was destroyed and almost all the thousand or so knights of the military Orders were either killed or taken prisoner.[34] Although its consequences appeared less serious, or less immediate, at the time because of the disunity of the Muslims and, as we shall see, the invasion of the Mongols in the Near East as well as Europe, for the Franks the outcome of La Forbie was as tragic as the battle of Hattin had been on 4 July 1187.

In 1187, the defeat at Hattin, followed by the surrender of Jerusalem, had created a shock wave. This in turn had given rise to the third crusade, in which the emperor, the king of France and the king of England had all taken up the cross. In mid-December 1244, however, when he uttered his vow, Louis IX had not yet been informed of the disaster at La Forbie, although he was aware of the threats which hung over the Holy Land. The letters sent by the authorities in the Holy Land (the Patriarch of Jerusalem, the bishops, the representatives of the military Orders) did not arrive in the West until January 1245; although the Prior of the Hospital had written to Louis in November, the king had not received this letter when he made his vow.[35] His decision to crusade was taken before the announcement of these dramatic occurrences. The king's choice, therefore, was not dictated by events; it was simply his will.[36]

Whatever the reasons, the king's decision came as no surprise. The Holy Land, Jerusalem, Christ's tomb, had long occupied an important place in the thoughts and spirituality of Louis IX, and many historians agree that the crusade was the central idea, even the turning point, of his reign.[37]

The king had encouraged and partly financed Thibaut de Champagne's crusade in 1239, but could only have been alarmed by its mediocre results. His interest in the Holy Land manifested itself more keenly, however, in another direction. In 1236, the Latin emperor of Constantinople, Baldwin II, approached the West for help in defending his moribund empire, one of the Latin States of Greece, born of the diversion of the fourth crusade in 1204. Early in 1237 he went to meet Louis IX in Paris, telling him that, having run out of resources, he was obliged to borrow money against the relics with which Constantinople was still crammed, even after its sacking of 1204. Owing to his inability to repay the loans, these relics were at risk of falling into his creditors' hands. On two occasions Louis IX redeemed the pledge. The holy crown of thorns had been pawned to Venetian merchants; Louis repaid the loan in 1239, sending two Dominican friars to Constantinople to collect the precious relic and bring it back to Paris for storage. On 10 August 1239, Louis IX went in procession as far as Villeneuve-l'Archevêque, near Sens, to meet the cortège. Back in Paris, 'on the Friday following the Assumption of Our Lady, the king came barefoot' and went down in procession from Notre-Dame cathedral to his palace in the City,[38] where the crown of thorns was placed in a chapel. As J. Le Goff, recounting this episode, put it neatly: 'Nine years before leaving on crusade, Saint Louis experienced the ecstasy of the crusader.'[39]

In 1241, Louis completed his collection of relics connected with the Passion by buying from the Templars of Syria, who were holding them as surety, some fragments of the true cross, the tip of the holy spear and a few other items; and to give these relics a setting worthy of their value, in 1242 he had built within the royal palace the Sainte-Chapelle, which was both a vast reliquary and a sanctuary. The Sainte-Chapelle was consecrated on 26 April 1248, a few months before the king's departure for the crusade. 'France became the new Holy Land.'[40]

And so, it can be seen that Louis IX was fully prepared for the crusade both psychologically and spiritually, which makes it easier for us to understand fully both his choice and the singular way in which it was effected. Although he embarked upon it without reference to the situation in the Holy Land and without prior consultation with the pope, that did not prevent his decision, in this context, from being welcomed.

Nevertheless, his initiative received hardly any echo from either the papacy or the secular rulers. The king of Norway had taken the cross in 1237, and Louis IX was counting on his ships; but, alas, the king of Norway later managed to get himself released from his vow. The kings of England and Aragon had good reasons for staying at home. As for Pope Innocent IV, he showed very little enthusiasm; his encyclical of 3 January 1245, convening the Council at Lyon, mentioned the crusades among matters to be discussed, but in no more than general terms. It was only during the course of the Council that the Church officially took over Louis IX's project. Two envoys from the Latin East had come to the Council to ask urgently for help. So Cardinal Eudes de Châteauroux was appointed legate and given the task of organising the preaching of the crusade.

Emperor Frederick II, excommunicated and about to be deposed, was out of the running. On the strength of a Muslim text, betrayal of the king of France's plan has been read into a letter addressed by the emperor to the sultan of Egypt, Salih Ayyub. Relations between Frederick II and Louis IX, which had been very strained after the incident of the bishops, had returned more or less to normal. Frederick had no interest in alienating a king who might partly defend his cause with the pope, so it is unlikely he wanted to harm him. Maybe this letter contained a veiled appeal to the sultan, asking him to behave towards Louis IX as his predecessor, Frederick, had towards him, that is by being conciliatory and obliging.[41] Louis IX, meanwhile, needed Frederick II; he wanted to use the ports of southern Italy and Sicily for loading the supplies and equipment necessary for the crusade. At all events, in November 1246 Frederick responded favourably to the king's letters in which he had been asked to facilitate the movement of horses, weapons and wheat in his states.[42] He granted the requisite licences so that, from spring 1248, the loading of wheat could be carried out in the ports of southern Italy.[43]

The setbacks encountered in the diplomatic preparation for his crusade, however, did not dishearten the king, who planned his enterprise methodically and steadfastly. Preaching the crusade did not begin until the summer of 1245, with the arrival of Eudes de Châteauroux in Paris. At that time, Louis was contemplating leaving in the spring of 1247, but could not meet the deadlines.

Boats, supplies and money were needed. The sum often suggested as the cost of the crusade, 1,500,000 Tournois *livres* (coins minted at Tours, the *livre* varying in value depending on period and place), compares with a normal annual income for the royal Treasury of some 250,000 *livres*. In fact, the first figure probably underestimates the cost of six years of crusade; that said, the king and his Treasury were not responsible for the entire funding of the enterprise. Nevertheless, the king's 'ordinary' resources could not meet the cost; he would have to resort to 'extraordinary' resources.[44]

The king had to hire boats to ensure his army's passage from France to Cyprus on the first leg of this crusade or at least that part of it which was under his leadership. He turned to Genoa and Marseille, which provided him with some forty big, round-ended ships capable of carrying several hundred passengers.[45] At the same time, a large number of smaller craft were also mobilised. Many of the crusaders managed on their own account, following the example of Joinville and his cousin the Count of Sarrebruck, who chartered a boat at Marseille to transport themselves, their twenty knights, their equerries and servants, horses and luggage.[46]

Although the vessels were from Genoa and Marseille, the planned embarkation port was in France at Aigues-Mortes, a new port which had been developed on the Languedoc coast some years earlier. Following the Treaty of Paris in 1229, the Count of Toulouse, Raymond VII, had had to surrender all the Languedoc part of his county, which had been rearranged into two royal seneschalships: Carcassonne and Béziers, and Beaucaire and Nîmes. Henceforth the kingdom of France had at its disposal a Mediterranean front which Louis IX fully intended to use to his advantage. Aigues-Mortes thus became the symbol of the Capetian monarchy's new ambitions, commercial and political.

Cyprus was to be the base of operations for the crusade, so the king took care to stockpile supplies there. Joinville, his chronicler, marvelled at the spectacle of all those barrels of wine and wheat piled up on the island's plains.[47] The crusade's target was Egypt, as it had been for the fifth crusade in 1218, and should have been in 1202-4 had it not been diverted to Constantinople. There was no mistaking its ultimate goal –Jerusalem – but at the time it was considered that, in order to gain a lasting hold on the Holy city, Muslim might must be struck at its heart. That heart lay in Cairo, the Babylon of contemporary texts. The ports of the delta, Alexandria and, particularly, Damietta, looked vulnerable, and the Franks taking control of them could seriously weaken the sultan's economic interests.

In the summer of 1248, all was ready. On 25 August, the king embarked at Aigues-Mortes, and arrived at Limassol, Cyprus, on 17 or 18 September. In the days that followed, other boats, including Joinville's, reached the island. By now it was too late in the year to land in Egypt, so the king decided to put off the enterprise until the spring of 1249 and overwinter in Cyprus. This decision necessitated hiring another fleet, something which could not be taken for granted since the Genoese and Venetians were engaged in war, and were keeping their vessels for themselves.

The army left Cyprus on 30 May 1249 and arrived within sight of Damietta on 4 June, landing the following day. The men-at-arms who had travelled in the larger vessels had to climb into rowing boats, whereas the galleys could get very close to the shore. An officer of the king's chamber, Jean de Beaumont, describes in a letter how the knights disembarked, shields hanging from their necks, spears in hand, jumping into the water to take up their position, immediately on the beach in order to confront the troops from Cairo. The latter, who were few in number, quickly abandoned the site, possibly from panic, thus allowing the Franks to gain possession of Damietta without resistance.[48] The next day, boats specially adapted to transport horses unloaded the knights' mounts.

The king had planned to march on Cairo, but by now the delta was completely flooded, which meant he would have to wait all autumn for the level of the Nile to drop. This was unfortunate, but it allowed time for reinforcements brought from the West by the king's brother, Alphonse of Poitiers, to arrive on

25 October. Together with these reinforcements, the knights of the Latin States and the military-religious Orders, Louis IX had at his disposal 2,800 knights, more than 5,000 squires, 10,000 footsoldiers and several thousand archers and crossbowmen – close to 25,000 men.

The army set off in December but swiftly encountered difficulties in the form of both resistance and harassment from the sultan's troops, and problems with crossing the tributaries and canals of the Nile. At least the question of provisions did not arise, however, as long as the sea link with Damietta was maintained.

In February 1250, the king's troops found a ford which enabled them to position themselves opposite the Egyptian fortress of Mansûrah, the key to Cairo. But a precipitate attack on Mansûrah by the vanguard, led by the king's brother Robert of Artois (who had disregarded the advice of his companions-at-arms to be cautious) led to its destruction. On 9 February 1250, the count and a large number of Templars, including the Grand Commander, Brother Gilles, were killed. Mansûrah became the focus of Egyptian resistance. The interception by the sultan's ships of the Christians' supply vessels coming from Damietta caused famine, while scurvy and dysentery also contributed to a crushing defeat. On 5 April 1250, by now completely surrounded, the Frankish troops surrendered and the king was taken prisoner.

Negotiations proved difficult, slowed down further by a *coup d'état* by troops of freed Turkish slaves, the Mamluks, which eliminated the last representative of the Ayyubid dynasty, Turan Shah. An agreement was eventually reached, however, containing the following clauses: a ransom of 4,000,000 *livres*; the restitution of Damietta; maintaining the *status quo* in Syria–Palestine, and the release and exchange of captives held by both camps since the truce concluded in 1229 by Frederick II and al-Kamil.

Set free on 6 May, Louis IX reached Acre with what remained of his fighting troops. At the request of the barons of the Holy Land, and with the agreement of his advisers, the king decided to stay in Palestine. Two reasons prompted his decision, which he revealed in a letter addressed to all his subjects on 11 August 1250. For one thing, he did not want to leave the East until he was sure of the release of all his prisoners; but the Mamluks were not honouring their commitments, and allowed matters to drag on. Secondly, his presence and that of the surviving crusaders was considered indispensable for the protection and survival of the Latin States. 'If we stay,' he wrote to his subjects, 'we always have the hope that time will bring something good.'[49]

In the end, Louis IX's sojourn lasted four years.

At Acre, the king quite naturally rediscovered the spirit of pilgrimage. For every crusader en route for the Holy Land had left with the hope of visiting places made sacred by the presence of Jesus, the Virgin and the saints. Contemporary texts most often refer to the crusaders as *peregrini*, pilgrims. Louis IX visited all the holy places still in Christian hands, such as Nazareth. He could have gone to Jerusalem, since the truce concluded with the Mamluks allowed him to do so, but he refused to go to a place controlled by Infidels.[50]

He hoped to make use of the dissensions between the Muslim authorities: Aleppo and Damascus remained loyal to the Ayyubid princes, descendants of Saladin and his brother, and very hostile to the Mamluks of Cairo, the murderers of their relative. The Frankish alliance with Damascus against Egypt was traditional, but Louis IX rejected it, fearing that the masters of Cairo would use it as a pretext for interrupting the release of Christian captives. He preferred to negotiate with the Mamluks. Because he thought that new opportunities favourable to the Franks were unlikely to present themselves, Louis IX set up a vigorous defence programme for the kingdom of Jerusalem. He concentrated on the coastal towns and fortresses, consolidating and restoring their defence walls. Acre, the capital, and its suburb, Montmusard, were for the first time encircled with walls; Caesarea, Jaffa and Sidon were repaired one after the other.[51] Louis realised that the only trump card held by the Latins against their adversaries lay in their almost complete mastery of the sea, as a result of the hegemony of the Italian maritime cities in the Mediterranean. The coastal fortresses were therefore not turned against an enemy from the sea; they were defensive redoubts facing a foe from the interior. Louis IX made the same analysis as the military-religious Orders who, without releasing their grip on a few strongholds inland, such as Krak des Chevaliers, Beaufort and Safed, put more emphasis on the coastal fortresses of Arsur, Castle Pilgrim, Tortosa, and later, in 1262, Sidon, which would be sold to the Templars.

When he departed from the Holy Land in 1254, Louis left behind what was called the 'French regiment', a contingent of a hundred knights, with squires, servants and grooms all equally capable of fighting, which he funded entirely himself. Initially based in Jaffa, the 'regiment' was put under the command of Geoffroy de Sergines, one of Louis IX's best commanders during the crusade. In fact, permanent forces of this kind, similar to those formed by the military-religious Orders, rather than a temporary crusade, were what the Latin States needed. This French regiment remained operational until the fall of Acre in 1291. A little later, Edward I of England would imitate the French king by sending a contingent placed under the leadership of Otton de Grandson, a lord from the Franche-Comté who had entered his service. On several occasions this man's path would cross that of Jacques de Molay.

In short, Louis IX had explored an entirely new avenue to ensure the survival of the Holy Land – a possible Mongol alliance. First under the leadership of Genghis Khan (d. 1226), and then of his sons and their descendants, the Mongols had formed a vast empire stretching from China to the frontiers of central and eastern Europe. Proclaiming themselves sole 'masters of the world', they aspired to subject all peoples and kingdoms to their domination. Under the supreme authority of a Great Khan installed at Karakorum, in the heart of Mongolia, four *uhlus*, or khanates, were constituted, each governed by a khan. Two were of interest to the Franks –the Golden Horde, or Kiptchak, north of the Caucasus in the Russian plains; and Persia, or Ilkhan, covering the Iranian plateau, Mesopotamia and part of Asia Minor.

At the time of the Council of Lyon, and despite the horrors of the invasion which had ravaged central and eastern Europe in 1239–42, Pope Innocent IV had dispatched ambassador-informants to the Mongol powers. Apparently, their empire contained many Christians, and some khans, descendants and successors of Genghis Khan, he was told, were not insensitive to Christianity. Although Innocent IV had been the initiator of a true missionary policy, Louis IX took over and at the end of 1249 met emissaries of the Mongol khan of Persia in Cyprus. They passed on to him letters from the Great Khan of Karakorum, following which the king sent André de Longjumeau on an ambassadorial mission. He had already made a journey to Mongolia in 1245.[53]

The king renewed his approaches in 1253, when Guillaume de Rubrouck, a Franciscan, left Acre for Karakorum. On his return in 1256, he wrote a thrilling account of his journey for the benefit of the king, who had come back to France.[54]

For the time being, nothing concrete came of these approaches, but relations continued. In 1262, Hûlâgû, the khan of Ilkhan, suggested to the king of France they should form an alliance against the Mamluks – in spite of the fact that the Franks of the kingdom of Jerusalem had rejected such an alliance in 1260, and adopted an attitude of benevolent neutrality towards the Mamluks; the latter had been able to cross Frankish territories without impediment to go and inflict the defeat of Ayn Djalût on the Mongols. As a result the Mongols had developed the habit of addressing the West directly, either the pope or the king of France. Hûlâgû no longer demanded, as his predecessors had done, the submission of the king of France. A fresh strategy, based on the Mongol alliance, was therefore offered to the westerners in their quest for Jerusalem, and Louis IX was one of the architects of its adoption by all the Franks over the following decades. It is further thought that Louis IX's second crusade, directed at Tunis, was explained by the 'vicissitudes of the Mongol alliance': a delay by the Mongols in their offensive against the Mamluks might have made the king postpone his intervention in the East and, consequently, use this time for another operation which had not been planned originally.[55] This strategy, implemented in the last third of the thirteenth century, was to be the framework within which Jacques de Molay was to act later on when he became Master of the Temple.

Contrary to what has sometimes been written, therefore, whether in the field of defence or of Mongol policy Louis IX did not look back to the past; he opened up paths for the future, and his ultimate failure in no way diminishes their relevance.

Several times before, during and after his crusade, Louis IX had dealings with the military-religious Orders, especially the Temple, the tone of which it is worth establishing. Jacques de Molay was not a subject of Louis IX, but he had spent his youth in the reign of the crusader king, and had entered the Order of the Temple in 1265, shortly before the king went on crusade for the second time. So to what extent had not only the king's actions but also his relations with the Templar Order left their mark on the young neo-Templar?

The military-religious Orders played a very important role in the defence of the Latin States, seeing to the upkeep of its fortresses and maintaining a permanent force of hundreds of knights. This expenditure was financed by the incomes of the commanderies in the West, the military Orders thus ensuring a continuous link between their bases in western Christendom and the front in Syria–Palestine through the transfer of men, supplies, weapons, money and information. It was in this respect that Louis IX first had links with the Templars.

The king had been informed of the defeat of the Polish and Hungarians by the Mongols in 1240–1 by a letter from the Master of the Temple in France, Pons d'Albon. The Master of France had been told in person by brothers of the Temple of Poland, who had come to Paris to take part in the general chapter of the Order in the West: 'The news of the Tartars [Mongols] as we have heard it from our brothers from Poland who came to the chapter.'[56] On the financial plane, a good part of the funds required to finance the crusade had been trans-ferred to the East through the offices of the Templars,[57] and quite a number of crusaders had similarly entrusted their money to them; they were the ones who – quite involuntarily – had made up the shortfall in the sum needed to pay the first part of the king's ransom at Damietta. A Templar ship carried the strongboxes (*huches*) of these crusaders. The Templars refused to touch them, as the money did not belong to them, but Joinville came to an agreement with the Marshal of the Temple to seize it by force. The honour of the Temple thus remained unsullied.[58]

Since the second crusade, in 1147–8, French royalty had acquired the habit of entrusting the management of its treasury to the Temple in Paris. That was still the case under Louis IX, and the situation would last virtually without a break until 1307.[59] It is therefore not surprising that the financial transactions operated by Louis IX passed by way of the Temple. Concluding an agreement with Henry III of England in 1259, the king of France promised to finance 500 English knights for two years. 'The king of France will give us the equivalent of the reasonable upkeep of five hundred knights over a period of two years ... and he will be bound to pay these *deniers* in Paris, to the Temple, in six instal-ments ...'[60] And the king made the Temple, or the Hospital, or both, guarantors for this agreement.

During the crusade, Louis IX had no cause for complaint against the Tem-ple's military activity. Templars and Hospitallers, renowned for their discipline, found themselves systematically allocated to the vanguard or rearguard of the armies.[61] Advancing in the Nile delta in December 1249, the king had forbid-den any over-hasty actions against the enemy; yet on 6 December the Tem-plars, who were in the vanguard, responded to harassment by the sultan's troops with an impetuous charge which, in the end, proved successful. The king does not seem to have reprimanded the Marshal of the Temple, Renaud de Vich-iers, who had been guilty of disobedience.[62] On 9 February 1250, at Mansûrah, a strong Templar contingent formed the vanguard under the command of Robert of Artois, the king's brother. After crossing an arm of the Nile and gaining a foothold on the opposite bank, had they followed the king's orders they would have awaited the bulk of the army before proceeding further, but, having easily scattered a few Turkish contingents, the Count of Artois wanted to pursue his advantage without waiting for the king or heeding the advice for caution of Brother Gilles, the Grand Commander of the Temple. The disaster of Mansûrah followed; Robert was killed, together with nearly all the 280 Templar knights involved in the affair. Louis wept for his brother, though he was well aware of the latter's responsibility in this failure. The Latin chronicle of Guillaume de Nangis lays emphasis on the intervention of the Grand Commander of the Temple in favour of respecting the king's orders.[63]

The Grand Master of the Order, Guillaume de Sonnac, had stayed with the king; he was killed two days later, on 11 February. The Marshal of the Order, Renaud de Vichiers, who assumed responsibility during the interim period, according to the regulations laid down in the Rule of the Order, was then elected Grand Master. Louis IX maintained good relations with Vichiers and, according to Joinville, was in favour of this election.[64] But those good relations did not prevent the king from severely berating the Grand Master in a matter which shows that, although the king trusted the Orders in the military field, he did not at all care for their diplomacy or their, in his view, suspect relations with the Muslim powers. Already in 1259, Guillaume de Sonnac had been firmly brought to heel by Louis IX. Salih Ayyub, the sultan of Egypt, who at the time was at war with the emir of Aleppo, was worried about the arrival of the crusade and had asked for the intervention of his friend Sonnac in favour of a truce. Rumour had it that they had bled together, that they were, so to speak, blood brothers. Sonnac therefore wrote to the king.

> When the king read the letters, he was greatly displeased ... The king let it be known, through authentic letters sent to the Master of the Temple, that henceforth he should not make so bold as to receive requests from the sultan of Babylon [Cairo] without the king's special command, or to hold discussions with the Saracens on matters concerning the king and his barons.[65]

The affair with Vichiers was even more serious. The setting was Caesarea, the date was 1251. The king held a court of justice, as he would have done at Vincennes. Among the cases raised, the most grave concerned the Marshal of the Temple, Hugues de Jouy, whom the Master of the Order at that time, Renaud de Vichiers, had sent to negotiate a *condominium* agreement with the sultan of Damascus to work a vast and rich farming region. Hugues had come back with an envoy from Damascus to have the settled agreement ratified by the king of

France. When Louis IX heard the Master make this revelation, 'he flew into a towering rage, and told him that he had shown great audacity in entering into agreements or understandings with the sultan without speaking to him about it; and the king demanded that reparation be made'. In front of the entire army and the envoy from Damascus, Louis IX made the Master go back on his words, forcing him to humiliate himself publicly. Furthermore, he banished Hugues de Jouy from the kingdom of Jerusalem. Joinville adds: 'Neither the Master who, as godfather of the Count of Alençon, born at Castle Pilgrim, was the king's comrade, nor the queen, nor any others were ever able to come to the aid of Brother Hugues and prevent him from being forced to leave the Holy Land and the kingdom of Jerusalem.'[66]

The friendship between the king and this or that Templar was not at issue; nor was the Templars' place in Jerusalem. But what the king would not tolerate was any attack on his authority. He truly wanted to understand the subtleties of Near Eastern diplomacy, in order to save the Latin States, but he rejected those 'little arrangements between friends' which had long been practised in these parts and were the sources of conflict between the various communities who formed overseas society – Italian merchant communes, seigneuries, royalty, military-religious Orders. Nothing escaped the notice of the peace-making king. Unlike Frederick II twenty years earlier, Louis IX succeeded in the *tour de force* of imposing peace on the Latin East. But it was not to last; the moment his back was turned, the quarrelling broke out again, even worse than before, eventually degenerating into full-blown civil war, the war of Saint-Sabas (1258).

Jacques de Molay must have retained some memories of the episodes that had unfolded under Saint Louis, but there is documentation for only two. First, that of Mansûrah in 1250, showing the temerity of the Count of Artois and the wisdom of the Templars: 'If the said Count had believed the Master of the Order then in office [in fact, it was the Grand Commander], the Count, the Master and others would not have perished.'[67]

In his memorandum on the crusade, which he wrote at the pope's behest in 1306, Jacques de Molay recalls the words of the Mamluk sultan Baibars (1260–77) on the worthiness of his foes, adding, 'That is why, remembering these words and several more that I also heard, words of those who were at Damietta with Saint Louis …'[68]

Louis IX's first crusade was thus a significant point of reference in Molay's memory; he does not evoke the qualities of the saintly king, but the deeds of the

Templars, their courage or wisdom, supported to some extent by Saint Louis. The gross chronological blunder committed by Molay regarding the second Council of Lyon in 1274 has already been mentioned; he refers to Saint Louis' presence there when the poor man had been dead since 1270. It is all the more surprising as Guillaume de Beaujeu, the Master of the Temple under whose authority Jacques de Molay spent most of his career as a Templar, really had been present in person. One may ask the question: Was Molay, a Templar since 1265, still in the West at the time of the second Council of Lyon, or even at the time of Louis' death?

1265

JACQUES DE MOLAY,
RANK-AND-FILE TEMPLAR

When Jacques de Molay was received into the Temple in 1265, the Order had already been in existence for a century and a half.[1]

It had been founded in 1120 in Jerusalem by a group of knights led by Hugues de Payns, a native of Champagne. Their desire was to lead a religious life, following a Rule, whilst also protecting pilgrims travelling along the routes to Jerusalem and the other holy sites. The Rule of the new establishment had been set out at a Council held at Troyes on 14 January 1129, where Saint Bernard, the Abbot of Clairvaux and figurehead of not only the Order of Cîteaux but the whole of Christendom, had played a leading role.[2] Very soon, the brothers of the Templar Order expanded their activities to include a properly military function, defending the Holy Land and the Latin States which had been created in the wake of the success of the first crusade in 1099: the kingdom of Jerusalem, the county of Tripoli and the principality of Antioch (the county of Edessa disappearing around 1144–6). 'Although their original purpose was to help pilgrims coming to pray, and escort them on the roads, they subsequently went with the kings to war against the Turks.'[3] Modelling themselves on the Temple, other military-religious Orders sprang up, such as the Calatrava and Santiago in Spain and in the Holy Land itself the Teutonics. The Order of the Hospital of Saint John of Jerusalem, founded before the Temple as a charitable Order to assist and take care of pilgrims, was also transformed into a military Order.[4]

Because of its links with the crusades, the new Order quickly became successful. It received donations in the East, of course, but also increasingly from the West. The acquisition of lands, churches, properties and revenues enabled it to amass a large patrimony which it managed like an ecclesiastical seigneur, using its resources to finance its activities in the Holy Land – guarding and maintaining castles and fortified towns; purchasing arms, equipment and horses. The portion of its income from the establishments in the West allocated to the Latin States was known as the *responsio*. This position, between the 'front' line and the 'home base', was fundamental in the organisation and operation of the Temple, and indeed military-religious Orders in general. Setbacks, destruction and losses suffered during combat necessitated both a constant replenishment of men and a continual transfer of resources and money. The Templars' reputation for conscientiousness and their efficiency in these operations led them to provide themselves with a few vessels and set up a financial organisation which, although it never made bankers of them, enabled them to render services to others (porterage of cash, loans), as we have seen with Louis IX's crusade. Like the majority of clerics, secular or regular, Templars placed themselves in the service of kings and rulers; they managed the royal treasury in France; the king's Almoner was often chosen from their ranks; Templars and Hospitallers also provided *cubiculari* (servants of the bedchamber) to the pope, etc.[5]

The Order was open to any unmarried, adult free man who had no connection with any of the other religious houses. There were three categories of brothers: the knights, the servants or sergeants, and the priests. The first were nobles, although it is unlikely that those who joined before they were twenty were actually knighted. They fought on horseback and formed companies of heavy cavalry whose charge, when deployed in favourable conditions, proved fearsome to the enemy. The sergeants were divided into two sub-categories: those who fought, often on horseback and in the same way as the knights (and who, although they were not knights, were sometimes drawn from the nobility); and the working brothers who, like lay brothers in Cistercian monasteries, attended to the agricultural, practical and domestic tasks of the Templar house. Chaplain brothers were soon recruited to take care of the religious side in these same houses. The only clergy in the Order, as ordained priests they were not allowed to fight. The others, knights and sergeants, were all religious laymen who had taken vows of obedience, chastity and poverty, and who lived according to the Rule of the Order. They recited the Hours and attended Mass, but since they were not monks, they had no vocation to withdraw from the world to pray, meditate and give glory to God. The Temple was a military-religious

Order, not a monastic one; so the common and hackneyed expression 'soldier-monk' is incorrect.

All the brothers wore a habit, a uniform: a cloak adorned with the insignia of a red cross, plain or Maltese, on the shoulder. For knights, the cloak was white; for the rest, brown or black homespun. The chaplain brothers were tonsured and cleanshaven; knights and sergeants were bearded and wore their hair short. The Order's banner was 'baucent' – that is piebald, half black half white, whatever some etymologists may claim.[6]

The organisation of the Order was both hierarchical and decentralised. There were three levels. At the top, management of the Order was carried out by a Master, Grand Master or General Master, who was elected for life. He was assisted by dignitaries who carried out specific functions, namely, the Marshal (leader in war), the Grand Commander – who at that period was still the Order's Treasurer – the Draper, the Turcopolier (who commanded the Turcopoles, auxiliary troops of mounted archers who formed a light cavalry and fought Turkish-style). Finally, there were the wise and worthy men (*prud'hommes*), the Master's associates (*socius, socii*), who formed a small council.[7] The Order's headquarters, mother house or *maison chèvetaine* as it was called in the Rule, was originally in Jerusalem, on the esplanade of the Temple. King Baldwin II had given the first Templars the al-Aqsa mosque and its outbuildings from which, as it was said to be the site of the ancient Temple of Solomon, the new Order took its name: 'Knighthood of the Poor Knights of Christ of the Temple of Solomon'. When Jerusalem was lost in 1187, the Order's headquarters transferred to Acre; but when that too fell, in 1291, the Templars were forced to retreat to the Latin kingdom of Cyprus, founded in 1190 by Richard the Lionheart following his conquest of the island. There was never any question that the Order's headquarters would transfer to Paris after 1291, as we shall see when examining Jacques de Molay's deeds as Grand Master of the Order.

The kingdom of Jerusalem, the county of Tripoli and the principality of Antioch each constituted a province. The Templars in Tripoli and Antioch were organised along similar lines to the central organisation in Jerusalem, but the Masters of these two provinces were subject to the authority of the Grand Master. In the East, during the thirteenth century, Cyprus and Morea (or Romania, in Greece) were added, followed by Armenia, when Antioch was lost in 1268. Western possessions were grouped in provinces, which were formed in several stages. In the Iberian peninsula, as in the Holy Land, in the provinces of

Catalonia–Aragon and Castile–Portugal the Templars pursued a policy of military action against the Muslims during the *Reconquista*; elsewhere, the Templars were chiefly rural lords managing seigneuries. They were also present in towns: London, Paris, La Rochelle and Rome, for example. There were also the provinces of Germany, Hungary, Lombardy, Apulia (or Puglia) and Sicily, Provence, Aquitaine–Poitou, Auvergne–Limousin, France and England. At their head was a Master, also known as a *praeceptor*, or Commander. The vast size of some of these provinces led to the more or less formal constitution of bailiwicks in places like Normandy, Ponthieu, Burgundy and Scotland, headed by Masters or Commanders (here, again, the terminology was not really fixed). A commandery was basically an administrative district with a principal house, provided with a chapel and a variable number of subordinate houses.[8] The Master of the Order delegated two Visitors to the main provinces of the West, one to Spain, the other to France and England. The Order also had a procurator at the papal court.

Jacques de Molay was received into the Order in 1265 by the Visitor of France in the chapel belonging to the Beaune house. Beaune was in the duchy, not the county, of Burgundy. Nevertheless, whichever locality one believes was Molay's birthplace, Templar commanderies existed in the county. It has been possible to draw up an exact map of the Templar settlements in the county of Burgundy from the list of his fiefs which Count Otto IV had made in 1295: 'The Temple has these chapels in the county of Burgundy, *viz*.: Dole, Saales [Sales], Laynne [La Laine], Faye [Fay], Girefontaine, which said chapels and adjoining houses have a good 4,000 *livres* worth of land.'[9] The house at Salins must be added to this list. The principal house of a commandery was distinguished by the presence of a chapel, served by a chaplain brother; and indications drawn from the trial interrogations bear ample witness to the fact that those who asked to enter the Order were received in the chapel. In almost every instance the Commander was present, and often undertook the task of receiving the new Templar; but it could also be carried out by a neighbouring Commander or a dignitary of higher rank, Commander of a bailiwick or province, a Visitor, or even – though infrequently – the Grand Master himself.

Why Beaune, a town in the duchy of Burgundy and the diocese of Autun? It does not appear to have been a very important Templar house if judged by the fact that Jacques de Molay was the only person known to have been received there. Yet a certain number of Templars questioned during their trial seem to have originated from that town: Gautier de Beaune, but also Gérard,

Guillaume, Laurent, who were all said to be from Beaune, in the diocese of Autun.[10] A Templar house also existed at Dijon, and some men were received there, including one who joined at almost the same time as Jacques de Molay; Dominique de Dijon was received in 1261 or 1262 by Henri de Dole.[11] The Comtois Henri de Dole was present in Lyon in 1263 when Hugues de Pairaud was received by his uncle Humbert de Pairaud, the same Humbert de Pairaud who received Molay two years later.[12] Dominique de Dijon, who witnessed him receive another Templar at Dijon around 1280, gave him the title 'Master of the overseas passage', that is, he was responsible for the transportation and passage to the Latin East of the resources and men necessary for the Temple's activities. The Master of transportation had his headquarters at Marseille. Jacques de Molay may have been received in a house of perhaps little importance, but it was situated on the great Saône–Rhône route, used by a number of crusaders leaving to embark for the East at Marseille or the Italian ports, and obviously by recruits to the Temple and Hospital military-religious Orders. At Marseille, with the Master of the Passage, the Templar Order had at its disposal a veritable observation post for what was going on in the Mediterranean.[13]

Jacques de Molay gave a brief account of his reception during his first interrogation, on 24 October 1307. Here it is, according to the minutes drawn up by the royal judges and the Inquisitor:

Forty-two years earlier, he was received at Beaune, in the diocese of Autun, by Brother Humbert de Pairaud, knight, in the presence of Amaury de la Roche and several other brothers, whose names he cannot remember. He also states under oath that after he had made several promises relating to the observances and statutes of the Order, they placed the cloak around his shoulders. And the one receiving him had brought into his presence a bronze crucifix bearing the image of Christ and told and ordered him to deny the Christ portrayed there. And he did so, though against his will; and then the one receiving him ordered him to spit upon it, but he spat on the ground. Questioned as to how many times he did so, he said on oath that he spat only once; and he remembers that well.

Questioned about whether, on making his vow of chastity, he was told to have carnal union with his brothers, he denied it on oath, and declared that he had never done so.[14]

I am inclined to think that Molay is telling the truth. When he was interrogated on 20 August 1308, at Chinon, he expressed himself in the same terms.[15] The matter of his admission to the Order was not brought up when he appeared in Paris before the papal commission charged with judging the Temple, in 1309–10. That is a pity, as the depositions made before this commission are far more accurate and detailed than those made in 1307. It is not yet time to discuss the matter of admission to the Order as a key element in the accusations against the Templars, except to say that when a new Templar was received, a kind of initiation test was added – since when is another question – to a perfectly orthodox profession of faith.[16]

Fuller depositions clearly show two stages in the entry ritual: firstly, the postulant, admitted with all the brethren of the house in attendance, is rapidly instructed about the constraints that will weigh on him, the duties he will assume, the broad outlines of the Rule and the vows he will have to take. Once he has accepted all that, and has sworn that he is free, a knight or not, unmarried, not in debt and that he has taken no vows in another religious house, he receives the cloak which immediately makes him a brother of the Order. He is thus *ipso facto* subject to the duty of obedience, the first of the vows taken.

Immediately afterwards, he is taken to a secluded part of the chapel – most often behind the altar – or an adjoining room by his receiver or another brother appointed by the receiver; there, away from any other person, he is told to deny Christ, spit on and (or) trample the cross, then to kiss the receiver on the navel, small of the back or anus; lastly, he is advised that, rather than having any dealings with a woman, he should have carnal union with other brothers should he become 'overheated'.

The two people Molay said received him into the Order were both important dignitaries of the Temple. Humbert de Pairaud belonged to a noble family of Forez, in the Roanne region of the diocese of Lyon; he held the office of Commander of the bailiwick of Ponthieu (1257), Master of the province of France (attested between 1261 and 1264), Master of England and Aquitaine (between 1266 and 1271) and at the same time General Visitor of France and England.[17] The second, Amaury de la Roche, was from a branch of the Namur family, from near Autun. He was Grand Commander of the Order in the Holy Land and, Louis IX having put pressure on the pope and the Order to appoint him, became Humbert de Pairaud's successor as Master of France. On 26 February 1264, Urban IV wrote to the Grand Master of the Temple, Thomas Bérard, to remind him that the links between the king of France and the Master of the province were necessarily close and that the king's wishes should be satisfied;[18] Amaury held this office until around 1274–5.

We know nothing of what motivated Jacques de Molay. As a younger son, he may have been destined for the Church (to begin with, the Temple was a religious Order). It has been suggested that he sacrificed himself for the benefit of his brother, but since no documentary evidence exists, that remains pure speculation. It is known, because documentation provides many examples, that the crusaders were motivated by sincere faith, material reasons and a taste for adventure; but social pressures, from family or feudal connections, also played their part. In some noble families a genuine crusading tradition carried on from one generation to the next; and, naturally, when the seigneur took up the cross, his vassals had to follow him, whether they liked it or not. There are thus two clues regarding Molay.

The first relates to family: among the dignitaries of the Temple in the Holy Land at the time when Molay entered the Order, the name Guillaume de Malay, Molaho or Malart appears, described as Marshal of the Temple in 1262 (31 May and 18–19 December), and as Draper in 1271 (11 March and 2 June).[19] Were the Marshal of 1262 (Malay) and the Draper of 1271 (Malart, Molaho) two different people, or were they one and the same? The Templar *cursus honorum* would go in the Draper-to-Marshal direction rather than the other way round. There is nothing to prove that this man or these men had any link of kinship with Jacques. However, there were many instances of a son entering the Temple after his father, or a nephew after his uncle (Humbert and Hugues de Pairaud, for instance), cousins and so on (Pairaud again), and, if such were the case for the Molays, it would be a powerful reason for Jacques' entry to the Temple; but it is a very tenuous link.

Similarly, one might cite the interest of the Comtois (and more generally Burgundian) nobility in crusading and the military Orders. Ancient historians of the county doubtless exaggerated the number of Grand Masters of the Temple who originated from their province (they claimed five, whereas there is only one certain Grand Master – Molay).[20] It is none the less true that when Jacques de Molay became Grand Master a number of Comtois orbited around him: Aymon d'Oiselay, Marshal of the Order, Jacques de la Rochelle, already mentioned, and Otton de Grandson, although he was not a Templar.

Virtually nothing is known about Molay's early years following his entry to the Temple, and little is known about when he went East; however, at least a few theories may be put forward on this subject. Let us start once again from the depositions at the trial, in particular the testimony of Jacques de Molay himself. When he appeared before the papal commission in Paris, on 28 November 1309, Molay adopted the principle, to which he would cling from then on, of refusing to answer the commissioners' questions in order to accept the judgement of no one but the pope. He was, however, intent on making clear three things that were close to his heart: the Order maintained its churches perfectly, and correctly performed the divine service; the practice of almsgiving was widespread and consistent; the Order had paid a very heavy contribution to the defence of the Holy Land. At that moment, Guillaume de Nogaret, Chancellor of the kingdom, chief accuser of the Templars and main architect of their trial, entered the room and reported that, in the *Great Chronicles of France*, most compromising facts were to be found about links between Saladin and the Templars.

> Molay was utterly astounded by this, and declared that he had never heard it said, but he knew, however, that, being overseas at the time when the Master of the said Order was Brother Guillaume de Beaujeu, he himself, Jacques, and many other brethren of the convent of the above-mentioned Templars, young and eager to make war, as is customary with young knights who want to take part in feats of arms, and even others who were not of their convent, had murmured against the said Master because, during the truce that the deceased king of England had made between Christians and Saracens, the said Master had shown himself submissive to the sultan and kept his favour; but that in the end the said Brother Jacques and others of the said convent of the Templars had been content, seeing that the said Master could not have acted otherwise, since at that time their Order supervised and guarded many towns and fortresses along the frontiers of the said sultan in places that he named, and could not have kept otherwise, and which could even then have been lost had the said king of England not sent them supplies.[21]

The 'said king of England' was Edward I (1273–1307) who, while still only Crown Prince, took part in Louis IX's second crusade and, after the king's death at Tunis, departed with his men for Acre, where he stayed for nearly two years. Leaving Acre at the end of 1272, he contributed to the conclusion of a general ten-year truce with the sultan Baibars.[22] Guillaume de Beaujeu was elected

Master of the Temple on 13 May 1273; he was in Italy at the time and did not reach the Holy Land until 1275.

From Molay's statement it has been deduced that he arrived in the Holy Land between Beaujeu's election in 1273 at the earliest and the end of the truce in 1282 at the latest.[23] It is possible that he reached the Holy Land with Beaujeu after the second Council of Lyon in 1274, at which the latter was present. From the time of Hugues de Payns in 1129, every Grand Master returning to the Holy Land after a stay in the West came back well equipped with money, reinforcements and men. But Molay wrote that Saint Louis had taken part in the second Council of Lyon with Beaujeu, so it would be surprising, had he made the journey with the Grand Master, if the latter had not taught him a few rudiments of French history. And it would be even more surprising if, living in a Templar house in the West, he had known nothing of the king's second crusade, or of his death at Tunis in 1270.

In my opinion, certain data in this text have been wrongly interpreted. When writing about Molay belonging to the convent of Beaujeu, Barbara Frale suggests that Molay's use, twice, of the term 'convent' refers to a small number of the Grand Master's advisers. If the word is taken in this sense, it would make the young knight Jacques de Molay someone close to Beaujeu, an adviser, a member of his entourage, household or *familia*.[24] In the Order of the Hospital of Saint John of Jerusalem, the word convent indeed has this meaning of small council, but not in the Temple – or not yet. In the Rule, convent never has this sense; it designates the fighting brothers of the Order, knights and sergeants-at-arms as a whole. 'Here begin the descriptions of the brother knights and brother sergeants of the convent', we read at the start of the paragraphs in the Rule dedicated to the clothing and weaponry of the fighting brothers.[25] The chronicle of the Templar of Tyre tells us that 'in this year it happened that the Temple, and the convents of Acre, Safet, Castle Pilgrim and Beaufort, etc ...';[26] It was therefore a matter of numbers of fighting men. And in his deposition Molay uses the word no differently: 'The knights who were not of their convent' means 'those who did not belong to the Temple'. A distinction continues to be made between the religious knights (those of the military-religious Orders) and the secular knights (lay knights), according to Saint Bernard's terminology.[27]

When he arrived in the East, Jacques de Molay was a young knight eager to prove himself on the battlefield. There is no evidence to suggest that he was close to Beaujeu; he should rather be seen as an ordinary young knight. The text of his statement means no more than that he arrived in the Holy Land as a young man, was there at the time when Beaujeu was Grand Master and, in particular, experienced the period of the truce. He might very well have arrived, therefore, before Beaujeu became Grand Master, in 1270 or 1271. It is unlikely he would have got there any earlier, since Molay entered the Order in 1265, at one of the worst moments for the Latin States. Suffering repeated attacks from the Mamluks which would last until the truce concluded by Prince Edward, the Order needed all the men it could get and could not have afforded to allow its young knights to kick around in western commanderies.

The tragic decade 1260–70 opened with what might be called 'breakdowns' in Mongol strategy. In 1258, the Mongols captured Baghdad and put an end to the Abbasid caliphate; early in 1260, they seized Aleppo and Damascus, and thus came into direct contact with the Franks. Their first objective was Egypt and the Mamluk power base. The battle took place at Ayn Djalût, in Galilee, on 2 September 1260. The Franks of the kingdom of Jerusalem, who remained neutral, after coming to an agreement, allowed the Egyptian troops to pass through their territory. For the first time the Mongols were defeated, and fell back to their base in Mesopotamia. Shortly afterwards, on 24 October, the emir Baibars had the sultan Kutûz assassinated, and took his place – surely a missed opportunity for the Franks.

Seized with panic at the Mongol attack, the inhabitants of Aleppo and Damascus fled, some taking refuge in the Frankish states. Although they did not have the means for an autonomous policy, the Franks were presented with the opportunity to make an alliance with the Mongols. However, they failed to turn the situation to their advantage, for they were divided on this point. A rift appeared between the Franks of the kingdom of Jerusalem and those of Tripoli and Antioch which would last until the 1290s. The count of Tripoli and prince of Antioch (the two states had the same leader) and the king of the Armenian kingdom of Cilicia (or Little Armenia) submitted to the Mongols. They had paid tribute and supplied troops since 1247. Their king, Hethum I, went to Karakorum to offer his submission in 1253, and Bohemond VI was present in Baghdad in 1258. In contrast, the Franks of the kingdom of Jerusalem mistrusted the Mongols and opposed them. But their policy lacked coherence: early in 1260, shortly before the Mamluks asked for their neutrality, a contingent of Templars and knights of the kingdom launched an operation on the Muslim towns of Tibnin and Tiberias. Failure

ensued. Numerous prisoners were taken, including Guillaume de Beaujeu and
Thibaud Gaudin, future Grand Masters of the Temple, and a ransom had to be
paid to free them.[28] Not long afterwards, the Christian population of the region
of Montfort attacked Muslim subjects of the Mongols; among the victims was
the nephew of the general whom Hûlâgû, khan of Ilkhan, had left at Damascus during his journey to Mongolia. This general, named Kitbuga, although a
Christian, then led a reprisal raid on Sidon, a seigneurie on which the inhabitants
of Montfort were dependent. It was a curious notion of neutrality to provoke
both sides.

Letters sent to the West throw light on the attitude of the Franks at that
point. The bishop of Bethlehem speaks of the Mongol people, armed with bows
and spears, cruel and pitiless:

> Report of them reached us and our hands failed us, terror seized us ... There
> will be no surprise that we feared we would have to choose one of these three
> paths: to leave the Holy Land deserted and desolate; to give ourselves up into
> the hands of men who not only thirsted for blood, but took pleasure in it, to die
> at their swords; or to accept the perpetual yoke of Infidels who have no mercy
> whatsoever ...

And he finished his letter with a prayer asking God to deliver the Christians
from this 'Tartar scourge', as the Mongols were commonly referred to at the
time.[29]

The panic aroused by the Mongols in Muslim Syria spread to Frankish Syria.
This better explains why the Franks of the kingdom rejected the idea of an alliance with the Mongols. They chose what they considered to be the lesser of two
evils – the Mamluks. Meanwhile, the khans of Ilkhan – Hûlâgû until his death
in 1265, then Abagha his successor (1265–82), who were both very hostile to the
Mamluks – made direct approaches to the pope and western sovereigns to establish an alliance. In 1262, Hûlâgû wrote to Louis IX and, for the first time, abandoned the rhetoric of the 'masters of the world' (who recognised only peoples
and kings who had submitted) to address the king of France on an equal footing.
He proposed an alliance which would put the Mongols in a pincer grip. Louis
IX's second crusade may have been undertaken with that prospect in mind, following a new approach by Abagha, before straying to Tunis.[30]

For the Franks of the North and the Armenians, however, the choice was stark: to submit or see their states destroyed. The Mongols had reduced the Seljukid sultanate of Asia Minor (from the name of the eleventh-century Turkish conquerors) to the status of a tribute-paying dependency since 1243, and from that time on had exerted strong pressure on the principality of Antioch and the kingdom of Armenia. Northern Franks and Armenians had a more accurate perception of the new arrangements of Hûlâgû and Abagha.

The benevolent neutrality of the Franks of the kingdom of Jerusalem earned them no gratitude from the Mamluks. It comes as no surprise, then, that in 1262 Baibars set out to wreak revenge on the Franks of Antioch and the Armenians for, as he saw it, openly siding with the Mongols. He failed, but the following year he launched attacks on the kingdom of Jerusalem, ravaging the plain of Acre and, more generally, the few farming areas from which the Franks could still obtain supplies. Then, from 1265, he stepped up his operations by attacking the Frankish fortresses. In February 1265, he seized Caesarea; on 30 April, he took Arsur, which was defended by the Hospitallers; next, it was the turn of Haifa and, finally, the town of Athlit, adjoining the great Templar fortress of Castle Pilgrim. South of Acre, the Franks kept only Jaffa and Castle Pilgrim. From that moment on, it may be said, quoting J. Prawer, that 'the whole military, political and territorial framework of the Frankish kingdom was smashed. Muslim enclaves split up the coastal region' (though it would be more accurate to speak of Christian enclaves).[31]

In 1266, from Aleppo to Egypt, Muslim troops attacked on all sides. This time they targeted the inland fortresses, which fell one after the other: Ramlah in Judaea, Safed in Galilee (betrayed on 22 July), Tibnin and Hunin. Following a brief pause in 1267, 1268 again saw large-scale operations on all fronts: farthest south, Jaffa, on 7 May; farthest north, Antioch, whose fall on 20 May brought about the disappearance of the principality and the dismantling of the Templar border district on the confines of the principality and the Armenian kingdom of Cilicia. The Templars lost Baghras (Gaston), Darbsak, Roche de Roissel and Port Bonnel, hanging on to only Roche-Guillaume which, until it fell in 1298 or 1299, became the chief town of the Templar province of Armenia. On 15 June, Castle Beaufort, which the Templars had acquired from Julian of Sidon in 1260–2 (at the same time as he sold them his town of Sidon), was lost.

Amid this chaos, with each side acting in its own interests, the Franks pleaded for truces, which sultan Baibars granted to suit himself, to the humiliation of his foes, and without ever feeling in any way bound by them. The preparations for Louis IX's crusade, possibly combined with a Mongol attack, worried the sultan; hence his relative leniency in 1269 and 1270. But nothing came of them; recalled to his Caucasian frontiers, where the khan of the Horde was threatening him, Abagha postponed his offensive in Syria, and Louis IX was diverted to Tunis, where he met his death on 25 July 1270.

As early as 1271, Baibars resumed the offensive, this time targeting the county of Tripoli. Its defences collapsed one after the other: Safita, the White Castle of the Temple, on 15 February; the Krak des Chevaliers, pride and joy of the Hospitallers, on 30 March. Next Baibars targeted Acre and, on 12 June, seized the castle of Montfort, the headquarters of the Teutonic Order in the Holy Land. On 12 June 1268, the Grand Master of the Hospitallers, Hugues Revel, wrote to the Prior of the Hospitaller province of Saint-Gilles in Provence, listing the losses and in each case indicating the duration of the resistance: Jaffa fell within the hour, Caesarea in two days, Safed in sixteen days, while Arsur – valiantly defended by the Hospitallers – lasted out for forty-five days.[32]

Another text, recounting the fall of Safed, makes an eloquent comparison:

Know that the strongest castle called Safed, which belonged to the Templars, prodigiously supplied with arms and provisions and amply provided with soldiers – knights of the Orders and lay warriors – this castle to which the sultan Saladin laid siege for three years and four months [*sic*], and which he did not succeed in taking by force, Benedekdor [Baibars], sultan of Egypt, captured after six weeks of a cruel, ferocious and continuous siege, which he interrupted neither by day nor by night.[33]

Defeatism was winning the day, although the arrival of Prince Edward from Tunis early in 1271 brought a certain amount of relief. The few raids he carried out had no real effect; however, he did manage to persuade Baibars to grant a general truce to the then king of Jerusalem, Hugh III of Cyprus – a truce which was to last ten years, ten months, ten days and ten hours (to reconcile the Christian solar year with the Muslim lunar year) and be concluded on 21 April 1272. It was long thought that this truce had been established without Prince Edward's knowledge, but that is incorrect. He left Acre at the end of the summer of 1272, reassured about the immediate future.[34]

So why did Baibars grant this reprieve to the Frankish possessions in Syria–Palestine? Just like his successor, Kalâwûn, he was preoccupied by the Mongol threat, which lasted until the end of the thirteenth century. The Mongols of Ilkhan had not given up their attempts to quell Mamluk power, and renewed their forays into Syria, although after their setback at Ayn Djalût they had had to abandon Aleppo and Damascus. The Franks, on the other hand, were reduced to total powerlessness, isolated as they were in their coastal enclaves of Castle Pilgrim, Acre, Tyre, Sidon, Beirut, Tripoli, Gibelet, Tortosa and Margat. There was therefore no immediate threat posed to the Mamluks on that side. And so, in this way, the Franks gained a reprieve of some fifteen years.

This period of respite occurred in 1272–3, at the same time as Guillaume de Beaujeu took over from Thomas Bérard as head of the Order of the Temple. The changeover can be seen as a turning point in the Order's history or, at the very least, a reorientation. Jacques de Molay experienced this change from the inside, perhaps even in the East, if we subscribe to the theory of the young Comtois Templar's early departure from the West.

1273

THOMAS BÉRARD AND GUILLAUME DE BEAUJEU TWO MASTERS, TWO POLICIES FOR THE TEMPLE?

When Renaud de Vichiers died on 20 January 1256, he was succeeded as head of the Order of the Temple by Thomas Bérard. Bérard was very likely Italian, although the English also lay claim to him.[1] His Mastership coincided almost totally with the dismantling of the Latin States under Baibars' assaults and the loss of most of the Order's fortresses and domains in the Holy Land – although he cannot be held particularly responsible for this rout which, as we have seen, was general. Indeed, there are other aspects of his Mastership which have not previously attracted enough attention, more worthy of comment.

Spanning the years 1256–73, Bérard's Mastership more or less tallied with that of Hugues Revel at the head of the Order of the Hospital (1258–77). The two Orders were rivals; they had noticeably differing, sometimes diametrically opposed, policies, and had been in direct confrontation in the war of Saint-Sabas at Acre (1256–8) during which the Temple had fought alongside the Pisans and the Venetians while the Hospitallers had sided with the Genoese. Thomas Bérard, although not Hugues Revel, was Grand Master during this period of intense confrontations between the two Orders. It may be supposed, however, that Bérard and his counterpart in the Hospital became aware of the mortal danger threatening the Franks, since directly after the war of Saint-Sabas the two Masters came to an agreement.[2] They were to become the architects of a policy of *détente* in the relations between the two Orders and of reforms within their own Orders.[3]

On several occasions in the past, the military Orders had tried to scale down their differences, which were often of a territorial nature, either by reaching an amicable agreement or resorting to arbitration. Conflicts arising from the use of the waters of the Na'aman river, which turned the wheels of both the Templars' and the Hospitallers' mills at Recordane and Doc (near Acre), led Bérard and Revel to seek the arbitration of a commission composed of the papal legate, representatives of the Teutonic Order and Geoffroy de Sergines, commander of the French regiment, who had become seneschal of the kingdom of Jerusalem. An agreement was concluded on 19 December 1262. In the same year, other arguments were settled following an identical procedure, notably at Sidon and Margat.[4]

Naturally, these agreements were not always correctly applied, but the will to resolve conflicts prevailed. In 1266–77, a new procedure was inaugurated which was destined to endure. It was an internal procedure within the three great military Orders (Temple, Hospital and Teutonic) stipulating that, in the event of bilateral disputes, the matter would be referred to the arbitration of the third – a procedure which applied throughout the whole of the Latin territories as well as in Armenia.[5] Nevertheless, jealousies and rivalries persisted, even if they were less marked than in the past. In his letter to the Prior of Saint-Gilles, on 27 May 1268, Hugues Revel speaks of the place at Arsur which 'held out for at least forty days although it was weaker than other strongholds', whereas 'Beaufort, so powerful that it was believed it could hold out for a whole year, was taken in four days'.[6] Of course, Arsur belonged to the Hospital, and Beaufort to the Temple! But that did not prevent the three Orders from acting in concert, for the most part, during this period.

The two Masters, Bérard and Revel, were also reformers. Hugues Revel's Mastership was marked by the publication of numerous statutes, regulatory or legislative decisions adopted at the meetings of the Order's general chapters. The resolutions of the eight chapters held during his Mastership which are known resulted in the publication of 105 statutes, 51 of which were from the chapter of 1262.[7] As for Thomas Bérard, around 1260 he added 113 new articles (the equivalent of the Hospital's statutes) to the Rule of the Order, completing the section on the Temple's penalties; these were articles 544–656, published under the title 'Details and examples of penalties'. It was less a matter of innovating than of detailing exactly, complementing and illustrating by example the Order's legislation concerning the misdeeds committed by Templars and the punishments they incurred[8] – a sort of jurisprudence.

Like his Hospitaller counterpart, Thomas Bérard became conscious of the bad effect that the rivalry and disputes between the Orders, as well as their supposed (and sometimes actual) laxity in disciplinary matters, might have upon the governments of the West – the providers of men, money and aid for the Holy Land. The context of defeat in the face of the Muslim enemy reinforced the providential conception of history which was widespread at the time. In order to explain the repeated reverses suffered by the Christians, their sins were cited, while the Mamluks were regarded as the instruments of a just punishment from God. Ricaut Bonomel, a Templar of Provençal origin, expressed his anger and sorrow at the situation thus created: 'In truth, anyone who has eyes to see realises that God upholds them [the Infidels]. For God, who should be waking, is sleeping, and Bafomet [Mahomet] uses all his power for the benefit of the Melicadeser [Baibars].'[9]

Thomas Bérard died on 25 March 1273, 'and Brother Guillaume de Beaujeu was made Master on XIII day of May, who was overseas Commander of the Temple in Puglia'.[10] The Templar of Tyre proves more loquacious, not to say more precise:

> And in the year of the incarnation of Christ MCC and LXXIII [1273], Brother Thomas Bérard, Master of the Temple, died and Guillaume de Beaujeu was made Master, a very fine man, related to the king of France, and he was very generous and liberal in many ways and did many charitable works for which he was much renowned, and the Temple in his time was greatly honoured and feared, and when he was made Master he was a Commander in Puglia, and remained overseas for 2 years, visited all the Templar houses in the kingdom of France and England and Spain, and amassed great treasure and came to Acre.[11]

Guillaume de Beaujeu was then about forty. Was he a Comtois (that is, from Franche-Comté), coming from the *châtellenie* (land belonging to the owner of a château) of Beaujeu, not far from Gray?[12] A document dated 27 June 1286, a letter from Henry II, formally gives the lie to this identification. Henry II, king of Cyprus and Jerusalem, had just landed at Acre and found himself prevented from lodging in the royal palace 'by people of my lord the king of France' (in other words, the Angevins). Henry II deplored this state of affairs, and was approved by the Masters of the Orders and prelates of the Holy Land, each of whom had affixed his seal at the foot of the document. The Templar seal was not the one with the dome, but the seal with the horse mounted by two knights; on the reverse was the personal seal of Guillaume de Beaujeu: an azure shield with a black lion rampant, armed, and its tongue in gules.[13] These were the arms of the noble family of Beaujeu-Forez. But to which branch did Guillaume belong?

Guichard IV, lord of Beaujeu, had married Sibille of Hainaut, whose sister Isabelle had married the king of France, Philip Augustus, in 1180. The Beaujeu family were therefore well connected to the kings of France, and the Templar of Tyre is not mistaken when he says Guillaume is one of their relatives – a rather distant kinship, but real all the same. Guichard IV had two sons: the elder, Humbert V of Beaujeu, Constable of France, died at Damietta in 1250; the second, Guichard of Beaujeu, was lord of Montpensier. From that starting point, we can trace two possible ancestral lines for the Master of the Temple.

Perhaps he belonged to the senior branch. Humbert V left two children: Guichard V, lord of Beaujeu from 1250 to 1265, died without issue, so that Isabelle, his sister, inherited his rights and became lady of Beaujeu; she married Renaud I, Count of Forez in 1247. According to some genealogies, the couple had three sons: Guigues, the eldest, inherited the county of Forez; Louis, the second, the seigneurie of Beaujeu, and Guillaume, the third, was destined to become our Master of the Temple. This is genealogy number one. A sentence from the Templar of Tyre, who was Guillaume de Beaujeu's secretary, seems to lend a weighty argument in its favour. Remarking on the death of the French king, Philip III, at Gerona in Catalonia in 1285, and some days later that of Louis de Beaujeu, Constable of France, he adds, 'this Constable was the brother of the Master of the Temple, Brother Guillaume de Beaujeu'.[14]

Genealogy number two, meanwhile, connects him to the junior branch of the Beaujeu-Montpensier family. Guichard, Humbert's younger brother, married Catherine de Montferrand but died in 1256, leaving several children: Humbert, who took part in the Tunis crusade, became Constable of France in 1273 and died in Aragon in 1285; Guillaume, who was to become Master of the Temple; Heric or Henri, lord of Hermant, Marshal of France, who was slaughtered at Tunis in 1270; and Louis, lord of Montferrand, also present at Tunis, who died in 1280.[15]

Genealogy number one, which is the most frequently proposed of the two, attaches little importance to the cadet branch. It recalls only Humbert, the Constable, who died in 1285; but in that case it cannot make Louis, of the senior branch, a Constable. If we follow genealogy number two, however, then the Louis de Beaujeu of genealogy number one is the heir to all the possessions of his father Renaud and his mother, that is to say, Forez and Beaujolais; yet he did not die until 1296.

The Templar of Tyre was therefore mistaken about the identity of the Constable of France who died in 1285; it was Humbert of the Montpensier branch, not Louis of the Beaujeu-Forez branch. Guillaume de Beaujeu really was the brother of a Constable of France, but that Constable's name was Humbert. Perhaps the confusion arose from the fact that in Sicily, with King Charles I of Anjou, there was a Louis de Beaujeu, with property in Italy, but who had no connection with the Grand Master's family.[16]

But another fact can be picked out which may favour genealogy number one: the arms of Guillaume de Beaujeu on the seal do not bear a mark of cadency. According to J.-P. Lombard, that 'could [I emphasise the conditional] indicate that he was the head of the senior branch of his house, unless the mark of cadency is the later mark of the Dreux–Beaujeu alliance'.[17]

However that may be, he had a few distant family links with the king of France, and thus with Charles of Anjou; but chiefly he had political connections with the latter and so, in this respect, his presence in southern Italy in 1272 is significant. The Master of the Hospital, Hugues Revel, was not mistaken when, in a letter to the Count of Flanders, Guy de Dampierre, dated 17 May 1273, he informed him of the change that had occurred at the head of the Templar Order:

> It is true that God gave his command to the Master of the Temple, Brother Thomas Bérard, in the past month of March ... Whereupon, my lord, the valiant men of the Temple elected, as Master and governor of their house, Brother Guillaume de Beaujeu, in reverence to the lord king of France and to yourself ...[18]

Guillaume de Beaujeu entered the Temple before 1253; we know that he was in the East in 1260, because in that year he was taken prisoner in the wake of an unfortunate attack on Tiberias. He is thought to have been châtelain of Beaufort (a castle that fell into Baibars' hands in 1268), Commander of Tripoli (the province) in 1271, then, in 1272, Commander of Puglia, Apulia or Sicily (that is, the Templar province covering the kingdom of Sicily conquered by Charles of Anjou). He was there when he was elected Grand Master and people came to tell him the news. Still according to Hugues Revel, the messengers were, 'brave knights of the Temple [who] went there and brought him the purse and the seal', that is, the Order's seal. The *Éraclès* gives us the names of these messengers: Guillaume de Ponçon, who had substituted for the Master (he had been appointed lieutenant), and Bertran de Fox. Brother Gaifier had been Grand Commander, and by virtue of this had headed the Order in Beaujeu's absence.[19] According to the Templar of Tyre, Guillaume de Beaujeu carried out a visit to the commanderies in the West before taking up his post; this could have taken place between the summer of 1273 and the spring of 1274, or after the Council of Lyon, in late 1274 or spring 1275, although that tour may have had neither the scope nor the exhaustive nature implied by the chronicler.

At all events, the principal reason for Beaujeu's prolonged stay in the West was not his tour, but that Pope Gregory X kept him there. On 13 October 1273, the latter wrote to the Patriarch of Jerusalem to inform him that the new Master would not be returning before the Council, which was in preparation at Lyon, as the pope needed his advice in dealing with the matter of a crusade.[20] The Master of the Hospital was also summoned, but sent a representative, whereas Beaujeu attended in person. The second Council of Lyon took place from 7 May to 17 July 1274. Besides the question of the crusade, for the first time the matter of uniting the military Orders, or at least the three main ones – Temple, Hospital and Teutonic was to be dealt with. That was rejected, but would henceforward remain a matter pending, and one of the issues Jacques de Molay would inherit on becoming Grand Master. When the Council was over, the pope decided to preach for a general crusade, although the almost unanimous decision of the Council (including Beaujeu) had been to reject this kind of expedition, preferring what was then known as a 'special passage', in other words, a relief expedition carried out by seasoned fighters remaining permanently in the Holy Land. It was the pope's death in 1276 that interrupted preparations for this great crusade or 'general passage'.[21]

The Templars in the East were worried by the Master's prolonged absence during such a delicate period, but their urgent appeals to the pope achieved nothing. On 3 October 1274, they wrote to the king of England that they had had no news of the Master and that, in the meantime, the Master's temporary replacement had appointed Robert de Turvill as Master of England, and sent him to the West.[22] Not until the end of summer 1275 did Guillaume de Beaujeu finally arrive at Acre, not – as it is stated in the *Éraclès* – on 29 September but, as Beaujeu himself specifies in a letter to the king of England written on 2 October at Acre, on 15 September, after a rough crossing of the Mediterranean.[23]

The policy Beaujeu would follow right up to his death in 1291 reveals a serious shift from that of Thomas Bérard, although both were equal in their defence of the Order and its autonomy. Beaujeu contributed more panache, or daring, at the cost of more imprudence.

Three aspects characterise this policy:

* Beaujeu was a man of the Angevins, masters of Sicily.
* He dragged the Order into conflicts with the Christian authorities which were very damaging for the Holy Land and the Order's reputation.
* He neglected the Mongol option, preferring a policy of truces and understandings with the Mamluks which he considered to be more advantageous to the Franks and, first and foremost, to his Order.

These last two features of his policy were naturally in keeping with the interests of the Angevins.

But what did it mean to be a 'man of the Angevins'? In 1265 Louis IX's brother Charles, Count of Anjou and Maine and by now Count of Provence following his marriage to the heiress to the county, Beatrice (sister of both the queen of France and the queen of England), had been invested with the kingdom of Sicily by the pope, who charged him with conquering it and wiping out the last representatives of the Staufen dynasty, that 'race of vipers'. Frederick II had certainly been stripped of his imperial title, which was an elective office, in 1245; but it had remained very difficult to drive him out of his kingdom of Sicily, to the extent that after his death in 1250, his legitimate son Conrad IV (1250–4), then his bastard son Manfred (1254–66) managed to maintain a firm grip on the place. Using the weapons of the crusade against Manfred, the papacy found its champion in Charles of Anjou. Crowned in Rome, Charles entered the kingdom early in 1266 and defeated Manfred at Benevento on 26 February, thus securing a hold on southern Italy and Sicily. On 23 August 1268, he carried the day at the battle of Tagliacozzo over the last of the Staufens, the very young Conradin, son of Conrad IV, and had him executed. There was still Constance, however,

Manfred's daughter and wife of Peter III, king of Aragon, so the rights of the Staufen family were henceforward transferred to the crown of Aragon.

Having become king, Charles followed in his predecessor's footsteps. The rulers of Sicily had all nurtured grandiose Mediterranean plans: the Normans in the twelfth century, Henry VI and his son Frederick in the thirteenth, and Charles of Anjou had all succumbed to the 'Sicilian mirage'. For his part, Charles set his sights on Albania and Epirus; he wanted to re-establish the Latin Empire of Constantinople and acquire rights over the Frankish principality of Achaia.

At last, on 7 June 1277, he bought the rights which Marie of Antioch (whom the texts of the time call the 'demoiselle') claimed to have over the kingdom of Jerusalem; this forced him into a confrontation with Hugh III, king of Cyprus, who also claimed to be king of Jerusalem, invested as he had been by the High Court of the realm. Charles I had the support of the papacy, Guillaume de Beaujeu's Templars and the French regiment; his representative, Roger de San Severino, was thus able to install himself at Acre without meeting any resistance. Among the Italian communes, Venice accepted him at once. In July 1277, the seigneur of Tyre, Jean de Montfort, an ally of the Genoese and supporter of Hugh III of Cyprus, preferred to temporise with Charles I and became reconciled with the Venetians. To the latter he restored the villages ('*casaux*') of which they had been dispossessed in the neighbouring countryside. The agreement was concluded under the auspices of Guillaume de Beaujeu (but in the presence of Hospitaller witnesses) 'in the field', in the tent of the Master of the Order in the village of Somelaria [Sumeriya].[24]

In 1279, Beaujeu banned Hugh from entering Tyre, naturally provoking a riposte. The king of Cyprus had the Temple's possessions seized.[25] This decision created a lasting crisis in relations between the Temple and the Cypriot royalty, a problem that Jacques de Molay was also to inherit when he became Grand Master.

Like the late Frederick II, Charles I maintained cordial relations with the sultan of Egypt; that is how he came to intervene with Baibars, urging him to grant the truce of 1272. Following the defeat suffered by the Mongols at Homs in 1281, Roger de San Severino went in person to congratulate the conqueror, the Mamluk sultan Kalâwûn. He similarly made an effort to maintain good relations with the princes of the Maghreb, notably Tunis. In connection with this, it must be made clear that if the crusade undertaken by his brother, the king of France, was diverted to this town,[26] it was nothing to do with Charles.

Guillaume de Beaujeu was not merely the mouthpiece for Charles of Anjou; by upholding the latter's policy, he was ensuring the autonomy of his Order in the Holy Land – not without risk, as may be seen at Cyprus. He conducted himself like an independent seigneur and stepped up interventions in the affairs of the Latin States – or what was left of them.

The Order of the Temple played an active part, in particular, in the conflict between the count of Tripoli (still ruler of Antioch even after the fall of the principality in 1268) and his vassal Guy de Gibelet. The intervention of the Templars, who had the fortified town of Tortosa at their disposal, was brought about by the death in 1275 of Bohemond VI, and the minority of his son and successor, Bohemond VII. The young prince's mother had the regency entrusted to her, while the bishop of Tortosa was given guardianship of the prince. That annoyed the lay aristocracy, at the head of whom was the seigneur of Gibelet, Guy II (from the Genoese Embriaci family). At first, the Templars sided with the prince and his guardian, but they then changed their allegiance at the urging of the bishop of Tripoli, who was a fellow member of the Temple. A private matter – a promise of marriage that was not kept – also set Guy de Gibelet against the bishop of Tortosa, and it was following Guy's abduction of the daughter of a rich lord, who had been promised to his brother but eventually married a nephew of the bishop, that the seigneur of Gibelet took refuge at Acre with the Templars: 'And became a fellow member of the Temple, and was a great friend of the Master, Brother Guillaume de Beaujeu, who promised to help him as much as he could.'[27] That help was substantial: boats, men-at-arms, crossbowmen. On two occasions in 1277–8, Guy and the Templars tried to gain a hold in Tripoli, but in vain.

Then a truce was negotiated, thanks to the arbitration of the Master of the Hospital, Nicolas Le Lorgne. It lasted a few, incident-filled months, but the conflict resumed, for the worse, in 1281–2. Guy de Gibelet again tried to enter Tripoli, but misunderstandings with the Templars in the town led to failure on no fewer than three occasions. The third time, he managed to penetrate the town by night, but the Templars were waiting for him elsewhere and he was taken prisoner by the count's men. On 18 February 1282, transferred to the nearby castle of Nefin, 'sire Gui, formerly lord of Gibelet said and confessed that he had come three times to try to take Tripoli …' In this confession, made in front of a notary, Guy de Gibelet understandably blamed Guillaume de Beaujeu and the Templars for his situation. He made out that they were the instigators of the attacks on Tripoli, while he was the resigned and manipulated instrument of Beaujeu,[28] whose ambition it was to control Tripoli and in so doing add another coastal defence lair to the ones he already had at Castle Pilgrim, Sidon and Tortosa.

Bohemond VII was pitiless; Guy de Gibelet and his brother were shut up in a pit where they died of starvation, and all the Geonese captured in the town of Tripoli had their eyes gouged out. Guy's confession is interesting in that it throws light on the 'technological warfare' of the period: carrier pigeons and coded messages, visual signals and flares, secret rendez-vous – everything was tried to ensure perfect co-ordination between the Templars of Tripoli, Templars from outside and Guy de Gibelet, however, nothing worked out according to plan.

The actions taken by Guillaume de Beaujeu against the existing ruling powers in the kingdoms of Cyprus and Jerusalem, as well as in the county of Tripoli, are in part clarified by the policy he followed in regard to the Mamluks.

Guillaume de Beaujeu had been elected at a time when a general truce had been agreed between Baibars and Hugh III of Cyprus, under the auspices of Edward I of England. However, this did not prevent the arrangement of specific truces between the Mamluk government and this or that Christian territory. For Muslim states thought of their relations with non-Muslims in two ways: within the *Dar al-Islam* (the house of Islam), non-Muslims had the status of *dhimmi* (protected people) which guaranteed them freedom of worship and respect for their laws and customs, by means of the payment of a *djyẓia* or tribute. Outside the *Dar al-Islam*, everywhere was considered fair game, to be conquered and incorporated into the *Dar al-Islam*. There was no question of peace with the non-Muslims in those territories, merely truces recognising a relationship of strength that was always temporary and subject to change. In the last three decades of their existence, the Franks asked for truces on several occasions; there exist texts for eleven of them between 1267 and 1290, although at least two others are also known about.[29] Two were general truces: that of 1272, which was then renewed in 1283 (the text of which has been preserved).[30]

The most numerous, however, were the special ones. Baibars and his successor Kalâwûn had a good understanding of the political and territorial situation in the Frankish East: a juxtaposition, if it can be called that, since their occupation was intermittent, of principalities or seigneuries, and communities, where each looked after its own interests, trying to safeguard its position while sheltering under a truce which had been begged for from the sultans. The Templars and Hospitallers negotiated four such truces, two each.

The chronology of these agreements clearly reveals the reasons why they came about. In 1266, Baibars had just taken the Templar castle of Safed. Anxious for their own safety, the Hospitallers wanted to protect themselves in the north; the truce of 1267 offered such protection for their castles in the county of Tripoli, in exchange for which they agreed to cease levying the tribute they took from the territory of the Assassins sect. In 1271, however, the Krak des Chevaliers fell. Temple and Hospital jointly asked for truces to protect the fortresses they still held in the county: Tortosa for the Templars, Margat for the Hospitallers. As the chronicler al-Yunini (1242–1326) recorded:

> When the Krak des Chevaliers was taken, the seigneur of Tortosa wrote to Baibars to ask for a truce to be agreed, and sent him his keys. He made peace with him on the basis of the concession of half the grain produced on his territory, and installed a permanent inspector there. The Hospitallers' ambassadors arrived from Margat, and he made a truce with them on the same basis of a share in the revenues. This was on the 1st day of Ramaḍan 669 [13 April 1271] and the truce was established for ten years, ten months, ten days.[31]

Eleven years later, the Templars renewed this treaty, which dealt only with Tortosa, the town and its port, here again, for ten years, ten months, etc.[32]

Beaujeu's policy, therefore, lay in playing for time and extending the existence, at the price of concessions which further diminished them, of territories that were already stripped to the bare bones, but defendable because they were backed by solid coastal fortresses. The link between these enclaves was assured by the sea, as we saw in the relations between the Templars and Guy de Gibelet; from Acre or Sidon to Gibelet, from Gibelet to Tripoli, everything was carried by boat.

This 'system of truces' could last only on two conditions: that the Mamluks were engaged on another front, and that close relations were maintained with them.

The first condition was realised thanks to the Mongols. Hûlâgû's successors at the head of Ilkhan had not in fact given up their attempts to vanquish the

Mamluks. In 1277, Baibars suffered a defeat against them, though not a grave one. In 1281, the khan Abagha launched a new offensive against Syria; once again the Armenian king of Cilicia helped him, and once again the Franks of the kingdom of Jerusalem displayed what might be termed a 'hostile neutrality' towards the Mongols. Aleppo was occupied again, Damascus threatened, but in October the first battle of Homs ended in a fresh failure for the Mongols.

The Armenians once more suffered the wrath of the Mamluk sultan, and the Franks of the kingdom of Jerusalem did very little to help them. But Kalâwûn's response was moderate; the Mongols did not disarm and, on Abagha's death in 1284, the appointment of Arghun, who was both openly pro-Christian and very hostile to the Mamluks, as khan of Ilkhan could only incite him to concentrate on the principal enemy.

The repeated failures of the Mongols to beat the Mamluks need some explanation, however. Firstly, it was only ever Ilkhan that was concerned, and its masters were ever watchful of what was happening at Karakorum in the ever-delicate matter of the succession of the Great Khan. Moreover, there was much rivalry between Ilkhan and the Golden Horde (or Kiptchak). Both khanates controlled the last stretch of a major commercial route that allowed access to China and the Far East: the Mongol route in the north, which came out at the lower Volga, then the Black Sea; and the Silk Road which arrived at Ayas (or Lajazzo), the port of Little Armenia, by way of Tabriz, capital of Ilkhan. The Mongols of the Golden Horde, who had been converted to Islam very early on, tried to penetrate south of the Caucausus, towards Tabriz. Two camps began to form within the vast Mongol empire: the allied khanates of Ilkhan and China versus the khanates of the Golden Horde and the Djagathai (Central Asia); while outside the Mongol world, an alliance was created between the Mamluks, the Golden Horde and the Byzantine Empire. The Turkish slaves who made up the Mamluk army were basically recruited from the Kiptchak, so the khans of Ilkhan always had to keep an eye out on their northern front for the Golden Horde when they were fighting the Mamluks, and very often threats on this front (astutely set in motion by Mamluk diplomacy) compelled them to postpone, interrupt or shorten an offensive.

To this may be added a more general, military explanation. The Mongol army was an army of horsemen, which was hampered in providing food for its mounts by the desert nature of the vast territories of Mesopotamia and Syria that had to be crossed in order for it to attack the Mamluk empire.

And so, an alliance with the Mongols of Ilkhan must have seemed natural to the Franks. That is what was understood by the Christian states of the North, Armenia of Cilicia first of all, but also the county of Tripoli. Even the brothers in the military Orders in those regions adhered to this pro-Mongol policy, in particular the Hospitallers of Margat, who sent a contingent to the battle of Homs. Truce or not, Kalâwûn wanted to settle scores with those Hospitallers as soon as he possibly could; and on 25 May 1285, the last great Hospitaller fortress fell.

In the kingdom of Jerusalem, meanwhile, a Mongol alliance was still not on the agenda, and the Franks made efforts to maintain reasonable relations with the Mamluks. In 1281, while Kalâwûn was negotiating a renewal of the truce of 1272 with the Franks, a conspiracy was mounted against him. The Franks found out and warned the sultan. After the battle of Homs, Roger de San Severino went to congratulate the victor Kalâwûn in his camp. For a long time, truces made with the sultan contained the proviso that, in the event of a crusade from the West, the Franks could suspend them; but henceforward they would have to inform the sultan of the progress and aims of such a crusade.

Beaujeu was not to be left out, and went about maintaining good relations with the sultan Kalâwûn; good relations which were known to all and, at least in the beginning, caused little upset in the Latin East, since they sometimes proved very useful. For example, after the battle of Homs, in which they had supported the Mongols, the Armenians had everything to fear from the Mamluks. The reaction of the latter was, however, moderate – for reasons already explained; but Kalâwûn refused to have any dealings with the king of Armenia, Levon II, even though the king wanted to agree a truce. Levon appealed to the Templars. Here is how one Muslim writer recounted the episode, which took place in 1285:

> While our lord the sultan was laying siege to the castle of Margat, the Commander of the Templars of Little Armenia came in person to bring a message from the seigneur of Sis (capital of the kingdom). He brought a letter from the king and another from the Master of the Templars containing a request on the part of the seigneur of Sis, a request in which he asked pardon for his conduct and offered his apologies. The request was that Levon's ambassadors might appear at the sultan's court; and the reason the Master presented this request was that, each time the king's ambassadors presented themselves at court, they

were arrested and imprisoned and were never given an answer. So the king had astutely sought the help of the Master of the Templars, and consequently the Commander had come as mediator to bring matters to a successful conclusion.[33]

The end of the affair was a truce, with draconian conditions, which the sultan granted to the Armenians on 6 June 1285.[34]

Guillaume de Beaujeu was not naïve, however, and he expected his good relations with the Mamluks to have some payback – information. The Master of the Temple had informants in Cairo, in the sultan's council itself; in fact, he had 'honourable correspondents' more or less everywhere. In Cairo, one was the emir Salah, in reality Badr al-Din Baktash al-Fakhri, one of the sultan's trusted men in the field of armaments.[35] In 1289, therefore, when Kalâwûn unilaterally decided to break the truce and attack Tripoli (he had not forgotten the count's participation in the Mongol operations), Guillaume de Beaujeu was informed about it:

> ... there was an emir who was old, and one of the four who upheld the 'paynim' [heathendom] let my lord the Master of the Temple know this piece of news, and this emir was named Emir Salah, who was in the habit of informing the Master of the Temple for the sake of Christendom when the sultan wanted to do it harm in any way, and cost the Master fine gifts which he sent to him each year.[36]

Beaujeu's policy had its limits, however. His commitment to the Angevins became increasingly difficult to maintain when, beginning in 1282, King Charles I, confronted by a coalition which united the Byzantine emperor Michael VIII, the king of Aragon Peter III and the rebel Sicilians (the Sicilian Vespers of 30 March 1282), lost control of Sicily.[37] Engaged in a long and fruitless war of reconquest, Charles I, and then his son Charles II (1285–1309), hardly bothered any more with Jerusalem, leaving their representatives at Acre, Roger de San Severino then Eudes Poilechien, to manage by themselves. Consequently, on the death of Charles I in 1285, the king of Cyprus, Henry II, was able to reclaim the crown of Jerusalem without too much difficulty. He negotiated with Guillaume de Beaujeu, and, as the Templar of Tyre informs us: 'The matter was agreed, and the agreement was first written by my own hand.'[38]

The following year, Henry II was welcomed with enthusiasm and joy by the population of Acre. The Masters of the three military Orders, gathered at the Temple, came to an agreement to put pressure on Eudes Poilechien (who had retreated with his loyal followers to the castle) 'and arranged it so that Messire Eudes Poilechien promised to hand over the castle to 3 monastic institutions ... and 4 days later the castle was handed back and he [King Henry] went to stay in it'.[39] On 15 August 1286, Henry was crowned king of Jerusalem at Tyre, the traditional site for royal coronations. The Franks of the East had regained their unity, but very late in the day. The Angevin interlude was over, but the frenetic involvement of Beaujeu and the Templars in that alliance was never completely forgotten on the Cypriot side.

As for the policy of good relations with the Mamluks, it did not always attain unanimity, even if many of those who criticised it were themselves hypocrites. When emir Salah warned Beaujeu of the imminence of an attack on Tripoli by Kalâwûn, the Master of the Temple informed the town's authorities. Thinking themselves to be protected by the truce, 'those of Tripoli', in the words of the Templar of Tyre, did not believe him and some 'had ugly words for the Master, saying he did it to frighten them'. When the Mamluk army penetrated Frankish territory, Beaujeu resumed his attempts and sent Brother Redecoeur, an important knight of the Order who had been Commander of Tripoli, to put the town on its guard again. There was still argument as to whether 'to believe or not', before they finally gave him credence.[40] But too late. Tripoli fell on 26 April 1289.

Mistrust was still in evidence when, the following year, Kalâwûn began preparing his final attack on Acre. Here again, people thought they were covered by the truce. Kalâwûn cared little about it, however, having already started his preparations. Then, the foolish behaviour of a newly disembarked group of Lombard crusaders provided him with the justification he was looking for. The crusaders massacred some Muslim merchants at Acre (as well as some Syrian Christians who resembled them at the same time). Here again, however, Beaujeu's conduct was ambiguous. To the council which had assembled to accede to the demands set out by Kalâwûn after this attack, he proposed handing over all those who, in the prisons of Acre (royal prisons as well as those of the military Orders and the Venetians), 'were to die for their misdeeds, claiming that it was they who had broken the truce and killed the Saracen villeins [in the sense of non-noble]'.[41] Some approved, but many more rejected the idea, unwilling to hand over Christians, even criminal ones, to the Infidels. Nothing, therefore, was done.

Kalâwûn, then his successor al-Ashraf Khalil, continued their preparations while also concealing their intentions, but 'emir Salah, admiral [emir] who was a friend of the Master of the Temple, let the said Master know that the sultan would in any event come to besiege Acre, and the Master of the Temple let it be known to all the gentlemen of Acre, but they would not believe him'.[42] Only the death of Kalâwûn in October 1290 granted a short respite to the carefree inhabitants of Acre.

These practices of Beaujeu, or perhaps the over-ostentatious way he had of revealing them (since he was not alone in them), caused uneasiness even in the bosom of his Order. I have already quoted Jacques de Molay's testimony, but among the Templars questioned at the time of the trial, there were others who referred to these deeds. Pierre de Nobiliac, a sergeant from the diocese of Limoges who was interrogated on 10 May 1311 'also stated that the said Guillaume was very friendly with the sultan and the Saracens, for otherwise it would have been impossible for him to survive with his Order in Outremer'.[43] A sympathetic viewpoint; but that of Hugues de Narsac, on 8 May in the same year, was more critical. Speaking of the misdeeds of which the Templars were accused, he said that

> these misdeeds were born in Outremer, where there was often talk with the Saracens, and Guillaume de Beaujeu, erstwhile Master of the Order, and Brother Mathieu le Sauvage, knight, struck up a great friendship with the sultan and the Saracens; and the said Brother Mathieu had conversations with them, and Brother Guillaume had several Saracens in his pay when he wanted to; and they said they did so for greater safety for themselves. But others contradicted that.[44]

Hugues de Narsac, who had never been in the East, gleaned his information from the testimony of brethren returning to the West whom he may have met during the years since his reception into the Order in 1286.

Guillaume Textoris, a priest of the Order questioned on 30 March 1311, was frankly critical; he 'had frequently heard it said by brothers whose names he no longer recalls that the misdeeds he had confessed to had been introduced into the Order after the death of Guillaume de Beaujeu, Master of the Order, against whom great scandal, suspicion and slanderous remarks had appeared at that time'.[45]

These testimonies need to be treated with caution, since the Templars were being questioned at a time when the attempt to defend the Order by the Templars themselves had been stifled in May 1310 and when fifty-four of them had been sentenced to the stake. The answer may have been whispered to them, for in any case it was in the air; but as we know that, when questioned by the judges regarding the origin of the 'errors' introduced into the Order's practices, the majority of Templars replied that they knew nothing and there the matter rested, it is hard to see what these three Templars hoped to gain by striving to find an origin or explanation for the misdeeds they admitted to. In any case, it is not the real explanation, although it does refer to actual practices, used in evidence in the charges brought against the Temple, when they were commonplace – and not only among the Templars.

Much of the above may not appear directly relevant to a biography of Jacques de Molay. However, he did serve as a Templar under both these two Masters and, when he became Master of the Order himself, he carried on from where they left off. I shall return later to the short Mastership of Thibaud Gaudin in 1291–2. Almost no evidence is available about Molay during those years, but such experiences must have left their mark on him and his knowledge of the choices made by Bérard and Beaujeu must have helped him guide the Templar Order when he too became Grand Master. For, as we have just seen, Bérard and Beaujeu had not acted in the same circumstances; they had not behaved or reacted in the same way, or pursued the same policy. Molay the Templar was able to compare, pass a judgement and, later, make choices, taking his inspiration from one or the other.

Only three references to Molay himself can be found from 1265, the year he entered the Temple, to 1291: firstly, as previously mentioned, his declaration to the judges regarding Beaujeu (corroborated by the testimonies given above) on 28 November 1309; then two testimonies describing him as the 'receiver' of new Templars on two occasions in the years 1284–5.

It is puzzling that nothing else of a 27-year career has been recorded. Perhaps he performed no office at all in the Order, either as a rank-and-file member, in a commandery, or at the summit of the hierarchy, in neither the East nor the West. But his predecessors held responsible posts in the Order before becoming its Grand Masters: Renaud de Vichiers had been a Marshal; we do not know about Bérard, but Beaujeu had probably been governor (castellan) of the castle of Beaufort, a Commander in the county of Tripoli in 1271 and Commander or Master of Sicily in 1272; and Gaudin had been Grand Commander for more than ten years.

As nothing positive is known, some people have naturally credited Jacques de Molay with various offices. Laurent Dailliez plausibly maintains that Molay was a Marshal of the Order at the time of his election;[46] however, he could not have been one until after the death of Pierre de Sivrey, who was decapitated by the Mamluks towards the end of the siege of Acre in May 1291.[47] Prior to that, it is impossible, because almost all the Order's dignitaries in Beaujeu's time are known, and he is not among them.

Molay is said by some to have held the office of Master of England. In 1295, claims T. Parker[48] – although this is impossible, as he had been Grand Master since 1292; someone else proposes 1293 – impossible for the same reason.[49] And prior to those dates, the list of Masters of England is complete.

There exist two references to Molay for the years 1284–5, one of which emerges from the interrogation of Jean de Vila in Cyprus on 28 May 1310, and the other from that of Guy Dauphin, questioned in Paris on 8 January 1311. Jean de Vila, the last Draper of the Order, states that he was received into the Order of the Temple twenty-five years earlier (i.e. in 1285) by Jacques de Molay, Master of the Order (*sic*) in Paris; present were Hugues de Pairaud, then Master of France, and Aymon d'Oiselay, the last Marshal of the Order, also interrogated in Cyprus some days before Jean de Vila.[50]

Guy Dauphin, who was forty-one years old at the time of his interrogation, had entered the Temple thirty years earlier, in 1281. Twenty-six years before, in 1285, he had seen Brother Roncelin, a knight from Provence, received at Acre by Brother Guillaume de Beaujeu, in the presence of: 'Brothers Thibaud Gaudin, Commander of the Land of Outremer [or Grand Commander], and the present Master of the Temple [Jacques de Molay], Pierre de Sivrey, Draper [he subsequently became Marshal], Pierre de Montade [this was the Catalan Moncade], Commander of Acre, Florent de Villa, companion [*socius*] of the said Master'.[51] This list is illuminating in that Molay is named among a number of important dignitaries in 1285, without himself apparently having a title or office, not even that of Master's companion. Perhaps in Guy Dauphin's memory, Molay's current office (in 1311) of Grand Master had obscured a less obvious office which he might have held earlier. But at the age of fifteen one's memory is excellent, and

what Guy Dauphin says is otherwise precise and accurate (other sources corroborate his list of dignitaries); there is therefore no reason to impute error or
confusion to him.

Molay himself, in his first interrogation in 1307, said that he had not received
many Templars into the Order and, indeed, from the various interrogations of
the trial it is possible to trace barely a dozen.[52] It is understandable that he would
hardly have done so as Grand Master, and it seems to have been equally the case
with Beaujeu; however, if he had held the office of Commander, for instance,
his name would have appeared more often. If Molay is rarely cited, it is simply
because he was telling the truth: he had not often received new entrants, probably because he had exercised none of the functions which would have made him
a 'receiver', such as Commander of a house, Master of a province, or Visitor.

Unless the witness was confused, the fact remains that Molay had received a
Templar in Paris in the presence of the Master of France, who would normally
have had this honour. Having arrived in Paris from the East, perhaps Molay was
given the task of receiving the postulant out of deference, even if he did not
hold a leading post in the Order. Molay the rank-and-file Templar was obviously not some anonymous knight. Was he a rebel? Someone who upset the
establishment? I will come back to this.

No other indication is available relating to Molay's stay in the West in 1285.
Was it a short one? Was he on some kind of mission? Or was he at the end, or
beginning, of a longer sojourn? We do not know the exact dates, and therefore
in which order the two receptions mentioned, at Acre and at Paris, took place.
Some historians think that he was not at Acre at the time of the town's final siege;
others think the opposite – there is no proof to support either argument.[53]

From 1265 to 1291, Jacques de Molay did not get himself talked about.
Perhaps he was an unusually discreet and reserved man. There is another possibility, however, based on some very meagre clues. Perhaps Molay held no
important office in the Order because he did not belong to Guillaume de Beaujeu's 'team', and did not agree with his policies, even though, in his deposition
during the trial, he admitted that nothing else could have been done. He would
never have been Beaujeu's man, the man of the Angevins and consequently the
man of the king of France. One must be cautious, but the circumstances of his
election to Grand Master of the Templar Order, *a posteriori*, give some credence
to this theory.

1292

GRAND MASTER OF
THE ORDER OF THE TEMPLE

In 1285, Jacques de Molay was in Paris, then in Acre, or possibly in Acre, then in Paris. Where he was and what he did between 1285 and 1291 is not known. There is no proof that he was in Acre during the siege but this doesn't mean that he was *not* there.[1]

The account of the fall of Acre is well documented, in both Latin and Arab sources. On the Latin side, we have two first-hand witnesses: the Templar of Tyre and the anonymous author of the *De excidio urbis Aconis* (*On the destruction of the town of Acre*).[2] On the Arab side, Makrizi's[3] *History of the Mamluk Sultans* and the *Summary of the History of Humankind*, by Abu al-Fida, an eyewitness fighting at the head of the troops of Hamah, of which he was emir,[4] head a list of some dozen historical works cited by D. Little.[5]

In the summer of 1290, Kalâwûn decided to attack Acre, after his council had deliberated over whether the murder of Muslim merchants by crusaders from the West should be regarded as a *casus belli* bringing about a break in the truce; the council thought not, but Kalâwûn paid no heed, having made up his mind well before those murders. He immediately began making substantial preparations, mobilising all his emirs and all the provinces in his empire. He also stepped up the number of false alarms in order to lull the Christians' vigilance. Beaujeu had been informed of Kalâwûn's intentions but, as with Tripoli, no one believed him.[6] The sultan's death during the winter did nothing to slow down preparations, and in March 1291 his son al-Ashraf Khalil was ready. Troops from the provinces, supplies and siege material were methodically transported to Acre. As well as regular troops, al-Ashraf Khalil had received reinforcements of numerous 'fighters for the faith' mobilised by the jihad.

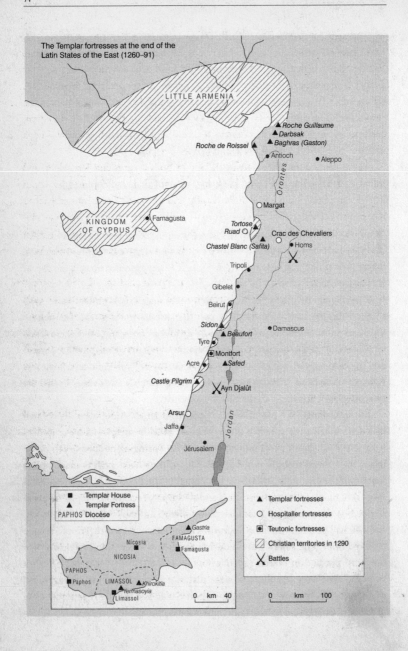

The Templar fortresses at the end of the
Latin States of the East (1260–91)

LITTLE ARMENIA

▲ Roche Guillaume
▲ Darbsak
▲ Baghras (Gaston)
Roche de Roissel ▲
● Antioch   ● Aleppo

Orontes

○ Margat

KINGDOM
OF CYPRUS   ● Famagusta

Tortose ○
Ruad ○   ▲ Crac des Chevaliers ○
Chastel Blanc (Safita) ▲   ✕ Homs

● Tripoli

Gibelet ●

Beirut ●

Sidon ◉
▲ Beaufort   ● Damascus
Tyre ●
Montfort ◉
Acre ●   ▲ Safed

Castle Pilgrim ▲   ✕ Ayn Djalût

Arsur ○

Jaffa ●   *Jordan*

Jérusalem ●

■ Templar House
▲ Templar Fortress
PAPHOS Diocèse

▲ Gastria
Nicosia ●   FAMAGUSTA
Famagusta ●
NICOSIA

PAPHOS
● Paphos   LIMASSOL ▲ Khirokitia
Yermasoyia ▲
Limassol

0   km   40

▲ Templar fortresses
○ Hospitaller fortresses
◉ Teutonic fortresses
▨ Christian territories in 1290
✕ Battles

0   km   100

The siege commenced on 6 April. The town was on a war footing, relying for its defence on the solidity of its walls and on being able to maintain its maritime links, notably with Cyprus. It is thought to have been housing some 100,000 people at that time, the usual population of about 40,000 having been swollen by an influx of refugees.[7] The defence of the double encircling wall was the responsibility of the various communities who made up the town's population, each taking charge of a sector or gate. There would also have been between 700 and 800 mounted knights and around 14,000 footsoldiers.

At the start of the siege, Henry II, king of both Cyprus and Jerusalem, and thereby natural commander of the army, was not there; so command was put into the hands of six men: Jean de Grailly and Otton de Grandson (the latter having arrived the preceding year), Jean de Villiers, Master of the Hospital, and Guillaume de Beaujeu, Master of the Temple, as well as the Masters of Saint Thomas and Saint Lazarus. Curiously, there is hardly any mention of the Teutonics in the defence of the town.[8]

Faced with the sultan, who had countless troops at his disposal, plus seventy-two machines which consistently demonstrated their effectiveness, at the start of the siege the Franks adopted the principle of active defence. Abu al-Fida writes that 'the Franks did not close the majority of the gates; on the contrary, they left them wide open, and it was there that they defended themselves'.[9] In this way they could conveniently carry out sorties and at any time threaten the Mamluk camp, which was excessively spread out over the whole of the area surrounding the town.

But the attempted sorties did not bring the expected results, and the arrival of Henry II on 4 May, with a small fleet and some assistance, scarcely altered the balance of power. The flow of projectiles from the sultan's mangonels, combined with the operation of the engineers on the weaker sectors of the ramparts, eventually got the better of the external defence wall. Al-Ashraf's troops were able to take a hold of part of the ditch between the outer and inner walls. On 15 May, Henry II, taking the view that the battle had been lost, returned to Cyprus.

Then came the final phase of the siege. On 18 May, the Mamluk troops launched a general attack on the inner wall. The King's Tower and the Accursed Tower capitulated, and the attackers were able to penetrate the town, in the Pisans' district; they advanced swiftly, massacring everyone in their path in the labyrinth of the old city. At one point they were blocked by a vigorous counter-attack mounted by Hospitallers and Templars at the level of the Saint Anthony gate. Dramatically recorded by the Templar of Tyre, it was here that the Grand Master of the Temple, Guillaume de Beaujeu, was mortally wounded:

> 'My lords, I cannot go on, for I am dead; see the blow', said he; his men jumped down from their mounts and supported him, took him from his horse and laid him on a shield … and carried him in through the Saint Anthony gate.

Under shelter, they removed his armour, his breastplate and shoulder-armour, and wrapped him in a blanket to take him to the shore. From there he was carried to the Temple, or rather, into the courtyard of a neighbouring house:

> And he remained there all that day without speaking, for after they had taken him down from his horse he spoke not except for one word to the Temple … and ordered that he be left in peace, and thereafter did not speak and rendered his soul to God … and was interred before his tabernacle, which was the altar where Mass was said, and may God keep his soul, for his death was a great pity.[10]

By evening the Muslims were masters of the town. The wounded Jean de Grailly, Otton de Grandson and Jean de Villiers all set sail for Cyprus, while other inhabitants and defenders fled to the port, attempting to find a boat that would take them to Cyprus or some other refuge. The sea was rough, dangerous; many were drowned, among them the patriarch of Jerusalem; meanwhile, others were massacred in the town. A large number took refuge in the vast house of the Temple and in a tower belonging to the Teutonics, as well as another belonging to the Hospital. The two latter held out for only a few hours. In contrast, the Temple's stronghold, situated on the shore, hung on for longer.

The Templar of Tyre's description again:

> The greater number of people, men women and children, crowded into the Temple and were over ten thousand in all, for the Temple was the strongest place in the town, and was by the sea on a large site, like a castle, for over its entrance was a tall, strong tower, and the wall was massive, 28 feet thick.

Protected for a while, the refugees in the Temple tower watched the boats draw away 'all together; those of the Temple who were gathered there uttered a very loud cry, and the vessels departed and went to Cyprus; and the good folk who had gone into the Temple were abandoned …'[11]

On two occasions, the defenders of the Templar tower tried to negotiate a surrender. The first time, al-Ashraf Khalil, who was anxious not to prolong a siege that was just as bloody for his own troops, agreed to let the Christians leave safely. The sultan's standard was hoisted, but some of the Mamluk soldiers refused to observe the agreement and began looting and attacking women. The Templars shut the gates again and slaughtered the intruders. Fighting recommenced; there were further negotiations. Once again, al-Ashraf Khalil gave assurances, pretending to condemn the conduct of his men the first time round.

> The Marshal of the Temple, who was a very gallant Burgundian named Pierre de Sevry [the only dignitary of the Order still present and in a fit state to fight], … trusted the sultan and surrendered to him, and there remained in the Tower some brothers who were upset by this. As soon as the sultan held the Marshal and people of the Temple, he had all the brothers and men beheaded; and when those brothers in the tower who were not so ill that they could not help themselves heard that the Marshal and the others had been beheaded, they made a defensive stand.[12]

The Mamluks mined the tower and eventually penetrated the defence wall. It was then that the great tower of the Temple of Acre collapsed, burying in its debris the last of the town's defenders, together with one or two thousand attackers.

The date was 28 May 1291. The Templars, Hospitallers and Teutonics had been decimated, the hierarchy of the Orders decapitated. For the Temple, the Grand Master and the Marshal had perished; for the Hospital, the Grand Master was wounded but safe, but the Marshal, Mathieu de Clermont, had been killed in the fighting. Shortly after Beaujeu's death, the Grand Commander of the Temple, Thibaud Gaudin, had taken a boat with a group of survivors to Sidon, another Templar stronghold, which was still holding out. Before looking at the conditions and reasons for his departure from Acre, though, let us consider the ways in which the defenders and what would now be called the 'civilian' population were evacuated from Acre. The Temple played a far from negligible role in this.[13]

The evacuation of women, children and old men had begun before the siege and continued throughout its first phase. These 'useless mouths' had been able to leave the town by boat (chiefly Italian) in a relatively orderly fashion. In contrast, once the walls of the town had been stormed, the departure of the rest of the population, combatant and non-combatant, had taken place in a state of panic. As for the last defenders of the Temple palace – the survivors, of course – they no longer had any opportunity to escape. Although the port of Acre was well sheltered, it was too small to harbour really large vessels capable of carrying 1,000 or even 1,500 people; these had to stay at anchor out in open sea, and the only way to get from the shore to the big ships was in boats or small vessels of the *linh* type. In heavy weather – as was the case after 15 May – this shuttle service would have been rendered difficult, if not impossible.

What boats were present off Acre in April–May 1291? The military Orders did not have their own ships permanently available at Acre or Cyprus;[14] they relied largely on hiring them from Italian or other shipowners. Neither the Hospitallers nor the Teutonics had boats at their disposal at the time. Those who were able to escape with the wounded Master, Jean de Villiers, in the evening of 18 May, did so on two barges which ferried them to a large Venetian vessel on the open sea. By contrast, the Temple had at least one ship on the spot, the huge *Faucon*, owned by Brother Roger de Flor. This boat helped to evacuate inhabitants of Acre, Florentine merchants, carrying them to the nearby Castle Pilgrim, probably running a shuttle service. Roger de Flor was afterwards accused of enriching himself at the expense of well-heeled refugees. Did he exceed the normal fare? It is possible, although not certain. In any case, in that first phase of evacuation, only those who already owned boats or were reasonably well off were able to leave. Given its size, the *Faucon* could certainly have taken plenty of people on board, but in the final phase of the siege it was no longer there.

Only Italian merchant ships, therefore, could be relied on, but there were not as many of those as might be expected – only a few had come in the preceding summer and not yet left for the West in the autumn. Save in exceptional circumstances, no sailing was done in winter, so April–May was the period when the western merchant fleets arrived in the ports of the eastern Mediterranean. However, the Pisan fleet was not yet in sight and the Venetian spring convoy, which had arrived, mainly evacuated its own nationals. The most effective boats in those final moments would appear to have been two Genoese galleys, which took on board free of charge the poorer inhabitants who had not had the wherewithal to quit the town earlier. Not until Acre's walls were crumbling had anyone bothered to think about them, by which time it was too late. The Temple's big ship was no longer there, although its captain cannot be accused of any negligence or failing.

Perhaps the last defenders of Acre, who had survived for ten days in the Templar house, thought that the ships would return to evacuate them. Maybe they hoped for help from the outside, a mobilisation from Cyprus – that final assistance was to be found wanting. In any case, the problem needs to be viewed from a wider angle. The Franks of Acre seem to have had boundless confidence in the strength of their position. Heedless of the warnings of Guillaume de Beaujeu, whom they did not trust, they had not seen the blow coming or been able to make best use of their strong point – the sea. Acre was cruelly short of boats at the crucial moment. For the mastery of the sea which the Franks incontestably enjoyed relied for the most part on the fleets from the Italian republics. The contribution of Cyprus, and of the military Orders, was hopelessly inadequate. The powerlessness to use this maritime superiority in 1291 compares with the failure, ten years later, of the Templars on the isle of Ruad. There, too, the Mamluks were able to slip a fleet through the net of the Christian defence. The rescue fleet took too much time to mobilise, and arrived too late.

So it was on a Venetian ship bound for Cyprus (business carried on as usual during the siege) that the little group containing the Grand Commander Thibaud Gaudin left Acre and reached Sidon on 18 May. Here, the Templars had a small flotilla at their disposal which a little later evacuated the defenders and population of the town to Cyprus.[15]

The group of Templars who reached Sidon with Thibaud Gaudin had not fled from Acre – theirs was a well-prepared and orderly evacuation. Gaudin had left with the valuables (archives) and the Order's relics. According to the anonymous author of the *Excidio*, Gaudin's withdrawal was deliberate. Shortly after the tower of the Legate was taken by the attackers, when Otton de Grandson and Jean de Villiers were evacuated to Cyprus and Guillaume de Beaujeu lay dying, the Templars decided to leave the Marshal at Acre and send the grand Commander to Sidon to organise its defence.[16] The Templar of Tyre indicates that the Templars were determined to keep up resistance in their castles and fortified towns, especially Sidon. After mentioning the appointment of the Grand Commander as Master, the chronicler writes that 'the new Master's name was Thibaud Gaudin, and it was thought at the start that he would never abandon the castle'.[17]

But what took place was a general retreat. In 1187, Tyre had resisted Saladin almost single-handedly until the arrival of Conrad de Montferrat, heralding the third crusade; but there was nothing like that in 1291. As soon as they saw the boats that had left Acre setting sail for Cyprus, the inhabitants of Tyre surrendered, on 19 May. Soon afterwards, the Mamluks laid siege to Sidon. The town was fortified and protected, on the sea side, by a castle built on an island. Thibaud Gaudin had joined the Templar garrison of this castle. But when the town was besieged, then attacked, by the Mamluk troops, the town's inhabitants took refuge in the castle, from which they were ferried to Cyprus. It was then that Thibaud Gaudin, with his council's agreement, left the castle to go and seek help in Cyprus. But he did not return, and the Templar of Tyre passes harsh judgement on his conduct: 'He took counsel with his brethren, and by their will, having promised that he would send help, went off to Cyprus, and when he was in Cyprus behaved in a cowardly way about sending them help …'[18]

In fact, Thibaud Gaudin sent no help at all. Under the circumstances, if we are to believe our (undoubtedly biased) chronicler here, Templars from Cyprus who were friends of those in Sidon warned the latter that there was no hope left. While the Muslims increased their pressure on the island castle by building a causeway, on the night of 14 July the Templars slipped away from Sidon unnoticed. Tortosa was abandoned on 3 August, and Castle Pilgrim on 14 August: 'When those of Castle Pilgrim saw that all was lost, they realised they did not have the means to defend the castle, so they left it and went to the island of Cyprus, and the Saracens razed everything to the ground.'[19]

Where, then, was Jacques de Molay during those decisive months? Possibly in the West; possibly with Gaudin; possibly in one or other of the garrisons of Tortosa or Castle Pilgrim. No one knows for sure.

Back in Sidon, among the Templars of the garrison and those who had come to join them with Gaudin after Beaujeu's death, a new Master had to chosen. 'This Commander of the Land made himself Master of the Temple by the election of the brethren he had with him'[20] – the wording suggests a self-proclamation validated by a small group of Templars rather than a choice (the first meaning of election) according to the procedure laid down in the Order's Rule. Neither those in charge of the provinces in the West, nor the Templars of Tortosa, Castle Pilgrim and Cyprus had been able to be present. This was not, however, an irregular appointment; with necessity dictating, the most experienced dignitary in the Order, probably the only survivor of Beaujeu's 'team', was chosen. The only opposition he could have encountered might have been the Marshal, but he had died at Acre a few days after Béaujeu's death and Gaudin's departure for Sidon. The Grand Commander automatically took charge in the interim between the Master's death and the election of a new Master.

Gaudin therefore represented continuity – which was an advantage, given the disorganised state of the Order at the time. As far as is known, no one in the Order protested or challenged his appointment, with the exception – indirectly, judging by the accusations he makes against him – of the Templar of Tyre (who was not a brother of the Order), who seems to have lost his job when Beaujeu died.

Little is known of Thibaud Gaudin; men did not enter a religious order to get themselves noticed, and the rule of humility applied to all. He was known as 'Gaudin the Monk', or *Monachus Gaudi*,[21] he came from a noble family from the Chartrain or Blésois region; one of his ancestors, also a Thibaud, is documented between 1181 and 1236, and a relative – an uncle, cousin or possibly a nephew – named Guillaume, a knight, was enrolled as a Templar and Master of the bailiwick of Chartres between 1285 and 1299. In the interrogations at the trial, this Guillaume is mentioned as having received new brothers into the Order at Arville and Sours (two Chartrain commanderies), and Châteaudun and Orléans.[22]

Thibaud Gaudin had been in the East since at least 1260, because in that year he was taken prisoner with Guillaume de Beaujeu during an expedition to Tiberias.[23] He was Commander at Acre and perhaps Castle Pilgrim, and had taken on the office of Grand Commander from at least 1279; 'then he was for a long time Commander of the Land of the Temple', says the Templar of Tyre.[24] In 1279, he is mentioned under the name *Monachus Gaudi preceptor terre ultramarine* (Commander of the Overseas Territory); at that time he was in Paris, where he presided over the reception of fifteen new brothers.[25] He could not have stayed long in France, given his responsibilities as Commander of the Territory. The Templar of Tyre refers to his 'humanitarian' intervention at Acre in 1286, where he obtained the release of 'poor sinners', people who had been taken prisoner as a result of the fighting between the Pisans and the Genoese.[26]

Having become Master of the Temple in these circumstances, he must have had to notify the pope of his election. But the news does not seem to have reached Rome when, on 28 July 1291, Nicholas IV wrote to 'André Mathie, brother and procurator of the house of the Knights of the Temple of Jerusalem, whom formerly Guillaume de Beaujeu, Master, and the convent of the house of the Knights of the Temple of Jerusalem, before their death in the war against the Saracens, had constituted their procurator-general, delegate and agent and special nuncio to the Roman court and elsewhere, confirming his procurator-ship and his authority to exercise those powers in the same way as before the decease of the Master and the above-mentioned brothers'.[27]

Beaujeu's demise was therefore known, but not the appointment of his successor. (Owing to the prevailing winds and currents, voyages from the eastern Mediterranean to the West were much slower than those in the opposite direction.)[28] And so, it was not until August that, by means of circular letters to the rulers and bishops of both Latin and eastern Christendoms, the pope launched an appeal for help following the fall of Acre.[29]

If the date supplied by Jean Serrand, a Templar brother questioned by members of the papal commission sitting in Paris on 31 May 1311, is correct, an important general Chapter of the Order was held in Cyprus in 1291. The witness claims to 'have heard at Nicosia from the lips of the Grand Master now in office [Jacques de Molay] that he wanted to eradicate from the Order all the things which displeased him, fearing that, if he did not do so, it would eventually harm the Order; and this was said by the Master in the year in which Acre was lost, in the general Chapter where about 400 brothers were present ...'[30] This Chapter, naturally and inevitably in the prevailing circumstances, could only have been held once the fighting was over and the Templar garrisons of Tortosa and Castle Pilgrim had retreated to Cyprus in August. The presence of 400 brothers is inconceivable without the participation of Templars from the western provinces. In view of the time lapse concerning the transmission of news and the length of the voyage, that would bring us to September or, more probably, October 1291. I will of course refer later to the significance of Jacques de Molay's intervention, and will raise just one problem here: this Chapter's purpose was to validate – perhaps legitimise – Gaudin's election and to choose new incumbents for the offices left vacant in the Order's leadership. If Jacques de Molay was ever Marshal of the Order, as Laurent Dailliez asserts, it could only have been at that moment.[31] Regardless, his intervention during the Chapter shows that he enjoyed a definite authority, and perhaps offered himself as someone who could possibly be called upon within the Templar Order.

Thibaud Gaudin's deeds as head of the Temple have left little trace. The Archives of the Crown of Aragon preserve four of his letters, dated August–September 1291. They concern two Catalan Templars, Bernard de Fontes and

Pierre de Saint-Just, to whom the Master gives leave to return to their country because they are wounded, authorising them to come back to Cyprus when they wish.[32] The Catalan Pierre de Saint-Just (not to be confused with his Picard homonym), present at the final conflicts at Acre, and at Cyprus, subsequently built a sustained and friendly relationship with Jacques de Molay, and it is highly possible that their friendship dates from that time.

The fact that almost nothing is known of Gaudin's activities means historians tend to consider them insignificant. However, his mastership was very short. Completely overlooked has been a document published in 1973 by A. Forey, which proves that Gaudin had died before 20 April 1292, the date on which, in a letter to which I shall return later, Jacques de Molay gives himself the title of Master of the Order.[33] In this document, the Master and dignitaries of the Order authorise the Templars of Aragon and Catalonia to sell a piece of the Templar patrimony in Aragon – a decision that would have been arrived at neither carelessly nor hastily. The dossier would have been the object of meticulous scrutiny, very probably when Gaudin was still Master of the Temple.

The entire Templar machine needed to be set in motion again, and Gaudin had done that. Action was urgently required on two fronts: on the one hand, to defend the Armenian kingdom of Cilicia, the last Christian State on the mainland and now directly under threat from the Mamluks; on the other, to protect the kingdom of Cyprus, which was less vulnerable because it was an island, but which was struggling to feed the mass of totally impoverished refugees who had fled there from Syria and Palestine. This humanitarian action had begun before the fall of Acre, and would continue for a long time afterwards. The journey Jacques de Molay was to make in 1293 aimed at solving this problem, among others. There is no reason to doubt that, in this undertaking, Molay was pursuing a policy begun by his predecessor. However, taking into account that Jacques de Molay became Master of the Order prior to 20 April 1292, a certain number of deeds or initiatives hitherto ascribed to Thibaud Gaudin must henceforward be credited to Molay. Such is the case for the attempt to give assistance to the kingdom of Cyprus, which was made in 1292–3. As for aid to the kingdom of Armenia, we shall see that this is problematic; for once again we are faced with inadequate documentation which has been treated by historians in a confused or erroneous fashion.

As regards Molay's appointment as Master of the Temple, the Templar of Tyre, previously such a precious source of information, is practically silent. He

continued to write until 1309, but he refused to say anything about the new
Masters of the Temple, Gaudin and Molay. A great admirer of Beaujeu, he
clearly disliked his successors. Apart from a few cutting remarks, which are difficult to accept at face value, he does not speak of them. Only in the year 1306
does he mention Molay's election, and even then only indirectly. In 1306, he
says, the pope 'sent for Brother Jaque de Molay, Master of the Temple, who was
made Master after Master Thibaud Gaudin, third after Brother Guillaume de
Biaujeu, the Master who was killed at the capture of Acre'.[34]

Until now, Molay's mastership was said to have commenced in 1293. In fact,
we have a falsely exact date for Gaudin's death. The Templars of the Reims
commandery left an obituary which indicates, month by month, the anniversary Masses they had to celebrate in their chapel. Thibaud Gaudin's anniversary is 'the 16 of the kalends of May'. The calends corresponds to the first of
the month, from which one counts backwards, so that 1 May is the first of the
calends of May; 30 April, the 2 of the calends of May; 29 April, 3 of the calends
of May, etc., which makes the 16 of the calends of May 16 April.[35] So Thibaud
Gaudin would have died on 16 April in a year unknown, although it can only
be 1292, taking into account a document found in the Archives of the Crown
of Aragon and published by A. Forey in 1973, which indicates that Molay was
already Grand Master on 20 April.[36] Written in French, this deed authorises
the Aragonese Templars to sell the outlying and not very profitable estates of
Puigreig and La Zaida. According to the Order's Rule, sale of even a portion of
the Templars' heritage could not take place without the consent of the Master
and the convent (in other words, all the fighting Templars). 'Brother Jacques
de Molay, by the grace of God the humble Master of the poor knights of the
Temple and the convent of this same knighthood' authorised the deal; and the
deed ends with 'We have had these letters sealed with our wax pendant seal
[representing the Dome of the Rock in Jerusalem, attached to a silk strand and
affixed at the foot of the document], with the guarantee of the worthy men of
the house [*prudes homes*, *prud'hommes*], namely ...', followed by the names of
all the dignitaries of what might be termed the 'governing body' of the Order.
Then, to finish: 'This was made at Nicosia in Cyprus, in the year one thousand
two hundred ninety and two of Christ on XX days of April.'[37]

This was therefore a document that had been drawn up with special care, and
its importance in Jacques de Molay's eyes is emphasised by the fact that all the
members of the Order's leadership undersigned it. From which we must con-

clude that the new Grand Master had been elected before 20 April 1292, but after 16 April of the same year – the date of Gaudin's death? That poses a problem, for this time lapse of three days at the maximum seems far too short. The Aragonese document dated 20 April turns out to be more reliable than the Reims obituary. In one of his works, Laurent Dailliez placed Gaudin's anniversary on the 16 of the calends of March, or 14 February.[38] That would fit perfectly, but, here again, we are obliged to bow before the original: it really was the calends of May. The argument that it was a 'copyist's error' is always possible, and sometimes verifiable; or perhaps the Templars of Reims celebrated the anniversary Mass in honour of Gaudin, not on the actual date of his death but on the day when they received news of it. I am always reluctant to use this kind of argument; there is a *certain* date – 20 April – which renders the other (16 April) unlikely, therefore questionable.

There are two arguments which favour a longer 'interregnum'. On the one hand, what is known about previous elections: Bérard died on 25 March 1273, and Beaujeu was elected in May; Sonnac died on 11 February 1250, and Vichiers was not elected until after the release of Louis IX and the return of the remnants of the crusaders' army to Acre in late April or early May; that said, Vichiers died on 20 January 1256 and the date of his successor Bérard's election is not known.[39] On the other hand, electoral procedure could not be completed in such a short time span. Although a case of *force majeure* might be invoked in respect of Gaudin's appointment, that was no longer so in 1292. We must return to the Rule.

Articles 198–223 of the statutes (*retrais*) are devoted to the procedure to be followed for the election of the Master. According to article 200, as soon as the Master's death is known, the Marshal must replace him, circulate the news to all the provinces of the Order and convene the Commanders (or bailiffs) to hold a Chapter; he must then organise the Master's funeral arrangements. Next, he must assemble the Chapter (himself, the convent and the brothers on this side of the sea) to designate a Grand Commander to stand in for the Master (article 198); the same people decide on the election day (203). All the brothers of the Temple on this side of the sea must then fast for three successive Fridays until the election. On election day, the convent (the fighting men) and the bailiffs of the provinces must gather together (206); a Commander of the election must be chosen and he must designate thirteen electors 'from various provinces and various nations', each of whom must be accompanied by a knight. Together they must form a council and 'no alteration may be made in the composition of this council of thirteen' (207). The subsequent paragraphs give details of how the day is to unfold and of the appointment procedure for the thirteen electors (208–9): the Grand Commander must summon the Commander of the election and his companion; these two must elect two brothers, then next those four elect a further two each so that there are now twelve in number (in honour of the twelve apostles); next, the twelve (who must consist of eight knights and four sergeants (210)) elect a thirteenth, in honour of Christ. The thirteen electors meet in another room (215) and begin to propose names, initially of 'persons this side of the sea or of the convent or the bailiwicks'; however, if they fail to choose any of them and 'if it happens that a more advantageous person be found in overseas parts, and with the agreement of all XIII or the majority, this man shall be elected Master of the Temple' (216). The chosen one is proclaimed (219–20), then takes the oath (221). Above all, the electing brothers must preserve rigorous secrecy about their deliberations (223).

It seems reasonable to envisage a lapse of some six weeks to two months between the death of a Master and the election of his successor, even if this does not allow the 'bailiffs' of the western provinces to arrive in time. Gaudin had been Grand Commander before his election, so his elevating himself to the office of Grand Master, especially in the absence of a Marshal, can be easily explained; but what of Molay in March/April 1292? We know nothing about Gaudin's 'governing body'; no names of dignitaries are available. Was Molay the Marshal of the Order, as Laurent Dailliez asserts?[40] It is not impossible; in which case he would have completed the first steps of the procedure. But then what? In the interrogations from the Templars' trial, there is one very interesting, though somewhat problematical, deposition: that of Hugues de Faur, a Limousin Templar questioned on 12 May 1311 in Paris. I quote it in its entirety:

As there was discord in the Chapter that was held across the water to create the Master, and the brothers from the Limousin and Auvergne province, who formed the majority of the convent, desired to have Brother Hugues de Pairaud as Master, and the minority the said Master [that is to say, in 1311, the then Master, Jacques de Molay], the said Master swore before the Master of the Hospitallers who was present and before the lord Otton de Grandson, knight, and several others, that he himself agreed with the choice of the said Brother Hugues and that he did not want to be Master. And as that majority had agreed that he should be made Grand Commander, as was customary after the death of the Master, the said Master [Jacques de Molay], as there were negotiations afterwards to make the said Brother Hugues Master, informed them that since he had been given the 'cloak' [i.e. made Grand Commander], they would give him the 'hood' [i.e. make him Grand Master], because, whether they wished it or not, he would be Master, and thus, through pressure, it was done.[41]

This is a fairly confused text, the various interpretations of which have failed to make any clearer.[42] The election must have been a source of argument – Jacques de Molay clashing with a rival, Hugues de Pairaud, but successfully manoeuvring to get himself elected despite a majority voting against him. However, the text gives no indication of how this sleight of hand was performed; it shows, though, that despite often being regarded as uninspired, Molay was an astute operator.

Taking a close look at the procedure described by Hugues de Faur, we discover that, in conformity with the Rule, the Chapter elected a Grand Commander following Gaudin's death, and that the said Commander was Molay; which means that, if Molay was a Marshal of the Order in Gaudin's time, he must have renounced that office in order to become Grand Commander and, by virtue of this, assume the role of Master. In the past (save for the exceptional situation in 1291), holding the position of Grand Commander provided no special advantage for becoming Master. Perhaps Hugues de Faur confused the office with that of Commander of the election, who would have, according to the Rule (210), together with the companion knight of his choice, initiated and thus steered the process of appointing the thirteen electors who chose the Master. How Jacques de Molay was able to win, despite not having the majority in the Chapter thus becomes clearer; however, it is hard to support this theory, as Hugues de Faur is obviously speaking about the *magnus preceptor* (Grand Commander).

Questions also arise regarding the background to the problem. It is not impossible that the Chapter was divided between two groups, who went on to field two candidates. More perplexing is the way in which Hugues de Faur gives a regional definition to the group which was hostile to Molay: a majority of the brothers forming the Chapter seem to have originated from the 'provinces' of Auvergne and Limousin; but at the time there was only one province, Auvergne, of which Limousin was a part, not two distinct provinces. There is no available indication of the geographical origin of the Templars who took part in the

Chapter in 1292, or of the Templars present in Cyprus, but it is highly unlikely that a majority came from the single province of Auvergne–Limousin, one of the Order's smallest, covering only the *départements* of Corrèze, Haute-Vienne, Creuse, Cantal and Puy-de-Dôme, and part of the *départements* of Cher, Loir-et-Cher and Allier;[43] besides, Hugues de Pairaud was not an Auvergnat, still less a Limousin! Like Molay, he belonged to the vast province of France, which extended as far as the Lyonnais, Beaujolais and Forez regions and which naturally included the two Burgundies, both duchy and county.[44]

Hugues de Faur gives no hint of the reasons for the rift between the so-called Auvergnat majority who favoured Pairaud and the minority who preferred Molay. A simple matter of personality cannot be ruled out for, as we shall see on subsequent occasions, Molay was not always easy to get on with. Perhaps Pairaud was more flexible? If there was a rift, it must have been for fundamental reasons.

Barbara Frale rightly points out that Pairaud's entire career had been in the West; he had never been to the East. Molay's profile was the exact opposite. But in 1291, what trump cards might Hugues de Pairaud have held within the Order? Firstly, he was the nephew of Humbert de Pairaud, who had been Commander at Ponthieu in 1257, Master of France in 1261–4, then Master of England, and lastly Visitor General of France and England. In the latter role, he had criss-crossed the commanderies of those two countries, and was therefore known to many Templars. In 1291, his nephew, Hugues, had not yet held any important office; he had been Commander of Épailly (1280–5), then Commander of the bailiwick of Bures (1289), both in Burgundy.[45] He is not mentioned as Master of France until 1292, and as Visitor General of France and England until 1294 or 1297,[46] that is, after Molay's election (at the time of which, the Visitor General was Geoffroy de Vichiers). Hugues de Pairaud was certainly someone who mattered in the West's Templar organisation in 1292, but he was not yet a leading dignitary. He might have been a serious rival for Jacques de Molay if the latter had been a nobody in the Order; but, despite the absence of information about this, that does not seem to have been the case. His intervention during the Chapter of 1291 emanated from a man of authority – one who had the advantage of being present in Cyprus.

Let us return to the electoral procedure followed in 1292, and to the Rule. The college of thirteen electors whose task it was to appoint the Master would have begun by putting forward and discussing names of brothers 'this side of the sea' who were capable of fulfilling the office; if no appropriate candidate could be found, overseas Templars would be considered 'if it happened that a more suitable person were to be found in overseas parts ... (216)'.[47] To interpret these articles correctly, it must be remembered that they had been drawn up at a time when the Order's headquarters were situated in the East, in Jerusalem, so 'this side of the sea' meant in the East and 'overseas' in the West. Sonnac, Vichiers, Bérard, Beaujeu and Gaudin had all pursued part of their careers in the East. Beaujeu, for instance, despite being Commander of Puglia in Italy at the time of his election, had served prior to that for a long time in the East. Hugues de Pairaud's election would therefore have been a 'first'.

Barbara Frale proposes a political explanation for this competition between Molay and Pairaud, based on the following two premises. The choice between the two men would have been first and foremost a choice between two future policies for the Order: a 'military' policy, slanted towards the reconquest of the Holy Land and Jerusalem in the tradition of the military Orders' original mission; and a 'diplomatic' or 'administrative' policy, better suited to the actual situation in the world at the end of the thirteenth century and more concerned with the general interests of Christendom (Church and States) than with the Holy Land alone. Molay embodied the first; Pairaud the second. Secondly, that choice was also between a policy of independence, or autonomy, for the Order and one of submission to the politics of the States, and primarily of the French monarchy. Pairaud would have been the candidate of a pro-French party manipulated by King Philip the Fair, whereas Molay would have been the defender of the Order's independence, and therefore the champion of an anti-French party. Deliberately forcing the point, Barbara Frale thinks that the choice offered in 1292 covered a 'nationalist' opposition between Limousins-Auvergnats and Easterners, coupled with a political opposition between 'militarist autonomists' and 'bureaucratic diplomatists'.[48]

This theory, though, is nothing more than an enticing construction built on very shaky foundations: too many doubtful or erroneous data, too many massed hypotheses, even if there is an element of truth in it. First, in 1292, Hugues de Pairaud was not yet the Pairaud of 1302 who supported – though not to extremes – Philip the Fair's violent attack on Pope Boniface VIII; at that time he was no more than a Commander in the West who knew nothing of eastern affairs; he was also, self-evidently, his uncle's nephew.

In 1292, the Order's primary concerns were the defence of Cyprus and

Armenia, coupled with an intense desire to reconquer the Holy Land. There
was no thought of switching to a new kind of enterprise. Neither the Temple,
the Hospital nor even the Teutonic Order wanted to bide their time in the West.
During this period, the strategy of a Mongol alliance was at its most successfully
developed, and the military-religious Orders, at the forefront of which was the
Temple, occupied an eminent place in it.

Lastly, although pressure was exerted on the Orders by western lay rulers
(that is, *all* the western rulers) regarding the appointment of provincial Masters,
the restriction of privileges and rights, and attempts to subject them to a tax, that
did not apply to the choice of Masters of the Orders. The case of Renaud de
Vichiers, supported by Saint Louis, had been exceptional, for the king of France
was then in the Holy Land. Even Guillaume de Beaujeu had more arguments in
support of his election than the backing of Charles I of Anjou. In 1292, Philip
the Fair was doubtless aware of what was happening at the summit of the military Orders; but to assume therefore that the Master's election was 'rigged' in
some way is a big step.

In any event, Molay's election, like that of Gaudin in the preceding year,
took place before the West had been informed of the Grand Master's death.
No western sovereign actually had time to intervene directly – but indirectly
perhaps, through some interposed agent?

It has often been assumed that Otton de Grandson, mentioned by Hugues de
Faur as having been present at Jacques de Molay's election, was acting as Philip
the Fair's agent in Cyprus.[49] That the election of Jacques de Molay, a Comtois
and thus a subject of the Empire, could hardly have delighted Philip is likely;
but that at that precise moment Philip had either the will, the means or the time
to thwart such an election is improbable; but that Grandson was his agent is
completely erroneous.

The presence of Otton de Grandson and the Master of the Hospital at
Molay's election, as recounted by Hugues de Faur, should be put into context.
Molay did not take the oath before them, as Faur relates, that he would not stand
in the way of Hughes de Pairaud; he swore only that he would not seek the
office of Grand Master. Neither the Master of the Hospital nor Grandson, nor
anyone else who was not of the Order, could intervene in the course of the electoral procedure. Only the Templars gathered in the Chapter and *in camera* were
allowed to take part. Jacques de Molay could only have made such a commitment (which moreover committed him to nothing) outside the Chapter, outside

the Temple and in front of persons external to the Temple. There is no evidence that Molay committed perjury, either then or at any other time.

That said, at the time of Molay's election, Grandson was indeed in Cyprus, not Armenia (see next chapter) as has been erroneously asserted by the Armenian historian Hayton of Corycos.

Otton de Grandson was a lord or seigneur of the county of Burgundy, whose estate was situated in what is now Switzerland, near Neufchâtel.[50] He entered the service of the king of England at a very young age and, in 1271, followed Prince Edward to the Holy Land, staying there until 1275. Returning to England to take up the post of governor of the Channel Islands, Grandson left again for the Holy Land in 1290 as head of an English contingent, funded entirely by the king of England and modelled on the French regiment of Saint Louis. If, as is likely, Molay pursued his career in the East, their paths must have crossed. Since he was in the service of the king of England, Grandson could not also have been a representative of Philip the Fair – especially as 1292 marked the start of a decade of conflict between the two countries. Moreover, Grandson belonged to the section of Comtois nobility who were hostile to French control over the county.

Philip the Fair exploited the rivalry within one noble family of two different branches, that of Count Otton IV on the one hand, and that of Jean de Châlons, seigneur of Arlay on the other. The former rallied to the king of France, following him on the Aragon crusade. This alliance was strengthened by two marriages: that of Otton IV himself to Mahaut d'Artois, and that of their daughter Jeanne to the king's second son, the future Philip V. In 1295, the Treaty of Vincennes ceded the county to French administration. Meanwhile, Jean de Châlons was brother-in-law of the emperor Rudolph of Habsburg, elected in 1273 after the 'great interregnum' that followed the death of Frederick II in 1250.[51] Consequently, Comtois lords who were hostile to French control formed a league, or confederation, maybe as early as 1289 but definitely by 1295. Among those lords, three brothers – Jehan and Étienne, knights, and Estevenoz, squire – members of the Oiselay family which was to provide the Templar Order with its last Marshal, Aymon d'Oiselay. It is said that this family was related in some way to Grandson, but this is unproven.[52]

Hugues de Faur's statement provides no evidence of any intervention by Grandson in Molay's favour, although a verbal intervention is always a possibility. However, it is not at all clear with whom he could have intervened. A deed from 1287 apparently proves some connection between the Temple and Grandson, but it was wrongly dated by the editors of the text, an error repeated by the historians who have made use of it. It concerns a gift of revenue made to Otton de Grandson by the Grand Master of the Temple, which was subsequently confirmed on two occasions.[53] It is impossible that, in 1287, Jacques de Molay was rewarding Grandson for supporting him in his election.[54]

There was no 'Limousin–Auvergnat majority' in the 1292 Chapter; however, there *was* a Comtois or, more broadly, Burgundian network, both within and outside the Temple, as there would appear to have been, as we saw in connection with his origins, surrounding the person of Jacques de Molay.[55] Perhaps it is here that we need to look for the reasons for his election.

Finally, the value of Hugues de Faur's testimony itself must also be questioned. Some historians have cast doubt on it or rejected it, whereas others have accepted it wholeheartedly. Whichever position is held, it cannot be taken at face value: neither an Auvergnat majority nor a head-on opposition between Molay and Pairaud is likely. The daring theories advanced by Barbara Frale lack foundation; however, Hugues de Faur's text suggests the existence of trends, divergences, perhaps even personal conflicts which can no more be ignored than another deposition in the Templars' trial – that of Brother Jean Serrand, who refers to Jacques de Molay's intervention in favour of a reform of the Order at the time of an earlier Chapter held the year before in Nicosia.

All those questions, however, were put at a time when historians thought that Molay had not been elected Master until 1293. One fact, however, cannot be ignored: Jacques de Molay was elected before 20 April 1292; and if Thibaud Gaudin's death is fixed at 16 April in the same year, then that leaves far too short a lapse of time for the development of such intrigues and manoeuvring. Even if, as would appear certain, Gaudin's death had occurred earlier, the length of time required for the news to circulate in the West makes any outside interference in the election impossible.

Until recently, Gaudin's death has been dated with near-certainty to 16 April 1293, although no such certainty has surrounded the date of Molay's election. It is now beyond doubt that Molay's election took place before 20 April 1292; consequently, the date of Gaudin's death can no longer be fixed at 16 April 1293, or even 16 April 1292. As ever, for the historian new certainties cast doubt upon the old.

1293

JOURNEY TO THE WEST

In Jacques de Molay, the Templars elected a man of action as their Grand Master: he knew what he wanted and he had pretty clear ideas about the situation in both the Holy Land and his Order. Jacques de Molay had objectives, in order to achieve which he would have to go to the West, to meet the pope, princes and brothers of the Order. Preparations for this journey would very soon take up much of his time and energy, but at the same time he had to assert his authority in Cyprus and continue with the policy of aid to the kingdoms of Cyprus and Armenia which had been started by his predecessor. He devoted the first year of his Mastership to these dual tasks.

The document in the Aragonese archives which informs us that Jacques de Molay was already Master of the Temple on 20 April 1292 also yields an interesting list of people as witnesses who undersigned the deed in question. It is nothing less than a list of what might be termed Molay's governing body. Hardly anything is known of Gaudin's 'government', but it may be assumed that, since the majority of dignitaries had perished in the aftermath of the fall of Acre, the next group of appointments which he made, with the assent of the Chapter, would have profoundly altered the leadership of the Order. It is not known either whether Jacques de Molay featured in Gaudin's government as Marshal; nor whether, among the dignitaries whose names appear at the foot of the deed of 20 April 1292, some were already in office under Gaudin. They were:[1]

Grand Master	*Jacques de Molay*
Marshal	*Baudouin de la Andrin*
Commander of the Land	*Berenguer de Saint-Just*
Draper (acting)	*Gaucher de Liencourt*

Turcopolier	*Guillen de la Tor*
Sub-Marshal	*Raymond de Barberan*
Commander of the Vote	*Guillaume d'Ourenc*
Treasurer	*Martin de Lou*
No specific post	*Bertran l'Aleman*
	Simon de Lende
	Ryenbaut de Caron

This is the complete list: all the posts are filled. The three without portfolios were there as advisers, of whom two, Simon de Lende (or Exemen de Lenda) and Ryenbaut de Caron (Raimbaud de Caron), would subsequently occupy important positions.

The geographical origin of some of these new dignitaries is known: three came from the States of the Crown of Aragon, namely, Berenguer de Saint-Just, Raymond de Barberan (Barbera[2]) and Simon de Lende, future Master of the province of Aragon–Catalonia. Gaucher de Liencourt, acting Draper (it is unknown who was the Draper in office at that date) was from Picardy. Guillen de la Tor, the Turcopolier, has his name spelt here as if he were from the south, although this is not certain. It is possible that he had some kinship link with a Guillaume de la Tour who was archbishop of Besançon between 1245 and 1268; however, the name is too common for this to be affirmed with absolute certainty.[3] Baudouin de la Andrin was probably the same person as Baudouin de Laudrana, cited by a Cypriot Templar, Étienne de Safed, when questioned in Nicosia in 1310, who said he had been present at Baudouin's reception in Nicosia in 1295;[4] however, nothing is known of his origins, nor those of Guillaume d'Ourenc or Martin de Lou. Bertran l'Aleman self-evidently originated from Germany, while Raimbaud de Caron was a Provençal, from a line of minor nobility which takes its name from the château of Caromb, near Carpentras.[5]

The composition of Molay's governing body seems to indicate an express desire for autonomy, as well as a very clear leaning towards the Templars of Aragon – a choice that would be confirmed subsequently. Although one cannot infer from this a formal alliance with the Crown of Aragon – it may merely have been a matter of circumstance – Aragonese affairs were to make many demands of Jacques de Molay in 1293–4, from the release of captives (including Aragonese Templars) on whose behalf James II, king of Aragon, had actively intervened with the Mamluk sultan, to questions relating to Templar property in the West.

In addition, in the summer of 1292 or 1293, a replacement would have to be found for the Turcopolier Guillaume de la Tour, who was killed in the naval confrontation between Genoese and Venetians which now takes centre stage.

Having formed his team relatively quickly, Jacques de Molay found himself, in the two years following the fall of Acre, still faced with continuing attacks from the Mamluks. For, having beaten the Latins, they now turned their attention to the Armenians. In June 1292, they seized Hromgla, a town which formed an enclave in Muslim territory and was the seat of the Patriarch of Armenia; in the following year, lacking adequate Mongol support, King Hethum II was forced to yield three fortresses in the upper valley of the Euphrates to the Mamluks and agree a precarious truce with them.

Meanwhile, in the West, Pope Nicholas IV swiftly became aware of the threat hanging over the Armenian kingdom and, early in 1292, tried to organise a proper crusade for the defence of the little realm. The series of Bulls, *Pia mater ecclesia*, which he issued on 23 January 1292 prove this. The first was a general one: as the kingdom was 'isolated in the midst of perverse nations like sheep in the midst of wolves who are enemies of the Cross', the pope granted to all who would come to its aid privileges and indulgences identical to those they would have received had they gone to the Holy Land; and he sent out envoys to the various dioceses of the West.[6] At the same time, he addressed the Grand Masters of the Temple and Hospital, asking them 'with the galleys which, by the mandate and order of the apostolic see, you must maintain at sea against the enemies of the Cross, exert yourselves in the defence and aid of the kingdom of Armenia'.[7] And with the same objective, he had several papal galleys equipped and placed under the command of Roger de Thodinis as captain-general.[8]

Did these papal Bulls produce the desired effect? Could we consider fitting out two galleys at Cyprus, as the Templars did, a sufficient response to the pope's appeal? The Templar of Tyre and the Genoese Annals give similar accounts of this episode, although the former places it in 1292, while the latter opts for the more likely July 1293. It happened at the start of the conflict between the Genoese and Venetians known as the 'War of Curzola'.[9] The Venetians equipped four galleys which set sail for Cyprus. On board were 'men-at-arms of two other galleys at Cyprus in the service of the house of the Temple'[10] – the Templars were thus to man their two galleys already in Cyprus with men-at-arms and crew (indeed, the text later mentions the 'chourme', or the crew of galley slaves) brought to them from the West on board the Venetian ships. At sea, these vessels came upon some Genoese trading galleys and attacked them. This was a grave mistake, for the Genoese emerged the victors from the confrontation and seized the Venetian galleys. Among the dead was the Templar official on the Venetian convoy, Guillaume de la Tour – surely the same man who witnessed Jacques de Molay's letter of 20 April 1292. If the episode occurred in 1292, that would fit in quite well with the papal demand for help for Armenia. If in 1293, it would have had more to do with the mobilisation of forces in defence of the island of Cyprus.

There was, however, another specific intervention in Armenia. As noted by several historians, there was an expedition to the kingdom led by the Grand Masters of the Temple and Hospital alongside Otton de Grandson, the head of the English contingent at Acre. It has been placed in 1292 or early in 1293, when the Master of the Temple is identified as Thibaud Gaudin.[11] However, sources that might provide proof of this expedition have been either poorly interpreted or wrongly dated and sometimes are just plain false. One chapter of an Armenian chronicle often cited is the 'Flower of the histories of the Eastern land' by Hethum or Hayton of Corycos (he was the seigneur of that town and its territory), known in the West as Hayton the Historian[12] – not be confused with King Hethum II, then reigning in Armenia, who also wrote a chronicle.[13]

It is necessary to make a detailed examination of Hayton of Corycos' text, which initially concerns Hethum II, who succeeded his father Levon II in 1289. He was a complex character forced to set his royal and dynastic obligations against his spiritual aspirations, which led him to enter the Franciscan Order. Having initially refused to let himself be crowned king, he abdicated three times and changed his mind as many times, either through circumstances or under pressure from the Armenian nobility, who were worried about the kingdom's weakness.[14] He abdicated for the first time in 1293 in favour of his brother Thoros, but had second thoughts, and in 1294 had his 'kingdom and seigneurie' restored to him by Thoros in a solemn ceremony.[15] On this topic, Hayton the Historian – who, as a great Armenian lord, had plotted against Hethum II in 1293, then been exiled by him in 1294 – tells us that Thoros convened the Armenian barons and numerous Cypriot lords, including Otton de Grandson,[16] at Sis, the kingdom's capital.

Continuing his account, Hayton comes to the years 1296–9, which were marked by Hethum's second abdication, still in favour of Thoros, but also by the usurpations of the two other brothers, Sembat and Constantine. At the same time, the Mongol Khan of Persia prepared for a huge offensive against the Mamluks, resulting in a victory at Homs in December 1299, which saved the Armenian kingdom. Hayton of Corycos personally intervenes in his narrative to say that, having returned from a pilgrimage to France, he spent substantial amounts of money re-establishing order and peace in the ruling family and in the kingdom. Then, to corroborate what he says, he calls upon the testimony of the 'noble and wise sire Otton de Grandson and the Masters of the Temple and Hospital and the brethren of their convent, who were at that time in these regions, and in general all the nobles and men and populations of the kingdoms of Armenia and Cyprus'.[17] 'At that time' means either 1298 or 1299.

Even if the chronology is not always specified by date, it can be understood pretty well in this text, which there is no reason to doubt: Otton de Grandson is named twice, in 1294 and 1298–9; the Masters of the Hospital and Temple are cited only once, on the later date. On the basis of this text, it seems unlikely that the joint expedition of the Masters of the Orders and Otton de Grandson can be placed in 1292–3. Charles Kohler, who has ascribed a treatise on the crusade to Otton de Grandson and delved into his life in minute detail, merely suggests a dating error on the part of Hayton the Historian.[18]

The Templar of Tyre has also been called upon to verify this combined expedition of the military Orders and Otton de Grandson's troops in Armenia. He confirms Grandson's presence in Armenia – in 1293 – but in circumstances unrelated to a military venture. The context is the war between Venice and Genoa. In order to avenge the crimes perpetrated by the Venetians on the Genoese at Famagusta and Ayas, a small Genoese squadron left Constantinople bound for the Armenian port of Ayas, with the intention of attacking the Venetian fleet then moored in the port. Sailing along the coast of Asia Minor, this squadron encountered offshore from Corycos 'an armed Cypriot galley, equipped by men from Syria, Pisans and Venetians, people who hated the Genoese ... on board which was messire Ote de Gualanson. And the said messire Ote de Gualanson, a knight of great renown from overseas, approached the Genoese and proposed going with them to settle the affair, but the Genoese would not hear of it.' So the Genoese rejected Otton de Grandson's offer to mediate between them and the Venetians, and asked him to go away. 'Messire Othe left them and went to Cyprus, for he had just seen and spoken to the king of Armenia.'[19]

Was Otton de Grandson returning from the re-enthronement ceremony of Hethum II at Sis? The dates do not correspond, since the Templar of Tyre places the incident in 1293, whereas the ceremony took place in 1294; but he also dates the event that brought about the death of the Templar Turcopolier a year too early. It is therefore necessary to know the exact date of the incident between the Venetians and Genoese. To recap:

In 1293, the Templars had certainly made an attempt to put two galleys to sea at Cyprus, but they had been victims of the war between Venice and Genoa and had lost equipment and men-at-arms intended for these two vessels.

There was no combined intervention in Armenia by the Masters of the Templar and Hospitallers' Orders with Otton de Grandson in 1292 or early 1293; however, Otton de Grandson really did go to Armenia in 1293 or, more likely, 1294 to attend the ceremony at Sis which re-established Hethum II as king of Armenia – but without the Masters of the Orders.[20]

Any intervention by the Templars and Hospitallers in Armenia – still with Otton de Grandson – must be deferred to 1298 or 1299. Whether such an intervention took place in conjunction with the offensive of the Mongol khan of Persia, Ghâzân, is another problem that will be examined in the next chapter. This chronology emerges from the text of chapter XLIV of Hayton of Corycos, which admits no ambiguity.

To return to the years 1292–3, while the appeal made by Pope Nicholas IV on 23 January 1292 was not a failure, it was hardly conclusive. The papal Bull addressed to the Templars was possibly received by Thibaud Gaudin, but more likely by his successor. The attempts made in Venice to fit out two Templar galleys at Cyprus were certainly down to Jacques de Molay, but they had nothing (or no longer had anything) to do with Armenia.

Jacques de Molay left Cyprus in the spring of 1293 and landed in May, probably at Marseille. The first document likely to mark a milestone in his journey, which historians usually date to May 1293,[21] was in fact written 'in Provence'. It is a letter to the king of England in which Molay indicates that he is in Provence, preparing to hold a general Chapter at Montpellier that he would like Guy de Forest, Master of England, to attend. The Chapter was to be held on 9 August 1293,[22] and it is from there that, having contacted the king of Aragon to deal with the important question raised during the Chapter[23] of the restitution of Tortosa, Jacques de Molay was to leave for Aragon. 'Was to', for it is not certain whether in the end he travelled there. Berenguer de Cardona, Master of Aragon, who had attended the Chapter and discussed the matter of Tortosa with Molay, was probably to have accompanied him to the king. But Berenguer de Cardona was ill, and postponed his return to Aragon. Did Jacques de Molay go there without him? He would have been coming from France, a country still at war with Aragon; the conflict born of the Sicilian Vespers had not yet been settled and, since the crusade of 1285, the two countries had not become reconciled. Therefore, on 24 August 1293, King James II, who had just arrived from Tarragona, had a safe-conduct delivered to Molay so that he could cross Catalan territory without being pestered by royal agents:

> As the venerable Brother Jacques de Molay, by our will and permission, is to enter our land, we command you that you must not present any hindrance to the said Brother Jacques, his companions, his horses and all his other effects ...[24]

In the absence of Berenguer de Cardona, it was the duty of the Commander of Ascò to bring the safe-conduct to the Master; it was also his task to escort him. The king of Aragon had left Tarragona for Barcelona by way of Lerida, having made a detour to Saragossa; he reached the Catalan capital on 19 September 1293. No Catalan document reports Jacques de Molay's actual arrival, not even the records of the proceedings instituted against Berenguer de Enteça, who was at the time in dispute with the Templars of the region of the Prades mountain. These have been meticulously analysed by F. Carrer y Candy, who seems, however, to give some credence to the idea that Molay made the journey.[25] Perhaps Berenguer de Cardona's recovery and his return to Catalonia had rendered the Grand Master's journey less urgent at this date?[26] The Montpellier Chapter had in fact given its agreement in principle to ceding Tortosa to the king; the methods had yet to be negotiated and compensation for the Templars yet to be found. These transactions were to take a year, and so Molay did not go to Aragon to conclude the negotiation until 1294.

During the last quarter of 1293, Jacques de Molay went to England. In a letter dated 8 December 1293, Edward I states that he spared Guy de Forest, Master of the Temple in England, a certain number of fines inflicted by the royal courts on Robert de Turvill, his predecessor, 'at the request of Brother Jacques de Molay, Master of the Knights of the Temple of Solomon'.[27] Though not entirely explicit, this letter seems a good indication that Molay was then staying in England and had interceded in person with the king. There is corroboration, too, in the testimony of John of Stoke, an English Templar questioned in London in 1311, in which he states that he was received into the Order eighteen years earlier (i.e., 1293), on 16 November, by the Master of England,

Guy de Forest; he adds that one year and fifteen days later, on the feast of Saint Andrew (30 November 1294), he was summoned by the Grand Master.[28] That date of 1294 is impossible, however, as Molay could not have been in London on 30 November and in Naples before 24 December; moreover, it is known that he left Aragon for Rome in the last quarter of 1294 (see below). The date 1293 is thus the only probable one, and so it must be assumed that John of Stoke was either confused or a year out in his reckoning.[29]

How long did Jacques de Molay stay in England? He was in Lincolnshire, in the Templar house of Eagle, in January 1294;[30] and he was still in Lincolnshire the same month, when he held a Chapter at Temple Bruer. He returned to the Continent early in the summer of 1294 at the latest, for by then he was preparing to return to Aragon. On 9 July, James II granted Molay a fresh safe-conduct and, on 22 July, informed his officers that the Master was on the point of entering the kingdom.[31] Jacques de Molay was actually in Catalonia in August. On 27 August, at Lerida, he concluded the procedure for the exchange of Tortosa, and empowered the Master of Aragon, Berenguer de Cardona, to go ahead with the handing-over.[32] He must have seen the king, who was also in town, that same day, but he must have departed soon after, for on that same 27 August, the king issued instructions to his agents to facilitate the Grand Master's journey to Rome.[33]

On 5 July, Celestine V, a pious Franciscan hermit, had been elected pope after the pontifical see had been vacant for two years. Totally unsuitable for such an office, he abdicated on 13 December 1294, and the conclave assembled in Naples on 24 December to elect Boniface VIII. Jacques de Molay, who was in the town at the time, having arrived in Italy in September, followed the new pontiff to Rome, where his coronation took place on 23 January 1295. A letter of James II of Aragon, dated that same day, shows that the king had been informed of the appointment of Boniface VIII by a missive from Jacques de Molay 'present at the Court of Rome'.[34] Molay must have spent a fairly long time in Italy, since in July–August 1295 he took possession of the Benedictine monastery of Torre Maggiore in the kingdom of Charles of Anjou, handed over to the Temple by the papacy.[35] However, his stay must have been interrupted by a few trips outside Italy, since it is also known that he went to the Templar house at Dijon, where he received one Brother Jacques de Doumanin, whom we shall meet again later in Cyprus.[36] It may be that he was travelling to or from Paris when he passed through Dijon, for he held a general Chapter of the Order in the French capital that same year, and these Chapters were almost always held on Saint John the

Baptist's day, 24 June, or occasionally on 29 June, the day of the apostles Peter and Paul.[37]

On 21 January 1296, Molay wrote from Rome to his friend Pierre de Saint-Just, Commander of Granyena in Catalonia, to say that, having agreed it with the pope and several other dignitaries he had met, he intended to return to Cyprus on the next feast day of Saint John the Baptist, but that he still meant to hold a general Chapter at Arles before embarking.[38] In fact, the Grand Master had to defer his return, for reasons unknown to us. However, the Chapter was indeed held at Arles on 15 August 1296, witnessed by a letter written by Jacques de Molay that day 'from Arles, in our general Chapter on the day of the Feast of the Assumption of Holy Mary in the year 1296', enclosed in a missive from Pope Boniface VIII.[39]

Did Molay then go back to Cyprus? He had plenty of time to join ship at Marseille so as to arrive comfortably (in theory) on the island before the bad weather set in. However, there are two indications that he was still in France in 1297: first, a letter from Jacques de Molay granting a revenue to Otton de Grandson which was sent from Paris in July 1297, on the Sunday following the Feast of Saints Peter and Paul (29 June);[40] secondly, the interrogation of Pierre de Saint-Just (a Picardian Templar and no relation to the Catalan Pierre de Saint-Just), who was received in Paris in the general Chapter by Jacques de Molay in person in 1297[41] – the general Chapters of the Order in Paris, of course, always being held on 24 or 29 June.

The coincidence of the dates thus argues for Molay's presence in Paris in June–July 1297. However, a date of 1297 for the letter making the gift does not bear close examination. M.-L. Bulst-Thiele has shown that in 1297 the Feast of the Apostles Peter and Paul fell on a Saturday, which means that the Sunday after it would have been 30 June not some date in July, therefore 1295 or 1296 is more likely than 1297.[42] Jacques de Molay's letter comes down to us from its transcription in a letter confirming the gift written by Clement V in 1308, several years later. The well-known 'scribe's error' could be to blame, although, if error there was, it could apply just as well to the day or the month as to the year. Fault lay with the editor of Clement V's records, M.-L. Bulst-Thiele and the papal scribe, in that order. The editor put the date 1277, while M.-L. Bulst-Thiele transcribed it as 1297, whereas the original, very clearly and without abbreviations or deletions, says 1287[43] – and in 1287, since the feast day of Saint Peter and Saint Paul fell on Sunday 29 June, the first Sunday after it was Sunday

6 July. The gift granted to Otton de Grandson would therefore have been made by Guillaume de Beaujeu. In which case, why does a document dated 1287 bear the name of Jacques de Molay as Grand Master? As Barbara Frale suggests, in 1308, as a result of the trial of the Templars and the seizure of their property and possessions, Otton de Grandson, in the service of the king of England, was worried about what would become of the concession previously made to him by the Templars in France. He sent a request to the pope, enclosing the Templar document bearing witness to that concession. It was a standard document for this kind of gift, with space left for date and names, which was then periodically confirmed. So, the original document of 1287 came from Guillaume de Beaujeu, but Otton de Grandson had it confirmed at an unknown date by Jacques de Molay – and it was this document that he must have sent to the Roman Curia in 1308. However, it would appear that the scribe who drew up this confirmation inscribed Molay's name, but forgot to alter the date and absentmindedly reproduced that of the original document. It seems likely that with this document, there was not one but three scribes' errors.

So, all that remains to prove Molay's presence in Paris in June 1297 is the testimony of Pierre de Saint-Just, which, like all trial testimonies, is based on memory. In any case, a letter from Boniface VIII, dated 23 February, to Pierre de Bologna, Procurator General of the Temple, proves that on this date Jacques de Molay was no longer in the West: 'As the said Master is absent and cannot easily be present, and therefore he cannot be presented with the said letter …'[44]

The fact also remains that there is no obvious reason why the Grand Master should have postponed a return that had already been delayed by several months, even a year, when he was already near his probable embarkation point of Marseille. Lastly, there is no documentation between 15 August 1296 and 24 June 1297 that mentions Molay's presence in the West, although equally there is none that mentions him in Cyprus either.

Jacques de Molay came to the West with two main objectives: first, to obtain help for his mission to the Holy Land, which meant among other things providing his Order with the means to fulfil its traditional goals, including the reconquest of Jerusalem. Secondly, to reform his Order so as to turn it into the driving force behind this reconquest. His presence in the West also enabled him to settle a few local and regional problems.

The letter written from Nicosia on 20 April 1292 settled one of these problems: it brought to a close an investigation in Cyprus into the sale by the Templars of Aragon of two not very lucrative out-of-town houses, Puigreig and La Zaida. Any large transfer of Templar property had to be authorised by the Master and the Chapter, and the letter of 20 April grants that authorisation. It is also proof that, in order to settle this kind of affair, there was no need for any travelling to be done. However, the sale of Puigreig and La Zaida involved no one but Templars, while the granting of the Templar property of Tortosa to the king of Aragon brought other interests into play. Molay's presence on the spot – on two occasions – would have made it easier to settle the matter, but also indicates to us the importance with which it was regarded.

In the last third of the thirteenth century, although the principal rulers in the West – the kings of England, France, Castile, Aragon and Sicily – were not hostile towards the Orders, they did seek to reduce the privileges that had been granted to them in the past by their respective states. In Catalonia, for instance, the king of Aragon , who was also Count of Barcelona, wanted to make himself absolute master of the lower valley of the Ebro, at the expense of the lay and ecclesiastical seigneurs who had been settled in the region since its conquest in the mid-thirteenth century. Among these seigneurs were Hospitallers and, to a greater extent, Templars who 'had converted this area into the main headquarters of their Order and the most extensive territorial seigneurie of all the Crown of Aragon'.[45] An agreement with the Hospitallers had already been concluded by King Peter III on 7 December 1280, under which the king regained Amposta, the seat of the Catalan priory of the Hospital (which, in this instance, bore the name of *châtellenie* of Amposta). By way of compensation, the king had given the Hospitallers castles in both Aragon and the kingdom of Valencia.

The agreement with the Temple, eventually reached in 1294, was followed almost immediately by an agreement with a lay seigneur, Guillaume de Moncada, who, like them, owned property in and around Tortosa. The Templar agreement had called for lengthy negotiations between the king and the Aragonese Templar authorities, as well as between the latter and the Order's central governing body. It had been raised at the general Chapter held by Jacques de Molay at Montpellier in August 1293, in which Berenguer de Cardona, Master of Aragon, had participated. The Chapter had given its consent to the exchange proposed by the king, but methods of its enactment remained negotiable. Next, in May 1294, a Chapter of Templars from Aragon met at Gardeny, to ratify the Montpellier decision.[46] Then, Jacques de Molay went to Lerida, from where, on

27 August, he authorised Berenguer de Cardona to conclude the agreement with the king.[47] This was done on 15 September, and a document was drawn up comprising two parts: in the first, referring to the agreement of the Grand Master and the Chapter, the provincial Master yields all his Order's rights over Tortosa; in the second, the king states that he is taking possession of Tortosa, in exchange for which he grants Peñiscola (in the kingdom of Valencia) to the Templars.[48]

Jacques de Molay also intervened in a dispute between the inhabitants of Monzon, where the Order had its headquarters in Aragon, and the Master of the province – perhaps this incident can be dated to his trip to Aragon. In 1292, Berenguer de Cardona had imposed a fine of 12,000 Jaca *sous* (money minted at Jaca) on the local population because on two occasions they had not fulfilled their military obligations. They in turn challenged the imposition of this fine and doubtless appealed to the Grand Master, who eventually reduced the fine to 8,000 *sous*. However, the affair was not concluded until 23 January (or 1 February) 1297, in the form of a letter of payment granted by the Commander of Monzon and made on behalf of the Order of the Temple and Jacques de Molay, 'Grand Master of the houses of the knighthood of the Temple'.[49]

Similarly, in England, Jacques de Molay made his presence known effectively. He intervened with King Edward I on behalf of the Templar Master in England, Guy de Forest, who was under pressure to pay fines which had been imposed on his predecessor, Robert de Turvill. On 8 December 1293, 'at the entreaties of Brother Jacques de Molay, Master of the Knighthood of the Temple of Solomon', the king pardoned Brother Guy.[50]

It was also through Molay's personal intervention that King Charles II of Sicily put a stop to the harassment to which Templars in the kingdom of Sicily were being subjected. On 3 July 1294, at the request of the Master of the Temple, the king forbade his agents in the ports of Puglia to demand the presentation of crossbows carried aboard Templar boats, or those chartered by the Templars, arriving from overseas (i.e. Cyprus), if it was proved contrary to custom.[51] On 12 January 1295, from the Saint Erasmus tower, near Capua, the king renewed this ban:

> On behalf … of the said Master and Brothers [of the Temple] it has been shown that, for ships and other vessels of the said house, and those that in the past were hired by it, coming from overseas parts to the kingdom, they have never formerly been accustomed to present crossbows or bows to our court …[52]

Jacques de Molay had been in Italy, or more precisely Naples, since at least December, if not September, 1294. It was doubtless a minor, secondary matter, but symbolic, given that Molay and Charles II were probably discussing such important questions as the crusade and the union of the Orders.

By the thirteenth century, the Holy Land, in the biblical sense, covered only part of Palestine – Acre, for instance, was not part of it. For convenience, however, the term was used to mean Palestine, or even the Latin States where they still existed. Its use also signified that the recapture of Jerusalem was still an element in any plans or attempts to recuperate all or part of the latter states. The expression *In subsidium terre sancta*, universally employed when referring to matters of aid, must therefore be taken in the broad sense in which it was understood at the time.

Aid for the Holy Land, with the underlying aim of reconquering it, remained the fundamental mission of the military Orders in the aftermath of the loss of Acre. A long historiographic tradition puts the date of the end of an under-taking which had been regarded as moribund for some decades, the crusades, as 1291. This same tradition, therefore, denies the military Orders (above all, the Temple) any *raison d'être* after that date. In 1291, however, public opinion – or what we can glean of it from the available documentation – did not swerve from either the Holy Land or crusading; they were neither anachronisms, nor dreams, or paradise lost. Conditions had changed, however; other preoccupa-tions became apparent; other 'adversaries of the Christian name', according to the phrase endlessly repeated in papal pronouncements, started to appear. Meanwhile, questions were asked about the crusades and their purpose, and many people criticised – often keenly – the ways in which they had been both conducted and used by the papacy and the Western states. Questions were asked about the military Orders, their responsibilities, their failures, their rivalries and their arrogance; consideration was given to merging, or even abolishing, them.[53] But, in the end, people still counted on them.[54]

By coming to the West, Jacques de Molay was pursuing his Order's aim of drumming up aid for the Holy Land. In material terms, this meant defending the surviving Christian states of Cyprus and Armenia; helping refugees flee from the Holy Land; and supporting the military Orders, who had been sorely affected by the losses they had sustained, so that they could continue to carry out their mission. Supporting the military Orders could be understood in two ways: carrying on supplying them with resources, continuing to give them donations, but also allowing them to use and transfer without hindrance their assets in the West; and as a corollary, aquiescing in their demand that those assets should not be diminished.

Jacques de Molay did not come to the West to persuade the pope and other rulers to launch a new crusade, even if that was his wish. Crusades were the pope's business. When Molay was elected Master in 1292, Pope Nicholas IV had been actively engaged in setting up such an undertaking; only his death had interrupted everything. As the papal see had remained vacant for two years, the project had been forgotten. The purpose of Molay's journey was to obtain from the western princes, with the pope's backing, a kind of 'freeing of trade' between the West and Cyprus. More precisely, he wanted the military Orders to be able to export freely to Cyprus (for him, it was merely a matter of 'transferring') the produce and income derived from their commanderies in the West; in other words, without having to pay export duties to the states in which they owned property. The European secular authorities, anxious to gain profit from trade, in fact levied customs duties on exports from their countries' ports.

In the realms of Sicily–Naples and England and, to a lesser degree, in the states of the Crown of Aragon, Jacques de Molay successfully interceded to obtain the freedom to export not only subsistence produce from the Templar estates to Cyprus, but also the money, arms and horses needed by the Templars on the island. On 12 January 1295, King Charles II of Sicily–Naples reminded his customs officers in the ports of Puglia (or Apulia) of 'the lamentable condition of the Holy Land' and his wish to remedy it by giving special assistance to 'the venerable house of the Temple' which continued to maintain men-at-arms over there. He therefore granted

> to the venerable and religious man, Brother Jacques de Molay, General Master of this holy house, our dear friend ... that every year as long as it shall please us, they may freely and without hindrance export 2,000 barrels of wheat, 3,000 of barley and 500 of leguminous plants at the current measure, from the harvests of the said house's estates in Apulia, leaving from the ports of the said province for the island of Cyprus or the Holy Land, for the succour of the people and men of the said house, by sea in suitable vessels and boats without paying exit duty.[55]

A later act, of 1299, shows in concrete form how these exports of grain from the ports of southern Italy were carried out. On 15 May 1299, a notary from Manfredonia recorded that the king's port authorities there authorised the export of the following quantities of wheat to the island of Cyprus: 123 barrels of wheat and 367 others belonging to the Temple, 1,700 barrels belonging to the Florentine company of the Bardi, 300 barrels belonging to Brother Guillaume, Master of the Hospital, and 230 others. The last three loads, namely 2,330 barrels of wheat, were intended for the Hospitallers on Cyprus. All were to be transported on a Templar vessel anchored at Manfredonia. No exit duties were to be levied.[56] Further acts in following years concerning the Hospitallers show the same intent.[57]

Jacques de Molay similarly interceded with the king of Aragon for a greater freedom of export: thus James II ordered his captain in the 'land of Otranto' (by which he meant the commander of the Aragonese fleet patrolling the waters of the Otranto channel, in the Ionian Sea) to cease impeding ships of the Hospital and Temple on their way to Cyprus.[58] He also approached the king of England.[59] His good relations with Pope Boniface VIII enabled him to obtain the papacy's unfailing support in this area. On 21 July 1295, when presumably Molay was still in Rome, Boniface VIII issued several Bulls in favour of the Templar Order, two of which are particularly relevant to the topic under discussion. One grants the same privileges to those who would make the 'passage' to Cyprus as to those who in the past had travelled to Jerusalem.[60] In the second, addressed to the king of England, the pope intercedes on behalf of the Temple, asking him not to hamper exports of produce from the Order's English houses. 'It is our good pleasure and by our orders that the Grand Master and the house of the Temple have settled in the kingdom of Cyprus in order to be better able to defend it,' writes the pope, exhorting the king to protect the Order and its possessions, and to 'permit these religious men to transport and remove from the lands under your authority, as freely as they did formerly, the goods that they need both for their upkeep and for the defence of the kingdom of Cyprus'.[62]

Jacques de Molay did not lose sight of his Order's interests. The prime objective of the measures he obtained from the western rulers was to allow the Templars of Cyprus both to rebuild their reserves and means of subsistence and to fulfil their charitable obligations.[63] By re-establishing their resources, they would in the future be able to act on behalf of the Holy Land and, more generally, on behalf of Christianity against the Infidels. The pope particularly stressed this point when he addressed 'those intrepid fighters for Christ charged with guarding the kingdom of Cyprus'.[64]

And so, what was good for the Temple was good for Cyprus and the Holy Land.

The success of Molay's enterprise in obtaining aid for the Holy Land rested, however, on his restoring the image of his Order after the disaster at Acre. To achieve that, he had both to reform the institution from within and improve its public relations. These two aspects of Jacques de Molay's journey cannot be separated; however, it would be unfair to doubt the sincerity of an action simply because it conceals a certain amount of calculation.

Hardly had he disembarked in Provence in 1293 when Molay assembled a general Chapter at Montpellier on 9 August. Each stage of his journey was punctuated by the holding of provincial (England, 1294; France, 1295 and 1296) or general (Arles, 1296) Chapters. For Montpellier and Arles, although letters of convocation would have been sent to those in charge of the Order's provinces, no such documents are known still to exist, whereas there are some regarding the meetings of the provincial Chapters, notably in the province of Aragon. On the other hand, there are in the royal archives letters from the Grand Master asking the king to give permission for the provincial Masters or Commanders to attend the Chapter, and the king's favourable replies. For England, we have both. In May 1293, Jacques de Molay wrote to Edward I informing him when the next general Chapter would be and that he needed Guy de Forest to attend, as his wisdom and counsel would be both valuable and essential.[65] For the Arles Chapter, we have the king's positive response to Molay's request. On 24 April 1296, the king sent two mandates to the Constable at Dover ordering him to permit Guy de Forest, former Master of the province of England, and Brian de Jay, the present Master, to embark for the continent in the company of the Cardinal-Bishop of Albano, the pope's legate in England; the first was authorised to go to Cyprus and the second 'to the council which is to be held with the Superior Master of the above-mentioned Order', that is, the Chapter.[66]

Only indirect information about the measures that were decided during those general Chapters still exists. In the Hospitaller Order, when a Chapter ended, its decisions were normally published in the form of statutes; it was probably the same for the Templars, except that the word *retrais* (revision, review) replaced 'statute'. But these statutes have not been preserved, at least in their original form: 'The *retrais* of such-and-such a Chapter …' or, in the case of the Hospital, 'of such-and-such a Master …' It is thought that they were periodically collected and added to the Rule. The latest of these *retrais* for which we have a date are those of Thomas Bérard. Again we must rely on the trial interrogations for information on the content of the decisions taken by those general Chapters. The papal commissions in particular were closely interested in these matters, so the minutes of the interrogations they conducted enable us to glean some idea of the reforming measures that Jacques de Molay wished to have adopted.

If we are to believe Guichard de Marsiac, former royal governor of Montpellier, and therefore present in the town at the time of the Chapter's meeting, or Guillaume d'Arrabloy, a Templar, the topics of those meetings were measures concerning 'methods of self-government, and food'.[67] Owing to the new situation created by their retreat to Cyprus, the Templars were no longer permanently in the front line; so Jacques de Molay intended to impose some restrictions regarding the Rule's regulations. Concerning food, the only known practical re-arrangement was to reduce the consumption of meat to one day a week instead of the three stipulated by the Rule.[68] Later, when opposing his Order's union with the Hospital, Jacques de Molay argued that the Templar Rule was stricter than that of its great rival; it was necessary to justify this aspect of Templar identity to use it as a weapon against criticism, and probably also to remedy a few abuses here and there.

The other matter which appears to have been raised at the Chapters was the question of the Order's charitable works. Fulfilling these in Cyprus, among other things, justified asking for assistance from the West. The duty of charity was incumbent on every religious Order, but varied in kind depending on that Order's vocation: to give alms and feed the poor was the duty of all; but hospitality, welcome and care for the poor and the sick were specifically the Hospitallers' calling. At the time of the Templar trial, an article of the act of indictment against the Order turned upon the fulfilment of this charitable obligation. The testimonies of the Templars themselves speak volumes. Questioned in Cyprus, Pierre de Torvone, knight, replied that 'it was not true that alms were not given. On the contrary, they were given in abundance, everywhere the Order had a chapel. They were given three times a week: one-tenth of the bread baked in the house and leftovers from the table, money and sometimes other items were distributed.' And, he added, 'the Temple is not obliged to offer hospitality [unlike the Hospital]. Nevertheless, if monks, knights or others came seeking hospitality at one of the Order's houses, they were given shelter and a warm welcome'.[69]

This was a sensitive issue, on which the Templars had already had to defend themselves, at the second Council of Lyon in 1274. Jacques de Molay justified himself in person on this matter during interrogation: 'He knew no other Orders where more alms were given than in the Order of the Temple, for in all the Order's houses, following the general Rule of the said Order, alms were given thrice a week to all who wished to accept them.'[70] There was one restriction, however: when the Grand Master made his journey to the West, because of the important needs of the Order in the East, he had asked that almsgiving should not be overdone but limited to what was laid down in the Rule.

During those Chapters, was the matter of the ritual of entry to the Order raised? This was one of the key elements in the accusations that were to be levelled against the Temple at the time of their trial, so was it possible that, when he took part in the 1291 Chapter in Cyprus to call for reforms in his Order, Jacques de Molay had included this subject in his agenda? The testimony of Jean Serrand, mentioned earlier, hints at it. Did the Grand Master encounter resistance within the bosom of the Temple that might have prevented him from proceeding further with his plans for reform? Or was he perhaps not very pugnacious on this point? These questions will be raised again in the chapter dealing with the trial.

The matter of merging the Orders took up much of Molay's attention while he was in the West. The Grand Master was himself opposed to it, as he later explained to Pope Clement V. However, the topic had been raised since the second Council of Lyon in 1274, and Jacques de Molay had discussed it with the pope, with King Charles II of Sicily, who in 1292 indicated he was in favour of it, and probably also with the kings of England, Aragon and France. The attitude of the first is not known, the second was hostile and Philip the Fair was in favour on certain conditions.

Finally, some historians have thought that, while Molay was passing through Aragon in 1294, there may have been some question of the Order's headquarters transferring to the West, specifically, Peñiscola. According to Laurent Dailliez, James I of Aragon had already wanted the Temple to settle in Ibiza, which had yet to be conquered. James II might again have proposed such a transfer.[71] As we have seen, in 1294 the Templars had received Peñiscola, in the kingdom of Valencia, in exchange for Tortosa. A very large number of deeds in the Archives of the Crown of Aragon, spread over the years 1294–1307, reveal the Templars' methodical take-over of the territory granted to them; domains, saltworks and rights of all kinds. In 1294, they undertook the construction of a mighty castle which, even today, leaves historians perplexed. Its site is, admittedly, superb, towering above the sea. But why build such a vast and carefully fortified place? Why there? And why then? Reconquest and the struggle against the Muslims of the kingdom of Granada are not persuasive arguments, as that front was situated much farther to the south. Muslim attacks from the sea were supposedly still also a threat, but Catalan maritime supremacy was overwhelming. Maybe the Templars wanted to make Peñiscola the seat of an Order whose mission would be redefined and centred on the struggle against the Moors in Spain?[72] There is no written documentation to support that theory. Is evidence in stone admissible? For it was a huge and costly castle that the Templars undertook to build in 1294; meanwhile, Jacques de Molay was travelling all over the West calling for aid for the Holy Land. The Holy Land was not in Spain, and Granada was not Jerusalem. The Templar Order's headquarters, the Order's governing body, were in Cyprus; and there they would stay as long as Jacques de Molay was Master.

The success of Molay's tour of the West could not be taken for granted. Conflicts between states, the primacy of western interests over all others, for the secular states as well as the papacy, formed sizeable obstacles: a lot of fine words and few commitments. But there was a further obstacle to be removed. The image of the Templar Order – of the military Orders in general – was not good. Despite their bravery, the Templars, even more than the Hospitallers, were held responsible for the disappearance of the kingdom of Jerusalem, simply because they had proclaimed themselves its best defenders.[73] To restore the tarnished image of his Order, Jacques de Molay had both to give evidence of humility and act with diplomacy while at the same time showing his determination to commit the Temple to the combat waged in the East. Given that nothing in the documentation surrounding his journey and his relations with either the pope or the secular rulers indicates any sign of imprudence, tactlessness or arrogance, he would appear to have conducted his affairs faultlessly.

Molay knew how to maintain friendships, as shown by the 'gifts' granted to several close associates of Pope Boniface VIII, with whom he seems to have enjoyed excellent relations.[74] It was a matter of exchanging courtesies. The pope, as we have seen, made a donation to the Temple of the Benedictine monastery of Torre Maggiore in 1295; on 7 April 1300, a chaplain brother of the Temple was delegated there to act freely in the monastery, to institute and dismiss, visit and discipline the clergy and other ecclesiastical subjects of the monastery.[75] On

20 July 1296, the pope also granted Jacques de Molay and the Temple a house and appurtenances at Anagni, on the pretext that the Templars had no refuge in maritime Campania.[76] But the Temple gave, too. On 9 March 1300, Boniface was thus able to reward two knights, a father and son, among his closest associates with a 'villa' or *castrum*, passed to the Roman church 'by the gift of brother Jacques de Molay'.[77] More directly, from Arles where he had assembled the Order's general Chapter, Molay conceded several of the commanderies and bailiwicks situated in Spain to a brother of the Temple, Jean Fernandez, who held the post of *cubicularius* (gentleman of the bedchamber) to the pope.[78]

These cordial relations with Pope Boniface VIII are evident in a series of Bulls issued on 21 July 1295. One grants the Templars in Cyprus the same liberties and immunities they had enjoyed in the kingdom of Acre; another exempts the brothers from presenting their procurations to the pope's nuncios and legates, unless the latter are cardinals. Another series of Bulls was sent to the European rulers commending the Order, its Master and members to them. A final, less conventional one was sent to archbishops, asking them to help bring back to the fold those troublesome Templars who had been disobeying their Master.[79] This is an intriguing Bull. Who were these rebels? What caused their rebellion? And what exactly was meant by the term 'rebellion'? Did Molay's attempts to reform certain practices within the Order trigger off bad-tempered attempts at subversion (rather than open revolt, no trace of which can be found) on the part of certain Templars? Such questions must remain unanswered. However, to ask them helps us to assess the significance of his journey. To recap, the objectives that Jacques de Molay had set himself were as follows: to gain assistance, in the form of greater facilities for obtaining supplies in the West, for his Order's mission in the Holy Land; a reform of the Order, although this is perhaps a rather grand word to describe what might have been no more than an intent to restore to working order a body that had been seriously shaken by the loss of the Holy Land and Guillaume de Beaujeu's possibly too-distant style of management. But among the aims pursued by Molay at that time, the organisation of a crusade in liaison with Mongol initiatives must not be included; in the first place, no pope was appointed before the end of 1294; next, the Mongol offensive did not become a reality until the accession of Ghâzân at the head of the Persian khanate.

Within these parameters, it could be said that Jacques de Molay was able to obtain the aid he wanted (after all, he was not asking the impossible). On the other hand, in the matter of reforming the Order, the results seem rather less successful, even taking into account that no one knows the exact scope and content of the reforms that Molay had in mind. We do know, however, the end of the story: the rites of entry to the Order were not altered; meanwhile, acts of charity received an encouraging impetus, even if at one point the Grand Master requested that they be limited to what had been laid down in the Rule. As for the reforms relating to life in the Order, most of the testimonies gathered during the trial interrogations suggest that they were applied, although there are exceptions.[80] It was no easy task to reform the Order, yet the notion that the Grand Master and the Chapter should be obeyed was widespread among the members of the Order. These questions were to lie at the heart of the trial. Many a Templar would come to regret the 'neglectfulness' of the Order as regards reform of its entry ritual. Yet it seems unlikely that Jacques de Molay would have been unaware of the need for such reform.

Before returning to Cyprus, probably at the pope's request, Molay delegated a large part of his authority, notably in financial matters, to Hugues de Pairaud, who was then Master of France. In all likelihood he also gave him the office of Visitor of France[81] although this is not specified in the pope's letter mentioning the matter, but may be inferred from his confirmation of the post. Hugues de Pairaud held both offices until 1300, when Gérard de Villiers became Master of France. Maybe Molay divided the roles along the lines of the East for me, the West for you (although it must be remembered that the office of Visitor of Spain also existed). Jacques de Molay may have been prepared to delegate but he abandoned neither his prerogatives nor his powers to control, which were in any case shared by the Chapter. We will have a chance to verify this when looking at his methods of government.

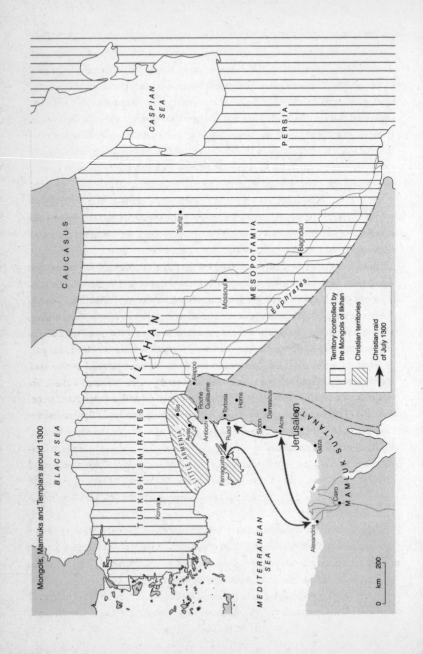

Mongols, Mamluks and Templars around 1300

CAUCASUS

BLACK SEA

CASPIAN SEA

TURKISH EMIRATES

ILKHAN

PERSIA

Konya

Sis

LITTLE ARMENIA

Aleppo

Roche Guillaume

Antioch · Ayas

Ruad · Tortosa

Horns

Tabriz

Mossoul

MESOPOTAMIA

Baghdad

Euphrates

Famagusta

Sidon

Damascus

Acre

Jerusalem

Gaza

MAMLUK SULTANATE

Cairo

Alexandria

MEDITERRANEAN SEA

☐ Territory controlled by the Mongols of Ilkhan

▨ Christian territories

→ Christian raid of July 1300

0   km   200

1300

THE ISLE OF RUAD

Jacques de Molay returned to Cyprus in 1296. No one knows what he did between 1297–8 and 1298, although it is likely that he devoted his time to defending his Order against the king of Cyprus, who was then attempting to diminish the privileges of both the Temple and the Hospital. He could also have been trying to recover some rights and re-examine concessions made by his predecessors in the past. This was the continuation of a dispute that would only worsen, and that Pope Boniface's pacifying efforts in 1298 were unable to extinguish altogether.[1] (I will return to this in Chapter 7). Not until 1299 does a still sparse documentation enable us to state that at that date, and for four years afterwards, Molay and his Order, together with the other Christian forces of Cyprus and Armenia, were wholly engaged in trying to reconquer the Holy Land, in association with offensives from the Mongol king of Persia, Ghâzân. And the Templars' two-year occupation of the isle of Ruad, off Tortosa, on the Syrian coast, must be seen solely in this light.

In the beginning, if we follow Hayton of Corycos, it was a Mamluk offensive against the Armenian kingdom of Cilicia that brought about the Mongol intervention, most likely at the request of King Hethum II. From then on, the Cypriot Christians tried to form a strategic alliance with the Mongols – although not without difficulty.

Hayton the Historian links the Mamluk attack to the enfeeblement of the Armenian kingdom caused by disputes within the royal family. In order for this to be fully understood, it is necessary to fill in some details on King Hethum II's recantations and their consequences.[2] In 1296, having chosen to abdicate the throne for a second time, again in favour of his brother Thoros, Hethum decided to go to Constantinople to visit his sister Rita, wife of the son of the emperor

Andronic II. Oddly enough, Thoros went with him. They stayed in the Byzantine capital for about six months, returning to Armenia in mid-1297. While they were away, their brother Sembat took advantage of the anxiety and discontent aroused in the Armenian nobility and clergy by the lack of obvious authority, and usurped the throne; and upon their return to Armenia, he had both his brothers arrested. Sembat reigned for roughly a year, between 1297 and early 1298. Meanwhile, a fourth brother, Constantine, indignant at the fate Sembat had meted out to Hethum and Thoros, rose up against him in order to obtain their release. Sembat reacted by having Thoros executed and Hethum blinded – although Constantine did manage to secure the release of the former king, caring for him so well that Hethum recovered his sight and granted Constantine a kind of delegated authority. Next, the two brothers reached an agreement with the nobility and the Church of Armenia that they would make Levon, younger son of the deceased Thoros, the future king. But, until he reached his majority, Constantine would run the kingdom. Sembat's supporters were captured and executed, and Sembat himself was imprisoned in late 1298 or early 1299.

Meanwhile – still according to Hayton – the 'Saracens who did not sleep' took advantage of these disputes and the kingdom's weakness to attack it: 'The enemies of the Christian faith occupied one-third of the whole kingdom of Armenia.' In particular, in 1298 or 1299,[3] they captured the castles of Servantikar and Roche-Guillaume, the Temple's last bastion on the mainland and its provincial headquarters in Armenia. Constantine did his utmost to ensure the country's defence, but Hethum, who had regained his sight (although not, it would seem, his perspicacity) 'was not happy with his brother's government'. At which point our Franciscan – Brother John, to give him his religious order name – had Constantine arrested during the night. He then forced his way back into power in the capital, Sis, before compelling his two brothers, Sembat and Constantine, to acknowledge once again that he was their lord and king. Next he dispatched the pair of them on a galley to Constantinople, under the guard of his brother-in-law the Greek emperor, so that 'they should never return to their homeland'.[4]

Luckily for the Armenians, the Mamluks were not able to take full advantage of these tragi-comic episodes, as they themselves were the victims of confusion. The sultan Lâdjîn was assassinated in 1298, bringing about the return to power of al Malik al-Nâsir Mohammed (Kalâwûn II), who had already been sultan in 1293–4. The Mamluk offensive in Armenia had to be interrupted for some months, but once the situation in Cairo was stabilised, military operations resumed.

It was now summer 1299. Hethum II then turned to Ghâzân, the khan of Persia, who, although converted to Islam, still regarded the Mamluks as his chief enemies. The latter left his capital, Tabriz, in October for the upper Euphrates, and in December captured Aleppo. He was soon joined by King Hethum, whose forces seem to have included Hospitallers and Templars from the kingdom of Armenia,[5] who took part in the rest of the campaign. On 24 December 1299, the khan and his allies carried off a brilliant victory over the Mamluk army at the second battle of Homs.[6] The Mongols pursued the routed troops southwards, but stopped level with Gaza. On 6 January, although its citadel continued to resist, Ghâzân seized Damascus.

Hayton of Corycos speaks of the presence in Armenia of Otton de Grandson and the Master of the Temple and Grand Commander of the Hospital at some point in 1298 or 1299. On two occasions during the first weeks of his expedition, Ghâzân made contact with the Latins of Cyprus, asking for their help. His first letter, dated 21 October 1299 and brought by messenger, reached Cyprus on 3 November. A second missive was sent at the end of November. Both were addressed to the king of Cyprus and the Masters of the Temple, the Hospital and the 'Germans' (the Teutonic Order).[7] According to Amadi, the Christians did not follow this up because of a falling-out between the military Orders; and in fact, no Christians took part in the expedition, apart from local Armenians, Templars and Hospitallers.

The generally held view is, therefore, that their missing the opportunity offered by Ghâzân to recuperate the Holy Land[8] should be blamed upon the traditional rivalry between the two Orders. However, this calls for closer examination. How can Ghâzân's letters and appeals for help be reconciled with the data in Hayton's text which, as shown in Chapter 6, were set in 1298 or 1299? Having returned to Armenia in 1298, Hayton was himself present at the battle of Homs and the various episodes that followed.[9] The historian is not only sparing with the exact details of the presence of the heads of the Orders in Armenia, but he says nothing about the activities of King Hethum II at the time either. Perhaps he does not want to cast a good light on the deeds of a king he detests? Western sources remain silent; the Templar of Tyre makes no mention of the sojourn in Armenia of the Orders' leaders, but equally says nothing about Ghâzân's approaches. And it is not Hayton who mentions the supposed ill-feeling between

Templars and Hospitallers, but Amadi, whose text comes much later and is usually modelled on that of the Templar of Tyre.

In my opinion, the presence of Grandson, Molay and the Grand Commander of the Hospital in Armenia was not connected with the Mongol offensive at all, not least for the simple chronological reason that it could not have been in response to Ghâzân's appeals, as they came later. These important personages no doubt came to Armenia, but shortly *before* the Mongol drive, at the time of the Mamluk offensives which preceded it. The castle of Roche-Guillaume having fallen to the Muslims in 1298 or 1299, Otton de Grandson, Jacques de Molay and the others would have made the journey to counter-attack the Mamluk invasion, not help the Mongols, who were not yet on the scene.

Ghâzân's request was belated because he was already on his way when he made it, and it might be thought – obviously without ruling out the possibility of differing views among Christians (although no contemporary sources such as the Templar of Tyre show this) – that the Cypriot Christians were not in a position to respond so rapidly. For what happened in the first months of 1300 indicates that there was neither bad grace nor procrastination on the part of the military Orders and Cypriots, but perhaps only a lack of preparation that prevented a speedy response to Ghâzân's appeal. Still, it is not clear why the khan of Persia waited until November to ask for help from the Christians when he had already been campaigning for at least a month.

The two letters he sent in late 1299 were not, however totally ineffectual. Seigneurs from Cyprus left the island to join him possibly as early as the end of 1299, but definitely by January 1300. Two knights of the realm, Guy d'Ibelin, Count of Jaffa, and Jean de Gibelet, landed with their entourages on the Syrian coast at Gibelet and settled in the castle of Nefin with the intention to reach Armenia and join Ghâzân. But after a few days they learned that the khan had terminated his campaign and gone back to his capital, Tabriz. This episode with the knights is a minor one, but it signifies none the less the Christians' willingness to become involved.[10] For even though the favourable conditions at the end of 1299 were not likely to happen again soon, the following year would see a better prepared attempt at common action between Mongol, Armenian and Cypriot forces. To which Jacques de Molay was to commit himself totally.

The idea of a combined operation by the Mongols of Persia and the Latins was not a new one, and its aims were fairly straightforward: lands taken from the Mamluks were to be divided between Mongols and Christians, the latter retrieving the territories of the former Latin States in the East and Jerusalem. This is reiterated in a letter sent by Thomas Gras from Cyprus on 4 March 1300:

> And the said Kasan [sic] sent his messengers to the king of Jerusalem and Cyprus and to the communes and military-religious Orders who supported him in Damascus or Jerusalem, saying that he would give them all the land which the Christians had formerly held in the time of Godefroy de Bolloin [sic].

Gras is referring to Ghâzân's offensive in the autumn of 1299, on the strength of which an optimistic rumour spread in the West early in 1300 that Jerusalem was once more in Christian hands. It was even said that King Hethum of Armenia had celebrated Mass at the Holy Sepulchre on the Feast of the Epiphany.[11] Ghâzân's attack and victories also raised great hopes in Cyprus, according to a letter from a Franciscan from Nicosia, dated 14 February 1300. He, too, says that Hethum prayed at the Holy Sepulchre; he further announces that 'our Minister and many of our brethren (of the Franciscan province) are preparing to go to Syria with the knights, footsoldiers and all the other monks'.[12] But the news of Ghâzân's retreat in the same month deferred such fine resolutions until later. Which brings us back to the problem of the Mongols' weak point – the difficulty of keeping such a vast army of horsemen mobilised, not because the men could not be kept, but because their mounts could not be fed. Breaking off his pursuit of the Mamluk army after his victory at Homs, Ghâzân had not been able to destroy totally the sultan of Cairo's army. The Templar of Tyre considers his pursuit 'feeble' and explains why: 'He began to follow the defeated army, but not very forcefully, for his horses were worn out from the long journey they had made, and the battle, and the shortage of fodder.'[13]

Returning to Tabriz, Ghâzân left Syria under the control of the emir Mûlay, whom the Templar of Tyre refers to as Molay, thereby leading to confusion with our Grand Master. Perhaps this is what lies at the root of the legend about Jacques de Molay entering Jerusalem – a legend I will return to at the end of the book. In reality, general command was exercised by Kutlushah, Mûlay being only the head of the army which got as far as Gaza and may have penetrated Jerusalem.[14]

Meanwhile, Ghâzân had announced that he would return the following November, this time to attack Egypt.[15] While he waited, during 1300, the khan stepped up his diplomatic initiatives with Cyprus and the West. The Templar of Tyre mentions the arrival in Nicosia, probably during the spring of 1300, of Mongol messengers whose leader is identified by Amadi as 'misser Chial', or 'Chiol'. He was in fact Isol the Pisan, an Italian merchant-adventurer from the Bofeti family of Pisa, who enjoyed a position of trust at Ghâzân's court and was an invaluable interlocutor in the Mongol khan's relations with western leaders, especially the pope.[16] By agreement with the Cypriots, a joint embassy was sent to the pope. In a report from Barcelona, dated 2 July, Romeo de Marimundo, adviser to the king of Aragon, indicates to his master that 'on behalf of the Tartars, the king of Armenia, the king of Cyprus, the Master of the Temple and other dignitaries from overseas, ambassadors are arriving to visit the sovereign pontiff; they are already in Apulia and are expected at any time at the Curia'.[17] The Mongols' envoy Vicarius was probably also Italian. It was doubtless to make the unity between Mongols and Franks evident to both Christians and Mamluks that raids by a Christian fleet on Egypt and Syria were organised, beginning on 20 July. Meeting in council at Famagusta, Henry II of Cyprus, Jacques de Molay and the Grand Commander of the Hospital decided to launch a fleet of sixteen galleys, six *sayettes* (fast boats) and a few other *panfiles* (small, rapid rowing-boats) against Egypt. Neither the Templar of Tyre's chronicle, nor Amadi's, which is more accurate, indicates that the king and Master of the Temple were on board any of these vessels. 'The king of Cyprus, his brother the Lord of Tyre, the Master of the Temple, the Commander of the Hospital and misser Chial, the ambassador of Cassan [Ghâzân], then went to Famagusta, where they held council to decide whether they should go on or not.'[18] They decided to cross, but there is no record that any of them went on the expedition, with the exception of the khan's ambassador, whose banner was hoisted on the boats. The flotilla sailed towards the Nile delta, attacking Rosetta and pillaging Alexandria before turning north in the direction of Acre and then Tortosa; a raid by the Hospitallers on Maraclea failed. The fleet then returned to Cyprus.[19] In military terms, the expedition had a very modest outcome, hauls of booty were not insignificant and as regards propaganda, it had its uses ('Something is being done'). Above all, this expedition made manifest the unity of the Cypriot Franks and, through a material act, put the seal on the Mongol alliance. Once mobilised, the Franks were able to make a rapid response to Ghâzân's new messenger, who came to Cyprus to announce the Mongol khan's decision to start campaigning in November 1300.

In the said year [1300] there came to Cyprus a messenger from Ghâzân, king of
the Tartars, saying that Ghâzân was to come that winter, and desired the king
and all the Franks to go and await his coming in Armenia, for which the king and
his people were making their preparations.[20]

On 30 September Ghâzân left Tabriz. He had contacted Hethum II, and this
time could rely on the consequent mobilisation of the Cypriot Franks.[21]

In fact, in November Amaury of Tyre, the king's brother, Guillaume de
Villaret, the Master of the Hospital (who had just arrived from the West), and
Jacques de Molay installed their knights on the isle of Tortosa, or Ruad, some
two miles from the Syrian shores. Amaury brought with him three hundred
knights and 'the Temple and Hospital had as many or more'.[22]

The Catalan Count Bernart Guillem d'Enteça, who had landed at Famagusta at the end of 1300, wrote to the king of Aragon, probably in March 1301,
recounting all that had happened on the isle during the winter:

When Ghâzân was in his own country, he sent several of his messengers to
Cyprus, to the illustrious king of Cyprus and the Masters of the Temple and
Hospital, to inform them that he would be coming to the land of the Infidels,
sons of Ishmael, commonly known as Shem [Syria], the next November. And
he asked the Christians to prepare to come with him with their entire army ...
Having heard this, the Christians ... made ready and went to the isle of Tortosa,
situated less than two miles from the coast. There were the honourable Lord
of Tyre, brother of the illustrious king of Cyprus, who had come with a large
number of men-at-arms; our Master of the Hospitallers, with all those who had
accompanied him on his journey, who did many fine and honourable deeds,
and with him people from Cyprus; and the Master of the Templars, with all
his convent, and many other men. From this isle they crossed to the mainland,
facing great perils and dangerous situations, and remained there for twenty-five
days or more; which means that, staying as long on the mainland as on the isle,
they remained four months or more. And there they daily awaited Ghâzân's
arrival.[23]

But Ghâzân failed to appear ...

In January 1301, only a Mongol vanguard led by Kutlushah showed up in
north Syria. The harsh winter had hampered the movement of too large a

cavalry. In February, an emissary from Ghâzân finally informed King Hethum that the khan had given up his undertaking and had decided to postpone the attack on Mamluk Egypt until later. At Hethum's side were Guy d'Ibelin and Jean de Gibelet, who, as previously mentioned, had initially landed in Syria early in 1300. Unless they stayed with King Hethum throughout that year – which seems unlikely – they must have returned with Amaury of Tyre in November and, because of their experience, been sent to the king of Armenia to find out more about Mongol troops' movements.[24]

By disembarking at Tortosa in December 1300, the Christian forces, led by Amaury and the Grand Masters of the Orders, thought they would be able to join Ghâzân around Aleppo, an almost obligatory staging post for Mongols coming from Mesopotamia to Syria. They stayed on the mainland for twenty-five days, laying waste towns and villages, plundering the populace and taking many captive, to be sold as slaves in Cyprus's markets. Then, as the Templar of Tyre writes, 'when they saw that the Tartars were taking too long to arrive and that the Saracens had a vast number of men to attack them, they returned to the said isle of Tortosa'.[25] Thinking it no more than a temporary hitch, they waited on the island. But in February 1301, King Hethum was informed that Ghâzân would not be coming. When the Franks on Ruad heard the news, they held council and decided to evacuate the bulk of their troops stationed there. Amaury of Tyre's knights and the Hospitallers regained Cyprus in late March or early April, but a contingent of Templars remained where they were, in the charge of the Marshal of the Order, Bartholomé de Chinsi (or Quincy).

It may appear that the occupation and defence of Ruad became the exclusive affair of the Templars, but the reality was rather different. Preparations for the landing at Ruad back in November 1300 had taken all year to organise by the whole of the Christian forces based in Cyprus, in the hope that all the promises made by the Mongol alliance would finally be realised. There are a number of documents from 1299–1300 which do not show categoric evidence of this but none the less indicate that Christian mobilisation took place. As early as mid-1299, the Hospitallers of Cyprus had asked Guillaume de Villaret, their Grand Master, to come to the island to hold a Chapter – the situation probably seeming rich enough in possibilities to merit the immediate presence of the Grand Master.[26] But the Hospitallers of the West were not to be left out, judging by this letter from a brother in Nantes, dated 4 May 1300: 'Upon this our Master ordered and commanded us to be ready to make this crossing with him in the month of August, and all our people were likewise commanded to be ready to cross with us.' He ends with a sentence that says far more about the 'rearguard's' state of mind than history's conventional words on the so-called decline of crusading: 'And know, my lord, that we felt very great joy at this command.'[27]

Guillaume de Villaret landed in Cyprus at the end of October 1300. On 5 November, he assembled a general Chapter of the Order at Limassol, from which he produced several new statutes, among them one which clearly reveals that the reinstallation of the Hospitallers' Order in Syria was envisaged at that time.

> It is established that as long as the Master and the convent are in the kingdom of Cyprus, a general Chapter shall be held at Limassol. And if the Master and convent went to Syria, the Master would hold a council with the convent or with the majority about the place where the general Chapter would have to be held.[28]

Among these statutes there is another, rather more ambiguous document, which is none the less revealing. On 25 February 1300, the 'Commander of the Temple' (it is not clear if this is Commander of the Land or Grand Commander or simply the Commander of Famagusta) hired a Genoese vessel equipped with fifty-five crew for the sum of 3,000 Saracen bezants. The ship having been chartered for a period from March to mid-July, the Templars were now able to 'leave the port of Famagusta for those of Syria, to reach the places indicated below, namely, Tortosa, Tripoli, Tyre and Acre. In those places, you and the said house will be permitted to have loaded on the said ship and unloaded from the said ship, boats, horses and all cargo, to go and come at your will or at that of the said house in the above-named places.'

It could have been a simple trading operation, but that seems unlikely, partly because the text does not indicate this at all, and partly because, in the context of 1300, such an operation would have been impossible, given the unequivocal attitude of the Grand Master on the subject of trade with the Infidels (an attitude which would reveal itself forcefully some years later in the plan for a crusade presented to Clement V). Most probably – especially given all the talk of unloading horses – the Templars were making ready a vessel for potential coastal raids. If so, at the end of February, when Ghâzân's retreat had become common knowledge but there was the possibility he might return in November, preparations were already being made for the expedition that would finally take place in July 1300.[29] On 19 April, the Master of the province of Aragon–Catalonia, Berenguer de Cardona, wrote from Saragossa to Pierre de Saint-Just, Commander of Corbins:

> We have received letters from the lord Master of Outremer [Jacques de Molay] asking us to spend this year in the Land [Cyprus] because the Tartars have conquered the Land and we must help the convent of the Temple ... Wishing to do our duty, we call upon your friendship to let us know your good will and to collect all the money that you have ...[30]

The Grand Master's letters mentioned above must date from the end of February or beginning of March. Berenguer de Cardona actually made his journey to Cyprus during the summer of 1300, but spent some weeks of the winter of 1300–1 at Ruad. There exist some interesting notarised documents which show that he chartered a Catalan vessel at Famagusta for his return journey to Barcelona in the company of another Catalan Templar, Berenguer Guamir.[31]

James II of Aragon's talented admiral-of-the-fleet, Roger de Lauria, had, since James' reconciliation with Charles II of Anjou to form an alliance against James' own brother, Frederick III of Sicily, become admiral of the Angevin fleet of Naples. On 27 April 1300 he wrote to his former (and to some extent current) patron informing him of the Templar and Hospitaller initiatives, and that for two years they had stockpiled in the kingdom of Naples and transferred overseas everything that was required for the arrival of the Tartars in the fight against the Saracens in the Holy Land.[32]

The lasting settlement of the Templars on Ruad, which began in April 1301, was no idle whim; nor was it a hazardous venture with no prospect of success. They had not been abandoned by the Cypriot knights, led by Amaury of Tyre (the king's brother and Constable of the kingdom of Jerusalem), or the Hospitallers. Since the preceding November, everything had been decided and carried out collectively. It was the same in March 1301; a group, in this instance of Templars, had been entrusted with the duty of watching over and preserving this advance post of Christendom, on behalf of all, while awaiting the next Mongol invasion and hoping that this time it would really take place. In any case, the island was too small and too poor to house a large garrison for more than a few months.

Ruad is the only island on the Syrio-Palestinian coast; consisting of arid sandstone, it is 700 metres long, 400 metres wide, and a mere 15 metres above sea level. Two tiny coves provide shelter for fishing boats. Seized from the Templars in 1302, Ruad has been populated by fishermen and trades people up until contemporary times; before the Second World War it was home to up to 3,500 inhabitants.[33]

Ruad was nothing like Rhodes, therefore, and the Templars did not seek to set up an independent fiefdom there, which would, in any case, have been unwise. There was not even the outline of a constitution of an *ordenstaat*, or 'Order's States' as Rhodes became for the Hospitallers and Prussia for the Teutonic Orders.[34] It is easy to be misled by the papal Bull of 13 November 1301, which grants the entire island to the brethren of the Temple. Ruad was dependent on Tortosa, whose Templars at the time of the Latin States shared their seigneurie with the local bishop. It was the same for Ruad, and in his Bull of 13 November, the pope grants to the Templars the entire seigneurie of the islet, including the bishop's share, arguing this was recompense for the expenses they had incurred defending it.[35] This arrangement bore no similarity to the concession of a conquered territory, such as that of Rhodes to the Hospitallers. Bearing in mind the strategic position of the island and what else was going on in 1301, the pope took a decision intended to strengthen the Christians' position, through the Templar Order, over a territory which he had never ceased to regard as belonging to Christendom since 1291. It was the continuation of a *de jure* situation dating from the twelfth and thirteenth centuries. Naturally, nothing in the Bull supports the idea that the Templars intended to make Ruad their new headquarters. Nor is there anything to suggest this in Jacques de Molay's actions or writings of the same period.

Ruad was to form a bridgehead for a massive landing on the Syrio-Palestinian coast which, it was hoped, would take place in the autumn of 1301 when Ghâzân returned to Syria; meanwhile, the little island served as a departure point for harassment raids on the same coast carried out by the Templars during 1301. Jacques de Molay took care to inform the western rulers of his Order's activities. On 8 April 1301, he told Edward I of the internal troubles Ghâzân had encountered, and was still encountering, as a result of a rebellion led by his cousin Porte-Ferri. But the Grand Master had also learnt that the khan intended to invade Egypt the following autumn: 'And our convent, with all our galleys and *'tarides'* [light galleys] [lacuna] has been transported to the isle of Tortosa to await Ghâzân's army and his Tartars ...' While they waited, the knights inflicted damage on the Saracens.[36]

A few months later, Jacques de Molay wrote to the king of Aragon to inform him that

> the king of Armenia had sent his messengers to the king of Cyprus to tell him ... that Ghâzân was now on the point of coming to the sultan's lands with a multitude of Tartars. Knowing this, we now intend to go to the isle of Tortosa, where our convent has remained all this year with horses and arms, causing much damage to the *casaux* along the coast and capturing many Saracens. We intend to go there and settle in to await the Tartars.[37]

But he did not go to Ruad, for once again Ghâzân failed to put in an appearance and the great Mongol offensive was adjourned. In July, and again in November 1301, Ghâzân had attempted to negotiate with the Mamluk sultan, but without success.[38] His failures, or semi-successes, combined with the increasing difficulties he encountered on his expeditions, had led him to behave in a less bellicose manner towards the Mamluks. That had produced no concrete results, but a nascent Muslim solidarity was becoming slowly apparent, and the Christians could expect nothing good to come of it.

So nothing actually happened at Ruad between November 1301 and March 1302. The Templar garrison made efforts to fortify the island, and kept up the raids and plundering, taking captives with the view of exchanging them against Christian prisoners, and – a further easily foreseeable outcome – beginning to seriously annoy the Mamluks in Cairo.

Nevertheless the Templars spent both the spring and summer of 1302 on Ruad; the strategy of a Mongol alliance was not yet quite dead. Ghâzân sent a delegation to the West for part of 1302 and early 1303. He also passed messages on to the kings of France and England (the latter's reply, dated 12 March, is preserved),[39] and to Pope Boniface VIII, to whom he indicated, on 12 April 1302, that he had not given up on an expedition to Syria but that he could not lead it until the following year; he was relying on the help of the Christians.[40] His ambassadors stayed at the court of Charles II in Naples, and with the pope in Rome, returning to Persia in April 1303.[41]

And so, the dilemma for the Templars on Ruad was, should they wait? The Mamluks, having re-established their authority over Syria, took advantage of the time wasted by Ghâzân to attack the islet. There was no long-drawn-out siege. In July 1302, the Syrian forces attacked Cilicia, and only after that did they set their sights on Ruad. The control of the sea flaunted by the Christians did not mean that no Mamluk vessel was afloat, and opportunities sometimes presented themselves. For instance, in September 1302, a Mamluk fleet of sixteen ships left Egypt for Tripoli, where it took soldiers on board; it then attacked Ruad and attempted a landing at two points on the island (probably the two coves). The Ruad Templars, under the command of the Marshal of the Order, Bartholomé de Quincy,[42] consisted of 120 knights, 500 archers and 400 men and women helping the garrison.[43] According to Amadi, the Templars repulsed the Muslims' first attempt and drove them back to their boats.[44] The Templar of Tyre is less positive, letting it be understood that the Muslims were certainly driven back, but that they clung on to the island. With the advantage of superior numbers, they pressed the defenders enough to force them to fall back to a tower in the centre of the island; consequently, the Muslims had room to manoeuvre and could dig themselves in solidly.[45] Having besieged the tower, they invited the defenders to capitulate, promising to take them to a Christian country of their choice. The Catalan Templar Hugues d'Empurias, who had already spent long years in prison in Cairo, conducted the negotiations leading to their surrender, on 26 September. Naturally, the Mamluks failed to honour their word, and executed all the Christians and Syrian bowmen; the knights of the Temple were taken into captivity and sent to Cairo, but the Marshal of the Order perished in combat. A rescue fleet assembled by the king of Cyprus and the Orders of the Temple and Hospital and led by their Grand Masters was preparing to weigh anchor when the news of Ruad's fall arrived. It stayed in port.[46]

This failure of the Templars alone, since they alone had stayed on Ruad, is reported in a neutral tone by the Templar of Tyre and the chroniclers who followed him, Amadi and Florio Bustron. The event raised merely a faint echo in the West, Jean de Saint-Victor being the only one to mention it.[47] The affair is referred to in one item from the Templars' trial, an indictment, written in French and presented by a brother of the Temple to his judges, indicating that at the time of the Order's last Chapter, held in Paris at Candlemas 1307 by Hugues de Pairaud, Brother Renaud de la Folie had made a serious accusation against Gérard de Villiers and another brother

because of whom the isle of Tortosa had been lost, and because of whom brethren and princes had been killed there; and he would throw down the gauntlet and
challenge them. All that happened because the said Brother Girart [*sic*] had left a
day earlier, taking his friends with him, and for want of the good knights he had
taken away, the battle was lost.[48]

This Gérard de Villiers was none other than the Master of the province of
France.[49] What was said about him is obviously unverifiable; the Templar of
Tyre makes no mention of anything in the nature of a betrayal or, at the least,
a desertion. A desertion that had happened a 'day earlier' seems unlikely – in
any case, a day earlier than what? The island was occupied and surrounded by
the attackers' fleet, and it is hard to see how Gérard de Villiers and his companions could have forced a passage. The Master of France may well have passed
through Cyprus and Ruad during 1301 or 1302, like many of the western Templars at that time, but there is nothing to suggest that he was there at the exact
moment of the Mamluks' final assault. Brother Renaud de la Folie's error or
confusion might have arisen from that. There is another possible cause for confusion – that Villiers had been sent to Cyprus to raise the alarm while there was
yet time. Lastly, a betrayal would not have passed without some disciplinary
consequences; but Gérard de Villiers was not punished. He was, and remained,
Master of France.[50]

The behaviour of the Templars on Ruad has been criticised. By retreating
to the tower in the centre of the island, it is claimed they left the field to their
enemies and engaged in a fight with no possible outcome other than surrender.
They have also been blamed for trusting their adversaries' word.[51] Perhaps they
were counting on imminent reinforcements from Cyprus and believed that if
they could hold out for a few days in the tower help would arrive; but it was not
ready in time.

Ruad was a grievous blow for the Temple, for one thing because its losses
had been so heavy, and for the other because one more failure could be laid at
the door of the military Orders. But, looking beyond such considerations, one
must place the failure at Ruad in the context of the strategy of the Mongol alliance. As long as a combined operation with Ghâzân could be envisaged, there
was some justification for holding Ruad and, despite the lack of success of the
two preceding operations, in September 1302 there was still hope. Ghâzân really
was preparing a new offensive for the following spring, and it did indeed take

place. The loss of Ruad did not prevent the Christians on Cyprus from continuing raids on the Syrian coast, even at the very beginning of 1303, when they ravaged Damur, south of Beirut.[52] But it deprived them of the bridgehead that would perhaps have enabled them to join the Mongol troops in 1303.

That said, such an expedition would probably have proved fruitless, for the third Mongol offensive against the Mamluks of Syria was also a failure. Ghâzân's generals, Mûlay and Kutlushah, were defeated at Homs on 30 March and at Shaqhab, south of Damascus, on 21 April, the two generals almost paying with their lives for the utter rout.[53] There were to be no more Mongol attempts on Syria. Ghâzân died on 10 May 1304. His successors sent one more delegation to the West, in 1307, promising a strong Mongol mobilisation, but that pious pledge would never materialise.[54] Thus ended the strategy of a Mongol alliance, in which Saint Louis had been one of the prime movers fifty years earlier.

There must be no mistake about the significance of the Ruad episode. The occupation of this island should be seen in the context of the first ever large-scale attempt to make this strategy a concrete, on-the-ground reality. At the heart of the Templar Order during those years Jacques de Molay supported this policy. The occupation of Ruad was the fruit of an initiative taken by all the Christian forces on Cyprus, proving that they were capable of uniting in spite of their differences (which, in any case, tend to be exaggerated).

The strategy of the Mongol alliance had failed, but the Cypriot Christians, the Temple and the Hospital were not the only ones responsible for its failure. It is true that, although the Christians had mastery of the sea, there was no fleet when they needed one. Moreover, it was the fleets of the Italian Republics which had earned them that maritime superiority; in comparison, the fleets that the king of Cyprus and the military Orders could mobilise were derisory. The Italian Republics, however, were less than enthusiastic about engaging in a war with Mamluk Egypt, the land of spices. The responsibility of the Mongols for the failure is just as great; their delays and hesitations weighed heavily. Last and not least, an enterprise on this scale was bound to run into practical difficulties that would have been hard to surmount: the problem of passing on news, communications, the transport of provisions, all the obstacles which, at the time, made it so difficult to mount combined operations.

During these four years, Jacques de Molay was the leader of one of the four forces — Temple, Hospital, and the kingdoms of Cyprus and Armenia — engaged in this strategy. More as political than military leader, he directed operations from Cyprus, and was rarely to be seen in the field: in Armenia in 1298 or 1299, perhaps; at Ruad in November 1300, definitely; but certainly not during the naval operations of July–August 1300 at Alexandria, Acre or Tortosa. Had the Mongol offensive expected for November 1301 taken place, he would have been at the head of his troops in combat. As it did not, the Marshal of the Order took charge in the field. Lastly, it is possible that Molay may have planned to join the fleet that was supposed to come to the assistance of the besieged Templars on Ruad in September 1302. On Cyprus, usually at the Order's headquarters in Limassol, he worked to mobilise the Templars in the West and have the resources that they needed – horses, weapons, provisions – brought over, as his correspondence during this period bears witness.

Jacques de Molay had no more intention of turning Ruad into a Templar Rhodes than he had of settling his Order's headquarters at Peñiscola, in the kingdom of Valencia. The Temple wished to stay in Cyprus, the last Latin state in the East. And so it is in Cyprus, in Molay's time and under his rule, that the government of the Templar Order must be viewed. We shall see later the consequences and drawbacks of this choice, when the strategy on which it was built was no longer valid.

1303

CYPRUS

Jacques de Molay was in Cyprus from the end of 1296 to the autumn of 1306. Apart from his two short forays to Armenia and Ruad, he stayed at the Order's headquarters in Limassol, in the south of the island. He sometimes went to Nicosia, the royal capital, or Famagusta, the big Cypriot port which could also lay claim to being a royal capital since the king of Cyprus had received the crown of king of Jerusalem there. As I have already said, Molay never intended to transfer the Order's headquarters to the West; it was in and from Cyprus that he ran his Order. The first question to arise, therefore, must be, What kind of relationship did he have with Cypriot royalty?

As previously indicated, the succession in Antioch and Tripoli, then the rivalry between King Hugh III of Cyprus and Charles of Anjou for possession of the kingdom of Jerusalem, had strained relations between the Temple and the Cypriot kingdom to such an extent that in 1279 King Hugh 'had the house of the Temple at Limeson [Limassol] destroyed and seized all their possessions in Cyprus'.[1]

The chronicler exaggerates; only the castles belonging to the Temple (Gastria and Paphos) were targeted, while the houses strictly speaking (commandery, headquarters) were left untouched.[2] The pope defended the Order, but Cypriot royalty was not to be intimidated. In a report that is undated but probably emanates from King John I (1284–5), the king complains to the Holy See about the ill-treatment meted out in the recent past to his father, Hugh III, by the Master of the Temple.[3] When Guillaume de Beaujeu ceased to support Angevin interests, around 1285–6, and acknowledged the new king of Cyprus, Henry II, as king of Jerusalem, relations improved only on the surface. Henry II, who suffered from epilepsy, was regarded as a weak king by some of the Cypriot aristocracy.

A similar situation prevailed at the same time in Armenia, with the voltefaces of Hethum II, the Franciscan king. Given the close links maintained by the two monarchies and aristocracies, this situation proved a breeding ground for all kinds of intrigues, including the attempt to depose Henry made in 1306 by his brother Amaury.

The military Orders did not remain aloof from these disputes. Before becoming known as a weak king, Henry II was a king like any other. The aftermath of 1291 was enough to worry him: on the one hand, the arrival of masses of refugees from Syria–Palestine raised serious accommodation problems; on the other – and chiefly – it was into his kingdom that the military Orders were transferring their headquarters, their central administrations and their quarrelsome and independent frames of mind. Having lost everything they still owned in the Holy Land, the Templars and Hospitallers (the Teutonics and brothers of Saint Thomas of Acre occupied a secondary position) had no intention of letting themselves be stripped of the incomes from their Cypriot domains. Henry II wanted to reduce the Orders' privileges and gnaw away at their revenues; above all, he forbade them to increase their property in his kingdom, and prevented them from acquiring new assets, by either donation or purchase. Henry II was acting exactly like a James II of Aragon or a Philip the Fair of France. In any case, his policy was not directed solely at the military Orders, as the Cistercian Order found itself equally targeted by these measures. Furthermore, the king was eager to subject the clergy's domains, and thus those of the military Orders, to royal taxation.

On Jacques de Molay's return to Cyprus in 1296, it would appear that the friction caused by the taxation and the ban on acquiring new possessions had taken a livelier turn, and the two sides appealed to the pope for arbitration. The Temple and Hospital naturally shared a mutual self-interest on these points. The papacy had already intervened in the past in an attempt to diminish the differences between the kings of Cyprus and the Temple. In 1284, for instance, Martin IV had asked Hugh III to 'cease attacking the Master and the brothers of the knighthood of the Temple ... Having confiscated their property, he had prevented them from using the resources of their domains and from managing them freely ...'[4] In 1295, Boniface VIII had confirmed all the privileges of the military Orders as they had been in the Holy Land.[5] He solemnly intervened with the king and Master of the Temple on 19 March 1298, when he replied, in two not identical but parallel letters, 'on the subject of concord between the

Templars and the king of Cyprus', to earlier missives sent by the two protagonists.[6] Jacques de Molay's letter had been conveyed to the pope by Geoffroy de Gonneville, a brother in the Order who was to become Master of Aquitaine, and that of the king by his messenger, the knight Baudouin de Mari. Addressing the Grand Master, the pope stuck to generalities; he invoked the interests of the Holy Land and preached humility, piety and patience. The king of Cyprus, meanwhile, was reminded of both the huge losses suffered by the Templar Order in the East and its great needs, stressing that the Order constituted an essential part of the protection of the kingdom of Cyprus. In both letters, he invited the Grand Master and the king to make peace and unite. It was a pious hope, for the disputes were concerned with material problems which the pope did not broach in his letters.

In fact, Boniface VIII did not wish to become too involved, for although he basically supported the Order of the Temple he had no desire to alienate the king by depriving him of his means of governing. It was in this frame of mind that he wrote again to Henry II, on 13 June 1298, to raise the question of the *testagium*, a poll tax of two bezants that had been levied for some time on all the kingdom's inhabitants except members of the Templar, Hospitaller and Teutonic Orders.[7] Originally, the king had imposed this tax on the serfs of the military Orders; then, realising that this was contrary to the Orders' privileges, he had backed down and sent a procurator to the pope to apologise.[8] In his letter of 13 June, however, taking into account the kingdom's great needs, the pope authorised the king to levy this tax on everyone, military Orders included, although it was contrary to the Church's previous constitutions.

Naturally, all the Orders protested. And so the following year – perhaps as a result of the Temple's and Hospital's engagement in Armenia in 1299 – the pope's interventions proved more favourable to the Templars and Hospitallers. On 10 June 1299, the pope asked the king to ensure that the *ordinatio* – a particularly solemn agreement made between the king and bishops of Cyprus on the one hand, and the military Orders on the other – was observed. This time he addressed the provincial ministers of the mendicant Orders in Cyprus, urging them to use their good offices 'between the king and the knighthood of the Temple'.[9] On the same date, Boniface also asked Henry II to allow the religious Orders to acquire, within modest limits, enough possessions in Cyprus for them to continue their mission against the Saracens and false Christians (that is, those who did business with the Infidels).[10] Finally, the pope ordered the king to stop levying the *testagium* on the Orders, thus going back on his decision of 1298.[11]

There was therefore plenty of room for dispute between Cypriot royalty and the military Orders. Papal Bulls and letters often only come down to us from a copy made by one of their many recipients, but what must not be forgotten is that what was valid for the Temple was equally valid for the Hospital, and vice versa. For instance, we have written proof that the king of Cyprus banned the fitting-out of Hospital ships without his authorisation; but should we really believe that this applied only to the Order of the Hospital simply because only the copy of the royal letter sent to the Hospitallers has been preserved?[12]

This fact must be borne in mind if we are to understand the attitude of the two Orders when faced with the problem raised by Amaury of Tyre's rebellion against his brother in 1306. The generally accepted historiographic tradition – a tradition which has, incidentally, been widely challenged recently – that, in the Latin States of the East, the Hospitallers were royalists while the Templars sided with the barons found new occasion to reveal itself in Cyprus in 1306. The Templar troublemakers supported the rebel, whereas the Hospitallers remained loyal to the legitimate sovereign. Writing his chronicle in the sixteenth century, Florio Bustron goes even further, implying that Amaury had been manipulated: 'The author of this enterprise was the Master of the Temple, Brother Jacques de Molay, and Pierre d'Erlent, bishop of Limassol.'[13] On the following page, by contrast, he tells how Jacques de Molay, in concert with the Master of the Hospital, intervened to impose a compromise between the king and his brother.[14]

What actually happened is rather different. As always with history, chronology and the order of events must be respected. The open political crisis involving King Henry II and his brother Amaury lasted four years, from 1306 to 1310, during which short space of time the Templars were arrested and tried, in both Cyprus and the West, and the Hospitallers conquered Rhodes. In 1306, the initiative for the revolt was taken by Amaury of Tyre, not the Templars. His following consisted mainly of Cypriot barons with connections in Armenia – Amaury was himself married to Isabelle (or Zabel), sister of Hethum II. The idea that these two Christian kingdoms would be better defended if they had capable rulers at their head, rather than a sick king and a Franciscan friar, was widespread at the time and generously hawked around by the Armenian historian Hayton.[15] The Templar of Tyre's chronicle is clear: the conflict between the king and his brother also set the two factions of Cypriot nobility at loggerheads.[16] At the council held on 26 April 1306, during which Amaury seized actual power, leaving Henry II with no more than a purely formal royal title, the two Masters, Jacques de Molay and Foulques de Villaret, who were both present, did not intervene. In contrast, the following month they were very active in the negotiations aimed at reconciling the two brothers or, at least, imposing a less humiliating compromise on King Henry II. They were successful and, on 16 May, affixed their seals alongside those of the island's other ecclesiastical and lay dignitaries on the document setting out this compromise.[17]

Foulques de Villaret then went off to Rhodes, returning in November to hold a general Chapter of his Order before leaving once more for the West, where Molay had already gone a short while earlier. This meant that the two Grand Masters no longer played any direct role in the development of the Cyprus situation. Whatever their feelings towards Henry II, or their differing approaches to the matter, they had united in trying to reconcile the factions. The Templars and Jacques de Molay may have had more to gain than the Hospitallers from the compromise and Amaury's coming to power, but in their venture to conquer Rhodes the Hospitallers would also receive help from Amaury, in the form of two galleys which he put at their disposal.[18]

The Templars' open hostility to Henry II was not revealed until a good year later, in early 1308. Before leaving Cyprus for France in the autumn of 1306, Jacques de Molay appointed the Marshal of the Order, Aymon d'Oiselay, as his second-in-command during his absence.[19] Aymon d'Oiselay is portrayed as a decided enemy of King Henry II and, together with the Master or Commander of Cyprus, Jacques de Doumanin, is held to be the instigator of a conspiracy, in January 1308, to abduct the king and force him to accept a treaty more favourable to Amaury than the one signed in May 1306.[20] The plot failed but the Marshal none the less joined forces with the Grand Commander of the Hospital to impose concessions on Henry II that were duly recorded in writing.

The Marshal 'could not conceal the spite and malice he felt towards the king, because in the presence of the barons who were at the royal palace, and of several prelates, he said, "*Quod scripsi scripsi*" ["What is written, is written"]. By his deeds and words he showed that he was very pleased and that he enjoyed the outrage and shame heaped on the king.'[21]

This frank enmity did not prevent Aymon d'Oiselay from intervening some months later on behalf of his cousin Rupin de Montfort, who was found guilty of supporting King Henry II, no less.[22] However, it is difficult to know whether the approach taken by Aymon, the Comtois whom Molay himself had appointed Marshal and then second-in-command, was his own or that of Molay and the entire Order. At any event, the Templars who remained in Cyprus gained nothing by Aymon d'Oiselay's backing of Amaury in such an outrageous fashion. In May 1308, Amaury resolved to apply the pope's orders commanding him to arrest the Templars in the kingdom. Aymon d'Oiselay reacted by flying into a bitter rage over Amaury's 'betrayal'. Under his leadership, the Templars tried vainly to put up some resistance, but eventually had to surrender on 1 June 1308.[23] Aymon d'Oiselay was to die in 1316 in the Templar castle of Akrotiri, which had become his jail. Ingratitude and reasons of state had swept him away. Meanwhile, the Hospitallers who, in August 1308, were still putting pressure on Henry II to abdicate in favour of Amaury, changed their tack at the end of that year and in 1309 openly rallied to the king – to such an extent that they were suspected of having arranged Amaury's assassination in 1310.[24]

Since it had given up direct governmental control of Cyprus in 1192, the Temple had settled in the kingdom created at that time by the Lusignan dynasty. In the first half of the thirteenth century, the latter had been increasing its donations. The disappearance of the Temple's central archives – probably in Cyprus when the Turks conquered the island in 1566 – prevents us from knowing the exact details of how this patrimony was constituted.[25] However, we have enough to go on from its content at the end of the Templar era, thanks to two very similar lists inserted by Florio Bustron into his chronicle relating to the years 1307 and 1313.[26] The historian makes the distinction between the churches with their *stanza* (houses with chapels which served as headquarters of the commanderies) on the one hand, and the fortresses and *casaux* (domains, villages) on the other. He mentions four houses, or commanderies: Nicosia, Limassol, Akrotiri and Famagusta, to which we must add Paphos (forgotten by Bustron). There were also three or four large fortresses: Gastria, Akrotiri, Yermasoia and perhaps Kolossi (although that seems doubtful, since Kolossi was a commandery of the Hospitallers, who farmed it and processed sugar cane there).

House	Castles	Casaux
Nicosia		12
	Gastria	2
Famagusta		6
	Kolossi (?)	1 + 14
	Yermasoia	8
Limassol		5
Akrotiri	Akrotiri	1
Paphos		

The 1313 list also mentions three bailiwicks, grouping different *casaux*, but that does not alter the map of these establishments. A good part of the Templar patrimony was concentrated in the south, around Limassol; there it had two (or perhaps three) out of its three or four fortresses. Not much is known about the income of these houses. Their inventory, carried out on the very day of the Templars' arrest, gives only an imperfect idea of what they possessed. At Nicosia, 970 crossbows, among other weapons, were found and 930 coats of mail, over and above the weapons and mounts of the Templar brothers. There were also provisions – vegetables, wine, cheeses – plus 120,000 white bezants (that is, gold coins with a high proportion of silver). But it appears that the Templars concealed the rest of their money so well that people are still searching for it.[27]

It is no easy matter to evaluate the financial resources available to the Templars in Cyprus. Jacques de Molay apparently had little difficulty in raising a sum of 45,000 silver *tournois* to pay the ransom of Guy d'Ibelin, seigneur of Jaffa, his wife, son and several of those closest to him, when they were captured in his domain of Episkopi by pirates from Rhodes and Monemvasia in May 1302.[28] It is also known that the Grand Master lent 40,000 white bezants to Amaury of Tyre.[29] Records of the Genoese notaries operating in Cyprus give some indications of the Templars' facilities and trading and financial operations around 1300.[30] From these we learn of the presence of two Templar ships in Famagusta waters in 1300–2: the *Faucon*, still in service since the siege of Acre in 1291, though Roger de Flor (still a Templar in 1301)[31] does not seem to be its captain; and the *Santa Anna*. The *Faucon* was hired on 24 February 1301 by the representative of a trading company from Piacenza to transport various products (sugar, cotton, etc.) from Cyprus to Marseille for the sum of

14,252 white bezants.[32] The *Santa Anna* was similarly hired by some Genoese on 2 November 1301, then on 3 March 1302, to carry a cargo of cotton.[33] The ship's captain, Brother Pierre Visianus, also agreed to do some money-changing: on 9 April 1302, he received from a citizen of Barcelona 900 Cypriot white bezants which he promised to repay at Genoa against 180 Genoese *livres*; on 10 April, he committed himself to another Genoese, Leonello, who stated that he had received from Giovanni Renulla 2,000 white bezants which Visianus was to repay at Genoa against 400 *livres*, two and a half months after the *Santa Anna*'s arrival. Leonello put up a quantity of ash and other products as security on the Templars' ship. The following day, according to a similar contract, the ship's captain undertook to transport another cargo 'at the risk and fortune at sea of the ship of the Temple called *Santa Anna*, presently on the point of leaving for Genoa'.[34] These vessels were round-bottomed sailing ships adapted for transporting cargo, not fighting galleys. The Templars used them to transfer goods and men from Cyprus to the West, and products from their western domains in the opposite direction. But as we know, their own ships were insufficient for their needs and they were obliged to hire or charter others. This was notably the case for Templars moving between East and West, a detailed example of which was the voyage of the Master of Aragon, Berenguer de Cardona, in 1300–1.

The Templars acted as owners of the boats which they used on their own account or hired out to third parties. They transported men, merchandise and currency ('porterage'); but it would be wrong to liken the Temple to a bank, even if it is true that it provided certain services which were also the business of banks or trading companies of the time (porterage, loans).[35] The Catalan Count Bernart Guillem d'Enteça, who came to Cyprus in late 1300 or early 1301, must have resorted to the Temple to pay Bernard Marquet of Barcelona, the owner of the ship *Saint-Nicolas*, for his passage; he supplied as security (for the sum of 16,350 silver *tournois*) 8,000 hogsheads of wheat which he delivered to Theodore, the Templar doctor who had handed over the sum to him with the consent of the Commander of the Vault.[36]

From these notarised deeds, which are rather contradictory and of which there are not very many (even fewer exist for the Hospital), let us try to pick out a guideline regarding the Temple's policy in this matter. In Cyprus, the Templars needed weapons, horses and money in order to maintain their fortresses and pay their mercenaries, but also to support their charitable works, such as the giving of alms and the release of captives. Since the resources derived from the island were inadequate, they called upon those of the West, from their own domains and others. The Temple bartered, bought and received pledges which it sold to recover currency; it lent money (and not gratis, that is for sure), did porterage; but it also, out of necessity, borrowed. It relied less on accumulation and hoarding than on the mobility and circulation of goods and money. It was a shrewd user of the commercial and financial techniques and tools of the time, but confined itself to what was indispensable: porterage, yes; loans and borrowings, yes, but investment and speculation, no. The Temple used its own ships, and hired them out to third parties, but also hired or chartered vessels itself. The handful of examples gleaned from the notaries' records clearly show the rule to be observed at all times: no dealings with Infidel countries. The Templars wanted to hunt down the 'bad' Christians who indulged in this trade; but not so that they could do the same. Boats were used to transport troops or provisions for raids and attacks on enemy coasts; and also for trading goods, but exclusively between Cyprus and the West, and for conveying men back and forth. The Order enjoyed great mobility between the 'home base' and the 'front'. It had been necessary to make up for the losses sustained both in 1291 and at Ruad in 1302; and the movement of men was accompanied by the transport of resources, weapons, horses and currency. Every Templar who went temporarily to Cyprus played a part in the hustle and bustle of this multiform network linking the centre (Cyprus) to the areas farther afield.

What part did Jacques de Molay play in relations between the centre and the peripheral Templar houses, between the Templar centre and the other Christian powers, or between this same centre and ordinary visitors? Although not plentiful, the documentation concerning his years as Master is explicit enough to show that there was a desire on Molay's part to develop these relations, and for it to be accepted, by the way in which he ran the Order, that he was a major agent in this development. His method of governing was based on the relations between the various structures of the Order and the men who directed them.

The movement of Templars between Cyprus and the West cannot be quantified. During periods of large-scale recruitment there was much travel to Cyprus, as at the time of the Chapter held in Paris on 29 June 1298, when 'it was ordered that 300 brothers should be sent overseas; the witness had been one of them, and he left and remained over there for two and a half years ...'[37]

There are many testimonies from the trial that suggest, like this one, numerous journeys. In the Cypriot trial, four entries to the Order can be picked out

– in France and England – in 1303 or 1304, and the impression clearly emerges that the four brothers thus recruited were transferred to Cyprus almost immediately, and possibly together, departing from Marseille under the leadership of Simon de Quincy, who was perhaps the Master of the crossing from Marseille at that time.[38]

Amadi (and Bustron, who followed him) states that there were 118 Templars in Cyprus in 1306–8.[39] This figure is corroborated by Humbert de Germilla in his deposition in Paris, when he says that he had been present at the reception of Antonio de Vercelli by Jacques de Molay in the presence of at least 120 brothers.[40]

Only seventy-six Templars were interrogated in Cyprus in 1310; some had left for the West in 1306 with Jacques de Molay, four of whom had been questioned in Paris in October–November 1307, including Molay himself and Raimbaud de Caron. Of the seventy-six in Cyprus, two provide no information about themselves; of the remaining seventy-four, twenty-one were received into the Order between 1267 and 1300, and fifty-one after 1300, including fourteen in 1303–4, that is, after the defeat at Ruad. I will make a distinction between three groups:

1   Ten had been received in the East (Cyprus, Armenia, Romania).
2   Twenty-one in the West, with the exception of France:
    Iberian peninsula: 11 (including 7 in the states of the Crown of Aragon)
    Italy: 7
    England: 4
    Germany: 4
3   Thirty-nine in the kingdom of France, divided as follows:
    South-east (Provence, Dauphiné): 6
    Centre and South-west: 6
    Province of France: 12
    Burgundy–Lyonnais: 15

If the four Cypriot Templars interrogated in Paris are taken into account, the figure for Burgundy must be increased by two units, that for Provence by one, and similarly one for the East.

Without ascribing more importance to these figures than they merit, one should note, on the one hand, the desire to recruit widely in all provinces; for instance, the presence in Cyprus of two Portuguese Templars, which contradicts the usually accepted notion of a quasi-autonomous Portuguese Temple in relation to the combatant structures and aims of the Order. On the other is the scale of recruitment in Burgundy and the Crown of Aragon, which obviously bears the stamp of Jacques de Molay, not least because all the Templars originating from Burgundy were recruited after 1290.

The journeys made by the Order's western dignitaries, sometimes only of short duration, also bear witness to this continual movement between the West and Cyprus. More accurate information is available thanks to the rich lode in the Archives of the Crown of Aragon. These crossings were sometimes motivated by the Temple's commitments (in 1300–1 for instance, with the Mongol offensives), but also out of concern for the Order's good management.

A type of schema for this sort of voyage would be as follows: The Grand Master takes the initiative by asking the Master of a province to present himself before him; he, in turn, requests his sovereign to authorise him to absent himself; generally, the king agrees, sometimes stipulating conditions (a quick return, for example). This is what happened in England in 1304: Edward I authorised the Master of England, William de la More, to leave, and gave instructions to the Constable of the port of Dover to facilitate the embarkation of the Master, his companions, horses and equipment, currency and other commodities necessary for the journey. William de la More made a contract with the Florentine company of the Mari, who were well established in London, and at the time paid them a certain sum of money which he was to recover in Paris from merchants of this same company, but the latter had fraudulently quit the kingdom of France before the Master's arrival.[41] In addition, while on the Dover road, William and his train were attacked by the inhabitants of Rochester (which incidental mishap is known from when the matter came to trial in 1305).[42]

The Aragonese archives enable us to see another aspect of this initial phase of the journey to Cyprus. The Grand Master asked those in charge of the provinces not only to come armed, with fully equipped horses and mules, but also to bring the *responsiones* (the share of income – in theory about one-third – to be paid to the Order's central authority) of their province or commanderies, together with provisions. Berenguer de Cardona, Master of Aragon–Catalonia, who went to Cyprus in the spring of 1300, thus asked Pierre de Saint-Just, Commander of Corbins, if 'in such great necessity and such great want as we are in, you can procure for us everything you can find in the world [sic] in the way of money, cured meats and everything connected with the event [the journey] …'[43] In 1296, Guy de Forest, for his part, was authorised by the royal Customs to carry to Cyprus 'Worsted cloth for the robes of the brothers of the knighthood living in Cyprus'.[44]

When he wanted to depart again from Cyprus, whatever the duration and reasons for his stay had been, the western Templar had to obtain the leave of the Grand Master. The four known letters of Thibaud Gaudin are such authorisations granted to Bernard de Fontes and Pierre de Saint-Just, two Catalan knights.[45] We have no letters of this kind written by Jacques de Molay, but Aymon d'Oiselay, who as Marshal of the Order was performing the duty of lieutenant to the Grand Master during his absence in 1306–7, granted similar permission to Pierre de Saint-Just once again, on 20 October 1306.[46] Occasionally, while granting this leave of absence, the Grand Master also authorised a Templar to return to Cyprus as and when it suited him. This happened to Pierre de Saint-Just in 1291. Thibaud Gaudin wrote to the Master of Aragon:

> This is to inform your group that we have given leave and permission to our friend in Christ, Brother Pierre de Saint-Just, bearer of these letters, to go to his country and return to these parts this side of the sea [Cyprus] as many times as he wishes.[47]

Berenguer Guamir came to Cyprus in 1300–1, and again in 1304. On 20 January 1305, he received from the Grand Master a similar authorisation, to which Jacques de Molay's personal wax seal was affixed.[48] Such authorisation was generally accompanied by an instruction to the Templar authorities in the western province concerned to provide a brother wishing to go to Cyprus with the necessary wherewithal for his journey: horses, mules, provisions or money. That was the case for Pierre de Saint-Just in 1306.

Berenguer de Cardona, Master of Aragon and Visitor of Spain, made two journeys to Cyprus in the period when Molay was Grand Master, in 1300–1 and 1306. The stages of the first trip are fairly well known. He was at Saragossa on 19 April 1300, when he informed the Commanders of his province that the Grand Master wished him to come to Cyprus in time for the great Mongol offensive which was then envisaged.[49] He must have left in May–June in the same year, and probably took part in the operations that led to the occupation of Ruad and the raids on Tortosa in November. He prepared for his return to the West in February 1301, hiring, together with Berenguer Guamir, the vessel *Saint-Nicolas* from Bernard Marquet of Barcelona in order to transport six knights and twenty-eight members of their train. But the ship's departure was deferred, Bernard Marquet apologising on 1 March for a delay for which he was not responsible.[50] Berenguer de Cardona probably returned to Catalonia before 1 May 1301; in fact, on that day he was at Gardeny, and wrote to Pierre de Saint-Just to inform him urgently that provisions, cured meats, cheeses, etc., were to be sent to Cyprus, to be loaded on to a boat at Tortosa (Catalonia).[51] It only remained to settle Bernard Marquet's bill, which was only to be achieved with some difficulty. On 10 July following his return, 125 Barcelona *livres* were still owing to the shipowner.[52]

In this controversial period of the Temple's history, when the question of its usefulness arises, a better measure is needed of the importance of these to-ings and fro-ings which was, in my opinion, considerable. There is a strong case for saying that they were proof of a political will – Jacques de Molay's – to continue to take action aimed at reconquering the Holy Land. And by gathering together the numerous, if not always precise, pieces of information scattered among the trial interrogations, it should be possible to complement the information gleaned from a repository of archives such as the one in Barcelona.

When they left the Holy Land, the Templars had taken care to transfer to Cyprus their treasures – that is, their archives (since lost) – and the relics from the chapels and churches in Syria–Palestine.[53] Despite the unfavourable situation, pilgrims still tried to go to Jerusalem. The papacy had banned such pilgrimages, as it meant the Mamluk sultan was able to levy taxes on the pilgrims at the entrance to Jerusalem and the Holy Sepulchre, but some, paradoxically, were prepared to risk excommunication to visit the Holy City. Cyprus was obviously an unavoidable port of call; but the island was also a destination for pilgrims in its own right, as several of its sites and relics were objects of worship. Therefore, pilgrims were still being received.

A pilgrimage to Jerusalem had sometimes been imposed as penitence on hardened sinners; however, because of its inaccessibility, Acre and then Cyprus had been assigned for such pilgrimages, as laid down by both ecclesiastical and secular courts. The penitent had to spend a certain time in the Holy Land, take part in crusading operations, then return to the West armed with a certificate validated by the Military Orders of the Temple and Hospital attesting that he had fulfilled his penance. Such was the punishment imposed in 1302 on Count

Henri de Bar by the courts of the king of France, though it is not known whether he carried out his penance.[54] Gérard du Passage, questioned at the time of the Templar trial, provides a colourful example. Having entered the Order in 1293, he had quit in 1305 and confessed the misdeeds imputed to the Order to a papal legate, who had imposed the penance of going overseas, that is, to Cyprus, with, of all people, the Hospitallers. He had been arrested by the king's agents just as he was making ready to depart.[55]

For the Military Orders, both pilgrims undergoing penance and their more pious brethren had to be welcomed, given lodging and sustenance and/or cared for. This mission belonged specifically to the Order of the Hospital which, in order to fulfil it, had a hospital built at Limassol, modelled on the ones at Jerusalem and Acre. We have seen that those Templars questioned about their Order's charitable works absolutely insisted on the fact that, unlike the Hospitallers, they were not obliged to assume this work of hospitality; for, as Jacques de Molay writes in his memorandum on the merging of the Orders, 'one was founded on hospitality, the other on military service'.[56] Nevertheless, the Templars provided hospitality, welcoming many guests in transit, whether pilgrims or others.

Late in 1301, the house at Limassol and the Grand Master received a notable guest in the person of the Majorcan Franciscan Ramon Lull, famous apostle of the peacemaking mission but also ardent supporter of the crusades (which is not the contradiction it may appear).[57] In the view of Ramon Lull, who had written treatises on the crusades, they were simply the necessary means of politically and militarily subduing the Infidels to develop the missionary action which would make their conversion to Christianity possible. On several occasions, Ramon Lull went to the Maghreb to try to preach for Christ, and it was with that missionary prospect that he came to Cyprus in 1301. Of course, it was the promise of the Mongol alliance and, in particular, the rumour of the restitution of Jerusalem that attracted him. He embarked at Majorca for Famagusta early in 1301, but on landing he must have been disappointed; Jerusalem had not been regained. He therefore spent the summer in Cyprus holding discussions with members of the Greek clergy on the island. September and October he passed in the Greek convent of Saint Chrysostom; but he soon fell ill and came back to Limassol, where Jacques de Molay housed him in his palace. Ramon Lull's anonymous biographer wrote in his *Vita coetanea* that, 'coming to Famagusta, he was received with joy [*hilariter*] by the Master of the Temple who was in the town of Limassol, and resided in his house until he recovered his health'.[58]

Once he had recuperated, Ramon Lull left for Armenia early in January 1302. Some historians have tried to suggest that his meeting with Jacques de Molay at Famagusta came about because he was then returning from Armenia;[59] but the evidence of his visit to the Cypriot convent of Saint Chrysostom is incontrovertible, and in this instance it is better to believe in a scribe's error.

Subsequently, in 1308, Ramon Lull rallied to the king of France, but without condemning the Templars. His amicable meeting with the Grand Master did not prevent his holding his own point of view, particularly on the union of the Orders, which he had always looked upon favourably. However, he had not been able to convince Jacques de Molay.

The latter doubtless received many visitors at his palace at Limassol, including a good number of Templars. In fact, the frequent passage of dignitaries from the West, like that of Templar friends, had its part to play in the Grand Master's method of governing.

The structures of the Templar Order, as set out in chapter 2, had scarcely changed during its two centuries of existence. Around 1300, however, of the eastern provinces, Jerusalem, Tripoli and Antioch disappeared, leaving only Cyprus, Armenia and Romania (or Greece). Cyprus, like any western province, was thus provided with a Master or Commander who, in 1307, was Jacques de Doumanin, although the Order's central organisation and the men who carried out its governmental duties remained. Unlike in the past, when the Order was still under the hierarchical structure of the Rule,[60] however, the Seneschal had gone, and it was the Grand Commander or Commander of the Land who took on the duties of the Master's first substitute. The Grand Commander had handed over to a Treasurer the financial tasks he had performed in the time when Joinville was recounting Saint Louis' crusade. He was the Order's central Treasurer, which the Treasurer of the Paris Temple was not. In Molay's time, there is mention of 'Commanders of the Palace', who had perhaps replaced the Commander of the City of Jerusalem.[61] They also performed the office of Almoner, which confirms the importance accorded by Molay to this sector of activity. By contrast, the posts of Grand Master, naturally, Marshal and Submarshal, Draper, Turcopolier, Commander of the Knights, Standard-bearer (or Gonfalonier) and Infirmarian had not altered.

A Commander of the Vault still existed; his duties lay with maritime affairs, which had developed considerably in the late thirteenth century, and the problems of providing provisions and transport between Cyprus and the West.

Regular supplies of provisions to the island had become a matter of priority for the Templars and their Grand Master – it is symbolic that a Commander of the Vault figures among those who put their signatures on the first known document of Jacques de Molay.[62] In the Order of the Hospital, which at that time was implementing an identical maritime policy, this development manifested itself in the institution of the office of admiral (mentioned in the texts of 1299), whose first holder was Foulques de Villaret.[63]

An admiral to the Temple is also mentioned shortly afterwards, in a notarised deed dated 16 June 1301. Lamberto de Sambuceto records a receipt given by an inhabitant of Famagusta to five people from Barcelona and Provence for a sum representing the guarantee they had provided to serve the Temple for two months, to a 'lord admiral or captain or Count of the Temple'. However, it seems that the term 'admiral' used here means nothing more than captain or skipper of a vessel.[64] So, the Temple had no 'admiral', although it did have a Commander of the Vault. The absence of such an institution has often been regarded as a mark of the Temple's backwardness or archaism, and its indifference to maritime matters. However, the Temple did not possess any boats of its own and it simply vanished in 1307–14, that is, probably before such terminology was current – and so it is hardly surprising that it did not use the term.

At the head of the Order, therefore, was the Master, or Grand Master or General Master; Master of 'Outremer' as he is also called in western documents. In his own letters, Jacques de Molay, like his predecessors, never awards himself any title other than 'humble Master of the knighthood of the Temple'. The Templar Rule describes precisely the Master's 'household', in other words, the staff put at his disposal to carry out his duties. These fell into three categories: firstly, the staff of the chapel, namely a chaplain and a cleric; then his domestic staff: a sergeant-brother, a gentleman valet to carry his shield and spear, a farrier/blacksmith, a Saracen scribe who also acted as interpreter, a turcopolier, a cook and two footmen;[65] and lastly, his advisers: two 'companion' knights (*socius, socii*) of the Grand Master, who had to be always at his side in every council or meeting of at least five or six persons.[66] On several occasions the Rule also mentions among the Master's entourage, and more generally that of the Templar dignitaries, his 'household counsellors' who held an advisory role and to whom I will return.

Running through the lists of the Order's dignitaries that can be established from Molay's letters or the trial interrogations, his entourage – those who formed his *familia* or '*maisnie*' – may be said to conform to the Rule, as regards its composition, even if words and names change. In 1295,[67] a Master's chaplain is mentioned, as well as a Provost of equipment and animals (Guillaume de Gy),[68] a Provost of garrisons (i.e. provisions and stores) (Pierre de Safed)[69] and valets (Martino Martin, Georgio).[70] Two further dignitaries cited as being in the Grand Master's service, but without any exact assignment are: Jacques de La Rochelle and Antonio de Vercelli.[71] Two men are also mentioned as guards of the Master's bedchamber: Aymon de Barbone, for three years, and Pons de *Bono opere* (Bonoeuvre?) 'guard of the bedchamber of the Grand Master overseas for a year and a half before the said Master came this side of the sea [the continent]'.[72]

Named as *socii* of Jacques de Molay are Guillaume de Barroer and Pons de *Magnocampo* (Grandchamp?) who, in the absence of any other dignitary of the Order, confirmed the authority given by the Grand Master to Berenguer de Cardona to conclude the exchange of Tortosa for Peñiscola in 1294.[73] There is also Geoffroy Picard, mentioned in 1303 by Pierre de Safed,[74] or the German Templar Count Frederick, who declares himself the Grand Master's companion.[75] As far as is known, there was no 'Saracen scribe' or 'writer' in Molay's entourage, and perhaps there was not one, his services no longer being required in Cyprus. In any event, the writer-interpreter of Guillaume de Beaujeu, author of the chronicle of the Templar of Tyre, failed to regain his employment in Cyprus.

Often named among the Order's dignitaries, but again without an exact specific role, are men who are not part of the *familia*. In 1292, Bertran l'Aleman, Raimbaud de Caron and Simon (otherwise known as Exemen) de Lenda are mentioned, the latter two later going on to forge successful careers within the Order. Perhaps they are the advisers who are often cited, but rarely named, in the documents. It may even be that, together with the dignitaries and the Master's companions, they formed an informal council which had the beginnings of a 'convent' as used in the limited sense by the Hospitallers. As I have already said, however, the word 'convent' as used in the Templar texts of the 1300s often retains its first meaning, referring to the whole of the combatant brothers in the Order, and often means the equivalent of 'Chapter'. But Molay's mastership could well mark an important stage in a development that was rudely interrupted by the king of France's bid for power over the Templars. In many of the statements made during their trial, the Templars say they believed that 'what had been commanded by the Grand Master with the convent was observed in the Order'.[76] Of course, this term could apply to the Chapter, but as these same Templars, when questioned, also use the word 'Chapter' in its first sense, it would seem they do indeed make a distinction between the words 'Chapter' and 'convent'.

The following tables show the names of the dignitaries for whom I have been able to collect documentation. The lists are incomplete, and there are not enough of them to give more than a general impression of Jacques de Molay's 'governing body'.

Office	1292	1294	1300
Marshal	Baudouin de la Andrin or de Laudrana	Baudouin de la Andrin	Bartholomé de Chinsi[77]
Grand Commander	Berenguer de Saint-Just		Florent de Villa (1299)
Draper	Gaucher de Liencourt (lieutenant)		Adam de Cronvalle
Turcopolier	Guillaume de la Tour (d. June 1293)		Dalmau de Timor
Sub-Marshal	Raymond de Barberan		
Commander of the Vault	Guillaume d'Ourenc		
Treasurer	Martin de Lou		
Infirmarian			
Com. of the palace			
Com. of the knights			Pierre de Bersi
Standard-bearer			
Others	Bertran l'Aleman Raimbaud de Caron Simon (or Exemen) de Lenda		Velasco Ferrandi, c. of Portugal R. de Caron, c. Limassol

Office	1302	End of 1304	1307–8
Marshal	Bartholomé de Chinsi (d. 26 Sept.)	Aymon d'Oiselay	A. d'Oiselay
Grand Commander	Raimbaud de Caron	R. de Caron	R. de Caron

Draper	Geoffroy de Charney[78]		Jean de Vila
Turcopolier	Dalmau de Timor	Bertrand de Gordo (or Barthélemy)	B. de Gordo
Sub-Marshal		P. de Aruyes (or Druyes)	
Com. of the Vault			
Treasurer		Pierre de Castillon (in 1305)	
Infirmarian			Jacques de Vallebrune
Com. of the palace			Martin de Lamusse
Com. of the knights			Jean de Lisivis
Standard-bearer			Pierre Borden
Others			

The *familia* of Jacques de Molay

Name	Date	Office	References	Geographical origin
Aymon de Barbone			Mich. I, 40	Dioc. of Troyes
Pons de *Bono opere*			Mich. I, 538	Received at Bures dioc. of Langres
Guillaume de Gy	After 1303	Provost of equipment and animals	Mich. II, 289 of	Hte.-Saône, dioc. of Besançon
Martino Martin		Valet		Spain
Jacques de Rupella (la Rochelle)		Mich. I, 562		Hte.-Saône, dioc. of Besançon
Pierre de Safed	After 1303	Provost of the garrisons	Mich. II, 294	Acre
'A chaplain'	1295		G. B., 117–18	Received at Dijon

Four – five, if we include the chaplain received at Dijon – of the known members of the *familia*, although probably only making up a tiny minority, had their origins in Burgundy and Champagne.

Most of the geographical origins of the central officers of the Order named in the tables can also be found. Jacques de Molay recruited them from the Order as a whole, but with a marked preference for people from Burgundy–Champagne, Provence and the lands of the Crown of Aragon, as the next table shows:

Origin	1292	1300	1302	1304	1307	Total
Catalonia–Aragon	3	1	1	1	1	7
Portugal		1				1
Provence	1	1	1	2	2	7
Toulouse					1	1
Burgundy–Champagne				1	3	4
Paris–Picardy	1			1	1	3
England		1				1
Germany	1					1

That is:

> Catalonia–Aragon: Berenguer de Saint-Just, Raymond de Barberan, Exemen de Lenda, Dalmau de Timor (2 times), Pierre de Castillon (2)
> Portugal: Velasco Ferrandi
> Provence: Raimbaud de Caron (5), Bertrand de Gordo (2)
> Toulouse: Pierre Borden
> Burgundy–Champagne: Aymon d'Oiselay (2), Martin de Lamusse, Jacques de Vallebrune
> Paris–Picardy: Gaucher de Liencourt, Geoffroy de Charney, Jean de Lisivis
> England: Adam de Cronvalle
> Germany: Bertran l'Aleman

It is not possible to check whether any strict rule existed regarding the duration of tenure of office. Four years are often cited, but there are exceptions. Nevertheless, there seems to have been a desire for mobility between offices held in the West and those held in Cyprus – and here again the Barcelona archives throw light on those movements. Berenguer de Saint-Just, Grand Commander in 1292, had previously been Master of the province of Aragon from 1283 to 1290 and would then become Commander of Miravet from 1297 to 1307; for some months he was the second-in-command to the Master of Aragon in 1300.[79] Dalmau de Timor became Commander of Barbera from January 1305 to July 1307 after holding the office of Turcopolier; he, too, had been second-in-command to the provincial Master in 1306.[80] Exemen de Lenda was Commander of Horta from 1296 to 1307, second-in-command to the Master of the province in 1296.[81] There are further examples outside this geographical zone: Geoffroy de Charney, who had become the Order's Draper probably soon after his crossing to Cyprus, may have returned to the West with Jacques de Molay (a new Draper, Jean de Vila, had been appointed) to take up the duties of Master or Commander of Normandy;[82] Aymon d'Oiselay is mentioned in various regions of France, and as Commander of the Templar houses in the county of Burgundy, before becoming Marshal of the Order,[83] Raimbaud de Caron, meanwhile, appears to have spent his entire career in Cyprus.

It is worth noting from the above both the concern for collegiality in the management of the Order, and Jacques de Molay's ability to delegate. It was usual for the Grand Master to appoint a second-in-command, or stand-in, during his absence. In October 1306, he chose Marshal Aymon d'Oiselay as his replacement;[84] he must also have chosen someone when he went on his first journey, but it is not known who. In both instances, he came to the West with members of his *familia*, but left all his management team in Cyprus. Only the two 'companions' were signatories to the deed by which he authorised Berenguer de Cardona to exchange Tortosa;[85] and in 1306 he took with him only Raimbaud de Caron, Grand Commander, and Geoffroy de Charney, although by this time he had given up his office of Draper.

In 1298, 1300 and 1303, a great many Templars made the crossing to Cyprus in connection with the Mongol offensives. Meanwhile, Jacques de Molay would have sent trusted men to the West to encourage and organise these movements. In 1300, Bertrand de Gordo (who was not yet Turcopolier) was in Paris,[86] while Bartholomé de Chinsi or Quincy, perhaps already Marshal, was staying at Sivré, or Sivrey, in Burgundy at Whitsun in the same year.[87]

Of course, changes in circumstance, such as the deaths of Guillaume de la Tour and Bartholomé de Chinsi, brought with them changes in Molay's entourage, but there was also a political will on Molay's part to encourage such mobility (the Catalan and Aragonese examples testify to this). The document of 1292 was doubtless an exceptional case, since it was one of the very first deeds (if not *the* first) of Jacques de Molay as Grand Master. On a matter concerning the Order's heritage in Aragon, he was resolved to assert his authority and that of this 'team', all of whom put their signatures to this document.

On his journeys to the West, during which he had to decide on matters concerning the Order's patrimony, he always acted in concert with the local dignitaries. On 9 June 1307, for instance, he accepted and ratified the donation made to the Temple by an inhabitant of Astaffort. This act involved primarily the Commander of the houses of Argenteins and Gimbrède in Agenais, who was at Jacques de Molay's side to handle the donation, Master of France Hugues de Pairaud and Bernard de Roche, Master of Provence (who was afterwards given the task of settling the practical details). Ratification took the form of a formal record by Jacques de Molay, dated 9 June 1307 at Poitiers, and undersigned by, among others, Jacques de Montaigu, Commander of Lombardy and *cubicularius* to the pope, who was evidently also present in Poitiers.[88] And so, in his relations with the Order's provinces, Molay displayed a genuine concern for dialogue, but he was also determined to remind them of his prerogatives.

There exists a file containing seven documents which pertain to the appointment of Exemen de Lenda as Master of Aragon on 8–11 September 1307. They show Molay's characteristic anxiety to respect form, but also to settle problems connected with it while at the same time reaffirming certain principles. He was then no longer in Cyprus, but in Poitiers; but that altered nothing – he continued to govern his Order.

Berenguer de Cardona had been Master of the province of Aragon since 1291, and Visitor of Spain since 1297. On the whole, harmony – even friendship – marked relations between Jacques de Molay and Berenguer de Cardona, as evidenced by the latter's joy at having met the Grand Master just before his departure for Cyprus in October 1306.[89] But that had not prevented a few minor problems in 1303–4, traces of which are to be found in the Exemen de Lenda dossier. Cardona came back from Cyprus around Easter 1307; he held a provincial Chapter at Horta in late May 1307,[90] and died some time in the following weeks, before 16 July. Molay, then in Poitiers, must have been informed of his death by the king's letter of that date, to which he replied on 4 August.[91] The king announced the Master of Aragon's demise and recommended Dalmau de Timor as his replacement. Jacques de Molay knew him well, as he had been Turcopolier in Cyprus, but he replied to the king that he could not defer to his wishes:

> It is an established custom that, when the Commander of a province dies, the brothers of that province, after informing the Master of what has happened, give their advice according to their knowledge and conscience for the appointment of a new rector. And because our brothers have not yet done that, we have not been able, without hearing their advice, to establish a new Commander.[92]

That is: the brothers propose, the Master and Chapter dispose. It seems at least a possibility that Molay made use of this 'tradition' in order not to yield to the king of Aragon; it smacks more of an excuse than of a strictly established rule.

On 8 September, the Grand Master made his decision. That day he sent out three letters, two to Exemen de Lenda, and the third to the Templars of Aragon informing them that he had appointed Exemen as Master.[93] Messengers had previously let the Master know the outcome of the Aragonese Templars' deliberations. Arnau de Banyuls, who was in Poitiers and whom he appointed Commander of Gardeny, was therefore instructed, together with Brother Gile, to take to the new Master the insignia of his office, the ball and the purse, in other words, the mould of the province's seal. The decision was Molay's: 'I think it for the best to make you Commander ...' he wrote to the newly promoted man.[94] In his second letter, he set out the powers with which he invested him: power of proxy, full powers in certain matters, etc.[95] The new Commander of Gardeny was also to make himself the bearer of letters to several people, including the royal family: one to the king[96] and another to Queen Blanche, both dated 10 September. 'We and our brothers thought to appoint Esemen de Lenda for this bailiwick.'[97]

Two other missives, one written on 10 September and the other on 11 September, are addressed to Exemen de Lenda, reminding him of certain management principles which his predecessor must have disobeyed, and informing him of some decision made concerning the province of Aragon–Catalonia. The letter of 10 September, which is fairly lengthy, calls on the Master to maintain the peace among the brothers, 'to keep himself honest in religion' (that is, watch over the Order honestly), to surround himself with advisers and expel or reprove evil men, and finally to maintain good relations with the king and the country's seigneurs.[98] He also commended the new Master and aforementioned advisers to the king.

Then the Grand Master told Exemen de Lenda of a few decisions relating to the States of the Crown of Aragon, in particular a 'movement', in the sense of administrative changes, in the commanderies. Pierre de Saint-Just was to move from Alfambra to Peñiscola; Berenguer de Olmos from Novillas to Alfambra; the bailiwick of Tortosa was to be entrusted to Gile Perez (the Templars still had at their disposal possessions in the town and its environs, notwithstanding the exchange that had been made with the king in 1294); lastly, he granted Gardeny to Arnau de Banyuls, hitherto Commander of Peñiscola, who 'has come to us'. These appointments were ordinarily the business of the Master of the province. Aware of this, Jacques de Molay wrote to him: 'And of all these bailiwicks that we grant, our intention is that you must be as glad of them as if you had granted them.' The Grand Master took advantage of the vacancy of the post to interfere in the normal procedure for appointing Commanders of the house, while also taking care to introduce a kind of 'without prejudice' clause.[99]

By making use, rightly or wrongly, of this procedure, Molay intended to settle a few specific problems and reward certain loyalties. Pierre de Saint-Just was a friend, so he gained promotion. Berenguer de Olmos had found himself in a difficult situation at Novillas (although it is not known how or why), so he changed places. Arnau de Banyuls did not lose out by transferring from Peñiscola to Gardeny, as that was the province's headquarters. Gile Perez was probably the 'mosire Gile' recorded as present in Poitiers in the letter of 8 September.

Jacques de Molay recalled two instances when his prerogatives had not been respected in the past by the Master at the time, Berenguer de Cardona. Firstly, he had given Bernard de Tamary, who was leaving Cyprus for home, the Commandery of Ribafora (or Ribaroja), but Cardona had made other arrangements. Molay indicated that 'when we grant any bailiwick, it is not a good thing if our letters are not adhered to'. The second, thorny problem raised by the Grand Master was that of Pierre de Castillon. Received into the Order in Roussillon in the 1280s, Castillon had crossed to Cyprus where he stayed until 1303, when he had returned to Catalonia. Molay had then asked Berenguer to provide him with a commandery, which he had failed to do. He was 'hard' with him, as the Grand Master wrote. Pierre de Castillon performed only secondary duties, substituting for the Commander of Miravet at Torres de Segre, a house which was dependent on Miravet, where his presence is attested from March 1303 to 1305, after serving for a time as substitute for the Commander at Ambel, Pierre de Saint-Just, in 1303. A letter from Pierre de Castillon to Pierre de Saint-Just, dated Christmas 1304 by its editor H. Finke,[100] which supplies important information about the central management of the Order, indicates that he had spent the Christmas festival at Miravet, at the governor's invitation, and was making ready to go back to Torres de Segre. With no prospect of promotion in Catalonia given the hostility of the Master of the province, he returned to Cyprus in 1305, when Jacques de Molay appointed him Treasurer of the Order. In 1306, he was back in Catalonia as the Grand Master's ambassador; and in 1307 he must

have left again for Cyprus, since Molay had granted him freedom to come to
Catalonia when he wished, and consequently asked Exemen de Lenda to supply
him with 'any good thing'. It is known from Amadi's chronicle that the Order's
Treasurer was in Cyprus with the Marshal, the Draper and others in 1307–8. But
was Pierre de Castillon still Treasurer? He does not figure among the Templars
questioned in Cyprus in 1310, but he was not dead, as there are mentions of him
in 1313 in Catalonia – at that time he received a pension based on the income of
the house of Aiguaviva, which was still Templar.[101]

Lastly – and this is the subject of the final letter addressed to Exemen de
Lenda on 11 September – Jacques de Molay asks the new Master to be 'friendly
and favourable to the household ['*maignie*'] of the late Commander'. No 'spoils
system', therefore, because 'it is not something that is commonly done in the
Temple'. Lenda would have to find new jobs for his predecessor's former servants.[102]

The file on the appointment of Exemen de Lenda shows the complexity
of the relations between the centre and the periphery in the Order, but it also
throws light on Jacques de Molay's concept of the Temple's relations with the
authorities – in this case secular, but ecclesiastic as well. In the letter to Exemen
of 10 September, there is a key sentence which I used as a preface to this book,
so perfectly does it seem to me to represent the whole basis of Molay's policy
as Master of the Temple. After advising the new Master of Aragon to maintain
good relations with the king and grand lords of the province, he mentions that
he is sending other letters, one addressed to the king, 'commending you and the
worthies [advisers] of our religious Order'. Jacques de Molay leaves Exemen de
Lenda the choice of taking this letter personally to the king or not:

> For we did not, and do not, wish the Temple to be placed in any servitude except
> that which is fitting.

The Temple – the Master, its dignitaries, Commanders of provinces and
houses – had to maintain good relations with the various rulers without calling
the Order's independence or autonomy into question. The appointment of
Masters of provinces was one of the criteria that enabled this autonomy to be
demonstrated. There were others: in England, for example, the king's accep-
tance of the journeys of Templar dignitaries when they were summoned by the
Grand Master. Jacques de Molay enjoyed good relations with Edward I. The

reasons for Guy de Forest's replacement by Brian de Jay as Master of England are not known, but there is nothing to suggest any conflict. In 1296, the former and the new Master, summoned by Molay, had to cross the sea together with Cardinal d'Albano, the papal legate, having obtained the king's authorisation without any problem.[103] In 1304, William de la More, who had succeeded Brian de Jay after his death in 1298, was summoned to Cyprus by the Master. After praising More's intelligence and virtues, the king commended him to the Master; he granted him permission to leave England, but asked Jacques de Molay to send him back soon 'to look after the Temple's possessions under the king's author-ity for his honour'.[104] The king also emphasised the gracious and praiseworthy services More had rendered to his kingdom.

This episode demonstrates the ambiguity at the heart of relations between the Temple and the various authorities. Like Hospitallers, Templars were at the service of rulers and the pope. In France, a Templar held the office of Treasurer or Almoner to the king.[105] In England, too, they played a role in guarding the royal Treasury. It was a guarantee for the Order, but also a means for the king both to meddle in its affairs and to exert pressure. To return to the appointment of provincial Masters, this had to be negotiated. In the case of William de la More, it had been easy; but for both sides a balance had to be maintained, an art of knowing 'just how far to go', that is well illustrated in a letter from Edward I, not to the Temple but to Guillaume de Villaret, Master of the Hospital, on 28 August 1299. The king asks him to promote a Knight Hospitaller, Fontanetus de Casa Nova, to a house or bailiwick, 'if the Order's rules permit'. In return, the king would be attentive to 'those things which he knows are dear to the Master'.[106]

In this kind of situation, it was necessary to show diplomacy, a quality in which Jacques de Molay was not lacking. One has only to see, for instance, how he resolved the delicate situation that arose in 1301–2 between the king of Aragon and the Master of the province, Berenguer de Cardona. Originally, a dis-agreement with an unknown cause cropped up between the king and the Master at the time of the meeting of the Cortes at Lerida (this was an assembly of the States of Catalonia, similar to the States General or Provincial in France).[107] On 9 April 1302, the king wrote to Molay asking him to dismiss Berenguer de Cardona. In fact, the king's main cause for complaint was that the Grand Master had appointed the latter as his second-in-command in those parts within the sov-ereignty of the Crown of Aragon (the islands of the western Mediterranean) without informing him (it is supposed that, in view of the way things turned out, Cardona should have been the one to do so). As Molay had not replied, the king sent a second letter, on 28 September.[108] The Grand Master's answer was dated 15 November 1302, from Limassol; after reassuring the king, Molay informed him that he could not dismiss the Master of Aragon because 'when the office is bestowed *ad terminum* [that is, for a specified duration], ... it is granted with the consent of our Chapter and until the end of that term it is not lawful to revoke it'.[109] He had, however, asked Berenguer de Cardona to apologise. In short, the Grand Master suggested that the king should bide his time until the next time the office came up for renewal. The king sent him a fresh letter on 31 January 1303, saying that he understood the Master's attitude and, as Cardona had apologised, the incident was considered closed; however, a similar event must not happen again.[110]

Jacques de Molay resorted to the customs and statutes of the Order to safe-guard its autonomy, and he succeeded pretty well, except, perhaps, in France. I have not been able to cite one example, one document, in which Jacques de Molay had any dealings with the king of France or with French Templar dignitaries; yet there must have been some. In view of the many exchanges of correspondence between Cyprus and the Catalan and Aragonese territories, it is unimaginable that a similar correspondence should not have existed with France, between Molay and the king, Molay and Pairaud. Yet there is not one single letter in existence between Molay and the Visitor of France and England, of whom Cardona was the counterpart in Spain. There is no reason to think that Molay disdained the kingdom. In Aragon and England, the Templar archives were seized at the time of the trial and, although some were later returned to the Hospitallers, one suspects that the royal chancelleries also kept some (in any case, those are the ones used today). Is it possible that in France they were deliberately destroyed?

In the kingdom of France, the provinces of France, Auvergne, Poitou and Provence had to be provided for, plus Normandy and several large baili-wicks. Had royal pressure been applied to obtain the appointment of provincial Masters who were loyal to the king? There is nothing to support the inference that Jacques de Molay yielded to royal pressure to appoint Gérard de Villiers in France, Humbert Blanc in Auvergne, Geoffroy de Gonneville (from England) in Poitou, Bernard de Roche in Provence or Geoffroy de Charney in Normandy. All that can be gathered is that Gérard de Villiers (who was doubtless no longer

Master of France at that time) and Humbert Blanc fled in order to escape arrest; that Geoffroy de Charney had been Draper in Cyprus and followed Molay to the stake in 1314. Meanwhile, Geoffroy de Gonneville, like Pairaud, held his tongue and escaped the ultimate punishment. Only Hugues de Pairaud may be classed as someone close to the king of France. His relations with Jacques de Molay are connected with the legal proceedings against the Temple, to which I will return in chapter 9.

1. Lecerf, 'Jacques de Molay',
nineteenth-century engraving

2. Chevauchet, 'Jacques de Molay',
nineteenth-century engraving

3. F. M. Granet, 'Jacques de Molay received into the Order of the Temple in 1265',
nineteenth-century painting

4. F. F. Richard (*1777–1852*), '*Jacques de Molay*'

5. A.-E. Fragonnard (*1780–1850*), '*Reading the sentence condemning the Templars*'

6. 'Jacques de Molay sentenced to the stake in 1314', from the Chronicle of France or of St Denis (fourteenth century)

7. 'The Templars before Pope Clement V (c. 1260–1320) and Philip the Fair (1268–1314)', from 'The Chronicles of France' by Boucicaut Master (1390–1430)

8. 'The arrest of the Templars in 1308' from the Chronicle of France or of St Denis

9. *Daniel Vierge (1851–1904)*, *'Templars at the stake'*, *engraving from Michelet*,
L'Histoire de France

1306

PLANS AND PROBLEMS

In late October or early November 1306, Jacques de Molay left Cyprus, never to return. He was responding to a summons from the pope, addressed to both him and the Master of the Hospital and dated 6 June.[1] There was a dual purpose for this convocation: the recurring problem of the crusade, and the merging of the Orders. The pontiff asked the Masters of the two Orders to offer him their ideas in the form of memoranda to be submitted before their arrival. We have the texts of the two memoranda written by Jacques de Molay, as well as that of Foulques de Villaret on the crusade (it is hardly likely, for reasons which will become apparent, that he wrote one on the matter of uniting the two Orders).[2] The latter problem no doubt took priority in the pope's eyes; its solution was at first envisaged as a pre-condition to the crusade's success, but it went much further and brought into play all the political and religious forces of the time. It was therefore heavy with consequences for the military Orders, in particular the Temple, as will gradually become clear.

On his arrival in France, late in 1306 or early in 1307, Jacques de Molay was put in the picture about another problem, of which he seemed totally oblivious – the rumours that were rife about his Order and the precise charges that were being assembled against it. The 1306–7 journey was thus undertaken in very different conditions from those that had prevailed on his first trip. It was not on the Grand Master's own initiative, but in response to a summons from the pope. However, there was nothing discourteous about it. Molay and Villaret were not 'on report'. They were coming to give expert advice on questions that concerned them both greatly. For this reason, Molay did not undertake a tour of the Templar houses in the West, as he had done before, but went only to France.

Before following him during his stay in France, I will set out the two problems of the crusade and the combining of the Orders that faced the Grand Master, and the solutions he presented to the pope. I will then deal with Jacques de Molay's third, and most formidable, problem – the defamation of the Order of the Temple.

The memoranda of Jacques de Molay and Foulques de Villaret belong in the line of 'treatises on the recovery of the Holy Land', which had flourished particularly since the 1270s and in which the word 'crusade' was used. Around 1300, more varied expressions were employed, depending on the nature and purpose of the 'crusade'. Two apply especially to the crusades whose aim was the liberation or reconquest of Jerusalem: the general crossing (*passagium generale*); and the special crossing (*passagium particulare*). The first applied to the great crusade in which, under the guidance of the Church, the kings and rulers of the West and their troops of knights joined together with fluctuating numbers of disparate non-combatants, whose presence was not really wanted but could nevertheless not be rejected. The term 'special crossing' was used in the first place for small expeditions undertaken by a king, prince or lesser lord between these great crusades. Paradoxically, Saint Louis' second crusade, which took him to Tunis, was said to be the 'first general crossing', whereas his first, which was uniquely French, was deemed a 'special crossing'.[4]

The meaning of a 'special crossing' developed in the second half of the thirteenth century; but to fully understand it, we must go back to its chronology and context and distinguish between post-1291 and pre-1291 when, although reduced, a portion of the Latin 'Holy Land' still survived and when, as on the eve of the first crusade, it was a matter of 'liberating', that is conquering, Jerusalem. The content of the crusading treatises is not the same before and after that date.

Prior to 1291, the proposals presented to Pope Gregory X at the second Council of Lyon in 1274 came from the clergy (Humbert de Romans, Guillaume de Tripoli, etc.) – laymen being invited to make their proposals orally. All the plans opted for a special crossing and rejected a general crossing, which was considered ineffectual. Meanwhile, the content of the special crossing took shape. What served as a model at that time was what I term the 'Saint Louis solution', namely, to send permanent troops similar to the 'French regiment' left behind by the king of France after his departure from Acre in 1254, and still present in the Holy Land in 1274. Since it was a matter of defending what already existed, and possibly reconquering further territory, the pope's advisers thought the most suitable solution would be a special crossing with new troops. The pope, however, paid no heed to this advice and launched into organising a general crossing; it was only his death in 1276 that interrupted preparations.

Post-1291, the context was radically different since, with the exception of Cyprus and the Armenia of Cilicia, the Holy Land no longer existed. The old places previously held by the Christians would have to be reconquered and, although Cyprus and Armenia formed useful bases, it would take an enormous military effort to regain a foothold on the Syrio-Palestinian coast.

At that time, treatises on the crusades proliferated, most of them combining, with varying degrees of realism, the two types of crossing – special and general. The earliest and, in my view, closest to the plans presented by Villaret (chiefly) and Molay, was that of Charles II of Sicily, dated 1292 or 1293.[5] It may be supposed that Jacques de Molay knew about it and had discussed it with the king when he met him in Naples in 1294 and 1295. However, there had been others, notably the three written by ardent defender of mission and conversion by word of mouth Ramon Lull, who knew from experience that the word of Christ could not be preached in an Islamic country unless the Muslims had been politically and militarily subdued beforehand. In 1292, he had written a 'Letter to the sovereign pontiff on the recovery of the Holy Land', enclosing a 'Treatise on the way to convert the Infidels', otherwise known as 'Lo passage'. His most important text, the *Liber de fine*, is dated 1305; lastly, in 1309, he published the 'Book on the acquisition of the Holy Land'. Hayton of Corycos, the Armenian historian whom the reader has already encountered, made the fourth part of his 'Flower of the histories of the Eastern Land' a crusade treatise which he presented to Pope Clement V at Poitiers in 1307, just when the treatises of Jacques de Molay and Foulques de Villaret were being discussed in the Roman court.[6] There were also two plans – or, more accurately, two reworkings of the same plan – ascribed to Otton de Grandson and composed at two different dates around 1300.[7]

Without going into detail, all these proposals took account, to varying degrees, of the following: the maritime superiority of the Christians and the connection of the special crossing with a general one. Naval superiority could be used for two purposes: effecting a blockade of Egypt and preventing the 'evil Christians' (merchants) from trading with the Infidels; and protecting Cyprus and Armenia. The special expedition would serve to carry out prior operations of harassment of the enemy with a view to weakening them, and setting up a bridgehead for the general crossing. The latter would allow a frontal attack on the enemy (the majority of the projects had Egypt as their target). As for Cyprus and Armenia, they were the home base, the place where the Christian army would be concentrated.

Foulques de Villaret's plan seems closer to this model than Molay's, but in my opinion other historians have exaggerated their differences, on the basis of inadequate analysis of the context and chronology.[8] Villaret, counselling the pope to be cautious if setbacks such as had occurred for more than a century were to be avoided, took as his model the first crusade commanded by both a religious leader and a military leader. It was up to the pope to launch and preach the merits of the crusade, setting a fairly short preparation period so that enthusiasm would not wane. At the same time, funds would have to be collected and vessels made ready. In the first instance a fleet would have to be equipped which, together with those of Cyprus and the military Orders, would take care of the blockade of Egypt. Another larger fleet (fifty vessels, including the '*huissiers*' which were fitted out to transport horses) would have the mission of harassing the enemy. Recruitment for the general expedition would follow. Foulques de Villaret counted on the support of paid mercenaries alongside the voluntary crusaders and brothers of the military Orders. The objective of this general crossing would be announced at the last moment. Lastly, the memorandum reviewed the various financial measures to be put into operation: tithes, collection boxes for the crusade in churches, indulgences and the redemption of pledges. Naturally, the crusaders would be placed under the safekeeping and protection of the Church.

Jacques de Molay's treatise is of almost comparable importance to that of Foulques de Villaret, but it is constructed differently.[9] In his, the Master of the Temple takes no futile precautions and from the outset rejects the idea of a special crossing (he speaks of a 'little crossing') and demonstrates its uselessness. A small army, if not rapidly supported, would be destroyed by the Mamluks. He similarly rejects the use of Armenia as a departure base for various reasons: the Armenian contribution is too weak; there are not enough resources; and the Armenians are not very reliable as combatants or allies.[10] He therefore proposes a general crossing with all the western rulers under the pope's leadership. His suggested means of transport is ships provided by the Italian republics (large rounded vessels better adapted than galleys for transporting men and equipment) and he envisages an army of between 12,000 and 15,000 cavalry and 5,000 footsoldiers. Cyprus, he thinks, would form the ideal base. From there, the 'large crossing' would head towards a secret destination which Molay would divulge to the pope in person. Finally, as an immediate measure, he asks the pope to have ten galleys fitted out as quickly as possible, during the winter, so that they would be operational by the spring, their mission being to defend Cyprus and undertake a blockade of the Saracen countries. Molay commits himself to funding these galleys. The Master asks the pope to punish severely those Christians who do business with the Saracens and supply them with dismantled galleys (that is, in 'kit form') and weapons. Venice, Pisa and Genoa are the targets of his reprobation, yet it is they who must be approached for the hire of the large transport vessels.

This memorandum bears the strong stamp of Jacques de Molay's personal experience; several times he reveals what he knows and what he has done. From agents of the Italian trading companies he has learnt of the huge profits which the sultan of Cairo derives from trade with Christian merchants in Alexandria and other ports. He knows the size of the armies the Mamluks are capable of mobilising, and therefore knows at what level the Christian response must be pitched (with regard to figures, he makes reference to Saint Louis' crusade). He knows which sites on enemy territory are suitable for landing and which are not.

The Grand Master's experiences, in Armenia perhaps in 1299 and at Ruad in 1300–2, were doubtless the reason for his rejection of Armenia as the destination of a small expedition, and of the small expedition in itself. In 1301–2, at Ruad, the Templars had found themselves in a 'small crossing' situation, during which they had not stood idly by; they had carried out those harassment operations and raids which, in his memorandum, Villaret proposes to use. But at Ruad a Mongol offensive had been expected; in the end it had not come, and in its place the Templars had seen the arrival of the Mamluks.

The argument can be extended: in Molay's view the small crossing made no sense and Armenia provoked no interest except within the strategy of the Mongol alliance. In 1306, when he was writing this memorandum, although a Mongol embassy went to Poitiers in 1307, that strategy was over and done with, and Molay, who had played an essential part in it in 1299–1303, had noted its demise.

The Master of the Hospital had been less personally involved than Jacques de Molay in the dramas of 1300–2. It is noticeable that his memorandum is more precise than Molay's; but perhaps that is due to the fact that the Master of the Temple leaves more room for informing the pope in person, his memorandum being conceived more as a working document. The main difference between the two, however, lies in Molay's rejection of the special crossing; by contrast, Villaret sets out his objectives with precision. His description matches what the Christian boats actually did in July–August 1300, when they ravaged the Egyptian and Syrio-Palestinian coasts and, after Ruad, when they occupied the Tortosa region for some twenty days – operations which notably continued after the Ruad episode.

One may wonder whether this was a matter of what might be called 'routine' action incumbent on the military Orders, and did not therefore count as a crusading project. The divergence between the two plans does not seem to me as wide as is often claimed. In fact, the points of convergence are just as obvious. Both men are planning on a general crossing. Jacques de Molay skips the stage of the special crossing, but not entirely, for there is nothing to prevent a small fleet of galleys blockading Egypt from carrying out raids. In both proposals, what matters is assured maritime superiority and the capacity to make use of it; on this point the two Masters are in agreement. A permanent flotilla is a necessity and, here again, there is no difference between them, except on one small point: Villaret makes a distinction between the fleet required for the blockade and the fleet to be used for the special crossing.

These two memoranda are without dates, although historians have suggested rather arbitrary ones – for instance, 1305 for Villaret's, which is very early. The simplest and most logical way to date these plans would be from Clement V's request in summer 1306, before the two Masters left for the West.[11]

The problem of the crusade is set out by both men in fairly traditional terms, because that was what they had been asked to do. Later on, once the legal proceedings against the Order of the Temple were under way, Clement V and Foulques de Villaret organised a special crossing, whose concealed objective was to support the Hospitallers in their conquest of Rhodes; a Hospitaller plan was even drawn up with this purpose in mind.[12] It resumed several aspects of the part devoted to the special crossing in the Master of the Hospital's treatise, but it was an independent project; it was conceived outside the framework of a general crossing.[13]

One topic must have however dominated the pope's conversations with the Masters even more than the crusade: the merging of the Orders. The matter had been cropping up since the 1270s, but now was a priority. As with the crusade, the pope had asked for a written opinion from the two Masters, but the only one we have is Jacques de Molay's.[14] Before we look at it, let us recall the birth of this project.

In the years 1250–70, the frequently keen rivalries between the Orders had sometimes degenerated into open conflict, as with the war of Saint-Sabas at Acre;[15] but also during this period the Orders had tried to establish a procedure for settling these fights. Their differences, which were known about in the West, had altered their image: the grave setbacks suffered in Baibars' offensive between 1265 and 1271 had been blamed on this rivalry. It matters little that in the historian's view such a judgement was widely inaccurate; what counts is their contemporaries' perception of it. In this context, the idea of combining the Orders had appeared to be the means of doing away with their disagreements and making them more effective, since it was none the less recognised that they were of some usefulness. The question had been openly raised at the second Council of Lyon in 1274, which was also dealing with crusading. The Grand Master, Guillaume de Beaujeu, had taken part and the Templars had intervened to defend their Order, which had been accused of, among other things, not practising enough charity. It was obvious that, in this field, the Temple could not hope to rival the Order of the Hospital, which was founded as a charitable Order.[16]

At the Council of Lyon, the discussion about union came to a sudden end. It is not known whether the Temple was convincing in its own defence; however, there were those in authority attending the council, such as the king of Aragon, James I, who were unenthusiastic and opposed the idea. In the end, the pope was forced to abandon the project. The king of Aragon had advanced a decisive argument: a unified Order would become too powerful, would carry too much weight in the kingdom; he had no wish to see a situation arise in his states like that which prevailed in the kingdom of Jerusalem. The other European sovereigns, such as Hugh III of Cyprus, took a similar view.

The matter returned to the foreground after the fall of Acre. Of course, people were not unaware of the courage of the last Templar and Hospitaller defenders, but that did nothing to alter the fundamental problem. In the eyes of some, the Orders bore a share of the responsibility for the defeat. Actively preparing a crusade, Pope Nicholas IV again took up the plan for union. In his Bull *Dura nimis*, issued on 15 August 1292 and requesting a reply by 2 February 1292, he asked the archbishops 'with their suffragans meeting together in provincial synod, to hold council on the union of the Templars with the Hospitallers, and let the apostolic see know the outcome of their deliberations'.[17]

The response of several of these synods is known: that of Milan, on 26 November 1291;[18] and that of Salzburg, which not only approved the merger and extended it to the Teutonic Order but also proposed that leadership of the crusade should be entrusted to Edward I of England.[19]

Others took up the question and proffered their opinions: Ramon Lull, in the same breath as speaking of the crusade, proposed the merging of all the Orders, including the Spanish and Teutonic. Jacques de Molay cannot have failed to discuss the subject during his journey in the West, for instance with Charles II of Naples, the author of a treatise on crusading in which he pronounced himself in favour of combining all the military and hospitaller Orders. He also spoke about it with Pope Boniface VIII in Rome in 1295. In his memorandum on union, he recalls the essential moments of the debate, the second Council of Lyon and Nicholas IV's Bull, before concluding that Boniface VIII 'spoke several times about this matter and, when all was said and done, gave up the whole affair, as you may learn from some cardinals who were with him at the time'.[20] Boniface VIII probably had his reasons for deferring a decision until later, but there is no doubt at all that Jacques de Molay had slowed down the process.

During the papacy of Nicholas IV, the project had been pushed mainly by the secular clergy. The pope had in any case addressed the bishops who had long protested against the privileges – exorbitant, in their opinion – accorded the military-religious orders. In 1274, the project had been wrecked by laymen, but the situation had changed in the last decade of the thirteenth century and the beginning of the fourteenth; the question of union, closely linked with that of the crusade, was again taken up by certain secular authorities, but diverted from its initial aims for political reasons.

Meanwhile, Charles II of Naples was in favour of the union, on the condition that a king or son of a king was made head of this dreamed-of combined Order, one who would become king of the reconquered Jerusalem. Perhaps his son Robert or, from the Capetians in France, Philip the Fair? The crusading project of the lawyer Pierre Dubois took shape in the environment of the Court of France; Ramon Lull's plans carried on from that. After 1305, the king of France became the widowed father of three sons and the notion of the Grand Mastership of the Order going to the king or one of his sons began to make headway.

The combined Order, therefore, would serve interests other than those of crusades and reconquest, objectives that were nevertheless solemnly proclaimed by
the entourage of Philip the Fair.

In the memorandum he sent to the pope in 1306, Jacques de Molay categorically rejects the idea of a merger. To understand his position, his memorandum
must be placed in historical tradition as well as in the changing – and changed
– context of the latter years of the Temple. As we shall see, Molay's argument is
weak; the Grand Master finds himself on the defensive, as his predecessor Guillaume de Beaujeu had done in 1274.

He begins by recalling the historical antecedents, of the second Council
of Lyon to Boniface VIII. Next, he presents the arguments against the union:
the two Orders are ancient; it is dangerous to force those who have chosen
one Order to blend with what would become another. Competition between
the two institutions has been beneficial; it has stimulated gifts, alms, commitments, enthusiasm in combat; but such competition would continue within a
single Order, and thereby poison its very existence. The Rule of a unified Order
would of necessity be a compromise between a strict Rule (the Temple's) and
one which was less so (the Hospital's); houses and chapels would be eliminated;
the two hierarchies would have to give way to a single one, causing rancour and
discontent (one cannot help thinking that here Jacques de Molay was defending
his own position). To conclude his argument, the Master of the Temple takes
the examples, positive in his view, of the healthy competition between the two
great mendicant Orders, the Dominicans and the Franciscans; or of the use of
the Temple and Hospital by the military leaders of the Latin East, as a vanguard
and a rearguard during the fighting in the Holy Land.

He then puts forward some arguments in favour of a merger. The Orders
have been criticised and attacked by both laymen and secular clergy; their patrimony is dwindling or damaged. A single Order would be 'so strong and so powerful that it could defend its rights against anyone'. Union would bring about a
reduction in operating costs. Although Molay's reasons for accepting the merger
are few, he does not close the door entirely. He finishes his memorandum by
affirming that he and his Order are and will always be ready to counsel the pope
and inform him of their will; the pope may then act as he pleases – which may
seem rather cavalier.

It is easy, of course, to mock the reasons, both good and bad, advanced
by Jacques de Molay for rejecting the merger. Although a few are based on

experience, many are not very sound. However, Molay is fighting a rearguard action here. He knows union is inevitable. The reasons he gives for turning the idea down are pretty mediocre; but he has others he cannot mention.

The first had to do with the fact that a united Order would, in its Rule, its offices, its way of life, be closer to the Hospital than to the Temple. The part of the memorandum devoted to the practice of charity, as distinct from hospitality which belonged specifically to the Hospital, is revealing. The Temple was accused, unjustly, of not giving alms; the proposal was to combine it with an Order in which charity – care given to the poor, pilgrims or otherwise – had been and still was its prime *raison d'être*, as opposed to the Temple which had been founded on 'military service'. It was a certainty that in any merger the latter would lose its identity.

Obviously he cannot disclose the second reason. In the context of the years 1305–6, he is sure that the new united Order would lose all autonomy, for it would come under the thumb of the king of France. Through union, the Temple would doubly disappear: in its essence and in its independence. Whatever its name might be, the unified Order would become no more than a variant of the Order of the Hospital; it would be managed, directly or indirectly, by the king of France, who, it must be said, was totally uninterested in the Holy Land. Despite being the grandson of Saint Louis, Philip the Fair was indifferent to crusading. Combining the Orders also represented a move in the struggle between French royalty and the papacy. Would the latter have sufficient resources and strength of character to retain supervision of the united Order and shield it from the king's ambitions? Perhaps Molay was being overly pessimistic as regards who would control the new Order. It was not all over yet.

At this point in history both Molay's intransigence and Villaret's silence are understandable. Villaret had not written a memorandum on the merging of the Orders because he had no wish, merely in the expectation of benefiting from that union, to be bound by a text at the very moment when, having taken on the conquest of Rhodes, he hoped to acquire the means that would enable him, with papal backing, to resist the ambitions of the king of France. In the summer of 1306, Jacques de Molay did not hold all the keys. Rhodes could not be regarded as conquered by the Hospitallers; as yet, it was still only a probability. It is therefore understandable that, glimpsing the worst, Molay's attitude hardened into haughty rejection; but by digging his heels in he alienated the king of France and was no help to the pope in resisting that same king's predatory ambitions.

For, although Clement V desired the uniting of the Orders, however feeble he was reputed to be, he certainly did not want a combined Order that would be under Philip the Fair's thumb.

We now come to the question of how these memoranda were ordered and drawn up, and how they were sent to their addressee, Pope Clement V.

Jacques de Molay and Foulques de Villaret were officially summoned by the pope on 6 June 1306; but in actual fact plans for a meeting between the three had been drawn up earlier. Here again, the Archives of the Crown of Aragon provide new information. On 26 and 27 January 1306, Molay wrote two letters, the first to his friend Pierre de Saint-Just, the second to King James II,[21] informing them that he was sending Pierre de Castillon, the Order's Treasurer, as ambassador to Aragon. A Catalan, the latter had held several secondary posts in the Templar commanderies in the province;[22] his mission was to deal with the business affairs of the house. To Pierre de Saint-Just, the Grand Master wrote that he had just remembered that 'we had asked you to come in person to the convent [Chapter, here?] on the next crossing [that is, in the spring]'. But, he added, 'in this instance we wish to do you a special favour and leave it to your discretion to choose whether to come or stay there' (Saint-Just would choose to go to Cyprus). It was therefore planned to hold a Chapter of sufficient importance for the Grand Master to call on certain Commanders in the West, not just the Masters of the provinces. In March, the Master of the province of Aragon, Berenguer de Cardona, told Arnau de Banyuls, Commander of Peñiscola, that he had received a letter from 'the lord Master of Outremer', in which the latter informed him that 'by reason of a letter from the pope about the general crossing', he asked him to come to Cyprus in August to confer about it.[23] In another letter, also addressed to Arnau de Banyuls, Berenguer de Cardona announced that he must go to Cyprus, accompanied by two other brothers and a valet of the Commander of Miravet.[24]

On 20 June 1306, Pierre de Castillon, the Grand Master's ambassador in Aragon, informs Pierre de Saint-Just, who has not yet departed, of important news:

> We would inform you, sir, that the lord Master of this land [Berenguer de Cardona] has had news from the Court of Rome [Poitiers] that the Visitor of France and the Commander of Portugal, by command of the pope … will come into his presence next All Saints' Day and that they must not go to Cyprus or

send anything there. The Grand Master is summoned before the pope on the said day. Furthermore, know that the Commander of Aragon will receive this command in a few days. The Grand Master of the Hospital and the other Commanders of the said Order have, or will have, this command for the purpose of dealing with the union of the said Orders; and of the other Orders which similarly own possessions.[25]

Pierre de Castillon was therefore aware of the pope's letter of 6 June convoking the two Grand Masters and other Commanders to Poitiers on the following All Saints' Day or within the subsequent fortnight.

So, before receiving this letter, Jacques de Molay had summoned the chief dignitaries of his Order in the West to come to Cyprus in August. The pope's letter of 6 June had thus interrupted a process in which the pope was already involved, probably as early as his coronation in November 1305; a process known to Molay, since it was on the strength of the information he possessed that he had organised the consultation with the dignitaries of his Order. The pope's letter set out the venue for the meeting (Poitiers) and its date (All Saints' Day), but it had the effect of forcing Jacques de Molay to forgo the consultations he had counted on holding in August before coming to see Clement V. It was obviously following these consultations that the Temple's position on the two subjects under discussion – the crusade and the merging of the Orders – was to have been settled and put in writing. In a letter dated 15 November 1306, Clement V reminded Hugues de Pairaud that he had asked him to cancel his journey to Cyprus in order to put himself at the service of the Holy See.[26] On the other hand, both Berenguer de Cardona and Pierre de Saint-Just had reached the island. They could not have failed to be informed of the latest events, so their journey was a matter of personal decision; in any case, it is doubtful whether the pope had given them any orders either way. Clement V did not have the close relationship with them that he had with Hugues de Pairaud.

Jacques de Molay's two memoranda were therefore written in Cyprus, with the Order's officers and 'advisers' present.

How did these memoranda reach the pope? Different historians have proposed one date, December 1306, and an intermediary, Humbert Blanc, Master of Auvergne–Limousin.[27] Although the latter assertion is without foundation, the date appears probable. The introduction of Humbert Blanc into the affair is the result of an arbitrary connection between the letter of 6 June and a group of three others from the pontiff, dated 13 June, concerning the Master of Auvergne. These three letters have identical sections: the first, addressed to the kings, princes, bishops and clergy, commends to them Humbert Blanc and Pierre de Lengres, a citizen of Marseille described as 'admiral of the galleys dispatched for the assistance of the Holy Land', and asks them to take a favourable view of their undertaking to help the Latin States. The two others are intended for these two men: since they have decided to fight the Infidels and impious Christians who trade with them, they can attack their boats and loot them; the pope grants them the further privilege of taking on board with them a priest able to hear the confessions of and absolve any captured evil Christians – only if they are repentant, of course.[28]

So, was this a personal initiative on the part of the two men or was it related to Jacques de Molay's proposed crusade? It could just have been a local initiative taken over by the papacy; in which case it would have been a privateering operation, and not simple piracy, sponsored by the Holy See and protected by the sovereigns of the West.[29] But it is unlikely the Master of the Temple would not have known about such an important mission by a provincial Master at a time when he himself was preparing for a crusade.

Is there a connection between this initiative and what Molay writes in this rather obscure passage from his memorandum on the crusade?

> Similarly, I am in agreement and strongly approve of your having ten galleys fitted out, as quickly as possible … so that they can defend the kingdom of Cyprus and guard the sea, thus preventing the evil Christians from provisioning the Saracens; … as for the necessary money, I will provide for it, secretly if you wish, as I see fit …[30]

If, as we have just seen, preparations for the meeting with the pope had begun in the spring of 1306, maybe even before, it is not impossible that concrete arrangements could have been put in place before being clearly set out in writing. In his memorandum, Molay is asking for ships to be chartered in the winter of 1306 so that they can be operational in the following spring. The Humbert Blanc–Pierre de Lengres initiative, revealed in the papal letters of 13 June 1306, may belong in this calendar. Setting up a small fleet to undertake the blockade of Egypt had become a commonplace, as we have seen, present in all the treatises on the crusade at that time, whatever the suggested solutions might be. As early as

March 1306, the Templars were aware that serious plans were afoot to launch a crusade; without waiting for its formal declaration, certain practical aspects could already have been organised.

Returning, however, to the three letters analysed above, nothing in them gives grounds for asserting that Humbert Blanc handed Jacques de Molay's letters to the pope. One of the Master's messengers left before him, and could well have brought the memoranda to the West; or perhaps they were sent earlier to arrive before December; or, quite simply, the Master brought them himself.

In October, Jacques de Molay made ready to leave for France. Except for Raimbaud de Caron, the Grand Commander, he left the entire governing body of the Order behind, and appointed the Marshal, Aymon d'Oiselay, as his replacement during his absence. This must have happened before 20 October, as in a letter dated that day concerning permission given to Pierre de Saint-Just to go home, Aymon d'Oiselay assumes the title,[31] as was customary practice, at central as well as provincial level.

Meanwhile, Berenguer de Cardona left for Cyprus after 10 August 1306, probably later than originally planned.[32] He landed at Famagusta some time before 8 October (the date on which he arrived at Limassol). There he met the Master, Molay, who was getting ready to leave for the West; three days later, the Master left. Realising that he had nothing more to do in Cyprus, Berenguer in his turn also decided to leave, but just as he was about to embark at Famagusta he fell ill with the quartan fever. Having postponed his departure, he returned to Limassol in order to nurse himself to recovery. He then set sail, but by this time the weather had changed and his ship had to overwinter at Candia, in Crete. It was from there that he wrote to his brothers in Catalonia, informing them that he would leave Candia in March 1307 and hoped to arrive in Barcelona before Easter.[33] That, in fact, is what happened.

Jacques de Molay appears to have left after 11 October but before 20 October. That would have given him enough time to arrive in France around mid-November, but certainly not by All Saints Day. Foulques de Villaret must have left later, since he held a Chapter of his Order at Limassol on 3 November.

When he left, Jacques de Molay could not have known that the planned meeting at Poitiers had been adjourned *sine die*. In fact, the pope had fallen ill at the end of August and had postponed all his audiences – as he made known in various letters, and was still doing on 5 November.[34] However, only when he landed in Provence did Molay learn about it.

On his departure from Cyprus, the Master had reason to be confident: the matter of the crusade was going to be tackled seriously, and he may even have continued to believe that the merging of the Orders would not take place if he rejected it. That was, however, a grave error of judgement; all the more so since, on his arrival in France, he was to find himself faced with a problem that he had not foreseen – rumours concerning his Order. This was something that dangerously weakened his position and, quite apart from any question of merging, directly threatened the Temple's existence.

1307

IN THE SNARES OF
THE KING OF FRANCE

Jacques de Molay landed in France in November or December 1306, very probably at Marseille, where there was a long-established Templar infrastructure, with a Master of Passage who supervised all transfers of men, goods and money to the East. Marseille was also the home port of Templar shipping in the western Mediterranean. It was here that Molay must have learnt of the impossibility of meeting the pope at Poitiers. The Grand Master of the Hospital, who had left later, perhaps did not arrive until the beginning of January. In a letter of 8 February 1307, King Edward I of England mentions to him that he has authorised the Grand Prior of the English Hospital, Guillaume de Tothale, to cross the sea 'to present himself to you at the Court of Rome [in Poitiers]'.[1] Although Edward evidently thought that Villaret might be in Poitiers at that time, it is doubtful whether he was, bearing in mind the postponement of the meeting with the pope to a later date; all the more so because Villaret might have been in Naples in April.[2] We are therefore reduced to conjecture about Villaret's whereabouts at the time, while absolutely nothing is known about Molay's.

The pope resumed holding audiences in January 1307; it may be supposed that it was he who took the initiative of proposing May of that year as the new date for a meeting. However, nothing is known about Molay's whereabouts or activities between December 1306 and May 1307. A Chapter of the Temple was held in Paris at Candlemas, on 2 February 1307. According to Ponsard de Gisy's testimony at the trial, Hugues de Pairaud had presided it. Was Molay present? Ponsard de Gisy neither confirms nor denies it; even the date is only vaguely indicated, making the year 1307 hypothetical.[3] Nor is there any trace of the Grand Master visiting any of the provincial Templar commanderies in the kingdom of France, for a reception ceremony into the Order, for example. Had he been present at one of these, the event would have been recorded in the trial depositions. No contemporary chronicle makes any mention of his possible movements. It is equally uncertain whether Jacques de Molay had planned a tour of inspection, unless he had decided to do so after his meeting with the pope. In a letter to the Grand Master dated 23 May 1307, Pierre de Saint-Just expresses his delight that Molay intends to go to Castile and Portugal, where, as he had gleaned from the brothers in those two kingdoms, a few problems had arisen.[4] In short, although nothing is known about his immediate activities, it is unimaginable that he would not have been informed, immediately upon his arrival in France, about the rumours concerning his Order.

Molay thus discovered a problem he never dreamed he would have to face. The rumours about the Order went far beyond the criticisms that had long been levelled at not only the Templars but also the Hospitallers and other military Orders, in fact all the religious Orders:[5] pride, arrogance, cupidity and (for the Templars) the absence of charitable works. If a non-Templar witness in the trial is to be believed, Molay was warned of the threats looming over his Order by letters from the Master of Passage at Marseille. A cleric of the diocese of Lyon, Étienne de Neyrac, giving evidence before the papal commission in Paris on 27 January 1311, stated that at the time of the Templars' arrest in Lyon (13 October, as everywhere else in the kingdom), a member of the secular clergy had been arrested with them, and the royal police had seized two pairs of sealed letters originating from the Master of Passage at Marseille.[6] In the first, the latter informed the Grand Master that the Order and brothers were the subject of serious accusations made to the pope and the king; he urged him to be careful and make sure the king remained favourable to the Templar cause. The other letters called into question knights from Gascony who, on being arrested, were said to have defamed the Order, and would therefore be the originators of the accusations brought against it. This is a single testimony, and one that is larded with improbabilities; however, as with all the trial testimonies, it cannot be dismissed. It is curious that the Master of Passage should inform the Grand Master by letter, when he could possibly have seen him in the flesh when he was passing through Marseille. But here is something even more curious: the letters were seized in Lyon on 13 October, which means that their bearer had left Marseille a few days earlier; in which case the Master of Passage would have informed his superior not shortly after the latter's arrival in France, but much later, just before the arrest of the Templars in October 1307. That makes no sense. At that particular time, Jacques de Molay knew what was going on. Maybe the Master of Passage, like so many other Templars, including the Master, had no suspicion of the magnitude of the threat.

Nevertheless, the witness cannot have totally invented this story of the letters (moreover, the events were recent, so it is unlikely his memory was faulty); but it must be a matter of distorted comments. In his testimony before the papal commission, on 27 November 1309, Ponsard de Gisy cites the four traitors who, in his view, were at the origin of the Temple's troubles: a monk; Sequin de Floyran, co-prior of Montfaucon (to whom I will return); Bernard Pelet, prior of the Mas d'Agen; and a knight of the Agenais region.[7] Could these have any connection with the Gascon knights mentioned above?[8] Whatever the truth may be, the historian cannot rely on this text to affirm that Jacques de Molay had been brought up-to-date – soon after his arrival, I stress – through this channel.

There were many other ways of informing the Grand Master. For instance, Raoul de Gisy (not to be confused with Ponsard) is supposed to have confessed the errors of the Temple (and therefore its turpitude) to a minor brother in Lyon, where he was shortly before the capture of the Templars, 'before having heard about that [sic]'.[9] Soon afterwards he had met Hugues de Pairaud, still near Lyon, and asked him to remedy those errors. Hugues de Pairaud was said to have replied 'that he would await the coming of the Grand Master, who was due to arrive from overseas, and swore … that if the said Master was unwilling to extirpate those failings, he himself would do so …' Once again, the witness suffers from memory problems: for him, 'shortly before the capture of the Templars' means 1306, before the Grand Master arrived from Cyprus.

The pope is known to have been aware of these rumours since the end of 1305. Since he had at his side a Templar as *cubicularius* (gentleman of the bedchamber), is it credible that he knew nothing? Is it believable that Jacques de Molay did not meet him?

We know where these rumours started and who propagated them. Two, partly fanciful, accounts exist: one by the Florentine chronicler Villani, the other by Amaury Augier, a cleric from Béziers and the author of a life of Clement V.[10] According to the first, a Templar who was imprisoned in a royal castle, prior of Montfaucon in the Toulouse area,[11] told his fellow prisoner the Florentine Noffo Dei about the misdeeds and vices of the Templars, which Noffo Dei subsequently reported.[12] According to the second account, a burgher from Béziers, Esquieu (or Sequin) de Floyran, had been imprisoned at the same time as a renegade Templar; they had confided in each other and the Templar was alleged to have told him 'that, upon entering the Order, and afterwards, many vices were committed', thereby revealing the many misdeeds against God and the unity of faith to be found within the Order. Esquieu, seeing it as a good way of lessening his punishment, persuaded his guards to let him be presented to the king, to whom he recounted everything.[13] Lastly, there is the testimony of Ponsard de Gisy, who cites 'Esquius de Floyrac, of Biterris, co-prior of Montfaucon' among those responsible for denouncing the Temple.

The Esquieu de Floyrac, or Floyran, in question did really exist, although it is not certain whether he obtained his information in this way, or that he had been prior of Montfaucon (a title which, in any event, signified nothing in the Order of the Temple, not least because Montfaucon in the Toulousain did not exist). A letter of 1308 from this Esquieu de Floyran to the king of Aragon, now residing in the Archives of the Crown of Aragon, reminds James II that when he visited him at Lerida early in 1305 he had given him information about the Order of the Temple. He says nothing, however, of how he came by this information – for which point one must refer to the texts of the chronicles just mentioned. Apparently, the king of Aragon had not believed him, but told him that if he managed to prove his allegations the king would give him money and secure him an income. In fact, the matter having assumed the importance we know, Esquieu was now writing to ask the king to keep his promise.[14]

So Esquieu de Floyran went to make his revelations to the king of France, who did as he always did – listened to him without saying a word, and probably without giving him too much credence, then turned the matter over to Guillaume de Nogaret to see what was going on.[15] Next, the king notified Clement V, whom he had met at the time of the coronation ceremonies in Lyon in November 1305. Wasting no time, Guillaume de Nogaret began his inquiries: he interrogated Templars who had broken with or had been expelled from the Order; he introduced 'moles' in order to build up a dossier, though probably without too clear an idea of its purpose beyond being certain that it would prove useful at some future date.

Thus the Templar affair was launched. At this stage, however, it was conceived by the king and his entourage more as a means of putting pressure on the pope and the Church than as an end in itself. The obsession of the king and his

chief councillors, in particular Guillaume de Nogaret since he was directly implicated in the Anagni assassination attempt, was to wipe out the repercussions of
that hideous crime and obtain the damnation of Pope Boniface VIII's memory.
In 1305, the abolition of the Temple was probably not yet on the agenda.

According to the rather fanciful rumours being spread at the time, the Templars were given to dubious and immoral practices: the denial of Christ, spitting
on the Cross, obscene kisses, sodomy, secrecy of the Chapters, lack of a spirit
of charity, etc. Not until full judicial procedure was under way would the accusations, already set out in the king's order of arrest, be clearly formalised. The
Bull *Faciens misericordiam* of 12 August 1308 lays out a double list: one of 87 or
88 accusations brought against individuals; the other of 127 accusations brought
against the Order.[16] It should be borne in mind that these lists contained both
traditional accusations – the problem of alms and charity, secrecy of the Chapters, wealth, arrogance, etc. – and new ones that were far more serious because
they touched on the faith (denial, spitting on the Cross, absence of consecration
in the Mass), or behaviour (obscene kissing, sodomy, idolatry).

However – and I return for a moment to the testimony of Ponsard de Gisy
– the investigators would focus on the matter of the ritual of entry to the Order.
Not a single interrogation would take place without this being brought up,
generally, at the very outset, just after details of identification had been stated.
Ponsard de Gisy's evidence, which seems plausible even if not totally accurate in
its detail, clearly shows that the Templars appeared vulnerable and embarrassed
when this point was raised. For the accusers, therefore, it was only reasonable to
concentrate their questions on the entry ritual, a technique they would apply to
Jacques de Molay, among others.

During 1306–7, when the idea of taking some resolution on the subject of
the Temple was gaining strength with both the king and the pope, the attitude
and actions of Jacques de Molay, who was present in France, would obviously
carry particular weight. His relations with the king, the pope and the Templars
of the kingdom, though not a determining factor, would influence the course
of events.

Even if he had wanted to, in 1292 the king of France had not been able to
exert much influence in the procedure that had led to the election of Jacques
de Molay.[17] The latter had probably had the opportunity to meet the king at the
time of his first journey, notably when he had come to Paris to preside over the
Order's Chapters, but there is no proof. And although all manner of things may

be imagined, nor is there evidence of grounds for conflict between the king and the Temple at the time, or between the king and the Grand Master, except on two points:

The relations between France and Aragon, over Sicily. Yet the situation was calmer in this area now than it had been, since James II of Aragon and the king of Sicily (southern Italy), Charles II of Anjou, were drawing closer. This would eventually lead to an alliance made in 1298 against Frederick of Sicily, James II's brother[18] – that conflict only ending with the peace of Caltabellota in 1302.

The question of the merging of the Orders as desired by Pope Nicholas IV in 1291. Given Molay's firm opposition to such a union, it may be thought that had the question been broached with the king there would have been disagreement. But in 1295–6 the king of France's position had not been clear cut; in any case, under the papacy of Boniface VIII the matter was no longer on the agenda. Around 1300, however, as a result of the confrontation between the king of France and Pope Boniface VIII,[19] major conflict arose between the Temple and the king. The conflict spiralled, leading to the event already mentioned, 'the Agnani assassination attempt' of 7 September 1303. The adversaries of Boniface VIII, the two Cardinals Colonna, joined by Guillaume de Nogaret, took the pope prisoner in his own palace at Agnani and threatened him. Guillaume de Nogaret's mission was to summon the sovereign pontiff to appear before a council ordered by the king of France to answer to various crimes, including heresy. The people of Agnani rebelled and forced the aggressors to give him up, but the pope died the following month. Naturally, the king and his councillors orchestrated an intensive propaganda campaign in France to denigrate the pope and support their cause. An assembly of estates (the first forerunner of the Estates General) met in Paris in 1302. The religious Orders, bishops and clergy in general had to make their choice: loyalty to the head of the Church or to the king. The Abbot of Cîteaux, Jean de Pontoise, remained loyal to the pope; but he was the exception, paying for it with a short term of imprisonment.[20]

The Templars' attitude was ambiguous. The Grand Master and governing body of the Order in Cyprus do not appear to have intervened. We know that Molay maintained good relations with Boniface VIII; and 1302 was still in the period of the Mongol alliance. The Temple needed the pope. On the other hand, the Templars in France had to choose. Like all the bishops and heads of Christian Orders, the Visitor of France, Hugues de Pairaud, was summoned to Rome by the pope in 1302. The king of France forbade the bishops and other clergy in his realm to go; many disobeyed the king, but not Hugues de Pairaud, who did not travel to Rome, delegating his nephew, Hugues de Chalon, to go in his stead. At the time of the meeting of the estates, Pairaud had upheld the royal position, although with minimal enthusiasm. In the minutes of the sessions held at the Louvre on 13 and 14 June 1303, during which Guillaume de Plaisians read the indictments against Boniface VIII, he was among the prelates, abbots and heads of Order who supported the request for a council to be convened to try the pope. But as Jean Coste, in charge of editing these texts, points out, the prelates preserved the pope's canonical title (unlike Guillaume de Plaisians), letting it be understood that their hand had been forced and they would not prejudge his guilt (again contrary to Plaisians); in short, they refused to behave like accusers.[21]

There was a kind of division of duties between the Grand Master and the Visitor of France which could not have gone unnoticed by the king and his councillors. Was it deliberate? At all events, as long as Molay was in Cyprus, as long as the means of achieving the crusade and the merging of the Orders were under discussion, even at a distance, nothing could happen; but once the Grand Master was in France, the problems that existed between the Temple and the king could no longer be concealed.

These were, of course, the ongoing problems of the crusade and the merging the Orders. Other new ones, however, were sprung on Molay the moment he set foot in France; chief among these was the dispute between the king and the Grand Master concerning the fate of Jean du Tour, Treasurer of the Temple in Paris and Treasurer to the king. The chronicle of the Templar of Tyre gives a brief, lively, if not wholly trustworthy account:

> This Brother Jacques de Molay, Master of the Temple, when he was over the sea (in the West), behaved in a very miserly way towards the pope and the cardinals, for he was an unreasonably mean man, but nevertheless the pope received him with great kindness, and the Master went to Paris and about in France, and asked the Treasurer of the Temple for his accounts; he found that the Treasurer had lent the king a great amount of money, said to be iiii^{c}m [400,000] gold florins, but I do not know if there were fewer. And the Master was very angry with the Treasurer, and stripped him of his habit. And drove him out of the religion [the Order], so he went to the king of France who was very angry that, through his fault, the man had been defrocked, and he sent a high-ranking man of France to

the Master, asking that for his sake he should restore the man's habit, and saying that he would willingly repay what he owed the house. The said Master would do nothing, and replied otherwise than he should have to the request of such a man as the king of France. And when the king saw that he would do nothing about his request, he wrote to the pope asking him to order the Master to return the Templar mantle to the Treasurer, and the said Treasurer in person carried the said letter from the pope to the Master of the Temple, who did nothing in response to the pope, and it is reported that the Master threw the said letter into the fire, which was burning in the hearth.[22]

The king had been annoyed. The pope had asked the Master to come back from Paris to Poitiers and enjoined him to give him a copy of the Rule. The Templar of Tyre connects this episode directly with the proceedings taken against the Temple. This account contains inaccuracies and a few improbabilities but, once again, probably also more than a grain of truth.

Jean du Tour (or de Tour) – here he is Jean du Tour the Younger – entered the Temple in 1275; he was received at Maurepas[23] by his uncle, Jean du Tour the Elder, Treasurer of the Temple of Paris from 1271 until his death in 1281. Jean du Tour the Younger became Treasurer in his turn in 1287 or 1289, having succeeded someone named Humbert in the post. He would thus appear to have lent the enormous sum of 400,000 florins to the king without informing the Master. The Temple's statutes were formal on this point: no loan of this size could be granted without the Master's authorisation. Having been informed of this misdemeanour, in accordance with the Templar Rule, the Grand Master expelled the culprit from the Order.[24] Note that the penalty inflicted was the loss of the habit – less serious than the loss of the house, in that it was a 'temporary' sanction, and could therefore be lifted. If this is really what happened, there is no reason to reproach the Grand Master.

Before going any further, however, let us pick out the structure of the Templar of Tyre's account: Jacques de Molay first sees the pope and appears petty or miserly; then he goes to Paris, checks his Treasurer's accounts and notices the illegal loan made to the king; he loses his temper with Jean du Tour and expels him. The king intercedes on his behalf (which is understandable, as Jean du Tour is also 'his' Treasurer), and the Grand Master responds improperly. Then Jean du Tour, whose cause has been upheld by the king, obtains a letter from the pope reinstating him in the Order. He takes it to Molay, who is still in Paris, and *he* throws it on the fire. So Jacques de Molay is guilty of meanness or miserliness towards the pope, violent rage against his Treasurer, unacceptable language regarding the king (written, or possibly verbal lapses) and lastly a gesture of rage insulting to the pontiff. By his actions, he alienates the pope, the king and an important personage in his Order. That seems a great deal for one man alone.

If this story is accepted, it must also be stated that Molay finished by giving in: Jean du Tour, whom he had expelled from the Order, must finally have been allowed to re-enter it, as he was arrested as a Templar in the great swoop of 13 October 1307, and was questioned by the Inquisitor of France on 26 October, two days after Jacques de Molay.[25] After saving a Templar because he was his Treasurer, Philip the Fair disowned his Treasurer without a qualm because he was a Templar.

Although he is generally trustworthy, the Templar of Tyre's account of this incident raises a problem. On the one hand, while a great admirer of Guillaume de Beaujeu, he did not know Jacques de Molay;[26] and on the other, his information about matters in the West, with the exception of the Italian maritime republics, is less than accurate.

It is also curious that western historical sources, notably those close to the Courts of Paris and Rome, make no mention of this episode. Nothing in the *Grandes Chroniques de France*, nothing in the 'Continuation of Guillaume de Nangis', nothing in Jean de Saint-Victor or in the *Lives of Clement V* collected by Baluze. However, there is a letter written by an Aragonese present at the Court of Poitiers during the weeks following the Templars' arrest which partially corroborates what the Templar of Tyre says. Probably someone close to the Templars, writing to the Commander of Ascò (in Catalonia) in November 1307, he gives an account of the arrest of the Templars in France, and the meetings that followed in Poitiers. He reports dialogues – possibly fictitious – between the pope and the Templars present in Poitiers, and between Jacques de Molay and Templars who were his fellow prisoners. To quote: 'And further know, according to what an equerry who has come from Paris told me, that the lord Master had strong and rough words with the king of France'; again, in his prison, the king having come to see him, 'they had very strong and harsh words'.[27]

As it is so often the case, the problem is chronological – when did this happen? The Aragonese evidence seems to place the events at the time of the arrests and in the days that followed. It has nothing to do with the Treasurer's troubles; all the information he gives is connected with the arrest, not with the circumstances that might have preceded it and could have been its cause. But is it likely that Philip the Fair would have met Jacques de Molay in his prison so soon after having him arrested? Of course not, but if that had been the case, a towering rage on Molay's part would have been very plausible.

The description by the Templar of Tyre places the incident earlier, almost turning it into the trigger that set off the infernal machinery which would crush the Temple. He reports a meeting with the pope in Poitiers (first incident), then a journey to Paris (anger at the Treasurer and clash with the king), and finally a return to Poitiers to meet the pope. This chronology could match the Grand Master's movements in May–August 1307, which some texts enable us to retrace.

The king of France arrived in Poitiers on 21 April 1307, and appears to have left again after 15 May. His interviews with the pope fundamentally concerned the indictment to blacken the memory of Boniface VIII, which he wanted to see set in motion quickly (although Clement V would not hear of it); he also mentioned the matter of the Templars.[28] On 14 May, Jean Bourgogne, King James II's procurator at the Court of Rome, wrote to his master giving him various items of information. He noted the presence of the king in Poitiers, saying that he knew little of what was said, except that Philip the Fair had asked, on the one hand, for the canonisation of Pietro di Morrone – in other words, Pope Celestine V, who had renounced the tiara and been succeeded by Boniface VIII – and on the other, for condemnation of the latter. Lastly, he indicated that 'the Master of the Knighthood of the Temple is to arrive here soon; he is expected, as well as the Master of the Hospital of Saint John of Jerusalem, and according to insistent rumour, the pope must deal with the merging of the two Orders, and intends to do so with them'.[29]

The king seems to have departed before the arrival of the two Masters; but he left Guillaume de Nogaret and Guillaume de Plaisians with the pope, their mission being to obtain the condemnation of Boniface VIII. It is therefore likely that, if Jacques de Molay and Foulques de Villaret had met up in Poitiers, they would have had the chance also to meet with the king's two councillors.[30] A passage in Molay's testimony before the papal commission in session in Paris, on 26 November 1309, reveals that the Grand Master knew Guillaume de Plaisians: 'The said lord Guillaume having spoken aside to the Master he liked and had liked, so he said, because they were knights …'[31] Perhaps that 'liking' or 'friendship' harked back to the stay in Poitiers? In any event, Jacques de Molay was still there on 9 June, staying in the town's hospital.[32] He then went to Paris to hold the general Chapter on 24 June 1307.[33] A letter from Molay to James II of Aragon proves that he was once more in Poitiers on 4 August,[34] and still there from 8 to 11 September.[35] He finally left again for Paris to attend the funeral on 12 October of Catherine of Valois, in which he was a member of the ranks of honour.

Molay could therefore have met the king before April, in late June or in July, or yet again, in early October. The incident reported by the Templar of Tyre could have occurred in June–July or, bearing in mind that a fire was burning in the hearth, in the winter of 1307 – February–March for instance, a hypothetical milestone in the chronological void of the first four months of 1307.

This date would have the advantage of leaving enough time for the incident – if it happened – to be either settled or forgotten when Jacques de Molay acted as pall-bearer at the funeral of Catherine of Valois, or even in June, when he opened up to the king about certain accusations that had been levelled at the Temple.

The question still remains: is it likely that, after such an incident, Jacques de Molay could go on to hold so great a position of honour at the Court? Possibly – Philip the Fair did not want to arouse the Master's suspicions when he was going to have him arrested the next day.

This story about the Treasurer slips through the fingers a little too often, however, to be credible. So, how should this single testimony be treated (the Aragonese letter of November 1307 ultimately having hardly anything to do with the episode)? Rejected outright? or accepted without further examination? That was the path chosen by Barbara Frale, who relies on this text to suggest an appealing sequence of events and an ingenious explanation.[36]

According to her, Jean du Tour must have been forced to promise that loan to the king, and thus to commit the irregularity in breach of his Order's Rule, probably when Philip the Fair had had to confront a riot when he was at the Temple in June 1306. The riot had been provoked by the (deflationary) monetary change the government had just introduced (Philip the Fair used and abused these monetary changes in order to get his hands on financial resources which he could not raise by taxation). An angry mob, knowing that the king was at the Temple (where the royal Treasury was kept), blocked its exits to prevent food entering.[37] Jean du Tour could not have Jacques de Molay's authorisation since he was in Cyprus and to ask for it would have taken too long. The king's need for money was immediate. Hugues de Pairaud, Visitor of France, who was then possibly in Paris could, if need be, substitute for the Master and grant the authorisation, thereby covering the Treasurer. Regarding this, we should recall Boniface VIII's letter of 8 February 1297 to Hugues de Pairaud, in which the pope asks for the sums owed by the Temple for aid to the Holy Land to be paid to the papal collectors, adding that, at his request, Jacques de Molay 'has informed us that he had sent you, in his place, to this side of the sea'.[38] The matter of the loan to the king would not have been concluded until February 1307, and in support of her theory Barbara Frale refers to an exchange of correspondence between the pope and the king mentioning a 'mysterious affair' which was, in her view, the affair of the loan.[39] This was the matter which Jacques de Molay uncovered on his arrival in France, when he checked the Treasurer's accounts.

But here again, a chronological problem arises, and it is not clear when these outbursts of anger from the Grand Master took place. He arrived in France in December 1306, so if the 'mysterious affair' ended in February, it was concluded without him, even though he was in France at the time and could have been consulted. So was he knowingly kept out of the picture? That would certainly be a good reason for him to become angry. But at what point?

There are too many 'probablys' and 'very likelys' in this line of reasoning, based not on proof but on a stacking-up of theories.[40] Certain statements in the Templar of Tyre's account arouse scepticism. The sum lent to the king is so large that the chronicler himself is careful to express doubt – indeed, it probably exceeded the financial capacities of the Temple. Jean du Tour was also a royal official and, as such, managed the royal Treasury, as distinct from the Temple of Paris Treasury. The sum lent to the king could only have been taken from funds belonging to the Temple;[41] indeed, he would hardly have been borrowing from his own Treasury, as it was empty, hence having to borrow.

I do not dismiss the theory that a financial incident took place involving the Temple and the king, but certainly not for the reasons given above on the strength of that one text by the Templar of Tyre. The analyses carried out by R. Kaeuper and S. Menache of the king's fiscal policy and the management problems of his Treasury invite us to seek the financial causes of the attack on the Temple[42] in another direction, more political and not solely technical. More generally, political reasons rather than personalities were at the root of the affair;

and among those political questions, Jacques de Molay's refusal to envisage the merging of the Orders seems to have counted for more.

Finally, if Jean du Tour was indebted to the pope for his reinstatement, it seems curious that he would present Clement V's letter to Molay himself. Such a letter should have been entrusted to an envoy of the pope, not to the man who stood to benefit from such papal benevolence. I also find it hard to believe that Jacques de Molay, a vastly experienced man who, in other places and circumstances, had shown proven level-headedness and a sense of diplomacy, should have let anger get the better of him to this extent. But I may be wrong.

In Barbara Frale's line of reasoning, and more generally in the genesis of the Templars' trial as she reconstructs it, Hugues de Pairaud plays a central role, perhaps even more important than that of Jacques de Molay. I tend to share this viewpoint, although I do not place the differences between the two men as early as she does, in 1292, and cannot find the same causes for the rift which seems to have developed between the Grand Master and the Visitor of France.

At the time of Molay's election, Hugues de Pairaud was as yet an insignificant member of the Order, a Commander of a house, albeit the nephew of a powerful, but dead, uncle. It was Jacques de Molay who made him Master of the province of France, then Visitor General of the Order in France and England. Holding the office of Master of a province together with that of Visitor was possible; Berenguer de Cardona was both Master of Aragon and Visitor of Spain. But for a clearer understanding of what happened in 1306–7, we need to know the details of Hugues de Pairaud's career in these two offices.

He is recorded as Master of France in 1293,[43] then in 1295 and 1300,[44] but not beyond. He is mentioned as Visitor of France in 1294 at the earliest;[45] he is formally attested as Visitor of England on 25 May 1294.[46] From then on, he is mentioned as Visitor of France some fifteen times until 1307. He held the offices of both Master of France and Visitor until 1300. A Cypriot witness at the trial, Brother Pons du Puits, from Laon, had been received then at Belleville[47] by *Bodo de Peraseo* (Hugues de Pairaud) 'at that time a Commander and Visitor of France'.[48] By 14 September 1300, he was only Visitor,[49] at which date Gérard de Villiers appears as Commander or Master of France. Hugues de Pairaud therefore no longer holds office except as Visitor of France and probably of England. He is still presented as Visitor of France by Gérard de Causse, who witnessed him receive Jehan de Prunay at the Temple in Paris – in the king's presence – about six months before the Templars' arrest.[50] Similarly, he is again found bearing this title at Candlemas 1307 in Paris, for the reception of Jean de Basemont.[51] This date would correspond to the Chapter held the same day and recorded in another deposition.

A letter from Pierre de Castillon, in the Archives of the Crown of Aragon, already mentioned in connection with the appointment of Templar Commanders and provincial Masters, provides some singular information. It bears no date, but was written after 27 December, certainly by January, at Torres de Segre, near Miravet. Pierre de Castillon had spent Christmas at Miravet, at the invitation of the Commander, Berenguer de Saint-Just; he had then returned to Torres, after 27 December, probably at the beginning of January. This letter, addressed to Pierre de Saint-Just, then Commander of Alfambra, informs him that a messenger from the Master overseas, the Castilian Domingo, who had first come to Gardeny (on 23 December), then to Miravet (on 27 December), had brought news of the Grand Master and reported some changes in personnel at the Templars' provincial and central administration. According to his informant, Hugues de Pairaud had been removed from the post of Visitor of France, but had been given the job of managing the provinces of France and Provence. Furthermore, Raymond (in fact, Simon) de Quincy, known as 'Le Chaperon', had been appointed to Puglia. Another item of news: Berenguer de Saint-Just, Commander of Miravet, has become Visitor of Spain. This same messenger also reported that the other dignitaries in Cyprus, the Grand Commander Raimbaud de Caron, Marshal Aymon d'Oiselay, the Draper Geoffroy de Charney, the Turcopolier Bertrand de Gordo and the sub-Marshal remained in office.[52]

As I mentioned in chapter 7, Pierre de Castillon's letter must have been written either just after Christmas 1304, or in early January 1305. I will not repeat the sound reasons put forward by H. Finke, who published the text, and A. Forey, but if this date is correct, the changes Molay seems to have made are not easy to interpret or understand, even if they really did take place. There is a problem with regard to Provence, as since 1300 – and without any subsequent interruption – Bernard de Roche had been the Master, [53] and still was on 9 June 1307, when he undersigned a letter from Jacques de Molay written in Poitiers. I will return to this. On the other hand, the appointment of Raymond de Quincy to Puglia matches the facts, except that it should be Simon, not Raymond. This was the same Simon de Quincy who presided at Marseille over the reception of the brothers whom he subsequently took with him to Cyprus. His tombstone may have been found at Barletta: 'Here lies Simon de Quincy, Master of the houses of the Temple in the kingdom of Sicily, who died on Wednesday 7 June 1307. May his soul live in Christ.'[54]

Had the two Visitors in the West been removed from office? Spain, first. Berenguer de Cardona had been confirmed in this post in 1300. We know from Jacques de Molay himself that it was not a permanent post; so it could have been the end of a four-year term and Cardona's replacement would have been perfectly possible. Yet Berenguer de Cardona remained Master of Aragon. Also, Molay's letter of 1300 confirming Cardona in the post of Visitor was enclosed with a letter from the latter dated 10 March 1306, in which he gives himself the titles Master of Aragon and Visitor of Spain. It is therefore almost certain that Cardona was never removed from his office of Visitor.

As for Hugues de Pairaud, the text of Pierre de Castillon's letter is unequivocal (he speaks of dismissal). Nevertheless, having lost the office of Visitor, Pairaud was to be given that of Master of France, in addition to being acting Master of Provence. It is therefore difficult to see the revocation of the post of Visitor as a form of punishment.

Should it be viewed as a gesture towards the king of France, since Hugues de Pairaud was so closely connected with him? His appointment would thus have been made to the detriment of Gérard de Villiers. But these decisions do not seem to have had any outcome; or else they were swiftly deferred. In the years that followed up to February 1307, Hugues de Pairaud bore the title of Visitor; similarly, there is a final mention of Gérard de Villiers as Master of France at a reception performed in mid-February at La Ferté-Gaucher,[55] although he is also once described as Visitor of France.[56]

Nevertheless, Jacques de Molay's letter written at Poitiers on 9 June 1307 is along the lines of these changes at the summit of the Order: Hugues de Pairaud undersigns it as Master, no longer Visitor of France; and beside him as signatory to the deed we find Bernard de Roche, Master of Provence.[57] The latter, who had been Commander of Vaour, had deputised for Hugues de Pairaud as Visitor on 13 June 1303.[58] The twenty-seven Templars held in the house of Jean Roscelli in Paris had a schedule sent to the inquiry officers in which they stated that they wished to meet the Master of the Order and Hugues de Pairaud, Commander of France.[59] But in the rest of the trial, notably in 1314 at the time of the final judgement concerning the Templar dignitaries, Hugues de Pairaud would be described in all the texts as Visitor of France.

It is therefore difficult to regard this revocation-cum-exchange of office as a sanction taken by the Grand Master against Hugues de Pairaud. It is also hard to see whether or not it was effective; it could almost be said to be the exact opposite. Hugues de Pairaud maintained excellent relations with the king throughout 1302–7. As we saw, he did not respond to the pope's summons in 1302. On 13 June 1303, in order to accomplish a mission in the king's service, he named Bernard de Roche as his lieutenant. On 10 August in the same year, the king granted Hugues and his people protection and privileges as a reward for helping him on various occasions, 'especially against Boniface'.[60] On 27 May 1305, a royal agent was paid 'for his expenses for travelling to the Dauphiné on the king's mandate in the company of Brother Hugues de Pairaud, Visitor of the houses of the Knighthood of the Temple ...'[61] This instance shows that, Visitor or not, Master of France or not, his title had virtually no influence on the quality of his relations with the king of France.

So, although there were probably some differences between Pairaud and Molay, they were not deep, certainly not sufficient to bring about a violent opposition between the two men. After all, it was in the interests of Jacques de Molay and the Temple to have a brother who was in favour with the Court of France. But obviously, in the event of open conflict between the Grand Master and the king (for example, on the matter of merging the Orders), or, if conflict existed – although I do not think this likely – on the affair of the Treasurer's loan, the king could make use of Hugues de Pairaud as mediator, or even baldly manipulate him against the Grand Master.

Pairaud was in Poitiers with Molay on 9 June; together they attended the general Chapter in Paris on 24 June. It is hard to imagine that they would have behaved secretively towards each other. If not jointly, at least in full awareness of what the other was doing, both interceded as much with the pope to ask for a commission of inquiry as with the king to discuss the rumours weighing on the Order.

Jacques de Molay seems to have spent the summer of 1307 in Poitiers. The conversations he had had in May and June had made him feel the situation was serious, but not desperate, provided he took the initiative. For that reason he made the first move, and spoke to the king about the problem of absolution by lay clergy which was sometimes practised within the Order. Later, once the Temple affair has been launched, Guillaume de Plaisians tells us that the interview did take place. In the speech he delivered on 29 May 1308 before the pope in Poitiers (a speech that is known to us from the report made by Jean Bourgogne to his master, the king of Aragon, the following day, [62] and from a document in the National Archives of Paris[63]) Guillaume de Plaisians says that the Master came before the king and

> in the presence of some of his council, wishing to excuse himself and his Order, uttered words which, if premeditated, smacked openly of heresy. He then explained several of the statutes of his Order and, among other things, that sometimes the brethren, for fear of the penance that might be imposed upon them, did not wish to confess their sins and that he himself, in Chapter, absolved them, although he was a layman and was not entitled to do so.[64]

It was for this reason that he had quite plainly and openly asked the pope to initiate an inquiry. This would have entailed interrogations, the public revelation of abuses, misdeeds, awkward situations here and there. Jacques de Molay could not have been unaware that the matter of the ritual involved in entry to the Order would be brought up, and the peculiarities of these rites made public. The Grand Master was taking risks; and by accepting his request and taking responsibility for setting up an inquiry, so was the papacy. It all happened as if Jacques de Molay, fully confident that he was within his rights though doubtless not overlooking the negative effects of the revelations that might be made, was sure that his Order was not at risk, that the rumours would die down and the accusations run out of steam. Only instances of individual shortcomings would be left, and the Order could say that he was the first to punish them. After all, Guillaume de Nogaret had built up his dossier by questioning renegade Templars, who had been expelled from the Order for their misdemeanours.

It might seem that the Grand Master showed little perspicacity, that his attitude bordered on recklessness; but neither he nor the pope could have imagined the extreme turn that the royal offensive would take. It matters little whether, on the king's part, everything was already prepared or whether the decision had been taken only on reading the papal letter ordering an inquiry; it would have been in the interests of both the Temple and the pope to act quickly. At that point, Jacques de Molay no longer had time to play with; the pope, yes, but he would not make use of that trump card.

On 24 August 1307, Clement V wrote to the king to announce the opening of an inquiry into the Temple, specifying that it had been requested by the Templars themselves:

> As the Master of the Temple and several Commanders, both from among your subjects and from foreign countries, have been informed of the slanders of which Your Majesty has also been informed, they came to throw themselves at my feet on several occasions and insistently implore me to inquire into the deeds with which they have been unjustly charged, so that they may be given penance if they are found guilty, or be discharged from this accusation if they are innocent.[65]

The Templar of Tyre, recounting the incident of the Treasurer, also writes that the pope had asked Jacques de Molay to let him have a copy of the Rule. With this inquiry in prospect, perhaps the pope actually made the request;[66] for, contrary to what is often stated in order to justify Philip the Fair's actions, the pope intended to tackle the fundamental problems and reform the Order should it prove necessary. He cannot be blamed for bad grace on the pretext that, in this same letter of 24 August, he also told the king that the inquiry could not really commence until the second fortnight in October. As he explained, he was seriously ill, and on 1 September must begin medical treatment that would oblige him to keep away from business matters; he also asked the king not to send him ambassadors before 15 October.

The king and his councillors could have waited and left the Church to conduct a serious inquiry which, without prejudging the culpability of the Templar Order, would not have left it unscathed, that is, they could have opted for the process of law. However, citing the gravity of events and convinced of the Templars' heresy, the king chose instead to act on his own authority, scorning the rights of the Church, and thus of the pope and the law, even though he used the Inquisitor of France as cover (the Inquisition was an instrument of the Church, that is, the pope, not the king). The Chancellor, Pierre Aycelin, Archbishop of Narbonne, disagreeing with the king's bid for power, resigned on 26 September, only to be replaced by Guillaume de Nogaret ...

Returning to the chronology: on 14 September, a royal letter denouncing the crimes of the Templars ('a bitter deplorable thing ... a detestable crime, an execrable infamy, an abominable act, a hideous scandal, a completely inhuman thing ...') and ordering their arrest, was addressed to all the bailiffs and seneschals in the kingdom, enjoining them to keep it secret until the day had been fixed for its execution. On 22 September, the Inquisitor of France sent instructions to his inquisitors throughout the realm. Discreetly, the royal agents kept a watch on the Templars, learned about their capacity for resistance and made inquiries into what they owned. On 13 October, they went into action.

Shortly before, in Poitiers in early October, Hugues de Pairaud seems to have confided in the pope, revealing the strange practices of the Order at the time he was received.[67] It was somewhat late for a man who, for twenty or thirty years, and more than many others, given the offices he had held in the Order, had practised this 'secret' ritual without any qualms. The pope had just written to the king on 26 September, asking him to provide what evidence he possessed to charge the Templars.

Meanwhile, the king diverted attention from his activities. On 12 October, the eve of his arrest, Jacques de Molay came to Paris to attend the funeral of Catherine de Courtenay, heiress to the throne of the Latin Empire of Constantinople and wife of the king's brother Charles of Valois, as a guest of honour.

Later, during the trial, Gérard de Causse, who had been present at a reception in the Temple of Paris about six months prior to the Templars' arrest – a reception where nothing untoward had occurred – when asked if he had had any suspicions about what was being prepared against the Order, had replied that he had had none.[68] Some, however, such as Gérard de Villiers *did* – and fled.

The Grand Master, however, had certainly not realised the likely violence of the imminent attack; and if he harboured any suspicions, he did not show them. But by asking for an inquiry, he had chosen not to shy away; and at that point in time, at least, he did not do so.

10

1309

ESCAPING THE TRAP

The aim of this chapter is to clarify Jacques de Molay's attitude in the course of the proceedings brought against the Order and its members, and to determine to what extent he was responsible in the development of the procedure and its conclusion – the dissolution of the Temple. It is therefore not a matter of presenting the history of the trial but, for a clearer understanding of my comments, it is necessary to mention its broad chronological outlines and gain a glimpse of the procedures that were followed.[1]

On 24 August 1307, Clement V wrote to the king of France announcing his decision to order an inquiry into the accusations levelled at the Order. However, sick and undergoing treatment, he specified that the process would not begin before October. Philip the Fair made the next move, less because he thought the pope was procrastinating and that the inquiry would become bogged down than because he had already made up his mind: he had decided to 'kill' the Temple by any means available. On 14 September, the king sent a letter to all his bailiffs and seneschals which was both a bill of indictment against the Templars and a command to arrest them; the king's officers had to keep the secret until the allocated day. It was therefore initiated by the king and his council, but executed by the royal agents. The intervention of the Inquisitor of France, Guillaume de France, who asked for the help of the secular arm, was merely for form's sake; the instructions he sent to the inquisitors on 22 September were illegal, for he should not have acted without the pope's direction. The inquiry ordered by the latter was to be conducted by bishops, not inquisitors; Clement V was not prejudging the Templars' heresy.

While waiting to go into action, the royal agents were to keep a discreet watch on the Templars in their district. A massive swoop in the small hours

Templar church, south view, (seventeenth-century engraving), Commission du Vieux-Paris.

of 13 October resulted in the arrest of nearly all the Templars in the kingdom, although some managed to flee, including the former Master of France, Gérard de Villiers, with a group of forty brothers and the Master of Auvergne, who went across to England.[2] On 16 October, the king informed the western rulers of the reasons for his action; he also asked them to do likewise in their states, but they refused. When he was informed, the pope was appalled.

The initial phase of the proceedings commenced, with interrogations conducted throughout France by the inquisitors of accused Templars who had previously been handled by the royal agents, who were in any case never very far away, having been given the task of guarding the Templars. These interrogations took place in the last fortnight of October and in November. In Paris, starting on 19 October, 138 Templars were questioned, including the principal dignitaries of the Order who were in France. Philip the Fair triumphed; the Templars confessed and admitted to some of the accusations brought against them and their Order, including Jacques de Molay and the dignitaries. That was enough to justify both the king's action and its rapidity. According to the king, the Templars' heresy was manifest; nearly all of them admitted the scabrous practices of the ceremony of entry to the Order: the repudiation of Christ, spitting on the Cross, obscene kisses, the advice to commit sodomy among the brothers 'should the blood become overheated'. Added to that were accusations about the sacraments, forgotten in the celebration of Mass, the absolution of sins by laymen, the secrecy of Chapters, and even idolatry (indeed, the Templars were accused of worshipping an idol in the shape of a head with four paws, or a cat – black, obviously).

The admissions of Jacques de Molay, Hugues de Pairaud and Raimbaud de Caron enabled the king of France to relaunch his offensive, this time involving neighbouring sovereigns and the pope. Gradually, the kings of England, Aragon and Castile were to change their attitudes towards 'their' Templars, and the pope's intervention would assist them. On 22 November 1307, Clement V issued the Bull *Pastoralis praeminentiae*, by which he ordered the arrest of the Templars throughout Christendom. The pope was anxious to regain the initiative and bring back to the Church an affair that he saw as entirely its own (the Temple was under the pope's direct jurisdiction). He wanted the guarding of the incarcerated Templars to be entrusted to the Church, as well as the safekeeping of their possessions, which had been seized. Two cardinals were sent to Paris in December to hear Jacques de Molay and the other dignitaries. By the end of

1307 and early 1308, all the Templars in Christendom had been arrested. They put up a resistance in Aragon, however, and also in Cyprus, but were forced to surrender on 1 June 1308.

Then a kind of Indian-wrestling match began between the pope and the royal camp. Guillaume de Nogaret and Guillaume de Plaisians turned everything they could to good account: consultation with the University of Paris on the legality of the action taken by the king (the reply was disappointing); incendiary libels to discredit the Templars and Molay;[3] convocation of the Estates General at Tours to uphold the king's action. Lastly, the king came in person to Poitiers, and Guillaume de Plaisians, in two speeches of tortured rhetoric, on 29 May and 14 June 1308, proffered scarcely veiled threats against the pope.[4] This situation between king and pope dragged on throughout the first half of 1308. At the pope's urging, however, the king agreed that a certain number of Templars imprisoned in Paris, including the Master and the chief dignitaries, could be brought to Poitiers to be interrogated there by the pope and cardinals. In fact, the five dignitaries, among them Jacques de Molay, would not go to Poitiers, but the admissions of the seventy-two Templars hand-picked by the king's agents and presented at Poitiers, swayed the pope, who ended by yielding. Only partly, though, for in his Bull *Faciens misericordiam* of 12 August 1308, he begins a procedure that would be acceptable to the king but leave the business of settling the affair to the Church.

By specifying the accusations brought against the Temple, the Bull set in motion a dual procedure, one against each of the Templars individually, the other against the whole Order. The investigation of the first, which rested on a catalogue of 87 or 88 accusations, was entrusted to diocesan commissions; a council of the province would subsequently pass judgment. The second was handed to papal commissions set up in each state (there would be several in Italy), who would work on the basis of a catalogue of 127 articles.[5] Based on the work they carried out, a general council was summoned in the autumn of 1310 at Vienne (Dauphiné) in order to decide on the fate of the Order, although it was later postponed for a year. Lastly, the pope reserved for himself the judging of five of the Order's dignitaries imprisoned in Paris: Jacques de Molay, Hugues de Pairaud, Geoffroy de Charney, Geoffroy de Gonneville and Raimbaud de Caron. The Temple's possessions, under royal confiscation since the start of the affair, were to be put to the service of the crusade; the pope wanted them to be handed over to the Order of the Hospital, but at that date the king of France opposed it.

The diocesan commissions were starting to be put in place in the spring of 1309, whereas the papal commissions were not ready until the end of 1309, or even 1310–11. The Paris commission met for the first time in November 1309 (Molay appeared before it on 26 and 28 November), but most of them did not get down to serious work until February 1310. Neither the Church nor the kings showed much enthusiasm for assembling them. Were they buying time, or fearful of what might come to light?

We have the interrogations of some of the diocesan commissions – Nîmes, Auvergne, Lerida, Navarre, Elne, London and Ravenna.[6] Generally speaking, the work reached its term, the outcome of which was a provincial council which absolved and reconciled with the Church those Templars who confessed the error of their ways while the rest were sentenced to prison. Such was the case for the provinces of Sens and Reims, where certain Templars were condemned as relapsed because, when they came before the papal commission judging the Order, they retracted the admissions they had made earlier before the diocesan commission.[7]

The workings of the papal commissions proved more erratic. Those of London, Rome and Cyprus are known,[8] but those of Paris are the most important, precise and detailed.[9] Here, the papal commissioners did their work with the utmost care, and with a clear concern for impartiality. The commission had launched an appeal throughout the kingdom for Templars who wished to testify about the Order and defend it to come to Paris. The movement started slowly but, in February 1310, a veritable groundswell brought nearly six hundred brothers to the capital, the majority wishing to defend the Order and clear it of the accusations levelled against it. The Templars gave four of them, chosen as procurators, the task of representing them: two priests, including Pierre de Bologna, former procurator of the Order at the Court of Rome, and two knights. The latter would have liked to have kept in the background behind the Grand Master but, as we shall see, the defence system chosen by Jacques de Molay did not allow it.

There was obviously panic in the king's camp. The counter-attack came from one of the king's chief advisers, the Archbishop of Sens, Philippe de Marigny, brother of Enguerrand de Marigny. Trying the Templars of the diocese of Paris (Paris was still only a suffragan bishopric in the see of Sens), he played on the connection between the indictment of individuals and that of the Order to pick out the contradictions between the Templars' testimonies before one court and the other. He thus improperly gave himself the power to declare relapsed those who, after admitting the error of their ways before the diocesan commission, defended the Order before the papal commission. Handed over to the secular arm, fifty-four of them were burnt in Paris on 12 May 1310. The Templars' resistance was smashed outright.

The papal commission continued its hearings until 26 May 1311. It had not given up bringing the practices of the Temple into the full light of day, but its objective was very different from the king's. A comparison of the interrogations carried out in 1307 under direct royal authority and those conducted by the papal commission in 1310–11 speaks volumes, and therein lies the interest of Barbara Frale's work.[10] The royal agents tried to amass as many facts as possible against the Templars, often resorting to torture: for them, admissions of denying Christ, spitting on the Cross, obscenities and so on, were just so many proofs of heresy, even of magic practices and sorcery,[11] which justified the procedures engaged by the king of France in defiance of the rights of the Church. In their eyes, that was enough to condemn the Order and abolish it. For the papal commission, and thus for the pope, the problem was different: it involved a careful examination of the conditions in which the scandalous (but not in themselves heretical) practices of the entry ritual had been perpetrated, seeking the reasons behind those practices and checking whether, besides this entry ritual, the liturgy followed within the Order was orthodox or not – the question of absolution by laymen, consecration of the Host, etc.

The members of the papal commission in Paris finally reached the conclusion that the Templars were orthodox; and for that reason all those who had acknowledged the unworthy acts of the entry ceremony (a kind of initiation 'rag'), and had made an act of contrition, were absolved and reconciled with the Church. But the Order must be purged of its debased practices; it must be reformed. The Temple's Rule and statutes, which those in charge had allowed to become degraded, had to be gone over with a fine-tooth comb to detect where the errors or confusions lay. And it had to be cleansed of those shameful practices, introduced no one knew when, which formed an unseemly 'sequence' in the course of an orthodox and sound ritual of admission, which aspiring Templars were told belonged to the Order's statutes.

These illicit acts imputed to the Templars did not form the nucleus of a blasphemous ceremony of admission, but were rather juxtaposed 'intruders', or better, appended at the close of a traditional and perfectly legal rite attested in the written Rule.[12]

The reports of the papal commissions formed the basis of the work of the Council that met at Vienne on 16 October 1311, one year later than originally planned. The debates were stormy, most of the Fathers seemingly unconvinced of the Order's guilt and declaring themselves ready to listen to its defenders, who were outside the Council, before passing judgment. But the pope, still under pressure from the king, who had come with his army as far as Lyon, had decided to put an end to the affair. He had to sacrifice the Temple in order to save the Church and the papacy, and once and for all bury the indictment of Boniface VIII's memory which Philip the Fair wanted to obtain from him. So, by the Bull *Vox in excelso*, issued on 22 March 1312, he decided to pronounce the abolition of the Order of the Temple 'not by way of judgment but by way of apostolic provision or decision'. The Temple had not been sentenced; it had been dissolved because, too weakened and too defamed, it could not get back on its feet and was therefore no longer of use.[13] Shortly afterwards, the pope gave the Temple's possessions to the Order of the Hospital, thereby effecting – in very particular circumstances – the union of the Orders. On the advice of Enguerrand de Marigny, Philip the Fair eventually accepted this solution. The king had got the Temple's 'scalp', but had been unable to remove from the pope's authority the unified Order which the Hospital had now become.

Clement V had reserved judgement of the Templar dignitaries for himself. He waited until 22 December 1313 to delegate to three cardinals the task, not of judging, but of announcing sentences of life imprisonment for the leaders of the Order. This was done on 18 March 1314 in Paris. Jacques de Molay, however, went back on all his admissions, proclaiming the innocence of a sound Order. Geoffroy de Charney joined him; Hugues de Pairaud and Geoffroy de Gonneville remained silent; Raimbaud de Caron, meanwhile, was apparently no longer there, probably dead. That very evening, the king ordered the Grand Master and Geoffroy de Charney to be burnt at the stake. Pairaud and Gonneville escaped death, but ended their days in prison.

Arrested at the Temple of Paris on the morning of 13 October 1307, Jacques de Molay[14] was kept prisoner there by the king's agents. Such was the fate of all the Templars, everywhere in France. Having spent a grim week or ten days being worked over by the royal police, the Templars were presented to the inquisitors for questioning. In Paris, interrogations began on 19 October, Molay undergoing his first one on 24 October.[15] He admitted that at the time of his reception in Beaune in 1265 he had denied Christ, unwillingly, and that he had had to spit on the Cross, though he had spat to one side. He stated that no one had suggested to him that he should have carnal relations with other brothers should he become 'overheated', and that he had never done so.[16] Lastly, he stated that he thought admissions to the Order took place in that way; in any case, that was how he had conducted them, although he had not carried out many himself, leaving to one of his assistants the task of taking aside the new Templar in order to 'do what had to be done to him'.

This is the sum total of the Grand Master's admissions – although he is never asked anything else. Either the inquisitor was handling Molay with great tact – although it is difficult to see why – or the inquisitor and Philip the Fair's advisers judged that these admissions, though incomplete, were sufficient to ruin the Temple's prestige, provided they were fully exploited. In any event, the admissions obtained from other Templars would reinforce Molay's testimony.

In fact, the next day, 25 October, Guillaume de Nogaret arranged a public session at the Temple in Paris. In the presence of a large number of clergy and, in particular, theologians and other members of the University of Paris, Molay repeated his admissions, without adding to his statement of the day before. By now everyone knew what the ceremonies of entry to the Order entailed. This is how the continuation of the chronicle of Guillaume de Nangis depicts that day:

> These crimes appear unbelievable, because of the horror they inspire in the hearts of the faithful, yet the Grand Master, brought to the Temple in the presence of doctors of the University, confessed to them, so it is said, expressly in the following week, except that he gave assurance that he had never been sullied by the depravity of sodomy and had never, in his profession of faith, spat on the image of the crucifix, but on the ground to one side. It is stated that he made known to all his brethren, in his own handwriting, that repentance had led him to this confession, and he exhorted them to do likewise.[17]

Not only were what few admissions he had made public but, even better – and this was a masterstroke[18] – the accusers had obtained from the Master (probably by some devious manipulation) a letter bearing the seal of the Temple enjoining the brothers, by virtue of the principle of holy obedience, to acknowledge the scandalous practices they had been subjected to when they had been received into the Order.[19]

It was perhaps at the close of this day that Molay, who until then had been put under house arrest in the Temple of Paris, was imprisoned and placed in solitary confinement at Corbeil. He was later to complain of the conditions of his imprisonment and his isolation. Pope Clement V, who had protested against the king of France's actions but decided on 22 November to order the arrest of all Templars in an attempt to regain the upper hand, was doubtless shaken by these admissions, but he did not want to be tricked. The king was urging him to abolish the Order; however, before taking that decision he wanted to be sure of the sincerity of the confessions obtained, especially those of the Grand Master, so he sent two cardinals, Bérenger Fredol and Étienne de Suisy, to Paris to find out the truth. At first, the king refused to present the Grand Master and other dignitaries to them; the pope sent them back to Paris again, with a letter he had written to the king. This time, the cardinals let it be understood that a fresh refusal by the king would mean excommunication.[20] The royal council therefore agreed to let the pope's envoys see the Grand Master, Hugues de Pairaud and several other Templars, and a letter from the king, dated 24 December, informed the pope accordingly.[21] The meeting was held, in camera, at Notre-Dame, probably on 27 December.

Jacques de Molay and the other Templars retracted their confessions and complained of the tortures and ill-treatment they had suffered. Two texts, dated spring 1308 and preserved in the Archives of the Crown of Aragon, give details – to be viewed with caution – of this session at Notre-Dame. The first comes from a cleric, probably the pope's treasurer, who is writing to inform his brother, the Templar Arnau de Banyuls, Commander of Gardeny;[22] the second, anonymous, comes from a cleric residing in Paris, who is writing to his brother, Bernard F. of Majorca.[23] The two letters give an account of the session, the second describing the stratagem employed by Jacques de Molay to afford the greatest possible publicity to his retraction.

The two cardinals asked him 'if what they had heard said, what he had confessed, was the truth. And he answered that it was the truth'; Molay added 'he would confess even greater errors' if all the people of Paris, rich and poor, could be assembled before him.[24] If this text is to be believed, the cardinals complied and opened the doors of Notre-Dame to the crowds. Then Jacques de Molay, perched on a dais, is said to have addressed the assembly as follows: 'Sirs, every-thing that the Council of France has told you, that I and all the Templar broth-ers who are here, and yet others, have confessed, is true.' Next he opens his cloak and strips off his clothing: 'You see, Sirs, how we were made to say what they wished'; at which point he reveals his arms, emaciated to the bone, and the traces of the torture he has undergone. Then he retracts his admissions. This account is probably too dramatic to be true, at least in its entirety; however, on 25 October,[25] in front of the cardinals sent by the pope, Jacques de Molay went back on his confessions. So, was he tortured like the rest of the Templars? I will return to this.[26] Molay is also supposed to have slipped wax tablets to the Tem-plars who were presented to the two cardinals with him, telling them to retract their admissions since they were now under the pope's protection.[27]

The outcome of these retractions is known: the pope deferred judgment and decided to suspend the procedure engaged in by the king and inquisitor in order to regain control. Despite coming under increasing pressure from the king, Guillaume de Nogaret and Guillaume de Plaisians, he succeeded in having several Templars, including the dignitaries, transferred to Poitiers to be inter-rogated there under his authority.

The king and his police took precautions, and sent only hand-picked Tem-plars to Poitiers; however, as if by chance, it was noticed that the dignitaries were in too weakened a state to make the whole journey. They stopped at Chinon, where the king obligingly put them up in his château. Between 28 June and 2 July 1308, seventy-two Templars were questioned at Poitiers; the inter-rogations of forty-two of them, during which they renew their admissions, are preserved.[28] As for those at Chinon, the pope had to resign himself to sending three cardinals, including Bérenger Fredol and Étienne de Suisy, to question them. This interrogation was published in part.[29] The original minutes, recently discovered by Barbara Frale in the Vatican Archives, confirm that they took place on 17–22 August.[30] Their content was incorporated into the Bull *Faciens misericordiam*, which was however issued by the pope on 12 August, therefore earlier, but reproduced in several dozen copies in the subsequent days and weeks. The dignitaries were thus interrogated after the publication of the first versions of the Bull. The pope had decided on the procedure to be followed for the rest of the trial without waiting for their hearings. It is known that in this Bull he reserved the sentencing of these dignitaries for himself, but without fixing a date. Forced to yield partly to the king's pressure (on the guarding of the prisoners and the sequestration of the Temple's possessions), the pope nevertheless tried to gain time in standing up to him.

Jacques de Molay therefore testified again before the cardinals at Chinon. He returned to his first admissions, neither subtracting nor adding anything: denial, spitting, but nothing on sodomy or obscene kisses and nothing on idolatry.[31] He breathed not a word of his retraction in December 1307. But why did he come back to those first confessions?

After his brief appearance in August 1308, Molay appears to have remained silent for over a year (at least, no one reported any of his utterances). As we have seen, setting up the diocesan and papal commissions occupied all that time. It must be remembered that he could appear only before the papal commission charged with trying the Order since, as an individual, he would be judged by the pope. The commission for the kingdom of France sat in Paris, and comprised the Archbishop of Narbonne, the bishops of Bayeux, Mende and Limoges, Master Mathieu de Naples, the apostolic notary and archdeacon of Rouen, the archdeacons of Trente and Maguelonne and the Provost of the church of Aix-en-Provence. It held its first meeting on 8 August 1309, summoning to appear by 12 November all witnesses who wished to defend the Order of the Temple or not, among them, of course, the Templars imprisoned throughout the kingdom. Messengers set off to deliver this summons so that it could be circulated in all the provinces. The Templars were informed of it in their prison cells, while it is known to have reached the bishopric of Bazas, in Guyenne, where the summons was read out on 6, 7 and 8 September 1309.[32]

The commission met on 12 November, but no one appeared; or in the days that followed. The commissioners had to remonstrate with the bishop of Paris, then the provost of the town, to show evidence of a little more zeal. The first witness did not turn up until 22 November. On 26 November, following on from Hugues de Pairaud, who had nothing to say, Jacques de Molay presented himself.[33] After reading him the summons to appear, the commissioners asked if he wished to defend his Order. Molay's reply was off the point. It would be astonishing, he began by saying, if the papacy wished in this arbitrary fashion to destroy so ancient an Order to which it had granted so many privileges. More-over, he did not possess the necessary abilities to defend his Order; he would like to, it was even his duty to do so, but he was the prisoner of the pope and the king, without means and without counsel. How could he?

He therefore requested assistance and advice, and the commissioners declared themselves willing to grant him some time in which to find it; but they reminded him that he was appearing at a trial for heresy and that he had made admissions, so he had better be careful. To help him reflect in full awareness of the facts, they read out to him and translated into the 'vulgar tongue' the Bull *Faciens misericordiam* and other apostolic letters; he thus heard what he had confessed before the cardinals at Chinon. During the reading he twice showed surprise; and when it was finished, he declared that he would be ready to say something if 'you were not who you are', before adding enigmatically 'that the same fate should be meted out to such perverts as that reserved for them by the Saracens and Tartars; *they* beheaded perverts'.

To this the commissioners replied that they contented themselves with trying heretics. Noticing among those present Guillaume de Plaisians, who had entered the room uninvited, Molay asked to speak to him. There seems to have been a certain complicity between Plaisians and the Grand Master, unless the attention paid to him by the king's counsellor was feigned. Plaisians having advised him to be careful not to contradict his earlier confessions, Jacques de Molay then asked for a two-day period for reflection, so as 'not to come a cropper',[34] and this the commissioners granted.

There has been much pondering over how to interpret the surprise evinced by Molay upon hearing the deposition he had made at Chinon. P. Viollet has even suggested that the minutes of that statement had been completely 'doctored' by the cardinals for Molay's sake; that he had, in fact, stood by his retraction, which led him directly to the troubles of which Guillaume de Plaisians reminded him when he took him aside at the hearing on 26 November. Fredol and Suisy would thus have concocted a fake testament to get him off the hook.[35] This is a rather far-fetched explanation, which has been dismissed by G. Lizerand.

Whereas Molay had seemed hesitant on 26 November, he showed great firmness on 28 November.[36] For an instant, an 'irrelevant' intervention by Guillaume de Nogaret, who was also 'passing through' without the commission's invitation, threw him off balance. When he was again asked if he wished to defend the Order, he replied that he was a poor unlettered knight (that is, he knew no Latin) and, as he had understood that the pope had reserved the right to try him, he wanted to say nothing more before the commission. Of course, he referred to the texts that had been read out to him two days earlier and to the procedure set up by the Bull *Faciens misericordiam*. At the commissioners' insistence, he then replied clearly that he did not wish to defend the Order, and asked the commissioners to intervene so that he could make his appearance before his judge more quickly, 'because only then would he, to his utmost ability, tell the lord pope something worthy of Christ and the Church'.[37]

But to salve his conscience, he set out three points regarding the Temple. There was not a single other Order in which the places of worship, the ornaments and worship itself, were as fine, as well maintained or as well celebrated; not a single Order which gave as much in the way of alms; and not a single Order that had spilt as much blood in the defence of the faith. The commissioners retorted that this was all well and good but that, without faith, it availed nothing for the salvation of the soul. To which Jacques de Molay 'replied that this was true, and that he himself believed in one God in three persons, and the other tenets of the Catholic faith; and that he had one God, one faith, one baptism and one Church, and when the soul was parted from the body it would be seen who was good and who evil, and that everyone would know about the matters presently being raised'. A profession of faith of perfect orthodoxy and already, perhaps, an appointment fixed before God at the Last Judgement for those 'perverts' he had mysteriously denounced two days before.[38]

It was after this declaration that Guillaume de Nogaret intervened, citing the chronicles of Saint-Denis (that is, the *Grandes Chroniques de France*, although this particular quotation is not to be found in it), which told that Saladin had already denounced the sodomy and apostasy of the Templar Order. Taken aback, Jacques de Molay replied that he had never heard of it, which was when he mentioned the instance of Guillaume de Beaujeu, who agreed truces with the sultan, but only with the aim of saving whatever could be saved. Lastly, the Grand Master requested to be able to celebrate Mass regularly, and to have a chapel and chaplain put at his disposal.

It was the watershed. Jacques de Molay had found what he believed to be the means of escaping the trap in which he had been struggling since his confessions of October 1307. He would say nothing more; but by keeping silent in this way, he would have no part in the groundswell which, in the spring of 1310, would raise the hopes of Templars and cause the accusation to waver.

When Jacques de Molay was brought before the commission one last time, on 2 March 1310, he held to the position he had adopted on 28 November: that he would speak only before the pope. The commissioners pointed out, quite rightly, that he was confusing the two procedures: the pope would judge him as an individual, whereas they had the task of trying the Order, and by refusing to speak before them he was challenging their legitimacy. Molay was not the only one to confuse these. When the archbishop of Sens, Philippe de Marigny, condemned fifty-four Templars as relapsed and sent them to the stake in the following May, he wittingly made the same confusion; they had confessed before the diocesan commissions, or perhaps even earlier, in 1307 before the inquisitors, then had gone back on their admissions before the papal commission. This sentence had been illegal, but Marigny, Nogaret and the king could not have cared less.

On the same 2 March, when Hugues de Pairaud, Jean du Tour, Geoffroy de Gonneville and a few other Temple notables were brought before the papal commission, they stood by their first statements and refused to defend the Order. The Temple was thus betrayed by its dignitaries, and the Templars abandoned by their leaders.

Jacques de Molay would not appear again in person before anyone whatsoever. He vanishes from the minutes of the papal commission, at least as a defendant (for he is cited in the depositions of the Templars who would continue to appear until the spring of 1311). He was never to see the pope, and was no longer an actor in the drama that continued to be enacted. He only cropped up again some four years later, when his Order had already been abolished.

Before we come to this last act in the life of Jacques de Molay, an attempt must be made to understand his attitude or, rather, attitudes, during 1307–10; understand and explain, leaving aside the common moralising *a priori* with which the Temple's historiography is burdened:[39] was he foolish, short-sighted, cowardly, etc.? Of course, that has to be taken into account, but it is not the problem. He was the Grand Master of an Order which, at a certain point, the king of France decided to destroy, the pope did not manage to defend and he himself was unable to save.

Why?

Molay's intriguing change of attitude during these interrogations needs some explanation. Had Jacques de Molay expected the king's bid for control? No. He was convinced of his Order's innocence, and that the papal inquiry would reveal the truth. Therein lies one of the reasons for the Templars' passivity at the time of their arrest; the royal agents had been careful to say that they were acting under orders from the king and the pope, which was a lie. At Poitiers, the Templars present at the papal Court – Hugues de Pairaud and some fifteen others – were arrested and shut up in the royal fortress of Loches;[40] in contrast, the Templar staff employed in the Curia, Clement V's *cubicularius*, Jean de Montaigu, Master of the province of Lombardy, and the pope's treasurers were not harassed. A letter from one of them, dated November 1307 and sent to the Templar Commander of Ascò, shows that they were at the pope's side.[41] The latter was not in Poitiers, however, even when the arrests were made; he returned to the town and held a consistory on 15 October, then made efforts to calm the anxiety of the Templars in his service, advising them under no circumstances to try and flee. According to the treasurer's letter, the *cubicularius* reaffirmed his trust in the pontiff on behalf of them all:

> Holy Father, we are not afraid, because you will defend us and preserve justice, and because all we brothers of the Temple are good Christians, Catholic and strong in the faith. And the brothers of the Temple have always died and fallen prisoner to the Saracens for the Catholic faith, and still do so today. And we do not fear death, because for a good 190 years the Order has been in existence; and that could not have happened had there been any wickedness, and without someone knowing about it.[42]

The same correspondent also reports that he has learnt from an equerry from Paris that Jacques de Molay could have taken the opportunity to flee but had refused to do so.[43] Here again, his letter provides this item of information in the form of direct address, although its content is less reliable than that of the *cubicularius*.

> The brothers who are with him [the Master] said to him, 'Since you, Sir, are able to escape, go, so that you can report to us the advice of the pope and the cardinals.' The Master replied, 'It is not my intention to do so because we all know we will be vindicated; so I tell you that if I were in Germany or Spain or England, and learned that you had been captured, I would come to you and go … to prison with you. It is not good to flee, because none of us is guilty and our Order is good and honest, and we are Catholics who hold a very strong faith, just like the pope, the cardinals and all the Christians in the world. And I beseech you, brothers, to hope'; the *cubicularius* spoke in the same way to the pope.[44]

The document does not say who it was who originally offered them flight. It is not unlikely that Jacques de Molay could have benefited from some collusion at the Temple in Paris where he was imprisoned, but his response was to be expected. Molay and the Templars thought they had nothing to hide, and put their trust in their natural protector, the pope.

Can Molay's partial admissions be explained by the fact that he had undergone torture? It is generally accepted that torture was fairly widely used in the king's prisons in the days following the arrests, in order to obtain some significant confessions rapidly. Since the middle of the thirteenth century, torture had formed part of the battery of methods used by inquisitors at heresy trials, so it is unlikely the royal agents would have deprived themselves of such an instrument. And while historians may quibble over whether this or that person was or was not tortured, there are enough testimonies in the Templar trials to prove that torture was widely employed. In many cases, the mere threat of it sufficed; and there were other ways of 'conditioning' people – isolation, ill-treatment, deprivation of both material and spiritual food, and so on. To give the clergy their due, however, some rejected these means and refused to recognise the validity of confessions obtained in this way - the archbishop of Ravenna, Rinaldo da Concorrezzo, for example, and the cardinals who were sent to interrogate Jacques de Molay in Paris in December 1307 and at Chinon in August 1308, Bérenger Fredol and Étienne de Suisy, who admitted that one could go back on confessions extorted under threat of torture without being considered 'relapsed'.

People ridiculed these valiant warriors, full of courage in combat or Mamluk jails, but who gave in so easily to torture. Apparently, that was not the same thing. The idea that Molay was tortured, however, is generally rejected. The chronicler Jean de Saint-Victor, making a distinction between the three categories of Templars – those who confessed, those who denied the accusations and those who confessed but afterwards recanted because their confessions had been extracted under torture – excepts Jacques de Molay from the last category: 'In third place, those who at first confessed but said later that they had lied because of cruel torture. The Master was not among those because, without torture, he had fully acknowledged his misdeeds.'[45]

Similarly, an anonymous document produced by someone in the king's entourage – which immediately renders it suspect – indicates that the Grand Master spontaneously admitted his errors and those of his Order, and that one day, weeping, 'he asked to be tortured so that his brothers could not say that he had freely caused their downfall', a scarcely veiled way of saying that he had not been tortured himself.[46]

Other documents, however, state the opposite.

The first is a letter from the Commander of Miravet and the Mas Deu, Raymond Sa Guardia, addressed to the Master of Aragon, Exemen de Lenda. In this letter, dating from late November 1307, Sa Guardia tells him of information he has come by, which a Catalan Dominican in Paris, Romeus de Bruguera, had conveyed to his prior in Barcelona. The king

> had the Master of the Temple seized, together with the other brothers of his seignory. And they were under guard in our house in Paris, kept separate from one another; and the Master was the first to be tortured, so he confessed publicly in the presence of many prelates and bachelors of law in Paris that the Order of the Temple had long been in the custom of ...[47]

Romeus de Bruguera, member of the Parisian *alma mater*, had perhaps attended the session on 25 October 1307.

The second is the text, also in Catalan, that I have already cited with regard to Molay's retraction at Notre-Dame in December 1307. True, it is a second-hand testimony, made by someone who was not an eyewitness, but if all testimonies of this type were dismissed out of hand, we would have little left. The veracity of this episode cannot be doubted: in his first speech at Poitiers, made before the pope and cardinals on 29 May 1308, Guillaume de Plaisians makes a barely veiled reference to the retraction made by some after 'collusion among them, as the lords cardinals sent to Paris learned and, thanks to the encouragement they received both orally and in writing from certain persons whose names will be revealed at the right time and place, and some of whom are held to be among the most considerable in this country'.[48]

As for the theatrical and extravagant scene portraying Jacques de Molay stripping off his garments to exhibit his tortured body, it probably did not take place, but that does not mean the Grand Master was not tortured.

In my view, the question is left in the air. The Catalan documents are important, and what they report is reliable. The problem is that they simultaneously record precise facts, rumours and hearsay, and it is not always possible to sort out which is which. For instance, another document records a piece of information passed on by a Hospitaller who recounts 'that the Master of the Temple is dead and many Templars subjected to torture'.[49] Looked at from another angle, the legal establishment in those days had no scruples about using torture and stating that it had done so; in which case, why not believe it when it says it has *not* done so? But it may have been judicious for the king's agents to conceal the fact that the Grand Master had been tortured in order to give more weight to his skimpy admissions.

That said, it is unlikely to have been a determining factor in the case of Jacques de Molay. Nogaret and Plaisians had no need of a large number of confessions from the Master; it was enough for them to give maximum circulation to those he had consented to make – admitting that he had denied Christ and had spat on the Cross. To obtain those, the threat of torture alone could have sufficed. In any event, when Molay himself made his complete retraction in 1314, he declared that it was fear of torture rather than torture itself that had led him to confess. Of course, it is possible he was being disingenuous, justifying changes in attitude that were difficult to explain and, above all, open to interpretation. Whether advised or not, and having been 'coaxed' by the king's agents (as one would say in 1314), Jacques de Molay could well have wanted to clear the ground and show goodwill by expressing his concern to see the inquiry and reform of the Order brought to a conclusion, by acknowledging practices that were undoubtedly scandalous but also irrefutable because they were so widely known. In the days preceding his interrogation on 24 October 1307, then on that day and the following, when put before the learned assembly brought together under the aegis of Nogaret, Molay doubtless found himself in the same situation as he had with Philip the Fair in June 1307, when he had told him of some of the abuses and manifest misdemeanours in the Order, especially the absolution of sins by laymen – a venal sin which, incidentally, not all theologians actually considered to be a sin.[50] But in the mouth of Guillaume de Plaisians, whose text I quoted in the preceding chapter,[51] that admission became clear proof of heresy.

Such distortion of the few misdeeds to which he had admitted probably did not give Jacques de Molay a good start to his trial, notably with regard to his brothers in the Order. If they had any basis in truth, the instructions which he twice issued to his brothers followed the same lines. After his public confessions on 24 October, his accusers obtained a letter from him, addressed to all the imprisoned Templars, asking them to acknowledge all the errors to which he himself had admitted, in the name of the sacred obedience due from any monk to his superior.[52]

In late December 1307, when he appeared at Notre-Dame before the cardinals sent by the pope, Jacques de Molay seemed once again to have transmitted his instructions to the brothers who, along with himself and other dignitaries of the Order, were to be brought before the pope's representatives. There exist two testimonies by Templars presented and interrogated at Poitiers in 1308. According to Brother Jean de Châlons, in an attempt to save the Order, a priest of the Order named Renaud had urged the Templars to recant their confessions, using a clandestine letter, sealed with a lead seal, probably in the hand of the Grand Master. He had managed to have this message passed to sixty Templars; the Grand Master's brother, dean of the church of Langres, was supposed to have conveyed the instructions.[53] Another Templar questioned at Poitiers, Jean de Folliaco (probably one of the 'moles' sent by Guillaume de Nogaret to infiltrate the Order before the Templars' arrest) meanwhile, wrote that he had heard it said that 'the Master of the Order or someone appointed by him, by means of wax tablets passed from room to room before the entry of the king and cardinals, had asked all the brothers to revoke their confessions'. There was no name on the tablets to allow identification of the author of the message, the contents of which were as follows: 'Know that the king and cardinals are coming here tomorrow; other brothers have denied their admissions; revoke yours and give these tablets back to the bearer.'[54]

It seems likely, then, that in the first instance, either on his own initiative or fairly astutely 'advised' by the king's agents (i.e. threats of torture and promises of pardon), Jacques de Molay had admitted some misdeeds which, in his eyes, appeared harmless enough. Then, in a second phase, embarrassed by the way in which royal propaganda had exaggerated his admissions out of all proportion, and given confidence by what appeared to be the favourable attitude of the two cardinals, Bérenger Fredol and Étienne de Suisy, he had persuaded himself that the pope would protect him and he therefore needed to place complete trust in him, if he was to obtain salvation and save the Temple. Another document relating to Molay's appearance in Notre-Dame is significant: the text is now lost, but Pierre Dupuy saw it and inserted it into his work in the seventeenth century, according to which the two cardinals dined with Hugues de Pairaud, who had also recanted, and gave him assurances on the matter.[55]

And so, Jacques de Molay and the Templars chose to put their trust in the pope – and, to be fair to them, the latter's attitude during 1308 reinforced their choice. However, Clement V's resistance to pressure from the Court of France had its limits, and in the summer of 1308 the Indian-wrestling match between king and pope ended in compromise. In such circumstances, Molay's room for manoeuvre was diminished, but his clear-sightedness at this point is also in doubt. By returning at Chinon to his first admissions, the Master of the Order sowed seeds of doubt and wearied those in the papal camp who might still have supported him. Was it fear of torture, fear of being condemned as relapsed or fear of the stake? Some good advice at that moment might well have encouraged him to have more – not just courage but perceptiveness.[56] At that time he was not being threatened – unlike in 1309–10.

He thus found himself in an impasse; he could not confess before Nogaret and Plaisians, the king's agents, then go back on those admissions before the pope's representatives when the royal police were not around. The dual procedure established by the Bull *Faciens misericordiam* had certainly provided the king with a weapon: to play on the contradictions between a statement made before the diocesan commissions and that made before the papal commissions. And so, thanks to the decision made by the archbishop of Sens in May 1310, the king of France was able to turn around the course of events. But it also gave the Templars an opportunity: to make the most of the seriousness with which the papal commissions – at least, the one in Paris – did their work; in their consideration, the Temple had not been condemned in advance.

The rank-and-file Templars sensed that possibility better than their leader. At first with fear and hesitation, then with growing assurance and determination, they defended their Order, going beyond individual cases. Paradoxically, like Philippe de Marigny, archbishop of Sens, Jacques de Molay had confused the two procedures; the papal commissioners, somewhat displeased, had in any case already pointed this out to him. Marigny and the royal camp did not have the law on their side, but they had the power, the strength, the initiative; the commission and the pope had right on their side, but not the strength; and Molay found himself with neither.

On 26 and 28 November 1309, Jacques de Molay missed his chance. He was conscious of this, as his hesitations on those two days prove. He had immured himself in silence too soon. Who knows what might have happened if in 1310 he had placed himself openly and resolutely at the head of his troops, as they had wanted him to do, in defence of his Order? When he did so, on 18 March 1314, it was no longer of any use.

1314

BURNT AT THE STAKE

I n his Bull of 12 August 1308, the pope reserved for himself the trial of the dignitaries of the Temple as individuals. We have already seen how, from 28 November 1309, Jacques de Molay used this declaration as an excuse to take no further part in the proceedings against the Order and to cease replying to the questions of the papal commission's investigators. The pope, notably in 1309, recalled that he had fully intended to honour his commitment;[1] but whereas on 26 and 28 November 1309, Jacques de Molay had insistently asked that this judgment should take place quickly, the pope had allowed matters to drag on. Most of the Templars who appeared before the papal commission had already been tried by the diocesan commissions and, most often, had been absolved by the bishop and reconciled with the Church. They had come before the papal commission cleanshaven and without their cloaks, thereby signifying that they had broken with the Order of the Temple. Sometimes the two procedures crossed paths. Such was the case in Paris, in May 1310, when the royal government was able to regain the upper hand by sentencing to the stake those Templars who had defended the Order before the papal commission having already confessed to crimes at the diocesan commission, or even earlier to the inquisitors.

Jacques de Molay and his companions had to await the pleasure of the pope who, as he gradually succeeded in imposing some of his views on matters which had remained in abeyance between the Church and the king (the condemnation of the memory of Boniface VIII, the transfer of the Templars' possessions to the Hospitallers), showed less and less inclination to re-open the affair. For that was what it was all about; Molay was only waiting for that moment to reveal all.

It is therefore understandable that the pope should first try to settle the fate of the Order before embarking on the individual trials of its dignitaries. The Council of Vienne had had three objectives: to pass judgment on the Order of the Temple as an Order; the crusade; and reform. The first item had eclipsed the other two, but they were all important. Judgment on the Order was to take place after a commission had made a synthesis of the inquiries by the papal commissions. The Fathers of the Council were divided, as we saw, so it would have been easy to give the Templars who wished to defend the Order (who were prowling around the outskirts of Vienne) a chance to speak; a figure of 2,000 brothers has been mentioned, although that is clearly an exaggeration. But the king of France and his army were also camped nearby and Clement V wanted to have done with the affair; he had had enough. He could not take the risk of provoking a debate in the Council, for he was not absolutely sure of the outcome; so he put an end to it and decided 'not as a sentence but as a provision' to abolish the Order of the Temple. He was not condemning it but, judging that it had been too greatly defamed to recover and serve the Church's cause, he dissolved it (in his Bull *Vox in excelso*) and gave its assets to the Hospital (in the Bull *Ad providam*). This decision led to grave problems, including the slow and incomplete devolution of the Order's possessions.[2] The major part was effected in 1313 but, in certain cases, operations dragged on – nothing was settled before 1319 in Spain, for instance, where the papacy had to accept some bending of the rules of devolution to the Hospital and approve the creation, on the ruins of the Temple, of the Order of Montesa in the kingdom of Valencia (Crown of Aragon) and the Order of Christ in Portugal.

Still to be dealt with were the Templar dignitaries, of whom, in fact, there were only five: the Grand Master; the Grand Commander Raimbaud de Caron; and three provincial dignitaries, Geoffroy de Charney (who until nearly the end had been the Draper of the Temple but now appeared as Commander of Normandy), Geoffroy de Gonneville (Commander of Aquitaine–Poitou) and Hugues de Pairaud (Visitor of France). Any other arrested dignitaries had been tried in either Cyprus or their respective provinces. Of the five, after 1308 there appear to have been only four left; Raimbaud de Caron, still present in August 1308 at Chinon, was not mentioned subsequently, and probably died in prison. The surviving four had therefore spent four years in prison at Gisors, the royal château that had become a state prison, between their last vain appearance before the papal commission in March 1310 and March 1314. Not once during those four years did they show themselves, either because they were unable to or because they did not wish to do so. And it was not until 1313 that the pope finally decided to draw a line under the Templar affair.

On 22 December 1313, in order to try the four dignitaries Clement V appointed a commission of three cardinals, comprising Nicolas de Fréauville, Arnaud d'Auch and Arnaud Novelli.[3] That is, he would not be trying Jacques de Molay himself.

As regards the legal situation of the Grand Master and his companions, at the Council of Vienne, according to the Bull *Consuderantes dudum* of 6 May 1312, the Templars were put into three categories: those who had confessed and had never gone back on their statements; those who had consistently denied, and those who had confessed but later retracted their confessions, pleading that the latter had been extracted under torture. The first were absolved and released fairly quickly; the second were sentenced to life imprisonment;[4] the fate of the third category was not specified. However, if they were considered to be relapsed, as the archbishop of Sens had declared in 1310, then the punishment was for them to be burnt at the stake. In his brief evocation of Jacques de Molay's demise, Jean de Saint-Victor takes up these three categories and, with regard to the third, writes as follows: 'The third is composed of those who in the first instance confessed, but afterwards said they had lied because of cruel torture. The Grand Master was not one of those, because he had fully admitted his faults without torture.'[5] The Grand Master had certainly retracted his confessions once in December 1307, but he had returned to his first statements in August 1308 at Chinon, and it was on that deposition – his last, since he had said nothing before the papal commission – that he was going to be tried.

The three cardinals met in Paris in March 1314. The most accurate of all the contemporary sources to record the event is the continuator of Guillaume de Nangis:

The Grand Master of the Order of Templars and three other Templars ... all four openly and publicly admitted the crimes with which they were charged in the presence of the archbishop of Sens [Philippe de Marigny] and several other prelates and men who were learned in canon and divine law, specially assembled for this purpose following the pope's orders, by the bishop of Albano and two other cardinals, and to whom the opinion of the counsel for the accused had been passed. As they persisted in their confessions, and seemed to want to persevere to the end, after mature deliberations, on the advice of the said counsel, the said assembly sentenced them, on the day after the feast of Saint Gregory [Monday 18 March], on the public foreground of the church of Paris [Notre-Dame], to life imprisonment. But lo and behold, when the cardinals believed they had finally concluded this affair, all at once two of the Templars, namely the Grand Master of Outremer and the Grand Master of Normandy, defended themselves stubbornly against a cardinal who was then speaking and against the archbishop of Sens, and without any respect began to deny everything they had confessed, which came as a great surprise to many people.[6]

The other chronicles of the times, those of Jean de Saint-Victor and Bernard Gui and the *Grandes Chroniques de France*, give very short, undetailed accounts of that 18 March which, if we follow Nangis, saw the four dignitaries at first confirm their confessions. One may well wonder if it was on the same 18 March that this new confession took place; would it not more likely have been the day before, or even the day before that, with the pope's envoys taking their precautions before pronouncing sentence? If that was so, had the cardinals made the four Templars repeat their earlier confessions, or merely been content to recall the events, obtaining from the accused only a silence which was interpreted as assent? Did Jacques de Molay understand at that point that he could expect nothing more and he would do better to keep quiet in the hope of receiving a lighter punishment?[7] Or was he waiting for the real opening of the trial he had hoped for in order to speak? Whatever its genesis, on the morning of 18 March, it was not a trial in right and due form that opened. Gathered on the forecourt of Notre-Dame, those present, like the Templars placed on the scaffold, heard the cardinals sent by the pope pronounce their sentence: prison for life. Then the Grand Master rose up, followed by Geoffroy de Charney; Hugues de Pairaud and Geoffroy de Gonneville continued to keep silent. Each knew what he was doing; each knew what awaited him: the stake for the Grand Master and Charney; life imprisonment for Pairaud and Gonneville.

In this unprecedented situation, which came as such a surprise to the cardinals, the king was the swiftest to react, once again showing scant regard for the law. Here again is Guillaume de Nangis' continuator:

When the cardinals had handed them over to the provost of Paris [a royal agent] who was present, only so that he could keep them under guard until they could deliberate more fully over them the next day, as soon as these things reached the king's ears in the royal palace, he consulted with his own advisers and, without speaking of it to the clergy, made a prudent decision to have the two Templars consigned to the flames towards evening on that very day, on a little isle in the Seine, situated between the royal garden and the church of the Hermit Brethren.[8]

As was pointed out by another chronicler of the time, the Dominican Bernard Gui (who was also an inquisitor), the king 'waited for no other judgment from the Church as two cardinals were then present in Paris'.[9]

All the contemporary chronicles highlighted the determination, calm and courage of Jacques de Molay and Geoffroy de Charney at the hour of their execution, Nangis' continuator like the rest stressing the admiration and amazement of those present. The verse chronicle by Geoffroi de Paris introduces a new element when it mentions Jacques de Molay's words from the pyre. Contemporary with events, it is a first-hand work by a king's cleric who witnessed the scene. Geoffroi first recounts the words uttered by Molay before the cardinals. There he defends the Order, affirming that the Templars were good Christians, that they had never fled and that they had suffered death for God, justice and 'uprightness'. Then comes the account of the stake:

> The master, who saw the fire ready,
> Stripped with no sign of fear.
> And, as I myself saw, placed himself
> Quite naked in his shirt
> Freely and with a good appearance;
> Never did he tremble
> No matter how much he was pulled and jostled.
> They took him to tie him to the stake
> And without fear he allowed them to tie him.
> They bound his hands with a rope
> But he said this to them: 'Gentlemen, at least
> Let me join my hands a little
> And make a prayer to God
> For now the time is fitting.
> Here I see my judgment
> When death freely suits me;

God knows who is in the wrong and has sinned.

Soon misfortune will come

To those who have wrongly condemned us:

God will avenge our death.'

'Gentlemen,' he said, 'make no mistake,

All those who are against us

Will have to suffer because of us.

In that belief I wish to die.

That is my faith; and I beg you

To turn my face

Towards the Virgin Mary,

Of whom our Lord Christ was born.'

His request was granted.

And so gently did death take him

That everyone marvelled.[10]

Next it was the turn of Geoffroy de Charney to mount the pyre, praising the by now martyred Master. Geoffroi de Paris again made a poem about it and, for good measure, tells us there was a third Templar close to the pyre who was not burnt but led back to prison: the Templar who had admitted the errors and crimes of the Order. That in no way detracts from the value of a testimony which is both measured and moderate. Of course, one line sketches the theme of the curse; but Jacques de Molay did no more than consign his persecutors to God. Nor is there any sign of repentance on his part in Geoffroi's poem.[11] This is only recounted in a third, later, account which, as we have already seen, could be sometimes fanciful – that of Villani, the Florentine chronicler who came by his information from a relative who happened to be in Paris at the time:

> The Grand Master of the Temple rose, shouting to be heard; and when the people had fallen silent, he said that never had the heresies and sins imputed to them been true and that the Order and their house were holy, just and Catholic, but he himself fully deserved death and wished to suffer in peace, because he had previously made confessions through fear of torture, and because of the wheedling of the pope and the king of France.[12]

Here again, there is no hyperbole in this measured testimony. Jacques de

Molay had made admissions, that could not be denied. The text suggests that promises had been made to him (by the king? his advisers? the pope?), and that his trust in the latter had been betrayed. That is all, but if Villani is to be believed it is a great deal inasmuch as Molay thus recognised that his defence tactics had been wrong.

Villani also points out a fact that should be taken seriously:

> It must be noted that, during the night following the martyrdom of the Grand Master and his companion, their corpses and bones were collected as holy relics by brothers and other monks and sheltered in holy places.[13]

This sentence compares with the *Grandes Chroniques de France*, which devotes only four lines to the burning, but specifies that 'their bones were burnt and reduced to dust',[14] as if the royal police had feared that events such as those reported by Villani might occur. Perhaps they did not intervene quickly enough?

These testimonies are still a part of history, but it is obvious how many fruitful sources they provide for legend. The stake was set up on a small island at the tip of the île de la Cité, below the gardens of the king's palace (the present-day place du Vert-Galant). This islet belonged not to the king but to the abbey of Saint-Germain-des-Prés. In the days that followed, the Paris parliament, the highest court in the land, gave a decision at the request of the Abbot of Saint-Germain, specifying that the king had not intended to flout the Abbot's rights by 'having two men who were formerly Templars burnt on the isle in the Seine adjoining the point of our garden, between our said garden on one side of the river and the religious house of the brothers of the Order of Saint-Augustin of Paris, on the other side of the river, over which he had full legal jurisdiction'.[15]

Today, on a plaque set at the foot of a stairway into the place du Vert-Galant, the following inscription may be seen:

On this spot
JACQUES DE MOLAY
last Grand Master
of the Order of the Temple
was burnt on 18 March 1314

In 1363–4, Giovanni Boccaccio, author of the *Decameron*, devoted a chapter of his moralising work *De casibus virorum illustrium* to the Templars. Boccaccio's book was translated into French by Laurent de Premierfait early in the fifteenth century under the title *Des cas des nobles hommes et femmes* (*Cases of noble men and women*),[16] which in its 1409 version enjoyed immense success. There are eighty known manuscripts of it, often richly illuminated, and one of these illuminations represents the Templars at the stake.

Using the example of illustrious men, this work was intended to illustrate the theme of the Wheel of Fortune, whereby one reached great heights before plummeting to the depths – of which there could be no finer example than the rise and fall of the Templars. Boccaccio gives a rapid history of the Order from its beginnings, which were very humble but soon followed by an extraordinary development which was accompanied by the elevation 'to a title of very special honour [of] the office of mastership'. The original ideal then became lost: 'And it is a sure thing that the holiness of the Templars declined as their power increased.' Boccaccio gives much space to Jacques de Molay: he recalls his origins, his entry into a powerful Order, his elevation to the Mastership and then his conflict with Philip the Fair. After a detailed narration of the execution of the fifty-four Templars burnt in Paris in May 1310, he returns to Molay, describing his end: his rebellion when faced with the 'judgment' of the cardinals, and his execution. In this the Italian author refers to his father, a Florentine merchant present in Paris when these events were taking place.[17] Boccaccio's text in fact appears close to that of Villani, and there is nothing in it likely to feed a legend.

Meanwhile, the historiographical study on the trial of the Templars conducted by A. K. Wildermann for the whole of Europe up to the seventeenth century gives little space to Jacques de Molay.[18] An unpublished study, made on the same subject but confined to the late Middle Ages and France, contributes useful additions to the preceding work, and lists the themes most often retained in the history of the trial by chroniclers and other writers in the fourteenth and fifteenth centuries: the arrests, the crimes and misdeeds imputed to the Templars, the Council of Vienne and the devolution of the Temple's possessions to the Hospital, not forgetting the burnings in 1310, far more than the death of the Grand Master.[19] The 1310 executions made a greater impact on minds than that of Jacques de Molay, which was mentioned only by writers such as the continuator of Guillaume de Nangis, Geoffroi de Paris, Villani and Boccaccio who had already written extensively on the Templar trial. In the fifteenth century, Molay's burning is referred to in only three chronicles. In 1381, the chronicle of the emperor Domitian contents itself with this sentence: 'In that year [1313] were burnt on the isle in front of the Augustins the general master of the Temple and another master of the order.'[20] The other two texts confuse Jacques de Molay with Guillaume de Beaujeu, in this instance given the forename Louis: they are an 'ancient chronicle of Flanders' and the *Chronographia Regum Francorum*. The latter text, although very extensive regarding the trial of the Templars, in addition confuses the burning in 1314 with that of the Templars in 1310.[21]

A fine example of historiography's very belated interest in Jacques de Molay is the famous curse uttered by the Grand Master as the flames began to envelop the stake. The last Capetians were accursed kings, for sure, but not for the reason given by Maurice Druon.[22]

If one follows the sources closest to the actual event – the continuation of Guillaume de Nangis, the chronicles of Geoffroi de Paris and Villani – they report that Jacques de Molay spoke first before the cardinals to proclaim his Order holy, then on the pyre – before it was lit – to proclaim himself a good Christian and call on God's judgement. A phrase here and there might have given rise to rash elaborations, but nothing of the kind emerged: no curse, no flowery discourse.

All the historiography devoted to the Temple since an already distant past cites a speech by Jacques de Molay, uttered on the pyre and skilfully composed, laying a curse on both the king of France and his descendants and the pope. So how did this legend arise, in which Molay is the one who utters the curse that heralds the imminent disappearance of the Capetian line? According to Colette Beaune, who has studied the genesis of this curse, 'it is because they [the Capetians] were looked upon as accursed in their own time and a reason for it had to be found, and someone to denounce them'.[23] A curse is a kind of appeal to divine judgement; and the appeal will have been heard if it results notably in the premature death of the person or persons against whom the curse is directed. This was certainly the case for the last of the Capetians: the adulteries of the king's daughters-in-law, the death of the king himself, then those of his three sons leaving no male offspring, and thus in 1328 the extinction of the direct line of the Capetians.

The reasons invoked to explain this curse by contemporaries of Philip the Fair and the last Capetians have nothing to do with the Temple. Instead, the burden of taxes and monetary changes are blamed; or the persecutions of Boniface VIII and the assassination attempt at Agnani. (This is the reason given by Villani, who makes the bishop of Ancona the one to utter the curse: 'I say by divine inspiration that this sin has condemned him by God to great perils and adversities, that he and his line will lose the kingdom.')[24] Most often, however, the curse is attributed to Boniface VIII himself.

It was also to fall on Clement V at much the same time that the Templars were undergoing the trial process initiated by him. After describing the Council of Vienne, an Italian chronicler from Vicenza, Ferreto de Ferretis, recounts that an anonymous Templar presented himself before the pope, protesting against his death sentence and declaring from the pyre: 'I call on the true and living God to witness your unjust sentence; within a year and a day, together with Philip, who is also responsible, you will appear before Him to answer my objections and offer your defence.'[25] (We are still close to the event – around 1330.) This story was taken up, but without the appearance of the Grand Master. Not until the seventeenth century was 'the death of Jacques de Molay gradually built up and dramatised'.[26] What he had said both before the cardinals and at the moment of death was thus gathered into a single speech delivered at the stake. In a historical work ordered by Francis I, the *De rebus gestis francorum*, published in 1548, Paul Émile became the first writer in France to put the famous curse in Molay's mouth: before the pyre, he utters his curse and summons the king and pope to appear before God's judgement; this was to be taken up by all historians in subsequent centuries, but uttered from the stake itself.

This curse, however, did little to bring Jacques de Molay out of a certain anonymity. People like Voltaire could write about the Templars and view their sentence as an act of barbarism without drawing particular attention to him. It was only at the end of the eighteenth century, and above all in the nineteenth, that he was to become a hero. This he owed not so much to the wild imaginings and forgeries of Fabre-Pellaprat and his friends, founders of the neo-templarism movement in the early nineteenth century (the so-called chart of succession of Larmenius, for example, is a crude forgery),[27] as to the development from the mid-eighteenth century onwards of a 'national theatre' always in search of patriotic themes.[28]

Jacques de Molay became one of the heroes of this national theatre, thanks to Raynouard, whose tragedy *The Templars* was staged with considerable success at the Théâtre-Français in 1805–6 (the celebrated tragedian Talma played one of the protagonists).[29] After the first performance, the *Courrier des spectacles* wrote: 'The theatre has long called for this national subject.'[30] The drama was distinguished by the confrontation between the king, who believed the Templars guilty but was prepared to pardon them if the Grand Master acknowledged this guilt, and Jacques de Molay, who rejected such a 'deal'. 'I would like to pardon you. I offer you your life,' says the king, to which Molay replies, 'Sire, offer us honour.'

A successful play often brought in its wake numerous sketches, light comedies or parodies; Raynouard's led to a number of emulators and, in 1807, a play entitled *Jacques de Molay* was offered to the Saint-Martin theatre, but turned down because it was too serious for a light comedy. Napoleon was also interested in Raynouard's play, although he reproached him for his bias towards Jacques de Molay; according to the emperor, the king appeared too weak and the Grand Master too perfect. In order to move the public, Napoleon basically claimed, the tragic hero should reveal a few human weaknesses. For him, the true hero was Philip the Fair who, through force of circumstance (the key word in Napoleon's reasoning and his concept of tragedy), acts as he does because he cannot do otherwise. The tragic dilemma of the statesman![31]

The play was staged throughout the nineteenth century and was re-edited in the popular series 'Good books', or 'One hundred good books at 10 centimes to form a library for every family', in which Raynouard's *The Templars* figured among the four titles representing French subjects (*Joan of Arc*, *Charles IX* and *The Siege of Calais*, alongside Racine and Corneille).[32]

This popularity in the nineteenth century, which the reservations of historians such as Michelet did nothing to weaken, was also made evident by Molay's entry into the crusade rooms in the palace of Versailles, a collection built up by Louis-Philippe. Jacques de Molay is represented in a bust by Amaury Duval in an 1840 painting, and figures in an action scene on a large picture by Claude Jacquand, dated 1842, which shows him at the head of his troops entering the reconquered Jerusalem in 1299.[33] It is, of course, a legendary representation, but one founded on a rumour that made the rounds of Christendom in 1300 and was connected with the offensives of the Mongol khan Ghâzân in 1299–1303. According to this rumour, khan Ghâzân, victor over the Mamluks in December 1299 at the time of the second battle of Homs, aided by the Christians of Armenia and the Masters of the Temple and Hospital Orders and their troops, was supposed to have handed Jerusalem back to the Christians. Laurent Dailliez (who has taken mischievous pleasure in muddying the waters) affirms that at that date Jacques de Molay was one of the three generals in the Mongol army, and would have had the honour of victoriously entering the Holy City.[34] Were it not for the text of the Templar of Tyre, who was well known, if not by his contemporaries, at least by later historians, it is possible that this assertion by the usually reliable Dailliez would be taken more seriously. On the basis of the correctly dated text by Hayton of Corycos, I have shown that Jacques de Molay was in Armenia in 1298 or 1299, therefore prior to Ghâzân's victorious battle against the Mamluks. The Templar of Tyre states: 'After Cazan had beaten the Saracens, he returned to his country leaving in his place at Damascus one of his admirals who had the name Molay …'[35] In fact, this was a Mongol general by the name of Mûlay, easily confused with Molay, and thus with the Templar Grand Master.

The contemporary western sources used by S. Schein in his study on the origin of the rumour current in the West, according to which the Holy City was handed back to the Christians by Ghâzân, never associate Jacques de Molay with this episode.[36] Might there have been a text which, at some time or another, made the connection between Molay and the supposed recapture of Jerusalem, perhaps based on the confusion caused by the Templar of Tyre's text? The painter Jacquand was not the only one to take the tradition at face value. This is what the article on Molay in the *Nouvelle Biographie universelle* of 1861, edited by Rapetti, has to say:

> Jacques de Molay had taken an active part in the great khan's action plan. What proves it is that he had command of one of the wings of the Tartar army. With the troops entrusted to him, he invaded Syria, took part in the initial battle in which the sultan was vanquished, pursued Malek Nasir in his flight as far as the Egyptian desert; then, under the leadership of Kutluk, a Tartar general, he had the joy of regaining from the Muslims, among other towns, Jerusalem, which the Tartars entered to celebrate the Easter festival.[37]

It is true that, in the Versailles rooms, he is not shown in a portrait like Hugues de Payns, the founder of the Temple, or Foulques de Villaret, his *alter ego* in the Order of the Hospital. But it is appropriate that he is depicted in action, even if that action is one in which he did not really engage, as it is closer to the reality of Molay's deeds in the crucial years of his Mastership (1299–1302) than has been suggested by many of the learned discussions held since the nineteenth century.

In the south-west of the Czech Republic lies the castle of Ruzemberk, on the Upper Vltava, which was confiscated from one of those defeated in the battle of the White Mountain in 1621 and given as a reward by the Habsburgs to a family of Flemish origin, the Bucquois. In the mid-nineteenth century, the owner had a 'crusades gallery' set up, modelled on the Versailles rooms, although obviously smaller. In 1855, he commissioned the painter Friedrich Ströbel to execute eight portraits to be hung on the walls of this gallery: of these, Jacques de Molay occupies a prominent place beside Godefroy de Bouillon, Philip Augustus and Saint Louis, while facing him are Richard the Lionheart, Leopold of Babenberg (Duke of Austria), Conrad III and Frederick Barbarossa.

CONCLUSION
A PORTRAIT OF JACQUES DE MOLAY

As this book closes, the reader may quite rightly ask the question, 'But when all is said and done, who *was* Jacques de Molay?'

The documents that enable one to discern his personality are rare, although they do exist. Few of them, however, provide certainties; they are contradictory and imprecise; their reliability must constantly be called into question, and the answers to those questions are not always possible or, even when they are available, are often unsatisfactory.

Nevertheless, since I have taken the risk of writing his biography, I must carry on to the end. Having meticulously analysed this rare and problematical documentation in an attempt to derive the maximum from it, I am taking the risk of pruning, choosing and affirming.

After a broad brush-stroke résumé of Jacques de Molay's life, I will try to determine his personality and draw his portrait. It will be 'my' portrait, inevitably and deliberately subjective, therefore open to criticism and likely to be retouched or revised at any time.

Like the historians of the medieval era who, having written a history sometimes summarised it, I will begin with a 'summary' of Jacques de Molay's life. Next, I shall attempt to draw my portrait of him; and to conclude, I will return to his failure and his share in the responsibility for the disappearance of the Temple.

Jacques de Molay was the offspring of an undistinguished family, probably minor nobility; he was born around 1244 at Molay (Haute-Saône) in the county of Burgundy, an Empire territory. He entered the Order of the Temple at Beaune in 1265, where he was received by Humbert de Pairaud, the Visitor of France and England, in the presence of Amaury de la Roche, Master of France, who were two leading men in the Order at that time. A brother knight, he soon went to the East, around 1270, independently of Guillaume de Beaujeu, who had become Grand Master in 1273 and with whom he is often mistakenly associated. His whole career as a Templar was spent in the East, but there is mention of him in France in 1285. It is not known if he held so much as an office of Commander or Master of a province in the West; nor is it known if he held any office in the East, unlike Guillaume de Malay, who was perhaps one of his relatives and was Marshal of the Order. This almost total lack of sources for the period 1265–91 leads me to think that, without necessarily being a self-effacing Templar, he was a discreet one, and did not belong in Guillaume de Beaujeu's 'team' or his sphere of influence: relatives, friends, vassals and clients. It is not known whether he was at Acre or in the garrison of a fortress when the capital of the Latin kingdom fell in May 1291.

Having retreated to Cyprus, like all the Franks who were still able to do so, he spoke at a Chapter assembled on the island in the autumn of 1291, offering himself as an alternative and as a reformer of the Temple. He was elected Master of the Order before 20 April 1292, as is formally attested by a document in the archives of the Crown of Aragon. This may have happened following an internal contest which set him against Hugues de Pairaud but, even so, no clear rift existed then between the two lines of policy regarding the Order's future, or in 'national' oppositions between groups of Templars. At that date, Pairaud was still an undistinguished member of the Order, who cannot be seen as the French monarchy's candidate against a Molay who was hostile to the kingdom of France and a defender of the Order's autonomy. In the two decades following the fall of Acre, indeed, the idea of a rapid reconquest of the Holy Land and Jerusalem was widely shared, all the more so because an alliance with the Mongols looked possible. If there was a rift, therefore, it must have been of a personal nature. In any case, there was not enough time, after Thibaud Gaudin's brief Mastership and before the election, for large-scale manoeuvres to be employed in order to put up a candidate in opposition to Molay.

Once elected, Jacques de Molay very quickly established his command of the Order and dealt with the most urgent matters first, in Cyprus and Armenia of Cilicia, which were threatened by the Mamluks. In spring 1293, he made a journey to the West which took him to Provence, Catalonia, Italy, England and France. There he settled several local problems, but chiefly he sought the help of the rulers in the West and the Church in recapturing of the Holy Land, strengthening the defence of Cyprus and rebuilding of the Templar forces; he also discussed plans for a crusade, and with various people broached the problem of uniting the Orders of the Temple and Hospital, a plan which he opposed and would continue to oppose consistently. He formed very close relations with Pope Boniface VIII, and relationships of trust with Edward I of England, James II of Aragon and Charles II of Naples; in contrast, nothing is known about his relations with the king of France. Lastly, he held provincial or general Chapters of his Order at Montpellier in 1293 and at Arles in 1296, at which he tried to impose reforms.

In the autumn of 1296, Molay returned to Cyprus, where he defended the interests of the Temple against King Henry II, with whom he had never got on well (here he was paying the price of Guillaume de Beaujeu's legacy). But above all, from 1299 to 1303 he pursued a Mongol alliance for all it was worth. With his Order and the other Christian forces from the kingdoms of Cyprus and Little Armenia (the king, other military Orders and the aristocracy of the two kingdoms), he tried to co-ordinate actions with the Mongols of the khanate of Ilkhan (or Persia). He intervened in Armenia in 1298 or 1299, probably after the capture by the Mamluks of Roche-Guillaume, the last Templar fortress in Cilicia. The Christian forces, however, were not ready to take advantage of the victory won by Ghâzân, the khan of Persia, over the Mamluks at the second battle of Homs in December 1299. In the summer of 1300, Jacques de Molay committed his Order to raids carried out along the Egyptian and Syrian coasts, then in November he took part in the occupation of the tiny island of Ruad, facing the Syrian town of Tortosa. He wanted to establish a bridgehead with a view to combining operations with the Mongols; but the Mongols failed to arrive, and the same occurred in 1301 and 1302. In September 1302, the Templars were driven out of Ruad and many were massacred by Egypt's Mamluk forces. The Ruad episode was wrongly interpreted as the failure of an absurd attempt by Jacques de Molay to settle his Order permanently in close proximity to Syria, whereas it was no more than an operation carried out within the framework of the strategy of the Mongol alliance. The failure of that strategy had doomed Ruad, and Molay finally abandoned it, as it became less and less tenable after Ghâzân's death in 1304.

At the start of his pontificate in November 1305, Pope Clement V had asked the Masters of the military Orders for their opinions on preparing for a crusade and on the plan for the merging of the Orders. On 6 June 1306, they were officially summoned to Poitiers, where Clement V had installed himself, to discuss these matters. At the pope's request, Jacques de Molay drew up two memoranda, one on each of these questions. They were written during the summer of 1306 and sent to the pope in the autumn. The interview at Poitiers, initially planned for the first fortnight of November 1306, was postponed owing to the pope's illness; but Jacques de Molay had left Cyprus around 15 October 1306 and landed in France in late November or early December. Nothing is known of his activities during the first six months of 1307; he may perhaps have made a brief stay in Paris. At all events, he was in Poitiers in the second half of May. On the crucial question of the merging of the Orders, the Grand Master was unwavering: he rejected the idea, which was awkward because he clashed with the king of France by thwarting his ambitions, and embarrassed the pope in his negotiations with the king over the thorny problem of condemning the memory of Pope Boniface VIII, which the king wished to achieve at all costs. Moreover, it upset the attempts to get a crusade under way. The Grand Master's intransigent position weakened the Temple at the very moment when – as Molay discovered during his journey – slanderous rumours concerning the Order were rife. The king and his councillors, prominent among whom was Guillaume de Nogaret, did not pass up the opportunity to exploit that weakness.

Jacques de Molay went to Paris for the Order's Chapter on 24 June; there he met the king, with whom he spoke about the accusations levelled at the Temple. Partially reassured, he returned to Poitiers, where he spent the summer, but asked the pope for an inquiry to be set up quickly to clear the Order of the suspicions that burdened it. On 24 August, the pope announced that he was initiating an inquiry with the agreement of the Order; but the king of France had no intention of letting himself be kept out of such imminent business. On 14 September 1307, in utmost secrecy, he set in motion the procedure which, on 13 October 1307, ended with the arrest of all the Templars in the kingdom and the confiscation of their possessions. Jacques de Molay was arrested in Paris, where he had returned in the preceding days to attend the funeral of Catherine of Valois.

When questioned on 24 October, Molay acknowledged that he had been received into the Temple following an illicit ritual that was inserted into a perfectly orthodox one, as laid down by the Rule. The Master admitted only to denying Christ and spitting on the Cross but, when forced to repeat his statement publicly the next day, he provided the royal propaganda against the Temple with sufficient arguments to discredit the Order and its members totally;

all the more so since the royal police obtained from him a letter addressed to all the Templars, in which he asked them to admit to these practices. On 22 November 1307, in order to regain his authority, Clement V ordered the arrest of all Templars throughout Christendom.

The pope nevertheless wanted to hear Molay; in December, he sent cardinals to Paris, and in front of them Jacques de Molay retracted his confessions. A power struggle ensued between the king and the pope, ending in a compromise in August 1308. The Bull *Faciens misericordiam* set out a dual procedure which aimed to try individual persons and the Order as an entity, following meticulous inquiries conducted by bishops and papal commissions. A Council, assembled at Vienne, would pass judgement on the fate of the Temple. Meanwhile the Order's dignitaries, including Jacques de Molay, were to be judged by the pope. Shortly afterwards, in the royal palace at Chinon, Molay was again questioned by the cardinals, but in the presence of royal agents, and returned to his admissions of 24 October 1307. Then for a whole year there was silence. The inquiry commissions were slowly put in place, and the papal commission for the kingdom of France began its hearings in Paris in November 1309. On two occasions, 26 and 28 November, Jacques de Molay made a deposition; he let it be understood that he did not acknowledge the accusations brought against the Order, but at that point opted for a defence tactic which he would not alter: to say nothing before the commission and to rely totally on the pope's judgement.

It was a turning point in a clumsily handled defence. For reasons that I will clarify later, Jacques de Molay had no other solution than this refusal to take part in the continuation of the inquiry. However, by doing so he condemned himself to silence and, after a last appearance in March 1310, to remaining apart from the great protest movement by the Templars who had come en masse to Paris to defend the Order. That movement was shattered by the sentencing by the archbishop of Sens, Philippe de Marigny, of 54 Templars to be burnt at the stake on 10–12 May 1310. The Order was abolished by the pope during the Council of Vienne on 22 March 1312. Clement V waited almost two years before sending three cardinals to Paris, their task being not to try the Templar dignitaries but to impose a sentence of life imprisonment on them. At that point, Jacques de Molay, feeling that he had been betrayed, rose up, retracted all his admissions and proclaimed his Order's innocence, before challenging the king and pope before God. This was on 18 March 1314; the king had him burnt that same evening.

It is difficult to discern Molay the man behind Molay the Grand Master, because documentation is both sparse and controversial; but he makes an appearance, none the less, and his picture is revealed as very different from the caricature history has imposed on him.

Jacques de Molay was humble, but not retiring. Of course, one must not take literally his declarations during the trial when, like many Templars, he defined himself as a 'poor, unlettered' man,[1] for he meant quite simply that he did not know Latin. As a prisoner, he found himself isolated and deprived of advice, and complained of having not so much as four deniers, and therefore being unable in such conditions properly to conduct his defence. He was a man of good sense, average intelligence and at times not lacking in shrewdness and perceptiveness, but he was not an intellectual. The long deposition on 12 January 1311 of Templar Gérard de Caux recounts that the current Master of the Order, whom he had seen overseas, had begged those brothers who owned copies of the Rule, statutes and regulations of the Order to hand them over to him; some of them he destroyed, others he divided among the elders of the Order, and yet more he kept for himself. He had, however, given Gérard de Caux a copy of the *De laude novae militiae* by Saint Bernard. Brother Gérard added, 'The elders said that the Masters Guillaume de Beaujeu and Thomas Bérard had acted in the same fashion, and they told one another that the Order had not greatly benefited from having cultivated persons in its bosom.'[2]

Molay was certainly a strong character, proud, sometimes arrogant, although not overbearing; he was probably not always easy to deal with and, as with his defence of the interests of his Order, could be intransigent. He recognised that in certain circumstances the Templars had without doubt acted over-zealously towards the secular authorities in defence of their rights, and probably included himself in their number. He was also inflexible in his conception of the Order and its mission: an independent Order, under the sole authority of the pope, with the mission of defending Cyprus and reconquering the Holy Land.

He may have been intransigent and consistent in his ideas and objectives to the point of seeming stubborn, but he was neither narrow-minded nor stupid. He believed in the crusades; he believed the recapture of Jerusalem was also possible. Contrary to what has been said in various places, in 1300 the crusade was not a lost cause, Jerusalem was not a daydreamer's illusion, and Jacques de Molay was drawing on practical experience. He knew what he wanted, but he was open to discussion. He was a capable negotiator, and not lacking in diplomatic, even pedagogic, talents – as may be seen from his relations with the king of Aragon. In the Cardona affair of 1302, as in the case of the appointment of Exemen de Lenda as Master of Aragon, he was able to settle delicate situations and put across his point of view without falling foul of the king, and he knew when to make the necessary concessions.

If we are to believe the single testimony of the Templar of Tyre, he may have been short-tempered, to the point of becoming violently angry with the king of France and the pope. The circumstances of the incident are known (an enormous loan granted to the king by the Treasurer of Paris), but they are problematic; and it is unclear at what precise moment in his second journey to the West it may have taken place. In any event, it is scarcely in keeping with his general attitude or behaviour in the relations he had with rulers and with Pope Boniface VIII. With Clement V, they proved more mundane, but it is hard to see on what occasions he would have flown into a rage; the tone of the two memoranda he addressed to him is deferential. His relations with Edward I, James II and Charles II were cordial, but they seem to have been more distant with Philip the Fair although this may be a view distorted by the absence of documents (unlike with his relations with the pope, James II chiefly and, to a lesser degree, Edward I). There was total disagreement between them over the merging of the Orders, but it was not the occasion for a violent display of anger. In any case, it is known that in June 1307 the Grand Master discussed with the king the problem of the accusations levelled against the Order but that no 'fireworks' were recorded. In any case, Philip the Fair did not provoke 'scenes'; he listened, often without uttering a word, but apparently deep in thought. Those who were granted audiences were listened to and might have gained the impression that they had been *understood*.

Naturally, Jacques de Molay had some failings: firmness and consistency in his ideas were good qualities, but hanging on to them obstinately soon became a flaw. I will return to this regarding the merging of the Orders. Although the two memoranda he wrote, on crusading and, chiefly, on uniting the Orders, sometimes reveal sound good sense, they also show a short-sighted policy. Similarly, the Grand Master evinces a rather naïve self-satisfaction; and he had a few very human weaknesses.

Another angle from which to approach the personality of Jacques de Molay is through the relationships he had within the Order, with the brothers, dignitaries and simple Templars. Once again, one must beware of the distorting lens of the sources: on the one hand, many items of information, most often in letters, from the Archives of the Crown of Aragon but almost nowhere else; on the other, the data extracted from the trial interrogations, where objectivity was not the principal quality.

Jacques de Molay was capable of forming bonds of friendship with members of the Order, and showed himself to be warm-hearted towards those – Templars or not – who visited him in Cyprus. The letters exchanged with the Catalan Templar Pierre de Saint-Just are those between two friends. Saint-Just held the office of Commander of Corbins, Maiorca, Ambel, Alfambra and, in the end, Peñiscola (owing this last promotion to the Grand Master). In the corpus of letters written by Molay, four are addressed to him;[3] and we also have letters from Saint-Just to the Grand Master. These sometimes have no other purpose than the relaying of personal news, such as a response to an inquiry into the correspondent's state of health. Thus, on 1 November 1300:

> Know that we have received your kind letters, from whose contents we under-
> stand that you are in good health, which pleases us greatly. And since you desire
> to know if our health is good, you may be informed of this and news of our land
> [Cyprus] by the men who come to your country.[4]

In another letter, Pierre de Saint-Just asks the Grand Master to order prayers for a Catalan brother, Dalmau de Roccabert, who was perhaps a prisoner of the Infidels or sick. Molay replies with a letter of thanks.[5]

With other Catalan or Aragonese correspondents, such as Arnau de Banyuls, Berenguer Guamir, Berenguer de Cardona, his tone is equally benevolent, even if the friendship tie is not as clear-cut as in the case of Saint-Just. Molay was loyal to his friends, and kept the promises he had made to them. He defended Berenguer de Cardona, whose dismissal the king of Aragon sought in 1302, but complained of his refusal to satisfy the Master's requests when he wished to reward loyal Templars such as Bernard de Tamary or Pierre de Castillon by installing them in a Commandery in Catalonia or Aragon.

In Cyprus, Jacques de Molay gave a warm welcome to visitors from the West: Ramon Lull was received with great joy (*hylariter*), the writer of *Vita coetani* tells us; Berenguer de Cardona, who went twice to Cyprus, in 1300–1 and 1306, recounted that he had met the Grand Master, who was making ready to leave for the West, and spent three days in his company, which had given him great happiness.[6]

In his manner of governing the Order, Jacques de Molay was not autocratic; he did not infringe its statutes, but governed with the Chapter. There is no trace of any conflict with the latter during his Mastership, as there was at the same time in the Order of the Hospital under Guillaume de Villaret.[7] During his two journeys to the West, he held general and provincial Chapters. He steered the Order with men whom he trusted and who trusted him; men he knew well, whom he had met and frequented within the West or in Cyprus; men from his own region, from the county of Burgundy, but others as well, notably those from the States of the Crown of Aragon. Was his choice of an Aragonese rather than a French alliance dictated by political imperatives?[8] Possibly, but here again, the Catalan and Aragonese links are better known because they appear more frequently in the wealth of documentation preserved in Barcelona. We can obtain a better grasp of those relations of trust and friendship that I described earlier by way of those documents which detail more closely the daily lives of the region's Templars. But there is nothing to say that such relations did not exist with the Templars in France, England or Italy. One must beware the *a silentio* argument. All in all, there was no known schism between Jacques de Molay and the Order's dignitaries. There may have been disagreements with Hugues de Pairaud, but they are to be guessed at rather than clearly stated in the sources. With the reservation that the latter are fragmentary, it may be claimed that throughout his Mastership Molay was not challenged within his Order, unlike the Masters of the Hospital who were his contemporaries, Eudes des Pins, Guillaume de Villaret and Foulques de Villaret (the last-named being dismissed a little later).[9]

From the minutes of the trial interrogations, a few pieces of information can be gleaned as to how the Templars regarded their Grand Master. The investigators put three questions that implicated him: the first concerned his having given absolution of sins when, as a layman, he had no right to do so. We know that he discussed this matter with Philip the Fair, admitting that he had sometimes done this. Generally speaking, the brothers questioned on this subject answered in the negative. A second question was about the authority he exerted, with his 'convent', over the Order, to which the replies were repetitive: yes, the orders he and his convent issued were obeyed;[10] but many of the Templars questioned viewed this almost total obedience to the Master as the cause of keeping alive in the Order those misdeeds for which it was blamed. The witnesses were also asked if they knew the Grand Master had admitted the faults of which the Order was accused. On the whole, the answers to these questions brought before the papal commission of Paris were positive: the misdeeds had persisted in the Order because the Grand Master and other dignitaries and commanders had allowed them to do so, which had resulted in the scandal; furthermore, other witnesses, following suit, admitted that 'they had heard that the Grand Master and others had confessed misdeeds, but did not know which ones'.[11]

Naturally, these replies came from the Templars questioned in Paris after fifty-four of their Order had been sent to the stake. That does not alter the truth of the matter: the Master had certainly made some admissions. But in Cyprus, the Templars who were questioned refused to believe it, and at Elne, where to a man they rejected the accusations, Pierre Bleda, Templar of the Mas Deu in Roussillon, vigorously expressed an opinion widely shared by his fellow prisoners, when he declared that 'if the Grand Master of the Order of the Temple made the confessions attributed to him, which for my part I shall never believe, he was lying through his teeth'.[12]

But before that fatal day of 12 May 1310, which saw fifty-four Templars consigned to the flames, and the resistance of those who had wanted to defend the Order shattered, another note made itself heard in the depositions and testimonies. Above all, as the Templars felt freer to speak, some indulged in less seemly remarks about the Grand Master. However, from testimonies gathered between February and May 1310 in Paris, it emerges that on the whole the Templars trusted their Grand Master. This can be clearly seen as regards the matter of designating procurators to defend the Order.

The papal commission had consulted the Templars in the many prisons where they were held, asking for an overall view on the matter and requesting them to appoint procurators for each detention centre. Pierre de Bologna and Renaud de Provins, the two chaplains who, with two knights, would eventually be appointed as procurators for the Order, began by asking, on 28 March, that the procurators be appointed by the Grand Master 'under whose obedience we are';[13] another declared that he would refer to the Grand Master to defend the Order;[14] the twenty-one Templars held in the house of the prior of Cornay stated that they 'had a head and superiors, in other words the Grand Master of their Order, to whom they owed obedience'; but they declared themselves prepared to defend their Order if the Grand Master did not.[15] There are plenty of references, but to end I will quote just three.

Before deciding on the designation of procurators, those Templars imprisoned in the house of Jean Rossel asked 'to see the Master of the Temple and Brother Hugo de Peraut, Commander of France, and all the worthies of the Temple, to get their advice ...'[16] The thirteen Templars held at Saint-Martin-des-Champs, meanwhile, stated that they 'had a leader to whom they owed obedience' and that 'they believed their Grand Master to be good, just, honest, loyal and free of the faults of which he was accused'.[17] At Mainz, Count Frederick, Commander of the trans-Rhine Temple, who had spent twelve years overseas, living for a long time with the Grand Master, whose companion he had been, and returning to the West with him, stated: 'He had always held him to be a good Christian, as good as any person can be, and still does.'[18]

From these testimonies, which are contradictory (among other reasons because they reflect different situations depending on times and places), it emerges that Jacques de Molay was not generally blamed personally, even by those who were most consistently unenthusiastic as regards certain of the Order's practices. When the Templars interrogated were asked at what moment the dubious practices had been introduced into the Order, they rarely gave precise replies. In a fairly confused fashion, this or that Grand Master was named – Beaujeu, Bérard, Molay himself – but even then very infrequently. Most often, the Templars informally implicated the Order itself or, more exactly, 'the system'. Nevertheless, that does not allow Jacques de Molay to escape his responsibilities, and I will conclude on this subject.

Molay was unable to save his Order. It is not certain whether he could have done so anyway, but a doubt persists. During his career as Master of the Temple, he had to confront problems and make choices; some were good, but others were less happy, even bad.

The idea of forging a Mongol alliance was a good one. Many historians who are not specialists on the crusades and military-religious Orders, or who are little versed in the research and publications of recent years by British and Israeli historians, continue to reiterate mechanically that everything was over in 1291; crusading no longer had any meaning, and the Templar Order (curiously, *only* that one) no longer served any purpose. For good measure, they add that the Templars who returned to the West in huge numbers displayed boorish ill manners: they drank (like Templars); they passionately kissed both men and women (beware the Templar's kiss!); in Germany they were said to be nothing short of brothel-keepers (Tempelhof); and, naturally, they were the

West's bankers. All attempts to modify, at the very least, these commonplaces have failed up to now. In 1291, therefore, the Temple became redundant; and in 1292 poor Jacques de Molay was elected head of an institution that was merely fit for the scrapheap, as a result of which what happened in 1307 was only too predictable. That there is no smoke without fire is a well-known adage, but historians should always ask themselves: who lit the fire? Everyone knows who lit the last fires of the Temple.

Yet all was certainly *not* over in 1291. The crusades, the concept of crusading, still had a present and a future, although perhaps no longer in the form in which it had prevailed in the twelfth and thirteenth centuries. The change had been set in motion by Saint Louis. Crusading would have to make way for mission, conversion by words; their adversaries were different, territories diversified. But to say that people no longer thought of Jerusalem and the other holy places in Syria–Palestine is not true. In the late thirteenth and early fourteenth century there was still an opportunity to be seized: the Mongol alliance. As long as that opportunity remained a reality – in other words, until the death of Ghâzân in 1304 – a crusade with Jerusalem as its objective was a possibility. I would even go so far as to say that the likelihood of success had never been so strong as in 1299–1303. And Jacques de Molay must be given his due, more than anyone else – pope, king of France, Order of the Hospital, etc. – for believing in it and for doing everything in his power for it to be realised.[19]

But after 1304, even though a Mongol delegation came to Poitiers in 1307, the strategy of the Mongol alliance lay dead and abandoned. Something else needed to be proposed, although admittedly an imaginative substitute was somewhat lacking: Molay's plan was classic, and Villaret's scarcely any fresher. At the time of discussing these plans with the pope, Foulques de Villaret undertook the conquest of Rhodes, something which would take four years to achieve. In 1306, when Molay, then Villaret, left for the West, no one could yet say what the outcome would be. The ever-wise Templar of Tyre had the necessary short hindsight when he wrote:

In this way God sent His favour to the noble Master of the Hospital and the valiant men of his house, who had great liberty and freedom in this place, having their own seigneurie outside the dominion of any other, and may God by His great grace keep them there performing good works, Amen.[20]

At that time, Molay was in prison and the Temple broken. His last years must not be judged in relation to Rhodes and the Hospitallers' initiative, but in regard to his attitude to the torment that had befallen his Order.

Jacques de Molay's initial error was in the first instance no more than a setback. He had failed to reform the Order of the Temple, and had certainly been mistaken about what should take priority in undergoing reform. He had doubtless proclaimed his willingness to undertake reform in the autumn of 1291 in Cyprus. At the start of his first journey to the West, at the time of the general Chapter in Montpellier in August 1293, he had had what might be called 'mini-reforms' adopted. This could have been the beginning of a process, but it was, in reality, the end. There was undeniably a malaise within the Order, of which Molay was aware, but of which he had not grasped the full measure or the possible consequences. That malaise was sparked by the scabrous ritual introduced into the admission ceremony. The Templars' statements at the time of the trial cannot be taken at face value, of course, and it should be remembered that Jacques de Molay had acknowledged only two things on this point – the denial of Christ and spitting on (or strictly, to one side of) the Cross. This ritual, somewhat similar to a student 'rag', occurred only once in a Templar's career, when he was received into the Order; it was not always practised in full, and more often than is believed it was not practised at all.[21] Of course, there were some perverted types who went too far, as in any rag, of whom Gérard de Villiers, the Master of France in the last years, was one.

In 1305, when the king of France and the pope were made aware of the problem, the question of reforming the Order assumed a dimension beyond that of knowing if meat should continue to be eaten three times a week or not. Reforming the Order meant eradicating these scurrilous practices from the admission ceremony; but Jacques de Molay had not done so.

Perhaps he had not been able to. I regard him as closer to Thomas Bérard, a great reformer, than Guillaume de Beaujeu. However, he may have encountered obstacles within the Order itself. For example, Hugues de Pairaud was not a strong enough rival or opponent to hamper Molay in his government of the Order or in conducting policies in keeping with his ideas (such as the Mongol alliance), but he had sufficient influence in France to block an ambitious programme of reforms. At all events, Molay did not push this programme hard enough, once the initial 'inspiration' and promises of the first journey to the West were over.

Perhaps he had not wanted to? Had never given it a thought? Neither he nor the other Templars had perceived the gravity of the matter. It was tradition, gave no cause for concern and it was not only the Templars who turned a blind eye. What about those Franciscan or Dominican friars who, according to many Templars who had made their confessions to them after undergoing these degrading and reprehensible practices at their entry, showed astonishment, indignation and, most often, incredulity – but were content to do no more than inflict a few additional fasts on their sinning brothers over the following year? Apparently, not one of those redoubtable pursuers of heresy, the Dominicans, had felt the need to take a closer look and denounce these practices. It is easier to understand how the idea that it was not all that serious could have become lastingly implanted in the minds of the Templars and their leaders. And indeed, it was not all that serious! With some relief, the papal commission reached the same conclusion. But in the meantime, the king and his councillors had judged otherwise, and turned these practices into the focus of their attack on the Temple. The work of the papal commission brought matters back into proportion, but it was too late – the Order was dead.

Jacques de Molay found himself trapped by this error of judgement. He could not fail to 'confess' those practices (even if he reduced them to the minimum), and therefore could not prevent their being exploited by the king and his agents against him and his Order. Henceforward he would no longer be master of his own destiny or that of the Order. He had to steer a course between Scylla and Charybdis: stand by his admissions and risk increasingly discrediting himself; or retract them and be perceived as a liar and considered relapsed. This reason, rather than cowardice or fear of torture, explains the waverings in his depositions, although here and there he did mention his fear of torture: he was dissembling. He tried unsuccessfully to escape from the trap which had been set by Nogaret and Plaisians, but for which the Temple had provided one of the components. He believed he had found the solution by refusing, from 28 November 1309, to take any part in the procedure set in place by the Bull *Faciens misericordiam* and refusing to collaborate in the work of the papal commission. However, immured in silence, he excluded himself from the trial and ceased to have any influence over the course of events.

Jacques de Molay had failed to reform his Order because he had been unable to make a correct assessment of the deleterious impact of the admission ceremonial on the Templars themselves. Evidence of this was the reproach made by many Templars that he had shown himself too negligent to denounce these misdeeds and eradicate them from the Order. Reproach cast on whom? The Masters, the dignitaries, but also themselves. The law of silence had worked perfectly within the Templar Order.

Molay did, however, die for his ideas; they were those in which he had been trained in the Temple, those in which, having become Grand Master, he had continued to believe: crusading, the Holy Land, the independence of the Order. But had not this faithfulness to his ideas, this stubbornness, also contributed to the downfall of the Temple? In part, yes.

In fact, Molay had committed another error, well before the trial, by rejecting the union of the Orders. His motives were not insignificant, though he set out his arguments against such a merger in very clumsy fashion. In Lampedusa's *Leopard*, young Tancred says to Prince Salinas, 'If we want everything to continue, everything first has to change.' It can be applied *mutatis mutandis* to the problem facing the Temple: the Temple had to disappear in order to survive. It needed to merge with the Order of the Hospital if an independent military-religious Order under the sole supervision of the pope was to have any chance of surviving. And this was not something to which Jacques de Molay could easily resign himself, for he had clearly seen what such a change would involve: 'It is to act in a very hostile and hard manner to force a man ... to change his life and habits or choose another Order if it is against his will.'[22] The Temple was not being asked to unite with the Hospital, but to meld into the Hospital, disappear into the Hospital; and everyone knew very well that the union proposed at that time was going to end up as a military Order subject to the king of France, and of which perhaps the king himself, although more likely one of his sons, would become head. Molay did not want this to happen. It is equally unlikely that Foulques de Villaret, Clement V, not to mention Edward I and James II, desired such a solution to the problem of merging the Orders.

The fact remains that, by rejecting the union of the Orders, Molay prevented the pope, Villaret and himself from playing a card which could have been a trump. A merging of the Orders negotiated with sufficient speed by the pope and the heads of the Orders could have cut the ground from under the king of France's ambitious feet and stopped the furthering of his hegemonic plans. Of course, it was risky; it might fail, and all the rulers in Christendom might demand what the king of France was demanding. The unified Order would then have been divided into just so many national Orders.

Nor did the dissolution of the Order of the Temple achieve the objective which Ramon Lull or Pierre Dubois ascribed to the king, namely, the creation of a single Order under his control. At Vienne, the pope had been able to impose the attribution of the Temple's possessions to the Hospital, contrary to the king of France's wishes. Paradoxically, in two states where, having rejected the union of the Temple with the Hospital, the rulers desired to obtain a single Order in their country, but without condemning or destroying the Temple, they partly succeeded. Within the Crown of Aragon, it was possible only in the kingdom of Valencia, with the creation of the Order of Montesa, which combined the possessions of the Temple and Hospital; conversely, in Catalonia and Aragon, it was the Hospital which received the Temple's assets. In the kingdom of Portugal, there was no fusion of Hospital and Temple; the possessions and houses of the Templar Order were bestowed upon the new Order of Christ, and ex-Templars became (or became again, since that had been their original name) Knights of Christ.

Jacques de Molay's final mistake, this time in the course of the trial, was to refer himself to the pope for judgement. I have given the reasons for his wavering during his interrogations. He tried to escape from the snare by placing himself completely in the hands of the pope, in November 1309. In any case, all the Templars shared the same naïve trust in the word of Clement V. By deciding to keep silent from then on in front of the papal commission, Molay ruled himself out of the game; so he took no part in the great Templar upsurge early in 1310, and remained apart from that pathetic attempt to defend and save the Order. He was its head, the Templars still trusted him, but he did not carry out his office to the bitter end; he betrayed their trust. At the time he no longer had much room for manoeuvre, but by taking the lead in the movement he could have strengthened it, and who knows what consequences that decision might have had? He also risked going to the stake. Perhaps he was not yet prepared for that?

Four years later, however, he was ready. The uprising had been in vain – but it had been magnificent. 'Molay lived in a period when the Order needed leaders who were heroes; unfortunately, he was no more than a poor and good man,' wrote Georges Lizerand.[23]

Until 1306, as long as it was a matter of taking on the mission for which the Order had been created – military service in the service of the Church, crusading and the liberation of Jerusalem – Jacques de Molay had filled his post brilliantly. But when it came to steering a course amid various political perils, disentangling the manoeuvres of the king, Nogaret and Plaisians, confronting the Inquisition, he was no longer up to the task. This was due partly to earlier mistakes, but also to the intellectual inadequacies of the Grand Master and, it must be admitted, of the Templars in general. He was no longer the right man for the job, but there again he had not been elected for that. Was there a man in the Order at that time who *was* right for the job? Hugues de Pairaud is a possibility. Yet apart from the fact that he was better acquainted than Molay with the mysteries of contemporary western politics, he does not seem to have had the necessary stature, and his attitude during the trial proves it.

Was heroism on the walls of Acre the same as that in the jails of Philip the Fair? I doubt it. How could one be heroic when faced with Guillaume de Nogaret? Molay was of good minor nobility, not a baron. The Templar Order favoured the emergence of new men, from the ranks of that minor and middle nobility. All the Grand Masters, including Molay, belonged in that category. He was doubtless not unhappy to have arrived where he was: at the head of one of the most prestigious religious Orders in Christendom. He was in contact with the pope, kings and princes, but he was not unduly overwhelmed. He was old (we must not forget that he had to tackle the storm that assailed the Order when he was between sixty and seventy), he had experience, he was cautious. For many a long year he guided his Order with wisdom, good sense and intelligence. In the end he had enough of the latter to realise that he had been caught in a trap, but was not clear-sighted enough to escape it. At least, unwillingly and unwittingly, by his sacrifice he had saved the Church. When Clement V deserted Jacques de Molay and his Order, he managed to wrest from Philip the Fair the abandonment of the indictment against the memory of Boniface VIII, the pope with whom Molay had got on so well.

NOTES

Abbreviations

Institutions

ACA	Archives of the Crown of Aragon (Barcelona)
AD	Archives of the départements
AHN	Archivio Historico Nacional (Madrid)
AN	Archives nationales (Paris)
BNF	Bibliothèque nationale de France (Paris)
CTHS	Comité des travaux historiques et scientifiques (Paris)
PRO	Public Records Office (London)
SHF	Société de l'Histoire de France (Paris)

Journals

AOL	Archives de l'Orient Latin
BEC	Bibliothèque de l'École des Chartres
ROL	Revue de l'Orient Latin

Works

Amadi   *Chronique d'Amadi et de Stambaldi*, ed. L. de Mas-Latrie

B.-T.   M.-L. Bulst-Thiele, *Sacrae domus militia templi* …

Baluze   E. Baluze, *Vitae papanum Avenionensium*

Bustron   *Chronique de l'île de Chypre par Florio Bustron*, ed. L. de Mas-Latrie

CH   J. Delaville Le Roulx, *Cartulaire général de l'ordre des hospitaliers de Saint-Jean de Jérusalem*

Éracles   *L'Estoirre de Éracles empereur*, RHC, Hist. Occ.

H. Finke, AA   H. Finke, *Acta Aragonensia*

H. Finke, *Papsttum*   H. Finke, *Papsttum und Untergang des Templerorden*

H. Finke, *Nachträge*   H. Finke, 'Nachträge und Ergänzungen zu den Acta aragonensia', *Spanische Forschungen* …

Grandes Chroniques de France   *Les Grandes Chroniques de France*, t. VII and VIII
Guizot   F. Guizot, *Collection des mémoires relatifs à l'Histoire de France*, t.
   XIII: *Guillaume de Nangis*, 30 vol.
G. Lizerand, *Le Dossier*   G. Lizerand, *Le Dossier de l'affaire des templiers*
Mich. (I, II)   Michelet, *Le Procès des templiers*, 2 vol., reissue.
Nangis   *La Chronique latine de Guillaume de Nangis* …, ed. H. Geraud
J. Prawer, *Royaume latin*   J. Prawer, *Histoire du Royaume latin de Jérusalem*
RHC   *Recueil des Historiens des croisades*, published by l'Académie des
   Inscriptions et Belles Lettres, Paris, 1841–1906
– Hist. Occ., Historiens Occidentaux, 5 vol.
– Hist. Or., Historiens Orientaux, 5 vol.
   Doc. Arm., Documents arméniens, 2 vol.
RHGF   *Recueil des Historiens des Gaules et de la France*, 24 vol., Paris, 1737–
   1904
Röhricht   R. Röhricht, *Regesta Regni Hierosolymitani*
R.T. 1   *Règle du Temple*, ed. S. Cerrini
R.T. 2   *Règle du Temple*, ed. H. de Curzon
T.T.   *Chronicle of the Templar of Tyre*

Chapter 1 1250 – Molay's Youth

1. Mich. II, p. 305.
2. H. Finke, *Papsttum*, t. II, p. 328.
3. *R.T.*1, Règle latine art. 59, pp. 214–15; règle française art. 4, p. 260.
4. This view is held by M. Barber, 'James of Molay, the Last Grand Master of the
   Order of the Temple', *Studia Monastica*, 14 (1972), pp. 91–124.
5. Mich. I, p. 415; see B.-T., p. 300, *n*. 30.
6. Mich. II, pp. 244–420; A. J. Forey, 'Towards a Profile of the Templars in the Early
   Fourteenth Century', *The Military Orders: Fighting for the Faith and Caring for the
   Sick*, Aldershot, ed. M. Barber, 1994, pp. 200 ff.
7. H. Finke, *Papsttum*, t. II, p. 324.
8. *Ibid.*, p. 325.
9. This is the date proposed by M.-L. Bulst-Thiele.
10. G. Duby, 'Les "jeunes" dans la société aristocratique dans la France du Nord-
    Ouest au XIIe siècle', *Annales: Économies, Sociétés, Civilisations*, 19 (1964),
    pp. 835–46.
11. *Dictionnaire national des communes de France, d'Algérie et des colonies*, Paris, 1897.

12. According to the manuscript peerage list of the county of Burgundy by Duvernoy in the library of Besançon, quoted by E. Besson and S. Leroy. P. Dupuy, *Traitez concernant l'histoire de France, à savoir la condamnation des templiers*, Paris, 1685, p. 65.

13. S. Leroy, 'Jacques de Molay et les templiers franc-comtois d'après les actes du procès', *Bulletin de la société grayloise d'émulation*, 3 (1900), pp. 133 and 136.

14. M. Rey, 'L'ordre du Temple en Franche-Comté ...', p. 95, *n.*5; the author refers to AD Doubs, 58 H 2. S. Leroy, ignored by M. Rey, had already mentioned this agreement, but gave another identification to the places cited in the document: according to him, they were Laître and Preigney, near Molay.

15. E. Besson, 'Étude sur Jacques de Molay', p. 484; taken up (and corrected) by S. Leroy, art. cit. (*n.* 13), p. 136.

16. Mich. I, pp. 65, 105, 117 and 562. The Gérard de Molay cited in 1233 was the vassal of a lord of La Rochelle, S. Leroy, *ibid.*

17. Mich. II, p. 289, and I, p. 564.

18. H. Finke, *Papsttum*, t. II, p. 337.

19. V. Thomassin, *Figures comtoises* ...; Bulst-Thiele and Dailliez lean towards this identification.

20. F. I. Dunod de Charnage, *Mémoire pour servir à l'histoire du comté de Bourgogne*, Besançon, 1740, p. 60.

21. J. Labbey de Billy, *Histoire de l'Université du comté de Bourgogne*, 1815, t. 2, p. 145. No will referring to Molay or Longwy is to be found in the publication of the *Testaments de l'officialité de Besançon*, ed. U. Robert, 'Collection de documents inédits de l'Histoire de France', 2 vol., Paris, 1902.

22. Besson, Leroy and Dugueyt (of whom only the 'positions' of their thesis are known and not the thesis itself) rely on this catalogue to reject categorically this Jura identification.

23. B.-T., p. 302, mentions the links between the Grandson and Oiselay families. The article by F. Funck-Brentano, 'Philippe le Bel et la noblesse comtoise', BEC, 49 (1888), pp. 1–36, on which it is based, never refers to Grandson. Oiselay is situated in Haute-Saône, canton of Gy. That rather tends to favour Molay, Haute-Saône.

24. B. Frale, *L'ultima battaglia dei Templari* ..., pp. 15–16.

25. A. Demurger, 'L'aristocrazia laïca e gli ordini religiosi-militari ...', *Militia Sacra. Gli ordini militari tra Europa e Terrasanta*, Perugia, 1994, pp. 55–84.

26. J. de Molay's memorandum on the merging of the Orders is published by G. Lizerand, *Le Dossier* ..., pp. 2–3.

27. On Saint Louis, I refer the reader to the two principal monographs, shown in the bibliography, by Jacques Le Goff and Jean Richard. On the crusades, see, among others, Volume II of *A History of the Crusades*, also shown in the bibliography.

28. *Les Grandes Chroniques de France*, ed. J. Viard, Paris, 1932, t. VII, pp. 46 and 72.

29. On all these aspects, see W. C. Jordan, *Louis IX and the Challenge of the Crusade* ..., Princeton, 1979.

30. *Grandes Chroniques de France*, t. VII, p. 80.

31. E. Berger, *Saint Louis et Innocent IV. Essai sur les rapports de la France et du Saint-Siège*, Paris, 1893.

32. J. Richard, *Saint Louis*, p. 193.

33. *Grandes Chroniques de France*, t. VII, p. 106.

34. A. Demurger, 'Templiers et Hospitaliers dans les combats de Terre sainte', *Le Combattant au Moyen Âge*, Paris, Publications de la Sorbonne, 1991, p. 80.

35. See the chapter devoted to these methods of information by S. Lloyd, *English Society and the Crusades, 1216–1307*, Oxford, 1988, pp. 248–55.

36. J. Le Goff, *Saint Louis*, p. 163.

37. For instance, W. C. Jordan and J. Richard; J. Le Goff, *op. cit.* (n. 36), p. 13, is less assertive.

38. *Grandes Chroniques de France*, t. VII, pp. 72–5.

40. J. Le Goff, *op. cit.* (n. 36), p. 145.

40. *Ibid.*, p. 142.

41. C. Cahen, 'Saint Louis et l'islam', *Journal asiatique*, 1970. The text is published in translation in C. Cahen, *Orient et Occident au temps des croisades*, Paris, 1983, pp. 241–2.

42. J. L. A. Huillard-Bréholles, *Historia diplomatica Frederici secondi*, 6 vol., Paris, 1852–61, t. VI, pp. 465–7.

43. J. Richard, *Saint Louis*, p. 190.

44. W. C. Jordan, *op. cit.* (n. 29), pp. 78–9.

45. Champollion-Figeac, *Documents historiques inédits tirés des collections manuscrites de la Bibliothèque royale et des archives ou bibliothèques des départements de France*, Collection des documents inédits sur l'Histoire de France, 5 vol., Paris, t. II, 1843, pp. 50–67.

46. Joinville, *Vie de Saint Louis*, Paris, ed. J. Monfrin, 1995, pp. 57–9, para. 113.

47. *Ibid.*, p. 65, para. 130–1. Joinville is the principal guide for Louis IX's crusade.

48. *Comte Riant*, 'Six letters sur la Terre sainte', AOL, t. II, 1884, pp. 389–90.

49. This letter is published in French translation in D. O'Connell, *Les Propos de Saint Louis*, Paris, 'Coll. Archives', 1974, pp. 163–72; J. Le Goff reproduces this translation, *Saint Louis*, pp. 901–6.

50. He was reminded of the example of Richard the Lionheart, who refused to go there because he had not managed to seize it from Saladin; Joinville, *Vie de Saint Louis*, pp. 174–7, paras. 555–8.

51. J. Prawer, *Royaume latin* ..., t. II, pp. 344–54.

52. C. Marshall, 'The French Regiment in the Latin East, 1254–1291', *Journal of Medieval History*, 15 (1989).

53. This letter is transcribed in *Les Grandes Chroniques de France*, t. VII, p. 124.

54. C. and R. Kappler, *Guillaume de Rubrouck, envoyé de Saint Louis: voyage dans l'empire mongol (1253–1255)*, Paris, 1985.

55. J. Richard, 'Saint Louis et la Terre sainte dans l'histoire de la Méditerranée', *La Méditerranée au temps de Saint Louis* ..., p. 114.

56. Letter included in a 'Chronique anonyme des rois de France', ending in 1286, RHGF, t. XXI, pp. 81–2.

57. W. C. Jordan, *op. cit.* (*n.* 29), p. 100.

58. Joinville, *Vie de Saint Louis*, p. 187, para. 381; A. Demurger, 'Trésor des Templiers, Trésor du roi. Mise au point sur les opérations financières des Templiers', *Pouvoir et Gestion*, 'Collection Histoire, Gestion, Organisation', no. 5, Toulouse, 1997, pp. 73–86.

59. A. Demurger, art. cit. (*n.* 58); G. Sivery, *Les Capétiens et l'argent au siècle de Saint Louis. Essai sur l'administration et les finances royales au XIII* siècle, Villeneuve d'Ascq, Presses du Septentrion, 1995.

60. *Grandes Chroniques de France*, t. VII, p. 212.

61. A. Demurger, art. cit. (*n.* 34), pp. 87–9.

62. Joinville, *Vie de Saint Louis*, pp. 90–1, paras. 185–6.

63. *Nangis*, t. I, p. 205; Guizot, t. XIII, p. 159.

64. Joinville, *Vie de Saint Louis*, p. 203, para. 413.

65. *Grandes Chroniques de France*, t. VII, pp. 135–6.

66. Joinville, *Vie de Saint Louis*, pp. 254–5, paras. 512–14 and *n.* 56.

67. Mich. I, pp. 42–5; G. Lizerand, *Le Dossier* ..., p. 167.

68. Baluze, t. II, pp. 156–60; translated by S. Leroy, art. cit. (*n.* 3), pp. 211 ff.

Chapter 2 1265 – Jacques de Molay, Rank-and-file Templar

1. See the general histories of the Order of the Temple: M. Barber, *The New Knighthood. A History of the Order of the Temple*, Cambridge, 1994; A. Demurger, *Vie et mort de l'ordre du Temple*, Paris, 1989; H. Nicholson, *The Knights Templar. A New History*, Phoenix Mill (England), 2001.

2. See *R.T.1*: S. Cerrini, *Une expérience neuve au sein de la spiritualité médiévale: l'ordre du Temple (1120–1314)*. 'Étude et édition des règles latines et françaises', typewritten thesis, 2 vol., Paris, Université Paris-IV-Sorbonne, 1998; *R.T.2*: H. de Curzon, *La Règle du Temple*, Paris, Société de l'Histoire de France, 1886; L.

Dailliez, *Règle et statuts de l'ordre du Temple*, 2nd ed., presented by J.-P. Lombard, Paris, Dervy, 1996.

3. *Chronique de Michel le Syrien*, ed. J.-B. Chabot, Paris, 1905, p. 203.

4. See an overall view in A. Demurger, *Chevaliers du Christ. Les Ordres religieux-militaires au Moyen Âge (XI°-XVI° siècle)*, Paris, Seuil, 2002.

5. A. Demurger, 'Trésor des Templiers, Trésor du roi. Mise au point sur les opérations financières des templiers', *Pouvoir et Gestion, op. cit.*; X. de la Selle, *Le Service des âmes à la cour. Confesseurs et aumôniers des rois de France du XIII° au XV° siècle*, Paris, 1995.

6. F. Tommasi, 'L'Ordine dei Templari a Perugia', *Bollettino della Deputazione di Storia Patria per l'Umbria*, t. LXXVIII, 1981, pp. 5–79.

7. In the Order of the Hospital, the word 'convent' was used to designate this restricted council. Not in the Temple, except perhaps at the very end of its existence; the word convent had the sense of a fighting formation. *R.T.*2, paras. 98, 138, 142. There is too often confusion between 'Chapter' and 'convent'; para. 80 of the Rule mentions the meeting of the Chapter and not the convent. There is a discussion on the problem of knowing whether, in the last years of the Temple's existence, the word convent was used in the sense of restricted council as with the Hospitallers, in A. J. Forey, 'Letters of the Last Two Templar Masters', pp. 157–8.

8. *La Commanderie. Institution des ordres militaires dans l'Occident médiéval*, Paris, 2002.

9. R. Locatelli, *Sur les chemins de la perfection. Moines et chanoines dans le diocèse de Besançon (vers 1060–1220)*, Saint-Étienne, 1992, plate XIII and pp. 431–41; quotation p. 440.

10. Mich. I, pp. 137, 174, 302, 591.

11. Mich. I, p. 632; II, p. 368.

12. Mich. II, p. 362.

13. ACA, Canc., CRD Jaime II (Templarios), 139, no. 334; Mich. I, pp. 458 and 564–6.

14. Mich. II, pp. 305–6; trans. G. Lizerand, *Le Dossier …*, p. 35.

15. H. Finke, *Papsttum*, t. II, p. 328.

16. B. Frale, *L'ultima battaglia dei Templari*, especially chapters 4 and 5.

17. *Ibid.*, pp. 13–14 and 34.

18. *Reg. d'Urbain IV*, t. II, p. 364, no. 760 and pp. 369–70, no. 765; B. Frale, *op. cit.*, (n. 16), p. 30.

19. B.-T., pp. 257–8; S. Paoli, *Codice diplomatico del sacro militare ordini gerosolimitano, oggi di Malta raccolto da vari documenti di quell'archivio per servire alla storia dello stesso ordine*, 2 vols., Lucca, 1733–7, t. I, pp. 194–5; Röhricht, no. 1378.

20. R. Locatelli, *op. cit.* (n. 9), pp. 434–5.

21. Mich. I, pp. 44–5; trans. G. Lizerand, *Le Dossier …*, pp. 168–71.

22. J. Prawer, *Royaume latin* ..., t. II, p. 504; J. Richard, *Histoire des croisades*, Paris, 1995, p. 446.

23. This is the opinion of M. Barber, M.-L. Bulst-Thiele and B. Frale.

24. B. Frale, *op. cit. (n.* 16), p. 16: 'Entrò a far parte del couvent di Beaujeu'.

25. *R.T.*2, p. 109.

26. T.T., p. 163, para. 305.

27. Saint Bernard, *Éloge de la nouvelle chevalerie*, ed. P.-Y. Emery, Paris, Ed. du Cerf, 'Coll. Sources chrétiennes', no. 367, 1990, pp. 47–61. Unfortunately, this document cannot be traced (probably a false or incomplete reference).

28. T.T., pp. 163–4, no. 304.

29. J. Prawer, *Royaume latin* ..., t. II, pp. 428–9.

30. J. Richard, 'Saint Louis et la Terre sainte', *La Méditerranée au temps de Saint Louis*, p. 214.

31. J. Prawer, *op. cit. (n.* 29) t. II, p. 469.

32. Röhricht, p. 91, no. 1358.

33. J. Prawer, *op. cit. (n.* 29), t. II, p. 490.

34. P. Holt, *Early Mamelouk Diplomacy* ..., p. 72.

Chapter 3 1273 – Thomas Bérard and Guillaume de Beaujeu

1.   B.-T., pp. 232–3.

2.   CH, II, no. 2902.

3.   M. Barber, review of 'H. Revel Master of the Hospital of St John of Jerusalem, 1258–1276' by G. Humphrey-Smith, *Medieval Prosopography*, 16 (1995), pp. 135–7.

4.   Röhricht, I, p. 345, no. 1322 and pp. 344–5, nos. 1317–19.

5.   J. Delaville Le Roulx, 'Inventaire de pièces de Terre sainte de l'ordre de Saint-Jean de Jérusalem', ROL, 3 (1895), p. 75, no. 312 and p. 89, no. 361.

6.   CH, IV, pp. 292–3; trans. in J. Prawer, *Royaume latin*, t. II, p. 484.

7.   E. J. King , *The Rule, Statutes and Customs of the Hospitallers, 1099–1310*, London, 1934, pp. 53–78.

8.   *R.T.*2, pp. 284–336, art. 544–656.

9.   J. Prawer, *Royaume latin*, t. II, p. 469 (translation).

10. *Éraclès*, Book XXXIV, ch. 17, p. 463.

11. T.T., pp. 201–3, para. 383.

12. M. Rey, 'L'ordre du Temple en Franche-Comté, d'après les documents écrits', *Académie des sciences, belles-lettres et arts de Besançon. Procès-Verbaux et Mémoires*, t. CLXXX (1972–3), p. 94.

13. AN, J. 456, no. 27. See J.-B. de Vaivre, 'À propos du sceau de Guillaume de Beaujeu', *Revue française d'héraldique et de sigillographie*, 30 (1963), p. 67; P. de

Saint-Hilaire, *Les Sceaux templiers*, Puiseaux, 1991, pp. 62 and 134. S. Leroy, *Jacques de Molay et les templiers francs-comtois* ... had already established that. But his article is for the most part overlooked by historians concerned with Jacques de Molay. This is a pity, as it is by far the most accurate and serious of the 'old' writings (1900) on the subject.

14. T.T., p. 218, para. 433.

15. B.-T., pp. 259–60.

16. *Ibid.*, p. 260, *n.* 6.

17. L. Dailliez, *Règle et statuts de l'ordre du Temple*, 2nd enlarged edition presented by J.-P. Lombard, Paris, 1996, p. 391.

18. Comte Riant, 'Six lettres sur les croisades et la Terre sainte', AOL, 2, 1884, pp. 390–1.

19. *Éraclès*, Book XXXIV, ch. XVIII, p. 464.

20. Röhricht, I, pp. 362–3, no. 393.

21. On these plans for crusades, see S. Schein, *Fideles Crucis. The Papacy, the West and the Recovery of the Holy Land, 1274–1314*, Oxford, 1991.

22. L. Dailliez, *Jacques de Molay* ..., p. 17, quotes this letter from a brother 'from Fychers ...' (*sic*) to the king of England, according to the PRO (London), Ancient Correspondence, XXI, 2. (Actually, SC 1, XXI, *n.* 2.)

23. C. Kohler and V. Langlois, 'Lettres inédites concernant les croisades (1275–1307)', BEC, 52 (1891), pp. 1–8, no. 2; *Éraclès*, Book XXXIV, ch. 21, p. 468.

24. G. Tafel and G. Thomas, *Urkunden zur Älteren Handels- und Staat der Republik Venedig*, 3 vol., reissued Amsterdam, 1964, t. III, p. 150, no. CCCLXIX.

25. N. Coureas, *The Latin Church in Cyprus* ..., pp. 128–9.

26. R. Lefevre, *La Crociata di Tunisi del 1270 nei documenti del distrutto archivio angioino di Napoli*, Rome, 1977.

27. T.T., p. 204, para. 391

28. L. de Mas-Latrie, *Histoire de l'île de Chypre* ..., t. II, pp. 662–8.

29. P. M. Holt, *Early Mamluk Diplomacy (1260–1290). Treaties of Baybars and Kalâwûn with Christian Rulers*, Leiden, J. Brill, 1995.

30. *Ibid.*, pp. 69–90: trans. in F. Gabrieli, *Chroniques arabes des croisades*, Paris, 1977, pp. 352–63.

31. *Ibid.*, p. 48.

32. *Ibid.*, pp. 66–8.

33. *Ibid.*, pp. 93–4.

34. *Ibid.*, pp. 95 ff.

35. J. Prawer, *Royaume latin*, t. II, p. 537.

36. T.T., p. 235, para. 474.

37. See S. Runciman, *The Sicilian Vespers*, Cambridge, 1958.

38. T.T., p. 218, para. 435.

40. *Ibid.*, p. 219, para. 438.

40. *Ibid.*, p. 235, para. 474.

41. *Ibid.*, p. 239, para. 481.

42. *Ibid.*, p. 240, para. 481.

43. Mich. II, pp. 214–16.

44. *Ibid.*, pp. 205–10.

45. *Ibid.*, pp. 129–32.

46. L. Dailliez, *Jacques de Molay* ..., p. 21, cites a chronicle and a large map of Cyprus *ad annum 1292*, with no reference, as is usually the case with this author.

47. T.T., p. 256, paras. 507–8.

48. T. Parker, *The Knights Templar in England*, Tucson, 1963, p. 125. It is only a table with no reference to sources.

49. G. B., pp. 139–40.

50. Mich., I, p. 420.

51. *Ibid.*, II, pp. 305–6.

52. *Ibid.*, pp. 305–6.

53. B. Frale thinks he was present at Acre.

Chapter 4. 1292 – Grand Master of the Order of the Temple

1. B. Frale, *L'ultima battaglia dei Templari*, p. 18, bases her opinion only on the fact that he was a close associate of Beaujeu, with no evidence to back it. But she is probably right, for had he been in the West during this period of time there would most likely have been some proof of it.

2. *Anonymi de excidio urbis Acconis*, ed. L. Martène and U. Durand, *Veterum Scriptorum ... Collectio*, 9 vol., Paris, 1729, t. V, col. 765 ff.

3. M. Quatremère, *Histoire des sultans mamelouks d'Égypte écrite en arabe par Taki Eddin ... Makriẓi*, 2 vol., Paris, 1845.

4. RHC, Hist. Or., I, Paris, 1872, under the title 'Résumé de l'Histoire des croisades', pp. 1–186; see chiefly pp. 163–4 and 168.

5. D. P. Little, 'The Fall of Acre in 690/1291. The Muslim Version', *Studies in Islamic History and Civilization in Honour of Professor David Ayalon*, ed. M. Sharon, Jerusalem–Leiden, J. Brill, 1986, pp. 159–81.

6. T.T., p. 240, para. 481.

7. T.T., p. 241, para. 484; M.-L. Favreau-Lillie, 'The Military Orders and the Escape of the Christian Population from the Holy Land in 1291', *Journal of Medieval History*, 19, 1993, pp. 203–4.

8.   J. Prawer, *Royaume latin* ..., t. II, p. 553.

9.   Abû al-Fidâ, 163–5, trans. in F. Gabrieli, *Chroniques arabes des croisades*, p. 376.

10. T.T., pp. 249–50, para. 498.

11. *Ibid.*, p. 253, paras. 501 and 503.

12. *Ibid.*, p. 256, paras. 507–8.

13. M.-L. Favreau-Lillie, art. cit. (*n.* 7) has made a meticulous analysis of the facts.

14. *Ibid.*, p. 208.

15. T.T., pp. 253 and 257, paras. 503 and 509.

16. *De excidio* (n. 2), col. 772; L. de Mas-Latrie, *Histoire de l'île de Chypre*, t. I, p. 495.

17. T.T., p. 257, para. 510; see also Makrisi, *op. cit.* (*n.* 8), p. 126.

18. T.T., p. 257, para. 510.

19. *Ibid.*, p. 258, para. 512.

20. *Ibid.*, p. 257, para. 509.

21. Mich. II, p. 313.

22. Arville and Sours are in Eure-et-Loir, Châteaudun in Loir-et-Cher and Orléans in
     the Loiret; see A. Trudon des Ormers, *Liste des maisons* ...,
     pp. 78–82 for references; B.-T., p. 292, *n.* 5.

23. T.T., p. 164, paras. 306–7.

24. *Ibid.*, p. 164, para. 306.

25. Mich. II, p. 313. See also Mich. I, p. 646, II, pp. 13 and 228.

26. T.T., p. 227, para. 454.

27. *Reg. Nicolas IV,* t. II, p. 778, no. 5763: *quem olim Guillelmus de Bellojoco, magister,
     et conventus domus militiae Templi Jerolomitani, priusquam in bello cum Sarracenis
     commisso decesserint, suum geralem procuratorem* ...

28. *Ibid.*, 23 August 1291, t. II, p. 899, no. 6778 and p. 904, nos. 6809–14.

29. J. Pryor, *Geography, Technology and War. Studies in the Maritime History of the
     Mediterranean 649–1571*, Cambridge, Cambridge University Press, 1988, pp. 12–
     24.

30. Mich. II, p. 139.

31. L. Dailliez, *Jacques de Molay* ..., p. 21.

32. ACA, Canc., Pergamine Jaime II, 129, no. 19 (B. de Fontes, 22 August), nos.
     26, 31, 36 (Pierre de Saint-Just, 29 August, 6 and 8 September); three of them
     are published by A. J. Forey, 'Letters ...', pp. 160–1 and the fourth by H. Finke,
     Papsttum, t. I, p. 21, *n.*3.

33. A. J. Forey, *The Templars in the Corona de Aragon*, pp. 405–6, no. XXXVI.

34. T.T., p. 329, para. 694.

35. BNF, *Ms lat.* 15054; published by E. de Barthelémy, 'L'obituaire de la commanderie
     du Temple de Reims', in *Mélanges historiques*, t. IV, Paris, 1882, p. 319: *obiit frater
     Theobaldus Gaudinus vicesimus secondus magister Templi.*

36. M. Barber and M.-L. Bulst-Thiele, relying on the first dated document concerning Jacques de Molay (8 December 1293) indicated the period April 1292–8 December 1293 as Molay's election date; but they were writing before the publication of A. J. Forey's book.

37. A. J. Forey, *op. cit.* (*n.* 33), pp. 405–6.

38. L. Dailliez, *Les Templiers, Gouvernement et institutions*, Nice, Alpes-Méditerranée Éditions, 1980, pp. 62–3.

39. B.-T., pp. 225–6, 232.

40. L. Dailliez, *op. cit.* (*n.* 31), p. 21.

41. Mich. II, pp. 224–5.

42. Frale, *op. cit.* (*n.* 1), pp. 17–19, accepts this; M. Barber challenges its historical value and M.-L. Bulst-Thiele does not discuss it.

43. A. Trudon des Ormers, *op. cit.* (*n.* 22), pp. 204–35. We must not confuse the Templar province of Auvergne with its Hospitaller counterpart (the great priory of Auvergne), which was much more extensive and included the Lyonnais and part of Burgundy (notably the county).

44. See the map in *l'Atlas des croisades*, p. 125.

45. Épailly, a commune of Courban, Côte-d'Or, canton of Montigny-sur-Aube; Bures, Côte-d'Or, canton of Recey-sur-Ource. See E. G. Léonard, *Gallicarum militie templi domorum*, Paris, 1932, pp. 154 and 150; Mich. I, p. 395; B.-T., p. 295.

46. E. G. Léonard, *op. cit.* (n. 45), p. 77; *Reg. Boniface VIII*, t. II, no. 2323 (8 June 1297).

47. Beware of the translation into modern French by L. Dailliez, praiseworthy in many ways but marred by too many errors; the passage I quote becomes 'But if it should happen, which would be more advantageous, that the person be found in overseas parts …' The positioning of the commas and the relative changes everything. L. Dailliez, *Règle et statuts de l'ordre du Temple*, ed. J.-P. Lombard, p. 174.

48. B. Frale, *op. cit.* (*n.* 1), p. 22.

49. Barbara Frale supports this idea: 'His links with the English sovereign and the presence of "many others" when Molay took the oath arouse the suspicion that certain western centres of power may have tried to steer the election towards a candidate who would be sensitive to their interests. Otton de Grandson was very probably acting on instructions from Philip the Fair, who tried to boycott the election of Jacques de Molay in favour of a candidate who was more inclined to the sovereign's intentions', p. 22.

50. This had been the site of the first defeat of Charles the Bold against the Swiss cantons in 1476.

51. R. Fiétier, *Histoire de la Franche-Comté*, Toulouse, Privat, 1985.

52. B.-T., pp. 302–3, *n.* 37, which gives no references and refers to an article by F. Funck-Bruntano which does not mention Grandson. F. Funck-Bruntano, 'Philippe le Bel et la noblesse comtoise', BEC, 49, 1888, pp. 1–36.

53. *Reg. Clement V*, t. III, pp. 137–8, no. 2938. The letter of confirmation from Jacques de Molay (badly dated) is enclosed in the letter of confirmation of Pope Clement V, this one dated 17 August 1308.

54. B.-T., p. 302. An unwise assertion.

55. See chapter 1.

Chapter 5 1293 – Journey to the West

1. ACA, AGP, parch., Cervera, no. 486; A. J. Forey, *The Templars in the Corona de Aragon*, p. 405.

2. P.-V. Claverie, '*La cristiandat en mayor peril* ou la perception de la question d'Orient en Catalogne à la fin du XIIIᵉ siècle', in *Les Templiers en pays catalan*, Perpignan, Editorial El Trabucaire, 1998, pp. 96–7.

3. R. Fiétier, *Histoire de la Franche-Comté,* Toulouse, Privat, 1985, pp. 54–5.

4. G.B., pp. 116–17. The date 1295 is false, for Jacques de Molay who, according to the witness, officiated at his reception, could not have been in Cyprus at this time.

5. A. Trudon des Ormes, *Liste des maisons …*, p. 18.

6. *Reg. Nicolas IV*, t. II, p. 913, no. 6830.

7. *Ibid.*, nos. 6834–5: *mandat ut cum galeis quas de mandato et ordinatione sedis apostolicae tenere in mare debet contra inimicos crucis ad regni Armeniae defensionem succursum impedat.*

8. *Ibid.*, no. 6836.

9. *Annales genuenses di Jacobo Auriaco*, ed. L. Muratori, *Rerum italicarum Scriptores*, t. VI, Milan, 1725, book X, col. 606.

10. T.T., pp. 275–6, para. 537.

11. B.-T., pp. 293–4 and 302; B. Frale, *L'Ultima battaglia dei Templari*, p. 18, quoting the Templar of Tyre, pp. 252 and 279 (no relevance to the question); C. Kohler, 'Deux projets de croisade en Terre sainte composés à la fin du XIIIᵉ siècle et au début du XIVᵉ', ROL, no. 10 (1903–1904), pp. 406–57.

12. Hayton, *Flor historiarum Terre orientis* (or *Fleur des histoires de la Terre d'Orient*); RHC, Doc. Arm., t. II, pp. 111–254 (French text) and pp. 255–363 (Latin text).

13. C. Mutafian, 'Héthoum de Korykos historien arménien. Un prince cosmopolite à l'aube du XIVᵉ siècle', *Cahiers de recherches médiévales*, 1, 1996, pp. 157–76.

14. On all this, see C. Mutafian, *La Cilicie au carrefour des empires*, 2 tomes, Paris, Les Belles Lettres, 1988, t. I, pp. 464 ff.

15. RHC, Doc. Arm., t. II, chap. XLIV, pp. 326–30; this chapter XLIV is not found in all the manuscripts of the 'Fleur des histoires'; it exists also in a French language manuscript, which is unfortunately truncated over the whole of its right-hand part: see *ibid.*, pp. 206–10.

16. *Ibid.*, p. 327: *Quo cumperto, frater ejus secundus, dominus Theodorus, convocatis domino Hotono de Grandisono et aliis etc. ..., fratri suo primogenito, domino Haytono, dominium restituit atque regnum ...* The date is either 1293 or 1294. Charles Kohler, art. cit. (*n.* 11), tells us that Grandson had gone back to England before December 1293; nevertheless, Hayton's text is clear: it was in 1294.

17. *Ibid.*, p. 330.

18. C. Kohler, art. cit. (*n.* 11), p. 419, *n.*3.

19. T.T., p. 280, para. 543.

20. A. Luttrell, 'The Hospitallers' intervention in Cilician Armenia 1291–1375', in T. S. R. Boase, *The Cilician Kingdom of Armenia*, Edinburgh, 1978, p. 121. The author also uses the passage from the text of Hayton the Historian relating to the events of 1298–9, but cites it as proof of the presence of the Grand Masters of the Temple and Hospital at the ceremony at Sis in 1294, which cannot be, at least for Molay, who was in the West at the time.

21. B.-T., p. 305, *n.* 49 and p. 356; the mention of Guy de Forest, Master of England, in this document validates this date: Kervyn de Lettenhove, who published it (in part), linked it with Molay's memorandum on the crusade and dated it 1306, wrongly. Kervyn de Lettenhove, 'Deux lettres inédites de Jacques de Molay', *Bulletin de l'Académie royale des sciences, des lettres et des beaux-arts de Belgique*, 43rd year, 2nd series, 38 (1874), p. 254.

22. L. Dailliez, *Jacques de Molay ...*, p. 23; B.-T., p. 305, *n.* 49.

23. ACA, Canc., Reg. Jaime II, 98, f. 218v; A. J. Forey, 'Letters ...', p. 156.

24. *Ibid.*, 98, f. 257v.

25. F. Carrer y Candy, 'Entences y Templers en les Montanyes de Prades (1279 a 1300)', *Bolletìn de la real Academia de las Bellas Letras de Barcelona*, II (1903–4), pp. 241–3.

26. A. J. Forey, 'Letters ...', p. 156.

27. PRO, *Close rolls*, 54/III/m.12.

28. D. Wilkins, *Concilia magnae Britanie et Hibernie*, London, 1737, t. II, p. 387: *fuit convocatus in cameram frater Jacobi de Molay tunc magni magistri ordinis.*

29. B.-T., p. 306, *n.* 52.

30. A. J. Forey, 'Letters ...', p. 156, *n.* 63.

31. ACA, Canc. Reg. Jaime II, 99, f. 264 and 302; A. J. Forey, 'Letters ...', p. 156.

32. ACA, Canc. Pergamine Jaime II, 136, no. 383; L. Pagarola, *Els Temple de les*

Terres de l'Ebre (Tortosa). De Jaime I fins a l'abolició de l'orde, 1212–1312, 2 vol., Tarragona, 1999, t. II, pp. 197–8.

33. ACA, Canc., Reg. Jaime II, 100, f. 53–53v.

34. *Ibid.*, 252, f. 12; edited by H. Finke, *AA*, t. 1, pp. 26–7, no. 17: … *in Romana curia existentes.*

35. *Reg. Boniface VIII*, t. I, col. 97, no. 264: letter from the pope dated Anagni 9 July 1295; Archives de Naples, Reg. 1272, E f. 137, *n.* 16: letter from the Queen of Naples dated 27 August.

36. G.B., pp. 117–18.

37. Mich. I, p. 626, interrogation of Raoul de Taverny.

38. H. Finke, *AA*, t. 3, p. 31, no. 18.

40. Archives of the Vatican, Registres Vat. 48, no. 617, f. 143v–144r; letter enclosed with a letter from Boniface VIII of 27 November 1296, *Reg. Boniface VIII*, t. I, col. 547–8, no. 1508 (Molay's letter is indicated but not published). My thanks to Yves Le Pogam, who was kind enough to transcribe this for me in Rome.

40. *Reg. Clement V*, t. III, *annus tertius*, pp. 137–8, no. 2938; B.-T., p. 307, *n.* 52.

41. Mich. I, pp. 474–5: the interrogation is that of 30 January 1311. Pierre de Saint-Just states that he was received ten years before the arrest of the Templars (1307), in Paris, during the general Chapter of 24 June.

42. B.-T., p. 307, *n.* 52.

43. Archives of the Vatican, Registres Vat. 55, col. 114r, no. 581: *Anno millesimo duecentesimo octuagesimo septimo.* My thanks to Barbara Frale, who was kind enough to check this with the Archives of the Vatican and, unwittingly, started a hare, as a new problem arose. Grandson and Beaujeu, Grandson and the Temple were already connected in 1287: where, how, for what reasons?

44. *Reg. Boniface VIII*, t. II, col. 31–2, no. 2429.

45. L. Pagarola i Sabaté, 'La fi del domini de l'ordre del Temple a Tortosa', *Anuario de Estudio medieval*, no. 28, 1998, p. 271; and by the same author, *op. cit. (n. 32)*.

46. *Ibid.*, art. cit., *(n. 45)*, p. 279

47. *Ibid.*, *op. cit.*, *(n. 32)*, t. II, pp. 197–8, no. 171.

48. *Ibid.*, *op. cit. (n. 32)*, t. II, pp. 198–209, no. 172.

49. Madrid, AHN, OM (San Juan), legojo 8277[1], no. 15, p. 31, quoted , under the old classification, by A. J. Forey, *op. cit. (n. 1)*, p. 331: *summus magister domorum milicie Templi*. My thanks to P. Josserand who was kind enough to check this document for me in the National Archives of Madrid.

50. London, PRO, *Close Rolls* 54/III/m.12; cited by B.-T., pp. 351 and 357.

51. C. Perrat and J. Longnon, *Actes relatifs à la principauté de Morée*, Paris, 'Collection des documents inédits sur l'Histoire de France', p. 96, no. 93.

52. *Ibid.*, p. 127, no. 127.

53. On these problems, see the general works on the crusades and the military Orders and B. Kedar, *Crusade and Mission. European Approaches towards the Muslims*, Princeton, 1984; S. Schein, '*Fideles crucis': The Papacy, the West and the Recovery of the Holy Land, 1274–1314*, Oxford, 1991; H. Nicholson, *Templars, Hospitallers and Teutonic Knights. Images of the Military Orders, 1128–1291*, London, 1991; N. Housley, *The Later Crusades from Lyons to Alcazar, 1274–1580*, Oxford, 1992.

54. A. J. Forey, 'The Military Orders in the Crusading Proposals of the Late Thirteenth and Early Fourteenth Centuries', resumed in *Military Orders and Crusades* (Reprints), Aldershot, Variorum, 1994.

55. L. de Mas-Latrie, *Histoire de l'île de Chypre* ..., t. II, pp. 91–2.

56. *Ibid.*, pp. 97–8. See other examples concerning the Hospitallers of southern Italy in 1300 in C., t. III, p. 800, no. 4495 and p. 808, no. 4512.

57. CH, t. IV, p. 9, nos. 4535–1536, p. 10, no. 4538, p. 49, no. 4589, etc.

58. CH, t. III, p. 708, no. 4362; N. Coureas, *The Latin Church in Cyprus* ..., p. 164.

59. CH, t. III, p. 708, no. 4362.

60. *Reg. Boniface VIII*, t. I, col. 160–70, no. 487.

61. *Ibid.*, col. 170, no. 489; M. Barber, *James of Molay* ..., pp. 94–5.

62. Translated by L. Dailliez, *Jacques de Molay* ..., p. 22, from Rymer, *Acta publica*, t. II, p. 683.

63. All the Templars questioned at Nicosia in 1311 at the time of the trial testified to the veracity of this charitable work in all the Cypriot Order's houses.

64. *Reg. de Boniface VIII*, t. I, col. 169–70, no. 487.

65. PRO, Anc. Corr., Sc1/21n f. 4; published in part and with errors by Kervyn de Lettenhove, art. cit. (*n. 21*), p. 254.

66. PRO, *Close Rolls*, C 54/113, m 9d. These are two different deeds, dated at Berwyk: *quod dilectio nobis in Christo fratri Briano de Jay, magistro milicie templi in Anglia licenciam dedimus transfretandi ad partem transmarinas ... ad colloquium habendum cum magistro superiori milicie supradicto.*

67. Mich. I, p. 187 and I, p. 513.

68. *R.T.* 1, art. 9 (Latin), p. 179; art. 13 (French), p. 269; *R.T.* 2, p. 35.

69. G.B., p. 240; see also pp. 201, 409, 412, 415, 428–9, etc.

70. Mich. I, pp. 42–5; trans. G. Lizerand, *Le Dossier* ..., p. 167.

71. L. Dailliez, *Jacques de Molay* ..., p. 24.

72. J. Fuguet Sans, 'De Miravet a Peñiscola (1294)' in *Acri 1291*, Perugia, 1996, p. 67.

73. H. Nicholson, 'Jacquemart Giélée's Renart le Nouvel: The Image of the Military Orders on the Eve of the Loss of Acre', *Monastic Studies*, no. 1, p. 183.

74. The Templar of Tyre's sentence concerning a clash with the pope can apply only to Clement V, not to Boniface VIII.

75. *Reg. Boniface VIII*, t. II, col. 662, no. 3514.

76. *Ibid.*, t. I, col. 411, no. 1153.

77. *Ibid.*, t. II, col. 643, no. 3479.

78. See *n.* 39.

79. *Reg. Boniface VIII*, t. I, col. 169–70, nos. 487–90.

80. Mich. I, pp. 182–1878 (Guichard de Marsiac, who thinks that they were applied); I, p. 503 (Guillaume d'Arrabloy, who does not think so).

81. *Reg. Boniface VIII*, t. I, col. 914, no. 2323. Some references in the trial give Pairaud the title of Visitor as early as 1293, which is too early. He succeeded Geoffroy de Vichiers.

Chapter 6. 1300 – The Isle of Ruad

1.   *Reg. Boniface VIII*, t. II, col. 37, n° 1438 (20 May 1298).

2.   I base my remarks on the text of Hayton of Corycos, already quoted and partly analysed in chapter 4; RHC, Doc. Arm., t. II, pp. 327–30.

3.   T.T., p. 292, para. 578. The Templar of Tyre gives the date 1299. But it is not certain that the four castles or fortified sites conquered at that time by the Mamluks, including La Roche-Guillaume, all fell in that year.

4.   T.T., p. 283, para. 552–3, is identical but shorter.

5.   A. Luttrell, 'The Hospitallers' intervention in Cilician Armenia 1291–1375', in T. S. R. Boase, *The Cilician Kingdom of Armenia*, p. 122.

6.   And not 20 December, the date put forward by T.T., p. 301, para. 608.

7.   Amadi, pp. 234–5; S. Schein, 'Gesta Dei per Mongolos. 1300. The Genesis of a Non-Event', *English Historical Review*, no. 94 (1979), p. 810, *n.* 6. The khan's letters are transcribed in a letter from the doge of Venice of 19 March 1300: L. Muratori, *Scriptores rerum italicarum*, t. XII, *Cronica veneta*, col. 513.

8.   The point of view of Barber, *James of Molay* ..., B.-T., and Luttrell, art. cit. (*n.* 5).

9.   C. Mutafian, 'Héthoum de Korykos historien arménien. Un prince cosmopolite à l'aube du XIVᵉ siècle', *Cahiers de Recherches Médiévales*, I (1996), p. 167.

10. TT, pp. 302–3, para. 614.

11. H. Finke, *AA*, 3, no. 41; S. Schein, art. cit. (*n.* 7), pp. 806–7.

12. S. Schein, art. cit. (*n.* 7), p. 816, *n.* 3. Letter preserved at the British Library: *Minister noster et multi fraters preparant se ad eundem in Siriam et milites et pedite et omnes alii religiosi.*

13. T.T., p. 301, para. 609.

14. T.T., p. 302, para. 611.

15. Ibn Taymiyya, *Épître à un roi croisé (al-Risâlat al-Qubrusiyya)*, trans. and notes by Jean R. Michot, Louvain-la-Neuve, Lyon, 1995, p. 43.

16. J. Richard, 'Isol le Pisan: un aventurier franc gouverneur d'une province mongole?', taken up in *Orient et Occident au Moyen Âge: contacts et relations (XIIe– XVe siècle)*, London, Variorum, 1976, XXX, pp. 186–94.

17. H. Finke, *AA*, t. 1, p. 86. This would relate to the month of June, leaving Romeu time to be in Barcelona in early July.

18. Amadi, p. 236.

19. T.T., p. 304, paras. 616–19.

20. TT, p. 305, para. 620.

21. Ibn Taymiyya, *op. cit.* (n. 15), pp. 52–3.

22. T.T., p. 305, para. 621.

23. H. Finke, *Papsttum*, t. II. pp. 4–5, no. 4: see P.-V. Claverie, '*La cristiandat en mayor peril* ou la perception de la question de l'Orient en Catalogne à la fin du XIIIe siècle' in *Les Templiers en pays catalan*, p. 108. Guillaume de Villaret arrived in Cyprus before 5 November, the date on which he held a Chapter of his Order at Limassol. The departure for Ruad would therefore fall in the second fortnight of November. At the time when Bernart Guillem d'Enteça was writing, the Christians were still on Ruad. The letter would have been written at the end of March or beginning of April. It must be specified that Bernart Guillem rejoined the ranks of the Hospital on this occasion; he pays tribute to the Masters of the Hospital and Temple, but has especial praise for the former. He belonged to a family who, in preceding years, caused a lot of trouble for the Templars of the 'mountain of Prades' in the region of Barberà, south of Barcelona. See F. Carrer y Candy, 'Entences y Templers en les Montanyes de Prades (1279 à 1300)', *Bolletìn de la Real Academia de las Bellas Letras de Barcelona*, II (1903–1904).

24. T.T., p. 306, para. 622.

25. T.T., p. 305, para. 621; Ibn Taymiyya, *op. cit.* (*n.* 15), p. 50. In the translation, the translator J. R. Michot thinks that the A. de Tyr, J. de Molay and G. de Villaret joined the Mongol general at Aleppo in January 1301. That is completely improbable.

26. CH. T. III, p. 766, no. 4461.

27. Original letter in the British Library quoted by S. Schein, art. cit. (*n.* 7), pp. 816–17, *n.* 5.

28. L. de Mas-Latrie, *Histoire de l'île de Chypre* ..., t. II, pp. 90–1.

29. Desimoni, 'Actes génois de Famagouste', AOL, t. II (1894), 2, pp. 42–3; quoted in J. Richard, 'La cour des Syriens de Famagouste d'après un texte de 1447', in *Croisades et États latins d'Orient. Points de vue et documents*, Aldershot, Variorum, 1992, XVII, p. 384; F. Tommasi, 'Fonti epigrafiche dalla *domus Templi* de Barletta ...', (*Militia sacra* ..., p. 179, also cites this document). Nevertheless, his idea that there might have been a sort of durable bridgehead at Tyre at this time rests on a

mistaken identification of the place where Bartholomé de Quincy is supposed to have been present on 23 May 1300 when Jean de Saint-Georges was received: *in Suro un domo dicti ordinis*; it was Sivré or Sivrey in Burgundy and not Tyre (Sur): G.B., p. 135.

30. H. Finke, *AA*, t. 1, p. 79.

31. Published by Desimoni and, more recently, by V. Polonio, *Notai genovesi a Famagusta ...*, pp. 256–8, no. 219 and pp. 305–6, no. 258; see also on the financial consequences of this journey, ACA, Canc., Pergamine Jaime II, 161, no. 1665 (10 July 1301).

32. H. Finke, *AA*, t. 2, p. 80. T.T., pp. 291–2, paras. 575–6.

33. X. de Planhol, *L'Islam et la mer. La mosquée et le matelot, VIIe–XXe siècle*, Paris, Perrin, 2000, pp. 300–1.

34. See A. Demurger, *Chevaliers du Christ. Les Ordres religieux-militaires au Moyen Âge, XIe–XVIe siècle*, chap. XIV; A. Luttrell, 'The Hospitallers and the Papacy, 1305–1314' in *Forschungen zur Reichs-, Papst- und Landesgeschichte (Mélanges Peter Herde)*, eds. K. Borchardt and E. Bünz, Stuttgart, A. Hiersemann, 1998, p. 596; in the wake of many others, A. Luttrell defends this viewpoint, which in my opinion is unacceptable.

35. *Reg. Boniface VIII*, t. III, col. 184–5, no. 4199.

36. PRO, Anc. Corr., Sc 1/55, f. 22; published in B.-T., p. 368.

37. ACA, Canc., CRD Jaime II, Ap. Gen. 128, no. 27; published in H. Finke, *Papsttum*, t. II, pp. 3–4, no. 3.

38. Ibn Taymiyya, *op. cit.* (*n.* 15), p. 55.

39. *Ibid.*, p. 55.

40. S. Schein, art. cit. (*n.* 7), pp. 812–13, *n.* 7 and 8.

41. Ibn Taymiyya, *op. cit.* (*n.* 15), p. 55.

42. G.B., p. 135, does not make the connection between the Bartholomé de Quincy named on this page and the Marshal of the Temple Chinsi or Quincy. A link of kinship may be suggested between this Bartholomé and Simon de Quincy, mentioned at Marseille in 1303 and future Master of the Temple in Puglia; F. Tommasi, art. cit. (*n.* 28), pp. 177–9.

43. Figures given by the Templar of Tyre, then Amadi and Bustron, when recounting the surrender and massacre of the garrison.

44. Amadi, pp. 238–9.

45. T.T., pp. 309–10, paras. 636–9.

46. T.T., p. 310, para. 327; Amadi, p. 239; F. Bustron, p. 133.

47. RHGF, t. XXI, p. 640.

48. Mich. I, p. 39.

49. A. Trudon des Ormes, *Liste des maisons ...*, pp. 55–7.

50. His presence in France is attested in 1300 and 1301: he carried out many receptions into the Order at that time; Mich. II, pp. 286, 390, 405, 416; G.B., p. 146. Gérard de Villiers was said to be a fierce defender of the practice of receiving candidates according to the informal initiatory ritual denounced by the inquisitors in the trial of the Templars; if he had the opportunity, he had those that had not been performed according to this ritual redone. This perhaps earned him some enmity within the Order and a bad reputation.

51. Amadi, p. 239; Bustron, p. 133.

52. Ibn Taymiyya, *op. cit.* (*n.* 15), p. 54.

53. *Ibid.*, pp. 56–60.

54. H. Finke, *Papsttum*, t. III, p. 28: some Mongol envoys arrived at Poitiers on 26 June 1307.

Chapter 7 1303 – Cyprus

1. T.T., p. 207, para. 407. On these relations, see the article by P.-V. Claverie, 'L'ordre du Temple au coeur d'une crise politique des années 1279–1285: *la querella Cypri*', *Le Moyen Âge*, t. CIV, 1998, pp. 495–511.

2. L. de Mas-Latrie, *Histoire de l'île de Chypre* …, t. II, pp. 108–9.

3. *Ibid.*,; N. Coureas, *The Latin Church in Cyprus, 1192–1312*, p. 130 and *n.* 3. P.-V. Claverie, art. cit. (*n.* 1) rightly suggests the attribution of this document to John I.

4. A. Potthast, *Regesta Pontificum Romanorum (1198–1304)*, Berlin, 1874–5, t. II, no. 22194; quoted by N. Coureas, *op. cit.* (*n.* 3), p. 129.

5. *Reg. Boniface VIII*, t. I, col. 169–70, no. 487.

6. *Ibid.*, t. II, cols. 38–9, nos. 2438–9.

7. *Ibid.*, t. II, cols. 143–4, no. 2609.

8. N. Coureas, *op. cit.* (*n.* 3), p. 167.

9. *Reg. Boniface VIII*, t. II, col. 411, nos. 3060–1.

10. *Ibid.*, cols. 411–12, nos. 3060–2.

11. *Ibid.*, col. 437, no. 3114.

12. CH, t. IV, nos. 4726–8.

13. Bustron, p. 138.

14. *Ibid.*, p. 139.

15. C. Mutafian, 'Héthoum de Korykos historien arménien. Un prince cosmopolite à l'aube du XIVᵉ siècle', *op. cit.*, pp. 157–76. Hayton, returning from the West, passed through Cyprus in 1307–8.

16. T.T., pp. 317–18, paras. 661–7.

17. L. de Mas-Latrie, 'Texte officiel de l'allocution addressée par les barons de Chypre

au roi Henri II de Lusignan pour lui notifier sa déchéance', *Revue des questions historiques*, t. XLIII, 1888, pp. 526–41; C. Kohler, 'Documents chypriotes du début du XIVᵉ siècle', ROL, t. XI (1905–8), pp. 448–9.

18. N. Coureas, *op. cit. (n.* 3), p. 169.

19. See a letter of 20 October 1306 in which Aymo de Monte Avium (Aymon d'Oiselay) gives himself the title *humilis marescalcus dicte milicie ac tenens locum domini nostri magistri in partibus cismarinis* ..., ACA, Canc. Pergamine Jaime II, no. 2337; published by A. J. Forey, 'Letters ...', p. 166.

20. Amadi, pp. 260–1.

21. *Ibid.*, p. 266.

22. *Ibid.*, p. 267.

23. *Ibid.*, p. 284.

24. N. Coureas, *op. cit. (n.* 3), p. 169.

25. R. Hiestand, 'Zum Problem des Templerzentralarchivs', *Archivitische Zeitschrift*, no. 76, 1980.

26. Bustron, pp. 170–1 and 246–7.

27. Amadi, p. 290: 'Il resto havevano nascoso cosi secretamente che alcun del mondo non ha possuto saver niente di quello.' Take heart, treasure-seekers, you must go to Cyprus!

28. Amadi, p. 238; Bustron, p. 134.

29. Amadi, p. 248, who says 50,000; Bustron, pp. 134–8; Leonce Makhairas, *Chronique de Chypre*, Fr. trans. by Miller, Paris, École des Langues Orientales, vol. III, t. 2, pp. 46–7.

30. These are the records of Lamberto de Sambuceto, *Notai genovesi* ...

31. H. Finke, 'Nachträge ...', pp. 443, no. 7 and 444–5, no. 8.

32. *Notai genovesi (1300–1301)*, ed. V. Polonio, pp. 291–2, no. 296.

33. *Notai genovesi (January–August 1302)*, ed. R. Pavoni, pp. 132–3, no. 104.

34. *Ibid.*, pp. 184–5, no. 155; p. 192, no. 162.

35. A. Demurger, 'Trésor des templiers, Trésor du roi. Mise au point sur les opérations financières des Templiers', *Pouvoir et Gestion, op. cit.*, pp. 73–95.

36. *Notai genovesi (1300–1301)*, ed. V. Polonio, pp. 170–1, no. 158.

37. H. Finke, *Papsttum*, t. II, p. 335: testimony of Étienne de Troyes, sergeant, received into the Order in 1297.

38. G.B., pp. 81–3, no. 6, 8, pp. 98–9, no. 20, p. 101, no. 23. F. Tommasi, 'Fonti epigrafiche dalla *domus templi* di Barletta ...', *Militia sacra*, p. 178.

39. Amadi, pp. 286–7.

40. Mich. I, p. 562.

41. PRO, *Close Rolls*, 32, m. 11 and 5; *Calendar of the Close Rolls*, Edward I, t. III, pp. 137–8 and 172.

42. *Ibid.*, *Close Rolls,* 33, m. 16 d; *Calendar,* t. III, pp. 346–7.

43. ACA, Canc., CRD Jaime II, no. 1171; published in H. Finke, *AA*, t. I, p. 73, no. 58. Letter of 19 April 1300.

44. See *n.* 43.

45. A. J. Forey, 'Letters …', p. 160.

46. ACA, Canc. Pergamine Jaime II, 172, no. 2337: *accedit iturus ad partes Catalania domino concedente de domini nostri magistri mandato et licentia speciali.*

47. A. J. Forey, 'Letters …', p. 160.

48. *Ibid.*, p. 164.

49. See *n.* 44.

50. *Notai genovesi (1300–1301)*, ed. V. Polonio, pp. 256–8 and 305–6.

51. ACA, Canc. CRD Jaime II, 137, no. 68.

52. *Ibid.*, Pergamine Jaime II, 161, no. 1665.

53. F. Tommasi, 'I Templari e il culto delle reliquie', in *I Templari: Mito e Storia,* Siena, 1989, pp. 191–200.

54. L. de Mas-Latrie, *Histoire de l'île de Chypre …*, t. II, p. 98.

55. Mich. I, pp. 219–20.

56. Lizerand, *Le Dossier …*, p. 6: *super hospitalitate fundata … super militia proprie sunt fondati.*

57. S. Garcias Palau, *R. Lull y el Islam*, Palma de Majorca, 1981, ch. IX: 'El viaje de R. Lull a Chipre y a Armenia', pp. 189 ff.

58. *Vita coetanea beati Raymundi Lulli*, ed. Hermogène Harada in *R. Lull Opera latina*, vol. VIII, Turnhout, 1980, pp. 272–309; I am quoting here from the translation of the edition of R. Sugranyes de Franch in *Raymond Lulle,* Actes du colloque Raymond Lulle, Université de Fribourg, 1984, Fribourg, 1986, pp. 109–10. See a useful edition: L. Costa Gomes, *Vie de Raymond Lulle, le docteur illuminé*, Fr. trans., Paris, 1995.

59. M. Batllore, *Obras essenciales de R. Lull*, Barcelona, 1957, t. I, p. 49.

60. *R.T.* 2, pp. 75–141, art. 77–197.

61. G.B., pp. 105–6 and 422–3; mentioned in the Cypriot trial are Martin de Lamussa and Jean de Lisivis; they are also entrusted with the care of alms.

62. Deed of 20 April 1292, A. J. Forey, *The Templars in the Corona de Aragon*, p. 406.

63. CH, t. III, no. 4515; P. Edbury, *The Kingdom of Cyprus*, p. 103, *n.* 8.

64. *Notai genovesi (1300–1301)*, ed. V. Polonio, pp. 493–4, no. 413.

65. *R.T.* 2, p. 75, art. 77.

66. *Ibid.*, p. 77, art. 79.

67. G.B., pp. 117–18.

68. Mich. I, p. 564.

69. *Ibid.*, p. 294.

70. *Ibid.*, and II, p. 207.

71. *Ibid.*, I, p. 562.

72. *Ibid.*, pp. 40 and 538.

73. L. Pagarola i Sabaité, *Els Templers de les Terres d l'Ebre (Tortosa)*, Tarragona, 1999, t. II, pp. 197–8, no. 171: *auctoritate nostra et conventus nostri, cuius nunc plenam et liberam habemus et gerimus potestatem, de consilio et assensu fratris Guillelmi de Barroer, fratris Poncii de Magnocampo, sociorum nostrorum ...*

74. Mich. I, p. 294.

75. J. M. F. Raynouard, *Monuments historiques ...*, p. 268.

76. Mich. I, p. 463: statement of Jehan de Bollencourt.

77. He is probably the same Bartholomé de Quinsey or Quincy as the one mentioned at Pentecost 1300 at Sivré or Sivrey on the Côte d'Or: G.B., pp. 134–5.

78. He was received at Étampes; he must have gone to the East in 1303 according to the testimony of Guillaume de Gy, who was received at Marseille in his presence, with a group of new Templars ready to go to Cyprus, Mich. II, pp. 190–5.

79. A. J. Forey, *op. cit.* (*n.* 63), pp. 421–2, 426.

80. *Ibid.*, pp. 422, 426.

81. *Ibid.*, pp. 421–2, 432.

82. A. Trudon des Ormes, *Liste des maisons ...*, p. 175; see also ACA, Canc., CRD Jaime II, ap. gen. 128, no. 102; published in H. Finke, 'Nachträge ...', pp. 445–6, no. 9 (under an inexact reference).

83. R. Locatelli, *Sur les chemins de la perfection ...*, Saint-Étienne, 1992, pp. 440–1.

84. A. J. Forey, 'Letters ...', p. 167.

85. See *n.* 74 on this.

86. G.B., p. 124.

87. *Ibid.*, p. 135.

88. Jacques de Molay's letter is enclosed in a letter of confirmation from Clement V of 1 July 1311: *Reg. Clement V*, t. VI, pp. 280–5, no. 7183.

89. ACA, Canc., CRD Jaime II (Templarios), 139, no. 242.

90. ACA, Canc., CRD Jaime II (Templarios), 137, no. 81; A. J. Forey, *op. cit.* (*n.* 63), pp. 415 ff.

91. ACA, Canc., CRD Jaime II, no. 2842.

92. ACA, Canc., Pergamine Jaime II, extra inventario no. 240; A. J. Forey, 'Letters ...', pp. 166–7.

93. *Ibid.*, n° 2471; A. J. Forey, *op. cit.* (*n.* 63), p. 419, no. XLVI.

94. ACA, Canc., CRD Jaime II (Templarios), 137, no. 46; A. J. Forey, 'Letters ...', pp. 167–8.

95. *Ibid.*, Pergamine Jaime II 173, no. 2471; A. J. Forey, 'Letters ...', p. 168.

96. ACA, Canc., CRD Jaime II (Templarios), 137, no. 48; H. Finke, *Papsttum*, t. II, pp. 43–4, no. 28.

97. *Ibid.*, no. 47; A. J. Forey, 'Letters …', p. 170 (letter to the queen).

98. ACA, Canc., CRD Jaime II (Templarios), 137, no. 86; A. J. Forey, 'Letters …', pp. 169–70.

99. A. J. Forey, *op. cit.* (*n.* 63), pp. 264–5.

100. H. Finke, 'Nachträge …', pp. 444–5, no. 9.

101. I am indebted to A. J. Forey for this information about the career of Pierre de Castillon, and thank him warmly.

102. ACA, Canc., CRD Jaine II (Templarios), 138, no. 158; A. J. Forey, 'Letters …', pp. 170–1.

103. See *n*. 43.

104. PRO, C 54/121 m. 11d; letter from the king, 13 May 1304, Stirling; B.-T., pp. 368–9.

105. X. Delasselle, *Le service des âmes à la cour, op. cit.*

106. *Calendar of the Close Rolls*, Edward I, t. II, 1296–1307, pp. 314–15.

107. J.-M. Sans i Travé, 'L'ordre del Temple als Països Catalans: la seva introducciò i organitzaciò (Segles XII–XIV)', *Actes de les primers Jornades sobre els Ordes Religioso Militars als Països Catalans*, Tarragona, 1994, p. 35.

108. ACA, Canc., Reg. Jaime II, 334, f. 53; H. Finke, *AA*, t. I, pp. 115–16.

109. ACA, Canc., CRD Jaime II (Templarios), 137, no. 123; see A. J. Forey, *op. cit.* (*n.* 63), p. 311.

110. ACA, Canc., Reg. Jaime II, 334, f. 162; H. Finke, *AA*, t. I, pp. 121–2.

Chapter 8 1306 – Plans and problems

1. *Reg. Clement V*, t. I, no. 1033.

2. Publication in Baluze, Lizerand, Petit, see below.

3. On the plans for the recovery of the Holy Land, refer to the works by S. Schein given in the bibliography , '*Fideles crucis …*', Oxford, 1992; A. Leopold, *How to Recover the Holy Land …*, Aldershot, 2001; J. Delaville Le Roulx, *La France en Orient …*

4. Jean Richard, 'La Croisade de Saint Louis de 1270, premier passage général?', *Comptes-rendus de l'Académie des inscriptions et belles-lettres*, 1989, pp. 510–23.

5. G. Bratianu, 'Le Conseil au roi Charles. Essai sur l'internationale chrétienne et les nationalités à la fin du Moyen Âge', *Revue historique du Sud-Est européen*, t. 19, (1942), pp. 291–361.

6. Hayton of Corycos, *Flor des estoires de la Terre d'Orient*, RHC, Doc. Arm., t. II,

book IV, pp. 226–54; the fourth part – the treatise on the crusade – is translated in *Croisade et pèlerinages,* ed. D. Régnier-Bohler, Paris, 'coll. Bouquins', 1997, pp. 859–78.

7. C. Kohler, 'Deux projets de croisade en Terre sainte composés à la fin du XIIIe siècle et au début du XIVe', ROL, 10, 1903–4, pp. 406–57.

8. The original of Foulques de Villaret's treatise may be found in the Vatican Archives, Miscellanea Vaticana, cassette 1305–6; it was published by J. Petit, 'Mémoire de Foulques de Villaret sur la croisade', BEC, no. 60, 1899, pp. 602–10.

9. AN, J 456, no. 36; published in Baluze, t. III, pp. 145–9; there is a translation in S. Leroy, 'Jacques de Molay et les templiers francs-comtois d'après les actes du procès', *Bulletin de la Société grayloise d'émulation,* 3 (1900), pp. 204–17.

10. There is something surprising about this formal attack on Armenia. It is true that other writers also advised against Armenia, fundamentally for reasons of climate. This was the case with Ramon Lull.

11. A. Demurger, 'Les ordres militaires et la croisade au début du XIVe siècle. Quelques remarques sur les traits de croisade de Jacques de Molay et de Foulques de Villaret', in *Dei Gesta per Francos (Mélanges J. Richard),* Aldershot, Ashgate, 2001, pp. 117–28; A. Luttrell, 'The Hospitallers and the Papacy, 1305–1314', in *Forschungen zur Reichs-, Papst- und Landesgeschichte (Mélanges Peter Herde),* Stuttgart, 1998, p. 601, *n.* 23: the author puts the date of composition of Foulques de Villaret's treatise nearer to that of the general Chapter of the Hospitallers held on 3 November 1306 at Limassol.

12. BNF, *Ms. lat.* 7470, f. 172v. –178v.; edited by B. Kedar and S. Schein, 'Un projet de "passage particulier" proposé par l'ordre de l'Hôpital, 1306–1307', BEC, t. 137, 1979, pp. 211–26.

13. A. Demurger, art. cit. (*n.* 11): a different position from that of Kedar and Schein on its dating and development with Clement V; an intermediate position in A. Luttrell, art. cit. (*n.* 11), p. 301, *n.* 24.

14. BNF, *Ms. lat.* 10919, f. 164–6; edited in Baluze, *op. cit.* (*n.* 9), t. III, pp. 150–4; published and translated by G. Lizerand, *Le Dossier* ..., pp. 2–15.

15. On this subject, see J. Prawer, 'Military Orders and Crusader Politics in the Second Half of the XIIIth Century', in *Die geistlichen Riterrorden Europas,* ed. J. Fleckenstein and M. Ullmann, Vorträge und Forschungen, 26, Sigmaringen, Jan Thorbeke, 1980, pp. 217–29.

16. On this question, see A. Demurger, *Chevaliers du Christ* ..., pp. 148–58.

17. *Reg. Nicolas IV,* t. II, p. 1042, no. 7626 and 7628: these are texts addressed to the archbishop of Split and the archbishop of Narbonne. See also p. 903, no. 6793–9.

18.   Mansi, *Sacrarum Conciliorum nova et amplissima Collectio*, Venice, 1780 (reproduced
       Paris, 1903), t. XXIV, (1296–9), col. 1079.

19.   *Eberhardi archidiaconi Ratisbonensis annales*, Monumenta Germanie Historica:
       Scriptores, t. XVII, Hanover, ed. G. H. Pertz, 1861, p. 594.

20.   G. Lizerand, *Le Dossier* ..., p. 4.

21.   ACA, Canc., CRD Jaime II (Templarios), 137, no. 99 and 139, no. 252; A. J. Forey,
       'Letters ...', pp. 164–5.

22.   A. J. Forey, 'Letters ...', pp. 146–7.

23.   ACA, Canc., CRD Jaime II (Templarios), 138, no. 142. This letter is from
       Gardeny, the Sunday *de latere,* without a year. See A. J. Forey, *The Templars in the
       Corona de Aragon*, p. 328.

24.   ACA, *ibid.,* no. 143.

25.   *Ibid.,* 137, no. 56; published in H. Finke, *Papsttum*, t. II, pp. 13–14, no. 11 (in
       Catalan).

26.   *Reg. Clement V,* t. II, no. 1540; A. Demurger, art. cit. (*n.* 11), pp. 121–2: a hasty
       reading of the text of 15 November led me to suggest an erroneous interpretation
       regarding the date of the reported deeds.

27.   L. Their, *Kreuzzugsbemühungen* ..., pp. 50–1; S. Schein, *Fideles crucis* ..., p. 200; M.
       Melville, *La Vie des templiers*, p. 289.

28.   *Reg. Clement V,* t. I, pp. 190–1, nos. 1034–6.

29.   I took up H. Finke's explanation, *Papsttum* ..., t. I, pp. 123–4, in my article quoted,
       n. 11, p. 123. But I no longer take it into account today.

30.   Translated in S. Leroy, art. cit. (*n.* 9), p. 213.

31.   ACA, Canc., Pergamine Jaime II, 172, no. 2237: letter in favour of Pierre de Saint-
       Just; published by A. J. Forey, 'Letters ...', p. 167.

32.   A. J. Forey, 'Letters ...', p. 154, *n.* 51, citing AHN (Madrid) Section des ordres
       militaires, San Juan, Legojo 310, doc. 18. See also A. J. Forey, *op. cit.* (*n.* 23), p. 154.

33.   ACA, Canc., CRD Jaimes II (Templarios), 139, no. 242.

34.   Baluze, t. III, pp. 61 and 72.

Chapter 9 1307 – In the Snares of the King of France

1.   CH, t. IV, p. 139, no. 4738.

2.   A. Luttrell, 'The Hospitallers and the Papacy, 1305–1314', *op. cit.*, p. 102.

3.   Mich. I, p. 39.

4.   H. Finke, *Papsttum*, t. II, p. 37, no. 24.

5.   A. Demurger, *Chevaliers du Christ* ..., chap. 13; H. Nicholson, 'Jacquemart

Giélée's Renart le Nouvel: The Image of the Military Orders on the Eve of the Loss of Acre', *Monastic Studies*, no. 1.

6. Mich. I, p. 458.

7. *Ibid*. pp. 36–7.

8. See *n*. 6.

9. Mich. I, pp. 401–2.

10. Villani, *Cronica*, 4 vols., Florence, 1845 (reissued Frankfurt, 1969), t. 2, book VIII, 92, p. 123; Baluze, t. II, pp. 89–106: *Sexta vita Clementis V auctore Amalrico Augerri de Biterris*. They were the subject of a close study by Piton, 'À propos des accusations contre les Templiers', ROL, no. 3, 1895, pp. 423–32.

11. There is no Montfaucon in the Toulousain; the expression 'prior' is very rarely used in Templar terminology. It could apply to the brother chaplain of an important Templar house, Paris for instance; but Le Mas d'Agen and the so-called Montfaucon leave one sceptical.

12. Villani, *op. cit. (n.* 10).

13. Baluze, *op. cit. (n.* 10), pp. 93–4.

14. H. Finke, *Papsttum*, t. II, p. 83.

15. G. Bordonove, *La Tragédie des Templiers*, Paris, 1993, p. 95.

16. See the list of the 127 articles in M. Barber, *The Trial* ..., pp. 248–52 (Eng. trans.); and for a French translation, G. Bordonove, *op. cit. (n.* 15), pp. 217–24. The two translations are made from Mich. I, pp. 89–96.

17. See chapter 4.

18. See, for example, the letter from James II to Florent de Velu, Grand Commander of the Temple, dated 1299 at Naples; ACA, Canc., Reg. Jaime II, 265, f. 204; H. Finke, *AA*, t. 1, pp. 55–6, no. 41.

19. See J. Favier, *Philippe le Bel*, Paris, Fayard, 1999; and chiefly J. Coste, *Boniface VIII en procès*, Rome, l'Erma, 1995.

20. *Nangis*, pp. 336 and 341; Guizot, pp. 247–8 and 252.

21. B. Frale, *L'Ultima battaglia dei Templari*, p. 21; J. Coste, *op. cit. (n.* 19), pp. 169–71: schedule of bishops, abbots and *de frater Hugo, visitator domorum ordinis militie Templi ac Sancti Iohannis Hierosolymitani in Francia et Sancti Martini de Campis parisiensis priores* ...

22. T.T., pp. 329–30, para. 695. Taken up by Amadi, pp. 280–1 and F. Bustron, pp. 163–4, who add a few details.

23. Département of Yvelines.

24. *R.T.* 2, pp. 77–8, para. 80; pp. 159–60, paras. 250–1; p. 286, para. 460; p. 310, para. 598.

25. Mich. II, pp. 315–16.

26. He seems to have transferred his admiration to Foulques de Villaret, to whom

he devotes a long development concerning the conquest of Rhodes by the Hospitallers. Indeed, Beaujeu and Villaret have features in common.

27. ACA, Canc., CRD Jaime II (Templarios), 137, no. 85; published in H. Finke, *Papsttum*, t. II, pp. 58–9, no. 39.

28. *Grandes Chroniques de France* …, t. VIII, p. 257: an eloquent, but untruthful, account: '… the king of France Philip left around Pentecost to go to speak with the pope and cardinals, and there many things were arranged by the pope and the king, and especially the arrest of the Templars.'

29. ACA, Canc., CRD Jaime II, Ap. Gen. 128, no. 80; published by H. Finke, *Papsttum*, t. II, p. 36, no. 23.

30. H. Finke, *Papsttum*, t. II, p. 38, no. 25, dated 26 June 1307.

31. Mich. I, p. 35; trans. Lizerand, *Le Dossier* …, p. 153.

32. *Reg. Clement V*, t. VI, pp. 280–8, no. 7183. This is a letter from Jacques de Molay enclosed in a letter from the pope (dated 1 July 1311, from the priory of Grauselle): *Actum Pictavis in hospicio, quo tunc morabatur frater Iacobus de Molayo* …

33. Mich. II, p. 279; M. Barber, *James of Molay* …, p. 109.

34. ACA, Canc., Pergamine Jaime II, *extra inventario*, no. 240; part publication, H. Finke, 'Nachträge …', p. 452, no. 14 (note); A. J. Forey, 'Letters …', pp. 166–7.

35. See the letters concerning the appointment of Exemen de Lenda as Master of Aragon, A. J. Forey, 'Letters …', pp. 168–71. See chapter 7 of this book.

36. B. Frale, *op. cit.* (*n.* 16), pp. 73 ff.

37. *Nangis*, pp. 355–6; Guizot, p. 264.

38. *Reg. Boniface VIII*, t. I, col. 914, no. 2323.

40. Baluze, t. III, p. 72: letter of 2 November 1306 from Clement V; E. Boutaric, 'Clément V, Philippe le Bel et les templiers', *Revue des questions historiques*, t. X–XI, 1872, p. 321: letter from the king in January; Baluze, t. III, p. 74: letter from the pope in February 1307, speaking of the happy ending of the affair.

40. Here we are close to the 'factoid' phenomenon – 'hypotheses or suppositions which have lost their hypothetical character through having been taken up and quoted in studies …', M.-L. von Wartburg, 'Production du sucre de canne à Chypre. Un chapitre de technologie médiévale', in *Coloniser au Moyen Âge*, eds. M. Balard and A. Ducellier, Paris, 1995, pp. 130 and 153, *n.* 28.

41. A. Demurger, 'Trésor des Templiers, Trésor du Roi. Mise au point sur les opérations financières des Templiers', *op. cit.*, p. 81.

42. R. W. Kaeuper, *War, Justice and Public Order. England and France in the Later Middle Ages*, Oxford, Oxford University Press, 1988; French translation, *Guerre, justice et ordre public. La France et l'Angleterre à la fin du Moyen Âge*, Paris, Aubier, 'Coll. Historique', 1994, pp. 99–100 of the French edition; S. Menache, 'The

Templar Order: A Failed Ideal?', *The Catholic Historical Review*, no. 79 (1993), pp. 19–20; A. Demurger, art. cit. (*n.* 41), pp. 81–5.

43. Mich. II, pp. 314–15.

44. *Ibid.*, p. 297 and G. B., p. 92.

45. Mich. I, p. 535.

46. *Calendar of the Patent Rolls*, Edward I, t. II (1292–1301), London, 1895, p. 4–19.

47. Belleville-sur-Saône, département of the Rhône.

48. G. B., pp. 110–11.

49. *Ibid.*, p. 124.

50. Mich. I, p. 390.

51. *Ibid.*, II, p. 335.

52. ACA, Canc., CRD Jaime II (Templarios), Ap. gen. 129, no. 102 (wanting); published by H. Finke, 'Nachträge …', pp. 445–6, no. 9.

53. E. G. Léonard, *Gallicarum Militiae Templi Domorum*, Paris, 1932, p. 28.

54. F. Tommasi, 'Fonti epigrafiche dalla *domus templi* di Barletta per la cronotassi degli ultimi maestri provinciali dell'ordine nel regno di Sicilia', in *Militia Sacra. Gli ordini militari tra Europa e Terrasanta*, p. 177.

55. Mich. II, p. 388.

56. *Ibid.* I, p. 448.

57. *Reg. Clement V*, t. VI, pp. 280–8, no. 7183.

58. B.-T., p. 296, *n.* 12.

59. Mich. I, p. 152.

60. B.-T., pp. 296–7, *n.* 14, publishing an extract from the text.

61. *Ibid.*, p. 297, *n.* 17.

62. H. Finke, *Papsttum*, t. II, pp. 141–50, no. 88.

63. G. Lizerand, *Le Dossier* …, pp. 110–25; also published by H. Finke, *Papsttum*, t. II, pp. 135–40.

64. H. Finke, *Papsttum*, t. II, p. 143.

65. Baluze, t. III, pp. 58–60.

66. B. Frale, *op. cit.* (*n.* 21), p. 68.

67. Mich. II, p. 372.

68. Mich. I, p. 390.

Chapter 10 1309 – Escaping the Trap

1. There are many far-fetched works on the trial of the Templars, and a few sound studies; I give here the more recent of the latter: M. Barber, *The Trial of the*

Templars, Cambridge, 1978; A. Beck, *Der Untergang der Templer*, Fribourg, 1992; G. Bordonove, *La Tragédie des Templiers*, Paris, 1993; B. Frale, *L'ultima battaglia dei Templari*, Rome, 2001; P. Partner, *The Murdered Magicians. The Templars and Their Myths*, London, 1981, French trans: *Templiers, Francs-maçons et sociétés secrètes*, Paris, 1992. The context can be gleaned from J. Favier, *Philippe le Bel*, Paris, 1999; R. W. Kaeuper, *War, Justice and Public Order. England and France in the Later Middle Ages*, Oxford, 1988, French trans., see *n.* 42, above; J. R. Strayer, *The Reign of Philip the Fair*, Princeton, 1980; S. Menache, *Clement V*, Cambridge, 1998. Overall view of the interrogations and their publications in A. Demurger, 'Encore le procès des templiers. À propos d'un ouvrage récent', *Le Moyen Âge*, no. 97, 1991, pp. 25–39.

2.   BNF, Ms. lat. 10919, f. 84v. and 236v.; published by H. Finke, *Papsttum*, t. II, pp. 74–5, no. 50.

3.   They bear the signature of Pierre du Bois, a lawyer from Falaise, whom people have been rather quick to make the king's spokesman. See G. Lizerand, *Le Dossier …*, pp. 84–101.

4.   *Ibid.*, pp. 110–37.

5.   See the references to these lists in chapter 9, *n.* 13.

6.   Some have been published. Nîmes: L. Ménard, *Histoire civile, littéraire et ecclésiastique de la ville de Nîmes*, Paris, 1750, t. I, *Preuves*, pp. 167–219; Auvergne: R. Sève and A.-M. Chagny-Sève, *Le Procès des templiers d'Auvergne (1309–1311)*, Paris, 1987: Lerida and Navarre: H. Finke, *Papsttum*, t. II, pp. 364–79; Elne: Mich. II, pp. 420–515; London: D. Wilkins, *Conciliae Magna Britanniae et Hiberniae*, London, 1737, t. II, pp. 329–407; Florence: J. Loiseleur, *La Doctrine secrète des Templiers*, Paris, 1872 (issued Geneva, 1975), pp. 172–212; Rome: A. Gilmour-Bryson, *The Trial of the Templars in the Papal State and the Abruzzi*, Rome, 1982; Ravenna: a detailed analysis of the trial in R. Caravita, *Rinaldo da Concorrezzo, arcivescovo di Ravenna, 1303–1321, al tempo di Dante*, Florence, 1964, pp. 265–307.

7.   *Nangis*, t. I, p. 388; *Grandes Chroniques de France*, t. VIII, p. 272.

8.   D. Wilkins, *op. cit.* (*n.* 5); for Cyprus, besides the old publication of K. Schottmuller, we now have available the English translation of the interrogations thanks to A. Gilmour-Bryson.

9.   This is the bulk of the Michelet publication: Mich. I and II, pp. 1–271.

10.   B. Frale, *op. cit.* (*n.* 1), chap. 4 and 5.

11.   The latter fact has been emphasised by Peter Partner (see *n.* 1).

12.   B. Frale, *op. cit.* (*n.* 1), p. 174.

13.   The texts of the Council of Vienne are now conveniently accessible in: *Les conciles oecuméniques. 2: Les décrets*, t. I, pp. 698–725.

14. G. Lizerand, 'Les dépositions du grand maître Jacques de Molay au procès des templiers (1307–1314)', *Le Moyen Âge*, t. XXVI, 1913.

15. Mich. II, pp. 305–6; trans. G. Lizerand, *Le Dossier ...*, pp. 34–7.

16. The depositions of Guillaume de Gy and Étienne Safed, members of his *familia*, contradict this denial by the Grand Master. Are they to be believed? It seems likely that had the sin of sodomy been committed, the investigators would have insisted further.

17. *Nangis*, t. I, p. 362; Guizot, p. 267.

18. B. Frale, *op. cit.* (*n.* 1), p. 108.

19. M. Barber, *The Trial ...* (*n.* 1), p. 65.

20. H. Finke, *Papsttum*, t. II, pp. 115–16.

21. Baluze, t. III, pp. 91–2.

22. H. Finke, *Papsttum*, t. II, pp. 110–11.

23. *Ibid.*, pp. 114–19.

24. *Ibid.*, p. 116.

25. M. Barber, *The Trial ...*, pp. 76–7.

26. It is easy to understand why the historians who take Molay for a fool cannot accept seeing him act in so clever a way! The Catalan witness thus becomes a second-hand witness who recounts hearsay; but was the Templar of Tyre under the table when Molay flew into a rage against the king? It depends what you want to prove.

27. M. Barber, *The Trial ...*, pp. 77–8; B. Frale, *op. cit.* (*n.* 1), p. 115.

28. The names are given in *Reg. Clement V*, no. 10402; K. Schottmüller, *Der Untergang des Templerordens*, 2 vols., Munster, 1907, t. II, pp. 9–72, publishes the interrogations of thirty-three of them; H. Finke, *Papsttum*, t. II, pp. 341–64, those of the other nine.

29. H. Finke, *Papsttum*, t. II, pp. 324–9.

30. Information supplied by Barbara Frale, whom I thank. See P. Viollet, 'Les interrogatoires de Jacques de Molay, grand maître du Temple. Conjectures', *Mémoires de l'Académie des incriptions et belles-lettres*, no. 38, 1909, p. 7; G. Lizerand, art. cit. (*n.* 14); both gave these dates.

31. H. Finke, *Papsttum*, t. II, p. 328.

32. A. Demurger, 'Encore le procès des templiers. À propos d'un livre récent', *op. cit.*, pp. 35–9.

33. Mich. I, pp. 32–4; trans. G. Lizerand, *Le Dossier ...*, pp. 146–55.

34. G. Lizerand translates as: 'Not to become entangled, or muddled.'

35. P. Viollet, art. cit. (*n.* 30), pp. 10 and 14. The author speaks of a useful, or compassionate, lie.

36. Mich. I, pp. 42–5; trans. G. Lizerand, *Le Dossier ...*, pp. 162–71.

37. *Ibid.*, p. 165.

38. *Ibid.*, p. 169.

39. The demand (readers) is as much to blame as the supply (historians)!

40. H. Finke, *Papsttum*, t. II, p. 114.

41. *Ibid.*, pp. 58–60, no. 39: this is a letter dated November, probably written by one of the pope's treasurers to the Commander of the Temple of Ascò in Catalonia; M. Barber, *The Trial* ..., pp. 72 and 270, *n.* 2.

42. H. Finke, *Papsttum*, t. II, p. 59.

43. *Ibid.* This same treasurer says he had the information from an equerry who had come from Paris.

44. *Ibid.*, p. 60.

45. RHGF, t. XXI, p. 658.

46. H. Finke, *Papsttum*, t. II, p. 102, no. 69 (AN,J 413, no. 37); trans. in G. Bordonove, *La Tragédie des templiers*, p. 178.

47. H. Finke, *Papsttum*, t. II, p. 61, no. 40.

48. G. Lizerand, *Le Dossier* ..., pp. 118–19.

49. H. Finke, *Papsttum*, t. II, p. 62, no. 41.

50. G. Lizerand, art. cit. (*n.* 14), pp. 82–3.

51. See chapter 9.

52. *Nangis*, p. 362.

53. H. Finke, *Papsttum*, t. II, pp. 338–9.

54. K. Schottmüller, *Der Untergang des Templer-Ordens*, t. II, p. 37.

55. Dupuy, *Traitéz concernant l'histoire de France*, Paris, 1685, pp. 91–2; quoted by M. Barber, *The Trial* ..., p. 75.

56. The problem has been chewed over for a long time: the Temple lacked jurists, theologians, educated people in general, capable of steering it through the procedural labyrinth. When the Templars, of whatever rank, said they were 'poor and unlettered' and thus incapable of defending the Order, it was not merely an evasion, it was true.

Chapter 11 1314 – Burnt at the Stake

1. *Reg. Clement V*, t. IV, p. 455, no. 5067 (22 May 1309).

2. For the essence of this, see M. Barber, *The Trial of the Templars*, 1978; and for a regional example: A. J. Forey, *The Fall of the Templars in the Crown of Aragon*, Aldershot, Ashgate, 2001.

3. *Reg. Clement V*, t. VIII, p. 482, no. 10337.

4. *Chronique métrique attribuée à Geoffroi de Paris*, ed. G. Diverres, ll. 5635–50, takes up this distinction but without specifying the fate that befell either group.

5. Jean de Saint-Victor, *Memoriale historiarum*, RHGF, t. XXI, p. 658 b.

6. *Nangis*, t. I, p. 402; Guizot, pp. 299–300.

7. G. Bordonove, *La Tragédie des templiers*, pp. 341–3.

8. *Nangis*, t. I, p. 403; Guizot, pp. 300–1.

9. B. Gui, *Flores Chronicorum*, French trans. of 1316, BNF, Ms. fr. 1409, f. 157.

10. *Chronique métrique attribuée à Geoffroi de Paris*, (n. 4), ll. 5711–42.

11. That being said, Geoffroi de Paris sometimes varies in his judgement on the Templars; he seems to hesitate, change his opinion: 'I prefer to speak of something else; this affair displeases me. The more one stirs up shit, the more it stinks. I no longer wish to write verses about such folk', ll. 3615–29; but elsewhere he writes: 'Who knows who is telling the truth and who lying ... The Church may be easily deceived, but in no way can one deceive God. I will say no more. Let him who wishes to, tell what follows', ll. 5766–70.

12. *Cronica di G. Villani*, t. II, book VIII, ch. 92, pp. 126–7.

13. *Ibid*.

14. *Les Grandes Chroniques de France*, t. VIII, p. 295.

15. E. Boutaric, *Actes du Parlement de Paris*, Paris, 1863, t. II, p. 122, no. 4272.

16. G. Boccaccio, *De casibus virorum illustrium*, in *Tutte le opere di Giovanni Boccaccio*, t. IX, ed. V. Branco, Milan, Mondadori, 1985, book IX, chap. 21, pp. 822–31. Translation by Laurent de Premierfait, *Des cas des nobles hommes et femmes*. Only Book I has been the subject of a recent publication, by P. M. Gathercole, Chapel Hill, 'North Carolina Studies in the Romance Languages and Literatures', no. 64, 1968. See *Dictionnaire des lettres françaises, Le Moyen Âge*, eds. G. Hasenohr and M. Zink, Paris, Fayard, 1992, pp. 202–4 and 922–4.

17. See the text in the Appendices, pp. 268–72.

18. A. K. Wildermann, *Die Beurteilung des Templerprozesses bis zum 17 Jahrhundert*, Fribourg (Switzerland), Universitätsverlag, 1972. A final chapter makes a rapid synthesis of the historiography of the trial up to the twentieth century.

19. C. Balasse, La Chute de l'ordre du Temple dans l'historiographie de la fin du Moyen Âge (Début du XIVe siècle-Fin du XVe siècle), dissertation given before the University of Paris 7-Denis Diderot, 1995, 2 tomes.

20. *Ibid.*, t. II, p. 88; BNF, Ms. fr. 4932, f. 214v.

21. *Ibid.*, t. I, p. 38 and t. II, pp. 78–80, 88 and 89.

22. M. Druon, *Les Rois maudits*, Paris, 1965.

23. Here I follow Colette Beaune, 'Les rois maudits', *Mythes et Histoire*, Razo, Cahier du Centre d'études médiévales de Nice, no. 12, 1992, pp. 7–24.

24. *Ibid.*, p. 19, *n*. 87.

25. *Ibid.*, quotation p. 21.

26. *Ibid.*, p. 22.

27. On these questions, see P. Partner, *Templiers, Francs-Maçons et Sociétés secrètes*, Paris, 1992; and R. Le Forestier, *La Franc-maçonnerie templière et occultiste aux XVIIIᵉ et XIXᵉ siècles*, posthumous work edited by A. Faivre, Paris, 1970.

28. M. H. Jones, *Le Théâtre national en France de 1800 à 1830*, Paris, 1975, especially chapters III and IV.

29. J. M. F. Raynouard, *Les Templiers*, tragedy in five acts (Paris, 1805) (reprint Nîmes, Lacour edn 1997). Raynouard also wrote a historical work on the Templars, the *Monuments historiques relatifs à la condamnation des templiers et à l'abolition de leur ordre*, which is still useful today. The author had had access to the Vatican Archives which had been transferred to Paris on Napoleon's orders.

30. Analysis by the *Courrier des spectacles* for 1805, bibliothèque de l'Arsenal, RJ 26.

31. *Correspondance de Napoléon Ier*, Paris, 1862, t. X, pp. 466–7 and t. XIV, p. 158.

32. J. F. M. Raynouard, *Les Templiers*, Paris, 1873, 63 p., Les Bons Livres, no. 97. Reprinted in 1875, 1877, 1879.

33. This great painting by Jacquand hangs in salle 4. This picture, and the one by Amaury-Duval, are reproduced in *Les salles des croisades. Château de Versailles*, by Claire Constans and Philippe Lamarque, Doussard (74), Éditions du Gui, 2002, pp. 161 and 162; see also E. Siberry, *The New Crusaders. Images of the Crusades in the 19ᵗʰ and Early 20ᵗʰ Centuries*, Aldershot, 2000, p. 210.

34. L. Dailliez, *Jacques de Molay, dernier grand maître du Temple*, pp. 27–8.

35. T.T., p. 302, para. 611.

36. S. Schein, 'Gesta Dei per Mongolos. 1300. The Genesis of a Non-Event', *English Historical Review*, no. 94 (1979).

37. Nouvelle Biographie universelle, Paris, 1861, t. XXXV, cols. 795–6, p. 795.

12. Conclusion - A Portrait of Jacques de Molay

1. Mich. I, p. 42; trans. G. Lizerand, *Le Dossier* …, p. 164; *ipse erat miles illiterates et pauper* …

2. *Ibid.*, p. 389; translated in R. Oursel, *Le Procès des Templiers*, Paris, 1955, p. 181.

3. See Corpus of Letters, no. 7, 8, 9 and 16.

4. *Ibid.*, no. 8.

5. *Ibid.*, no. 7. Dalmau de Roccabert was freed after the abolition of the Temple, in 1313.

6. ACA, Canc., CRD Jaime II (Templarios), 139, no. 242, dated 5 January 1307 at Candia.

7. A. J. Forey, 'Constitutional Conflict and Change in the Hospital of St John during the Twelfth and Thirteenth Centuries', in A. J. Forey, *Military Orders and Crusades*, Aldershot, 1994, X, pp. 15–29.

8. B. Frale, *L'ultima battaglia dei Templari*, p. 47.

9. A. J. Forey, art. cit. (*n.* 7), pp. 20–1.

10. Mich. I, p. 355, 7 January 1311: 'He believes that if the Master commanded anything it was observed throughout the Order'; *ibid.*, p. 367, 8 January 1311: 'He believes that whatever the Grand Master commanded with his convent on the other side of the sea was obeyed on this side of the sea.'

11. *Ibid.*, I, p. 465.

12. *Ibid.*, II, p. 436; trans. in B. Alart, *L'Ordre du Temple en Roussillon et sa suppression*, Rennes-le-Château, 1988, p. 26.

13. *Ibid.*, p. 102.

14. *Ibid.*, p. 124.

15. *Ibid.*, p. 125.

16. *Ibid.*, p. 152.

17. *Ibid.*, pp. 116–17.

18. J. F. M. Raynouard, *Monumens historiques* ..., p. 269.

19. Several others also believed in it: the kings of Cyprus and Armenia, Otton de Grandson, and Edward I of England.

20. T.T., p. 323, para. 678.

21. If one takes the course of not rejecting the testimonies without examining them, then this applies to all, to those who describe the scurrilous ritual as well as to those who deny it.

22. G. Lizerand, *Le Dossier* ..., p. 5.

23. G. Lizerand, 'Les dépositions du grand maître Jacques de Molay au procès des templiers (1307–1314)', *Le Moyen Âge*, t. XXVI, 1913, p. 106.

CONTEMPORARY POPES

Name	Date of election	Date of coronation	Date of death
Gregory IX	19 March 1227	21 March	22 August 1241
Celestine IV	25 October 1241	not crowned	10 November 1241
Innocent IV	25 June 1243	28 June	7 December 1254
Alexander IV	16 December 1254	16 December	25 May 1261
Urban IV	29 August 1261	4 September	2 October 1264
Clement IV	5 February 1265	15–22 February	29 November 1268
Gregory X	1 September 1271	27 March 1272	10 January 1276
Innocent V	21 January 1276	22 February	22 June 1276
Adrian V	11 July 1276	not crowned	18 August 1276
John XXI	8 September 1276	15 September	20 May 1277
Nicholas III	25 November 1277	26 December	22 September 1280
Martin IV	22 February 1281	23 March	28 March 1285
Honorius IV	2 April 1285	20 May	3 April 1287
Nicholas IV	22 February 1288	22 February	4 April 1292
Celestine V	5 July 1294	29 August	13 December 1294 (abdication)
Boniface VIII	24 December 1294	23 January 1295	11 October 1303
Benedict XI	22 October 1303	27 October	7 July 1304
Clement V	5 June 1305	14 November	20 April 1314
John XXII	7 April 1316	5 September	4 December 1334

GENEALOGIES

Kings of France

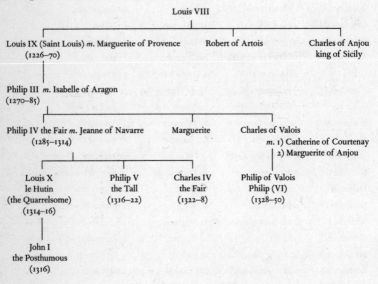

Louis VIII

Louis IX (Saint Louis) *m*. Marguerite of Provence
(1226–70)

Robert of Artois

Charles of Anjou
king of Sicily

Philip III *m*. Isabelle of Aragon
(1270–85)

Philip IV the Fair *m*. Jeanne of Navarre
(1285–1314)

Marguerite

Charles of Valois
m. 1) Catherine of Courtenay
2) Marguerite of Anjou

Louis X
le Hutin
(the Quarrelsome)
(1314–16)

Philip V
the Tall
(1316–22)

Charles IV
the Fair
(1322–8)

Philip of Valois
Philip (VI)
(1328–50)

John I
the Posthumous
(1316)

Crown of Aragon

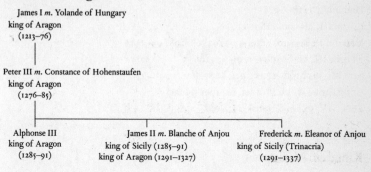

James I *m.* Yolande of Hungary
king of Aragon
(1213–76)

Peter III *m.* Constance of Hohenstaufen
king of Aragon
(1276–85)

Alphonse III
king of Aragon
(1285–91)

James II *m.* Blanche of Anjou
king of Sicily (1285–91)
king of Aragon (1291–1327)

Frederick *m.* Eleanor of Anjou
king of Sicily (Trinacria)
(1291–1337)

Hohenstaufens and Angevins in Sicily

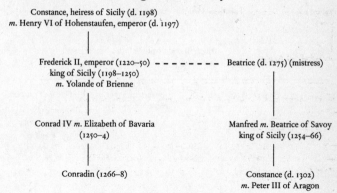

Constance, heiress of Sicily (d. 1198)
m. Henry VI of Hohenstaufen, emperor (d. 1197)

Frederick II, emperor (1220–50) – – – – – – – – Beatrice (d. 1275) (mistress)
king of Sicily (1198–1250)
m. Yolande of Brienne

Conrad IV *m.* Elizabeth of Bavaria
(1250–4)

Manfred *m.* Beatrice of Savoy
king of Sicily (1254–66)

Conradin (1266–8)

Constance (d. 1302)
m. Peter III of Aragon

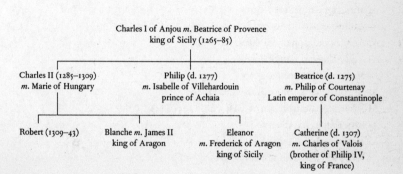

Charles I of Anjou *m.* Beatrice of Provence
king of Sicily (1265–85)

Charles II (1285–1309)
m. Marie of Hungary

Philip (d. 1277)
m. Isabelle of Villehardouin
prince of Achaia

Beatrice (d. 1275)
m. Philip of Courtenay
Latin emperor of Constantinople

Robert (1309–43)

Blanche *m.* James II
king of Aragon

Eleanor
m. Frederick of Aragon
king of Sicily

Catherine (d. 1307)
m. Charles of Valois
(brother of Philip IV,
king of France)

Kings of Little Armenia

Hethum I, 1226–69
Levon III, his son, 1269–89
Hethum II, his son, 1289–93, 1294–6, 1298/99–1305
Thoros III, his brother, 1293–4, 1296–7
Sempad, his brother, usurper, 1297–8
Constantine II, his brother, usurper (idem)
Levon IV, son of Thoros, 1304–08

Kingdom of Cyprus

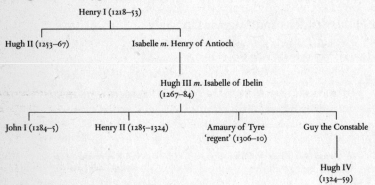

Henry I (1218–53)

Hugh II (1253–67)

Isabelle *m.* Henry of Antioch

Hugh III *m.* Isabelle of Ibelin
(1267–84)

John I (1284–5)   Henry II (1285–1324)   Amaury of Tyre   Guy the Constable
                                              'regent' (1306–10)

Hugh IV
(1324–59)

The Mamluk Sultans

Aybak, 1250–7
Al Malik al Mansûr Ali, his son, 1257–9
Al Muzaffar Kutûz, 1259–60
Al Zâhir Baybars, 1260–77
Al Sa'id Berke, son of Baybars, 1277–80
Al Adil Salâmish, son of Baybars, 1280
Al Mansûr Kalâwûn, 1280–90
Al Ashraf Khalîl, son of Kalâwûn, 1290–3
Al Nâsir Muhammad, son of Kalâwûn, 1293–4 (I)
Al Adil Katbugha, 1294–6
Al Mansûr Lâdjîn, 1296–8
Al Nâsir Muhammad, 1298–1310 (II)

Al Mansûr Baybars II, 1310–11
Al Nâsir Muhammad, 1311–41 (III)

The Mongols of Persia (Ilkhan)

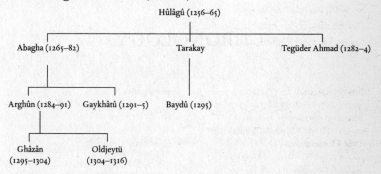

Hûlâgû (1256–65)

Abagha (1265–82)   Tarakay   Tegüder Ahmad (1282–4)

Arghûn (1284–91)   Gaykhâtû (1291–5)   Baydû (1295)

Ghâzân   Oldjeytü
(1295–1304)   (1304–1316)

(The last two tables were drawn up from data by J. C. Garcin *et alii*, *États, sociétés et cultures du monde musulman médiéval, X*ᵉ*-XV*ᵉ *siècle*, Paris, PUF, 'Nouvelle Clio', 1995, t. I, pp. CLIV and CLVIII, and t. III, *Index historique*, pp. 234–65.)

CHRONOLOGY

Historical context

1243 (2 July): The Mongols put an end to the
   Seljukid sultanate of Anatolia

1244 (23 August): Capture of Jerusalem by
   the Khwarezmians

1244 (17 October): Battle of La Forbie

1244 (mid-December): Louis IX vows to
   make a crusade

1245 (28 June): The first Council of Lyon
   deposes Frederick II

1248 (26 April): Consecration of the Sainte-
   Chapelle

1248 (25 August): Louis IX's crusade; the
   king leaves Aigues-Mortes

1249 (5–6 June): Louis IX captures Damietta

1250 (8 February): Battle of Mansûrah

1250 (5 April): Louis IX taken prisoner

1250 (6 May): Release of Louis IX; Damietta
   handed back to the Egyptians

1250 (30 July): Aybak, first Mamluk sultan
   of Egypt

1250 (13 December): Death of Frederick II

1254 (24 April): Louis IX leaves Acre and
   returns to France

1258 (February): Capture of Baghdad by the
   Mongols. End of the Abbassid khalifate.
   War of Saint-Sabas at Acre

1260 (24 January): The Mongols capture
   Aleppo

1260 (1 March): Capture of Damascus by the
   Mongols

Jacques de Molay

1244–5: Birth (version 1)

1249–50: Birth (version 2)

Historical context

Jacques de Molay

1260 (2 September): Battle of Ayn Djalût: the
Mamluks defeat the Mongols

1260 (24 October): Assassination of the
sultan Kutûz. Baybars becomes sultan

1261 (25 July): Reconquest of Constantinople
by the Greeks

1265 (February): Capture of Caesarea by
Baybars

1265 (8 February): Death of Hûlâgû; his son   *1265*: Reception into the Temple at Beaune
Abagha founds the khanate of Ilkhân in
Persia

1265 (30 April): Fall of Arsur

1266 (26 February): Battle of Benevento;
Charles of Anjou defeats Manfred and
seizes the kingdom of Sicily

1266 (22 July): Baybars takes Safed

1268 (20 June): Baybars takes Antioch

1268 (23 August): Battle of Tagliacozzo.
Conradin, last heir of the Staufens, is
conquered by Charles of Anjou   *before 1270*: Goes to the Holy Land (theory 1)

1270 (25 July): Death of Louis IX at Tunis

1271 (8 April): Fall of the Krak des
Chevaliers

1271 (12 June): Montfort, castle of the
Teutonic Order, taken by Baybars

1272 (22 May): Truce concluded at Caesarea
between the kingdom of Jerusalem and
the sultan

1273 (13 May): Election of Guillaume de
Beaujeu as Master of the Temple

1274 (May–17 July): Second Council of Lyon   *Between 1273 and 1282*: Goes to the Holy

1275 (11 May): Death of Bohemond VI, count   Land (theory 2)
of Tripoli. Crisis over the succession

1277 (15 July): Charles of Anjou buys back
the rights of Marie of Antioch to the
crown of Jerusalem

1277 (1 July): Death of Baybars

1279 (December): Kalâwûn becomes Mamluk
sultan

1280 (16 July): Agreement between the
Templars and Bohemond VII of Tripoli

1281 (December): First battle of Homs.
Defeat of the Mongols by the Mamluks

Historical context	*Jacques de Molay*
1282 (30 March): Sicilian Vespers. The Aragonese seize Sicily	
1283 (3 June): Ten-year truce concluded between Kalâwûn and Acre	
1284 (24 March): Death of Hugh III of Cyprus	
1284 (11 May): Coronation of John, king of Cyprus	
1285 (7 January): Death of Charles I of Anjou, king of Sicily	
1285 (20 May): Death of John of Cyprus	*1285*: Jacques de Molay present in France
1285 (October): Accession of Philip IV the Fair in France	
1286 (28 June): Henry II of Cyprus master of Acre	
1286 (15 August): Henry II of Cyprus crowned king of Jerusalem at Tyre	
1289 (26 April): Kalâwûn captures Tripoli	
1290 (11 November): Death of Kalâwûn	
1291 (6 April): Start of the siege of Acre	
1291 (18 May): The town is captured. Death of G. de Beaujeu	
1291 (28 May): Collapse of the Tower of the Temple	
1291 (14 August): Evacuation of Castle Pilgrim	*1291* (September–October?): Molay present at a general Chapter in Cyprus
1292 (23 January): The Bulls *Pia mater ecclesia* appeals for aid to the kingdom of Armenia	
	1292 (before 16 April): Death of Thibaud Gaudin
1292 (4 April): Death of Pope Nicholas IV	*1292* (before 20 April): J. de Molay is Grand Master of the Temple
1292 (June): The Mamluks seize Hromgla, seat of the Armenian patriarch	*1293* (May): Molay in Provence
	1293 (August): Holds a general Chapter at Montpellier
	1293 (24 August): Meets the king of Aragon at the frontier?
	1294 (January): In England
1294 (24 December): Election of Boniface VIII to the pontificate	*1294* (27 August): At Lerida (Crown of Aragon, to settle the problem of granting Tortosa to the king)
	1294 (24 December): At Naples; election of Boniface VIII
	1295 (January): In Rome

Historical context	*Jacques de Molay*
	1295 (24 June): Paris (Chapter); Dijon (reception of a candidate)
	1295 (9 July): In Apulia
	1296 (21 January): In Rome
	1296 (15 August): Chapter at Arles
	1296 (autumn): Return to Cyprus
1297 (11 August): Canonisation of Saint Louis	
1298/1299: Mamluk attack on Armenia of Cilicia; the Templars lose the castle of Roche-Guillaume	*1298 or 1299*: In Armenia
1299 (24 December): Second battle of Homs. Victory of the Mongols over the Mamluks	*1299* (20 October): Limassol (letter to Pierre de Saint-Just)
	1300 (20 July): At Famagusta. Raids on Egypt and the Syrian coasts
	1300 (1–10 November): Limassol (letters to Pierre de Saint-Just)
	1300 (after 15 November): At Ruad
	1301 (8 April): Limassol (letter to Edward I)
1301 (18 November): Bull *Unam sanctam*	*1301* (8 November): Limassol (letter to James II). Announces that he is ready to go to Ruad
	1301 (November–December): Receives Ramon Lull at Limassol
	1302 (1 May): Famagusta (reception of G. de Raval)
	1302 (26 September): Defeat of the Templar garrison on Ruad
	1302 (5 November): Limassol (letter to James II of Aragon)
1303 (12 May): The king of France calls on the Council to try Boniface VIII	
1303 (7 September): Assassination attempt at Anagni	
1303 (11 October): Death of Boniface VIII	
1303 (22 Oct.)–*1304* (16 July): Pontificate of Benedict XI	
1305 (5 June): Election of Clement V	*1305* (20 January): At Limassol
1305 (15 November): Coronation of Clement V at Lyon	
1306 (26 April): Dethronement of Henry II of Cyprus. His brother Amaury is governor	*1306* (26 April): At Nicosia (abdication of Henry II)
	1306 (6 June): Summons to Poitiers by Clement V

Historical context	Jacques de Molay
1306 (July): Expulsion of the Jews from the kingdom of France	*1306* (before 20 October): Leaves Cyprus
	1306 (November or December): Arrives in France
	1307 (after 15 May): At Poitiers
	1307 (24 June): General Chapter in Paris
1307 (7 July): Death of King Edward I of England	
1307 (24 August): The pope announces an inquiry into the Temple	*1307* (11 September): At Poitiers (appoints E. de Lenda to Aragon)
1307 (14 September): (Secret) order to arrest the Templars	*1307* (12 October): Funeral of Catherine of Valois in Paris
1307 (13 October): Arrest of the Templars in France	*1307* (13 October): Arrested in Paris
1307 (19 October): Start of the interrogations of the Templars in Paris	*1307* (24 October): First interrogation
	1307 (25 October): Public admission. Letter to the Templars
1307 (27 October): Letter from Clement V to Philip the Fair disapproving the arrest of the Templars	
1307 (22 November): Bull *Pastoralis praeminentiae* ordering the arrest of the Templars throughout Christendom	
1308 (February): Clement V removes the inquisitors from the inquiry into the Templars	*1307* (after 27 December): Retraction before two cardinals representing the pope
1308 (5–15 May): Estates general of Tours	
1308 (6 May): Order to arrest the Templars of Cyprus	
1308 (1 June): The Templars of Cyprus go to Limassol	
1308 (26 May): Meeting of Philip the Fair and Clement V at Poitiers	
1308 (12 August): Start of publication of the Bulls *Faciens misericordiam*	
1308 (17–21 August): Interrogation of the dignitaries of the Temple at Chinon	*1308* (20 August): Questioned by cardinals at Chinon. Returns to his admissions
1309 (8 August): Beginning of the work of the papal commission of Paris	
	1309 (26 November): First interrogation before the papal commission
	1309 (28 November): Second interrogation
1310 (28 March): Gathering of the Templars who wish to defend the Order in the gardens of the bishopric	*1310* (2 March): Third appearance

Historical context   *Jacques de Molay*

1310 (6–31 May): Interrogation of the
Cypriot Templars

1310 (12 May): Burning at the stake of fifty-
four Templars in Paris

1311 (5 June): End of the papal commission's
inquiries in Paris

1311 (16 October): Opening of the Council
of Vienne

1312 (20 March): Philip the Fair arrives at
Vienne

1312 (22 March): Bull *Vox in excelso*.
Abolition of the Order of the Temple

1312 (3 April): Publication of the Bull in full
council

1312 (2 May): Bull *Ad providam*, granting the
Temple's possessions to the Order of the
Hospital

1313 (April): Death of Guillaume de Nogaret

1313 (22 December): Clement V appoints
three cardinals to try Jacques de Molay
and the dignitaries

1314 (20 April): Death of Clement V   *1314* (18 March): Burnt at the stake

1314 (29 November): Death of Philip the Fair

1315 (30 April): Execution of Enguerrand de
Marigny

BIBLIOGRAPHY

Manuscript sources

ACA, Archives of the Crown of Aragon, Barcelona

– Fonds Cancelleria, reign of James II

– First series: Pergamines, carpetas nos. 129 to 174

– Second series: Registers, 81–2, 98, 189–190, 252

– Third series: Cartas reales diplomaticas (CRD): cajas 1 to 28; Apendice general 128–9; Templarios 137–42

PRO, Public Records Office, London

– Close rolls

Printed sources

Actes de les primeers jornades sobre els ordes religioso militars als Països Catalans (Segles XII–XIX), (Monblanc, November 1985), Tarragona, Diputacion de Tarragona, 1994.

Acri 1291. La fine della presenza degli Ordini Militari in Terra santa e i nuovi Orientamenti nel XIV secolo, ed. E. Coli, M. de Marco, F. Tommasi, Perugia, Quattroemme, 1996.

ALBERIGO, G., ed., *Les Conciles oecuméniques*, 2 *Les décrets*, t. 1: *De Nicée à Latran V*, Paris, Éditions du Cerf, 1994 (translated from the Italian edition, Bologna, 1972).

BALUZE, E., *Vitae paparum Avenionensium*, 4 vols., ed. revised by G. Mollat, Paris, 1913–22.

BARTHÉLEMY, E. de, ed., 'L'obituaire de la commanderie du Temple de Reims', in *Collection des documents inédits sur l'Histoire de France. Mélanges historiques et choix de documents*, 5 vols., Paris, Imprimerie nationale, 1882, fourth tome, pp. 305–32.

BLANCARD, L., 'Documents relatifs au procès des Templiers en Angleterre', *Revue de sociétés savants des départements*, 4th series, t. VI (1867).

Calendar of Close Rolls (Edward I), 3 vols. (1288–96; 1296–1302; 1302–7), London, 1904.

Calendar of Patent Rolls (Edward I), 3 vols. (1290–92; 1292–1301; 1301–7), London, 1895–8.

CERRINI, S., *Une expérience neuve au sein de la spiritualité médiévale: l'ordre du Temple (1120–1307)*. 'Étude et édition des règles latines et françaises,' typed thesis, 2 vols., Paris, Université Paris–IV, Paris, Sorbonne, 1998 (Brepols, 2002).

CHAGNY-SEVE, A.-M. and SEVE, R., *Le Procès des templiers d'Auvergne, 1309–1311. Édition de l'interrogatoire de juin 1309*, Paris, CTHS, 1986.

COSTE, J., *Boniface VIII en procès. Actes d'accusation et dépositions des témoins (1301–1311)*, critical edition, introduction and notes, Rome, l'Erma, 1995.

Cronaca del Templare di Tiro (1243–1314), ed. and Italian trans. L. Minervini, Naples, Liguorini, 2000.

Cronica de G. Villani, Collezione di storici e cronisti italiani, t. II, Florence, 1845 (reprinted Unveränderter Nachdruck, Frankfurt, 1969).

Chroniques d'Amadi et de Strambaldi, ed. L. de Mas-Latrie, Collection des documents inédits sur l'Histoire de France, 2 vols., Paris, 1891–3.

Chronique de l'île de Chypre par Florio Bustron, ed. L. de Mas-Latrie, Collection des documents inédits sur l'Histoire de France. Mélanges historiques et choix de documents, vol. 5, Paris, 1886, pp. 1–531.

Chronicle of the Templar of Tyre, see G. Raynaud, *Les Gestes des Chiprois*.

Chronique latine de Guillaume de Nangis de 1113 à 1300 avec les continuations de cette chronique de 1300 à 1368, ed. H. Geraud, 2 vols., Paris, Société de l'histoire de France, 1843.

Chronique métrique attribuée à Geoffroi de Paris, 1312–1316, ed. A. Diverres, Paris, 1950.

CURZON, H. de, ed., *La Règle du Temple*, Paris, Société de l'histoire de France, 1886.

DAILLIEZ, L., *Règle et statuts de l'ordre du Temple*, 2nd edn. Presented by J.-P. Lombard, Paris, Dervy, 1996.

DELAVILLE LE ROULX, J., *Cartulaire général de l'ordre des hospitaliers de Saint-Jean de Jérusalem (1100–1310)*, 4 vols., Paris, 1894–1906.

DESIMONI, C., 'Actes génois passés à Famagouste', *Archives de l'Orient latin*, t. I (1894).

Estoirre de Éraclès Empereur (L'), RHC, Hist. Occ., t. II, Paris, 1859.

FINKE, H., *Acta Aragonensia. Quellen zur deutschen, italienischen, französischen, spanischen, zur Kirchen und Kulturgeschichte aus der diplomatischen Korrespondenz Jaymes II (1291–1327)*, 3 vols., Berlin, 1908–22.

FINKE, H., *Papsttum und Untergang des Templerordens*, 2 vols., Munster, 1907.

FINKE, H., 'Nachträge und Ergänzungen zu den Acta aragonensia (I–III)', *Spanische Forschungen des Görresgesellschafte. Gesammelte Aufsätze zur Kulturgeschichte Spanien*, 4 band, Münster, 1933.

GABRIELI, F., *Chroniques arabes des croisades*, Paris, Sindbad, 1977.

GILMOUR-BRYSON, A., *The Trial of the Templars in Cyprus. A Complete English Edition*, Leiden, Brill, 1998.

— *The Trial of the Templars in the Papal State and in Abruzzi*, Città del Vaticano, Biblioteca apostolica vaticana, 1982.

Les Grandes Chroniques de France, ed. J. Viard, 10 tomes, Paris, 1932, t. VII and VIII.

GUIZOT, F., *Collection des mémoires relatifs à l'Histoire de France*, 30 vols., Paris, JLJ Brière, 1823–35, t. XIII, *Chronique de Guillaume de Nangis*, 1825.

HAYTON OF CORYCOS, 'Flor des estoires de la Terre d'Orient', RHC, Doc. Arméniens, t. II, Paris, 1906, pp. 111–254 (French version) and 255–362 (Latin version).

IBN TAMIYYA, *Lettre à un roi croisé (al-Risâlat al-Qubrusiyya)*, trans. from Arabic, introduction and notes by Jean R. Michot, Louvain-la-Neuve, Bruylant-Academia et Lyon, Tawhid, 1995.

JOINVILLE, J. de, *Vie de Saint Louis*, ed. J. Monfrin, Paris, Garnier, 1995.

KING, E. J., *The Rules, Statutes and Customs of the Hospitallers, 1099–1310*, London, Methuen, 1934.

KOHLER, C. and LANGLOIS, C.-V., 'Lettres inédites concernant les croisades (1275–1307)', BEC, 52 (1891).

LIZERAND, G., *Le Dossier de l'affaire des Templiers*, Paris, 1963. This is a reissue of a work that came out in 1923 and includes the Latin texts and their translation. An edition of the French text only has been recently published (Paris, Axiome, 1999). No reference is made to the original edition, or to the dates of publication; the author, G. Lizerand, is presented as if he were a living writer. This type of practice is reprehensible.

MICHELET, J., *Le Procès des templiers*, 2 vols., Paris, 1841–51, reissue Paris, CTHS, 1987.

Notai genovesi in Oltremare. Atti rogati a Cipro da Lamberto da Sambuceto (11 ottobre 1296–23 giugno 1299), ed. Michel Balard, Genoa, 1983.

— *Ibid. (1300–1301)*, ed. Valeria Polonio, Genoa, 1982.

— *Ibid. (January–August 1302)*, ed. Romeo Pavoni, Genoa, 1981.

PERRAT, C. and LONGNON, A., *Actes relatifs à la principauté de Morée*, Collection des documents inédits de l'Histoire de France, series in 8°, Paris, Bibliothèque nationale, 1967.

RAYNAUD, G., ed., *Les Gestes des Chiprois*, Geneva, 1887. Comprises three chronicles, including that of the Templar of Tyre.

Regestum Clementis papae V ex Vatecanis archetypis, editio, cura et studio monachorum ordinis sancti Benedicti, 9 vols., Rome, 1885–92.

Les Registres de Benoît XI, ed. C. Grandjean, Paris, 1883–1905.

Les Registres de Boniface VIII (1294–1303), ed. G. Digard, A. Thomas and R. Fawtier, 4 vols., Paris, 1884–1939.

Les Registres de Clément IV, ed. E. Jordan, Paris, 1893–1945.

Les Registres de Grégoire X (1272–1276), ed. J. Guiraud and L. Cadier, Paris, 1892–1960.

Les Registres de Honorius IV (1285–1287), ed. M. Prou, Paris, 1886–8.

Les Registres de Nicolas III (1277–1280), ed. M.-J. Gay, Paris, 1898–1938.

Les Registres de Nicolas IV (1288–1292), ed. E. Langlois, 2 vols. Paris, 1887–93.

Les Registres d'Urbain IV (1261–1264), ed. J. Guiraud and S. Clémencet, 4 vols., Paris, 1899–1958.

RÖHRICHT, R., *Regesta Regni Hierosolymitani (MXCVII–MCCXCI)*, 2 vols., Innsbrück, 1893–1904.

SCHOTTMULLER, K., *Der Untergang des Templer-Ordens*, 2 vols., Berlin, 1887.

Modern writing on the Templars

BALARD, M., *Croisade et Orient latin, XIe–XIVe siècle*, Paris, A. Colin, 2001.

BALASSE, C., *La Chute de l'ordre du temple dans l'historiographie de la fin du Moyen Âge (Début du XIVe siècle – Fin du XVe siècle)*, polygraphed dissertation given before the Université de Paris-7 Denis Diderot, 2 tomes, 1995.

BARBER, M., *The New Knighthood. A History of the Order of the Temple*, Cambridge, Cambridge University Press, 1994.

— *The Trial of the Templars*, Cambridge, Cambridge University Press, 1978.

— 'James of Molay, the Last Grand Master of the Order of the Temple', *Studia Monastica* (Barcelona), 14 (1972), pp. 91–124.

BECK, A., *Der Untergang der Templer*, Fribourg, Herder, 1992.

BESSON, E., 'Étude sur Jacques de Molay', *Mémoires de la Société d'émulation du Doubs*, 1876.

BOASE, T. S. R., *The Cilician Kingdom of Armenia*, Edinburgh, Scottish Academic Press, 1978.

BORDONOVE, G., *La Tragédie des templiers*, Paris, Pygmalion-Gérard Watelet, 1993.

BOUTARIC, E., 'Clément V, Philippe le Bel et les Templiers', *Revue des questions historiques*, t. X and XI (1871–2).

BRAMATO, F., *Storia dell'ordine dei Templari in Italia*, t. I, *Le Fondazioni*, Rome, 1991; t. II, *Le Fonti*, Rome, Atanòr, 1994.

BULST-THIELE, M.-L., *Sacrae Domus Militia templi Hierosolymitani Magistri: Untersuchungen zur Geschichte des Templerordens, 1118/9–1314*, Göttingen, Vandenhoeck und Ruprecht, 1974.

CARRER Y CANDY, F., 'Entences y Templers en les Montanyes de Prades (1279 a 1300)', Bolletìn de la Real Academia de las Bellas Lettras de Barcelona, II (1903–4), pp. 209–50.

CLAVERIE, P.-V., 'L'ordre du Temple au Coeur d'une crise politique des années 1279–1285: la *querella Cypri*', *Le Moyen Âge*, t. 104, 1998, pp. 495–511.

La Commanderie. Institution des ordres militaires dans l'Occident médiéval. First international symposium of the Conservatoire Larzac Templier et Hospitalier (October 2000), Paris, CTHS, 2002.

COUREAS, N., *The Latin Church in Cyprus, 1195–1312*, Aldershot, Ashgate, 1997.

Croisades et pèlerinages. Récits, chroniques et voyages en Terre sainte, X^e–XVe siècles, ed. D. Régnier-Bohler, Paris, R. Laffont, 'Coll. Bouquins', 1997.

DAILLIEZ, L., *Jacques de Molay, dernier grand maître du Temple*, Paris, R. Dumas, 1974.

DELAVILLE LE ROULX, J., *Les Hospitaliers en Terre sainte et à Chypre (1100–1310)*, Paris, E. Leroux, 1904.

— *La France en Orient. Les expéditions du maréchal Boucicaut*, t. I (the only one), Paris, 1885.

— 'La suppression des templiers', *Revue des questions historiques*, no. 98, 1890.

DEMURGER, A., *Chevaliers du Christ. Les ordres religieux-militaires au Moyen Âge (XIe–XVIe siècle)*, Paris, Seuil, 2002.

— *Vie et mort de l'ordre du Temple*, Paris, Senil, 1989.

— 'Jacques de Molay', *Dictionnaire d'histoire et de géographie ecclésiastique*, Paris, Letousey, t. XXVI.

— 'Les ordres militaires et la croisade au début du XIVe siècle. Quelques remarques sur les traits de croisade de Jacques de Molay et Foulques de Villaret', *Dei Gesta per Francos (Mélanges Jean Richard)*, Aldershot, Ashgate, 2001.

DUGUEYT, P., 'Essai sur Jacques de Molay', *Positions des théses de l'École des Chartes*, Paris, 1906, pp. 81–2.

DUPUY, P., *Traitez concernant l'histoire de France, à savoir la condamnation des templiers*, Paris, 1685.

EDBURY, P., *The Kingdom of Cyprus and the Crusades (1191–1374)*, Cambridge, Cambridge University Press, 1991.

— 'The Templars in Cyprus', in *The Military Orders I: Fighting for the Faith and Caring for the Sick*, ed. H. Barber, Aldershot, Ashgate, 1994.

FAVIER, J. *Philippe le Bel*, Paris, Fayard, 1999.

FAVREAU-LILLIE, M.-L., 'The Military Orders and the Escape of the Christian Population from the Holy Land in 1291', *Journal of Medieval History*, 19 (1993), pp. 201–27.

FOREY, A.-J., *The Templars in the Corona de Aragon*, London, Oxford University Press, 1973.

— *The Military Orders. From the Twelfth to the Early Fourteenth Centuries*, London, Macmillan, 1991.

— *Military Orders and Crusades*, Aldershot, Variorum, 1994.

— *The Fall of the Templars in the Crown of Aragon*, Aldershot, Ashgate, 2001.

— 'Letters of the last Two Templar Masters', *Nottingham Medieval Studies*, XLV (2002), pp. 145–71.

FRALE, B., *L'ultima battaglia dei Templari*, Rome, Viella, 2001.

FRIED, J., 'Wille, Freiwilligkeit und Geständnis um 1300. Zur Beurteilung des letzten Templergrossmeisters Johann de Molay', *Historisches Jahrbuch*, 1985, pp. 388–425.

FUNCK-BRUNTANO, F., 'Philippe le Bel et la noblesse comtoise', *BEC*, no. 49 (1888), pp. 136.

Die geistlichen Ritterorden Europas, ed. J. Fleckenstein and M. Hellmann, 'Vorträge und Forschungen', no. 26, Sigmaringen, J. Thorbeke, 1980.

HEFELE, C.-J., *Histoire des conciles*. New French Translation, H. Leclercq, t. VI, 1st and 2nd part, Hildesheim–New York, Georg Olms Verlag, 1973 (reprint).

HILL, G., *A History of Cyprus*, 4 vols., Cambridge, Cambridge University Press, 1948 (tome 2 concerns our period).

HILLGARTH, J. N., *Ramon Lull and Lullism in Fourteenth-century France*, Oxford, Clarendon Press, 1971.

A History of the Crusades, general ed. Kenneth M. Setton, vol. 2, *The Later Crusades, 1189–1311*, eds. R. L. Wolff and H. W. Hazard, Madison, University of Wisconsin Press, 1969.

HOLT, P. M., *Early Mamluk Diplomacy (1260–1290). Treaties of Baybars and Kalâwûn with Christian Rulers*, Leiden, 1995.

HOUSLEY, N., *The Later Crusades from Lyons to Alcaẓar, 1274–1580*, Oxford, Oxford University Press, 1992.

— *The Avignon Papacy and the Crusades, 1305–1378*, Oxford, Oxford University Press, 1986.

JORDAN, W. C., *Louis IX and the Challenge of the Crusade. A Study in Rulership*, Princeton, Princeton University Press, 1979.

KAEUPER, R. W., *War, Justice and Public Order. England and France in the Later Middle Ages*, Oxford, Clarendon Press, 1988.

KEDAR, B., *Crusade and Mission. European Approaches towards the Muslims*, Princeton, Princeton University Press, 1984.

KERVYN DE LETTENHOVE, 'Deux lettres inédites de Jacques de Molay', *Bulletin de l'Académie royale des sciences, des lettres et des beaux-arts de Belgique*, 43rd year, 2nd series, 38 (1874).

KOHLER, C., 'Deux projets de croisade en Terre sainte composés à la fin du XIIIe siècle et au début du XIVe', *Revue de l'Orient latin*, no. 11(1905–1908), pp. 406–57.

LANGLOIS, C.-V., 'L'affaire des Templiers', *Journal des Savants*, 1908, pp. 417–35.

— 'Le procès des templiers', *Revue des Deux mondes*, t. 103, 1891.

LECLER, J., *Vienne (1312). Histoire des Conciles oecuméniques*, ed. G. Dumeige, t. 8, Paris, Éditions de l'Orante, 1964.

LE GOFF, J., *Saint Louis*, Paris, Gallimard, 1996.

LE GRAND, M., *Le Chapitre cathédral de Langres de la fin du XIIe au concordat de 1516*, Paris, Letouzey et Ané 1931.

LEOPOLD, A., *How to Recover the Holy Land. Proposals of the Late Thirteenth and Early Fourteenth Centuries*, Aldershot, Ashgate, 2001.

LEROY, S., 'Jacques de Molay et les templiers franc-comtois d'après les actes du procès', *Bulletin de la Société grayloise d'émulation*, 3 (1900).

LITTLE, D. P., 'The fall of Acre in 690/1291. The Muslim Version', *Studies in Islamic History and Civilization in Honour of Professor David Ayalon*, ed. M. Sharon, Jerusalem-Leiden, J. Brill, 1986.

LIZERAND, G., 'Les dépositions du grand maître Jacques de Molay au procès des templiers (1307–1314)', *Le Moyen Âge*, no. 26, 1913.

— *Clément V et Philippe le Bel*, Paris, 1910.

LUTTRELL, A., 'The Hospitallers and the Papacy, 1305–1314', in *Forschungen zur Reichs-, Papst- und Landesgeschichte (Mélanges Peter Herde)*, ed. K. Borchardt and E Bünz, Stuttgart, A. Hiersemann, 1998.

MARSHALL, C., *Warfare in the Latin East, 1192–1291*, Cambridge, Cambridge University Press, 1992.

MAS-LATRIE, L. de, *Histoire de l'île de Chypre sous les règnes des princes de la maison des Lusignan*, 3 vols., Paris, 1852–61.

La Méditerranée au temps de Saint Louis, Records of the symposium at Aigues-Mortes (April 1997), ed. Gérard Dédéyan and Jacques Le Goff, Éditions du SIVOM de la région d'Aigues-Mortes, 1998.

MELVILLE, M., *La vie des templiers*, Paris, Gallimard, 1951 (reissued 1974).

MENACHE, S., *Clement V*, Cambridge, Cambridge University Press, 1998.

The Military Orders I. Fighting for the Faith and Caring for the Sick, ed. M. Barber, Aldershot, Ashgate, 1994. *The Military Orders II. Welfare and Warfare*, ed. H. Nicholson, Aldershot, Ashgate, 1998.

Militia Sacra, Gli Ordini Militari tra Europa e Terra santa, ed. E. Coli, M. de Marco, F. Tommasi, ed. San Bevignate, Perugia, 1994.

MUTAFIAN, C., *La Cilicie au carrefour des empires*, 2 tomes, Paris, Les Belles Lettres, 1988.

— 'Héthoum de Korykos historien arménien. Un prince cosmopolite à l'aube du XIVe siècle', *Cahiers de recherches médiévales*, 1 (1996), pp. 157–76.

NICHOLSON, H., *Templars, Hospitallers and Teutonic Knights. Images of the Military Orders, 1128–1291*, London, Leicester University Press, 1991.

PALOU, S. G., *Ramon Llull y el Islam*, Palma de Mallorca, 1981.

PARTNER, P., *The Murdered Magicians. The Templars and their Myth*, Oxford, Oxford University Press, 1982.

PRAWER, J., *Histoire du royaume latin de Jérusalem*, 2 vols., Paris, Éd. du CNRS, 1969–70.

PRYOR, J. H., 'The Naval Battles of Roger of Lauria', *Journal of Medieval History*, 9 (1983), pp. 179–216.

— '*In Subsidium Terrae Sanctae*. Exports of Foodstuffs and War Materials from the Kingdom of Sicily to the Kingdom of Jerusalem, 1265–1284', *The Medieval Levant. Studies in Memory of Eliyahu Ashtor (1914–1984)*, Asian and African Studies, 22 (1988), pp. 127–46.

RAYNOUARD, J. M. F., *Monumens historiques relatifs à la condamnation des chevaliers du Temple et à l'abolition de leur ordre*, Paris, 1813.

— *Les Templiers*, tragedy in five acts, Paris, 1805. Reprinted, Nîmes, ed. C. Lacour, 1997.

REY, M., 'L'ordre du Temple en Franche-Comté, d'après les documents écrits', *Académie des sciences, belles-lettres et arts de Besançon. Procès-Verbaux et Mémoires*, t. 180 (1972–3), pp. 93–120.

RICHARD, J., *Saint Louis*, Paris, Fayard, 1983.

— *Histoire des croisades*, Paris, Fayard, 1996.

— *Histoire du royaume latin de Jérusalem*, Paris, 1953.

RILEY-SMITH, J., *The Crusades: A Short History*, London, Athlone, 1987.

— *The Atlas of the Crusades*, London, Times Books, 1981.

— *The Knights of Saint John in Jerusalem and Cyprus*, c. *1050–1310*, London. Macmillan, 1967.

ROUSSEL, Curé de Vieux Bois, 'Les templiers du diocèse de Langres à l'époque de leur suppression', *Revue de Champagne et de Brie*, 16 (1883) and 17 (1884).

ROUX, J.-P., *Histoire de l'empire mongol*, Paris, 1994.

Les Salles des croisades du château de Versailles, ed. Claire Constans and Philippe Lamarque; introduction historique par Jean Richard, Doussard (74), Édition du Gui, 2002.

SANS I TRAVÉ, J. M., *Els Templers Catalans*, Barcelona, Pagès editors, 1996.

— *El procès dels Templers Catalans*, Lerida, Pagès editors, 1991.

SCHEIN, S., *'Fideles crucis': The Papacy, the West and the Recovery of the Holy Land, 1274–1314*, Oxford, Clarendon Press, 1991.

— 'Gesta Dei per Mongolos. 1300. The Genesis of a Non-Event', *English Historical Review*, no. 94 (1979).

SCHWARZ, W., 'Die Schuld des Jakob von Molay, des letzten Grossmeisters des Templer', *Welt als Geschichte*, 17 (1957), pp. 259–79.

STRAYER, J. R., *The Reign of Philip the Fair*, Princeton, Princeton University Press, 1980.

Les Templiers en pays catalans, Perpignan, Editorial El Trabucaire, 1998.

I Templari. Mito e Storia, Atti del Convegno internazionale di Studi alla maggione templare di Poggibonsi-Siena, May 1987, ed. G. Minucci and F. Sardi, Sinalunga-Siena, Casa editrice A. G. Viti, 1989.

THIER, L., *Kreuzzugsbemühungen unter Papst Clement V*, Düsseldorf, Dietrich Coelde Verlag, 1973.

THOMASSIN, V., *Figures comtoises; Jacques de Molay*, Paris, 1912.

TRUDON DES ORMES, A., *Liste des maisons et de quelques dignitaires de l'ordre du Temple en Syrie, en Chypre et en France d'après les pièces du procès*, Paris, 1900.

TRUNZ, A., *Zur Geschichte des letzten Templermeister*, Fribourg, Buchdruckereï Aug. Feyel, 1919.

VIOLLET, P., 'Les interrogatoires de Jacques de Molay, grand maître du Temple. Conjectures', *Mémoires de l'Académie des inscriptions et belles lettres*, t. XXXVIII, 1909.

WILDERMANN, A. K., *Beuteilung des Templerprozesses bis zum 17. Jahrhundert*, Fribourg (Switzerland), Universitätsverlag, 1972. The final chapter makes a rapid synthesis of the historiography of the trial up to the twentieth century.

INDEX

A

Abagha 45
Acre 13, 53, 55–9
Aigues-Mortes 10–11
Amaury de la Roche 4, 25
Amaury of Tyre 101, 114, 116
Aragon 63, 74, 83–4, 90–91
Armenia 75–8, 95–7
Arnau de Banyuls 134
Arnaud d'Auch 195
Ashraf Khalil, al- 49, 53, 57
Aycelin, Pierre 171
Aymon d'Oiselay 26, 71, 115–16, 122, 131, 152

B

Baldwin II 8
Bartholomé de Chinsi 131
Bartholomé de Quincy 107
Baudouin de la Andrin 74
Baybars 29, 31, 32, 43, 44
Beaujeu, Guillaume de: second Council of Lyon 19; Master 27–8, 33, 36, 39, 65; prisoner 30; genealogy 37–8; policy 40–44, 46, 47, 48, 49; career 51, 69; Acre 55; death 56, 59

Beaune 23
Bérard, Thomas 33, 34–6, 65, 69
Berenguer de Cardona: ill 78; Chapters 83, 84; Ruad 104; Cyprus 121, 122–3, 132, 134, 149; and JM 132, 134, 136–7, 213; Crete 152; remains Master of Aragon 168
Berenguer de Olmos 133, 134
Berenguer de Saint-Just 74, 130
Bernard de Roche 132
Bertran l'Aleman 74
Bertrand de Gordo 131
Blanc, Humbert 138
Bohemond VII 42, 43
Boniface VIII 80, 87, 91–2, 112–13, 146, 159
Brian de Jay 88, 136
Burgundy 4

C

Capetians 201
Castillon, Pierre de 134–5
Celestine V 80
charitable works 89–90
Charles I of Anjou 40–41, 47
Charles II of Naples 146

Charles II of Sicily 84, 86, 90

Clement V: memoranda to 144, 150; intends Templars inquiry 170–71, 173; orders arrest of Templars 175, 176; dissolves Templars 179, 194; and Court of France 191; individual trials of dignitaries 193, 195

coastal fortresses, military Orders 13

Constantine 96

Council of Lyon, second 39

crusades 2, 85, 140–44, 216–17

crusading treatises 140–44

Cyprus 11, 63, 111–38

D

Dalmau de Timor 130

Damietta 11

Dauphin, Guy 51

Dei, Noffo 156

diocesan commissions 176, 177, 183, 193

Dominique de Dijon 24

E

Edward, Prince 32

Edward I 14, 27, 135–6

Egypt 11–12

Eudes de Châteauroux 9, 10

Exemen de Lenda 130, 132, 133

F

Fernandez, Jean 92

fleets 109, see also ships

Foulques de Villaret: Rhodes 115, 217; memorandum on crusades 139, 140, 142, 144; special crossing (crusades) 144; union of military Orders 148; summoned by Pope 149, 152

France 137–8

Franks: Damietta 11; and Mamluks 14, 30, 31, 46, 48; and Mongols 15, 29, 30, 33; Acre 59

Frederick II 6, 7, 9–10, 40

'French regiment' 13–14

G

Gaucher de Liencourt 74

Gaudin, Guillaume 61

Gaudin, Thibaud: prisoner 30; career 51, 66, 69; Acre 57, 59; Master 60–61; letters 62–3, 122; death 64, 72

general crossing (crusades) 140, 142

Geoffroy de Charney 131, 138, 179, 194, 198

Geoffroy de Gonneville 113, 138, 179, 186, 194

Geoffroy de Sergines 13

Gérard de Causse 172

Gérard de Villiers 108, 137, 175

Gérard du Passage 124

Ghâzân: Mongol alliance 95; requests help 97, 98; diplomacy 99–100, 102, 106; leaves Tabriz 101; death 109

Gilles, Brother 17

Golden Horde 14, 45

Grandson, Otton de see Otton de Grandson

Gregory X 39

Guamir, Berenguer 122, 123
Guillaume de Barroer 127
Guillaume de Beaujeu *see* Beaujeu,
    Guillaume de
Guillaume de Gy 3
Guillaume de la Tour 74, 75, 76
Guillaume de Malay 26
Guillaume de Nogaret: intervenes at
    commission 27, 184, 185; inquiries
    into Templars 157; and Boniface
    VIII 158, 159; Poitiers 163, 176
Guillaume de Plaisians 163, 176, 184,
    189
Guillaume de Sonnac *see* Sonnac,
    Guillaume de
Guillaume de Villaret 101, 103
Guy de Forest 79, 84, 88, 136
Guy de Gibelet 42–3
Guy d'Ibelin 98, 102, 117

H

Hayton of Corycos 77, 97, 141
Henry II: Acre 36–7, 48, 55;
    Jerusalem 47; raids on Egypt 100;
    epilepsy 111; refugees 112; taxes
    113; and Amaury of Tyre 114
Henry III 5
Hethum II 75, 76, 95–6, 97, 102
Holy Land 85, 95, 141
Homs, second battle of 97
Hospitallers: founded 20; rivalry
    with Templars 34; and Peter III
    83; Chapters 88, 103; charitable
    works 89, 124; Armenia 97; Ruad
    102; Cyprus 112, 113, 114, 115,
    116; pilgrims 124; maritime policy

126; crusade plan 144; Templars
    dissolved 179, 194, 221
Hugh III 41, 43
Hugues de Faur 66–7, 72
Hugues de Jouy IX 17, 18
Hugues de Pairaud *see* Pairaud,
    Hugues de
Hugues de Payns 20
Hugues d'Empurias 107
Hûlâgû 14–15, 30
Humbert de Pairaud *see* Pairaud,
    Humbert de

I

Ilkhan 14, 30, 32, 44–5
Innocent IV 6, 9, 14
Isol the Pisan 100

J

Jacques de Doumanin 80, 115
Jacques de la Rochelle 3, 26
Jacques de Molay *see* Molay, Jacques
    de
James II 74, 80, 87
Jean de Châlons 71
Jean de Gibelet 98, 102
Jean de Grailly 55, 56
Jean de Longwy 3
Jean de Vila 51
Jean de Villiers 55, 56, 58, 59
Jean du Tour 160–62, 165, 186
Jerusalem 7, 13, 41, 47, 48, 203–4

K

Kalâwûn 43, 45, 46, 47, 48, 49, 53
Khwarezmians 7

Kiptchak *see* Golden Horde

Knighthood of the Poor Knights of Christ of the Temple of Solomon *see* Templars

Knights Templar *see* Templars

L

La Forbie, battle 7

Le Lorgne, Nicolas 42

Levon 96

Levon II 46

Louis IX: first crusade 2, 11–13; prepares for crusade 5–6, 9–11; reasons for crusade 7–9; and Mamluks 12, 13; Mongol policy 14–15; and military Orders 15; and Templars 15–18; death 32

Lull, Ramon 124–5, 141, 146

M

Mamluks: and Louis IX 12, 13; and Franks 14, 30, 31, 46, 48; attacks on Latin States 29; and Mongols 29; and Templars 43–5; Acre 55, 57; Tyre 60; Armenia 75, 95, 96, 97; Ruad 107

Marseilles 24, 154

Mathieu de Clermont 57

military Orders: coastal fortresses 13; defence of Latin States 15; history 20; differences between 34–5; rivalry 34, 144; union of 39, 90, 144–8; ships 58; policy 70, 85; trade 86–7; image 91; Cyprus 112–13; charitable works 124; pilgrims 124; Masters summoned

by Pope 139, *see also specific orders*

military-religious Orders *see* military Orders

Molay 2–3

Molay, Jacques de: birth 1–4; enters Templars 4, 23–6; and Louis IX 4; Louis IX's crusade 18; testimonies 27–8, 50–52, 180–82, 183–5; arrives in East 28–9; career 51, 66; appointed Master 63–72; policy 73, 82–4, 85–8, 92, 135; journeys to West 78–82, 85–6, 131–2; England 79–80, 84; France 80–81, 158, 160, 164, 169; Italy 80, 85; merging Orders 90; diplomacy 91–2, 135–7; delegation 93, 131, 152; Armenia 98; Jerusalem legend 99; raids on Egypt 100; Ruad 101, 109–10; Cyprus 111, 115; governing method 119, 125, 128–31, 132–5, 214; entourage 126–7; summoned by Pope 139, 149; memorandum on crusades 140, 142–4, 150, 151; memorandum on union 146, 147–8, 150; union of military Orders 146, 147–8, 150, 220; leaves Cyprus for France 152; learns of rumours concerning Templars 155; and Jean du Tour 160–62; requests inquiry 170; admissions 175, 179; arrested 179; interrogated 180–82, 183–5; retracted confessions 181; attitude during interrogations 186–92; trial 194, 195–6; burnt at stake

197–8; legends 201–4; summary
of his life 206–10; character 211,
222; relations with rulers 212;
relations within Templars 212–13;
fails to reform Templars 218
Mongols: alliance 14–15, 109, 217;
and Franks 15, 29, 30, 33; and
Mamluks 29, 32, 44–6; Armenia
95, 97; horsemen 99
Mûlay 99

N
national theatre 202–3
Nicholas IV 75, 86, 145, 146
Nicolas de Fréauville 195
Novelli, Arnaud 195

O
Order of Christ 194, 221
Order of Montesa 194, 221
Order of the Hospital *see*
Hospitallers
Otton IV 71
Otton de Grandson: and Edward I
14; and JM 26; Acre 55, 56; career
70, 71, 82; Armenia 76, 77, 97, 98;
crusade plans 141

P
Pairaud, Hugues de: enters Templars
24; and JM 67, 93, 132, 166, 218;
career 68, 138, 168–9; and Raoul
de Gisy 156; summoned by Pope
159–60; admissions 175, 186;
silence 179; trial 194
Pairaud, Humbert de 4, 24, 25, 68

papal commissions 176, 177, 178, 179,
183–6, 193
Pelet, Bernard 156
Perez, Gile 133, 134
Persia *see* Ilkhan
Peter III 83
Philip the Fair: agent 70; policy 71;
uniting Orders 90; and Clement
V 163; orders arrest of Templars
173; accepts abolition of Templars
179; audiences 212
Philippe de Marigny 177–8, 186
Picard, Geoffroy 127
Pierre de Bologna 177, 215
Pierre de Castillon 167
Pierre de Saint-Just (Catalan
Templar) 63, 122, 133, 134, 213
Pierre de Saint-Just (Picardian
Templar) 81
Pierre de Sevry 57
Pierre de Torvone 89
pilgrimages, to Jerusalem 123
Poilechien, Eudes 47, 48
Pons de Manocampo 127
Ponsard de Gisy 156

R
Raimbaud de Caron 74, 131, 175, 179,
194
Raoul de Gisy 156
Raymond de Barberan 74
Redecoeur, Brother 48
Renaud de Provins 215
Renaud de Vichiers *see* Vichiers,
Renaud de
Revel, Hugues 34, 35

Robert de Turvill 40
Robert of Artois 12, 16, 17
Roger de Flor, Brother 58
Roger de Lauria 104
Roger de San Severino 41, 46, 47
Ruad 101–2, 103–10

S

Salih Ayyub 17
Sembat 96
Sequin de Floyran 156, 157
Serrand, Jean 62, 72
ships 58, 117–18, 119, *see also* fleets
Sicily 40–41, 159
Simon de Lende 74
Simon de Quincy 167
Sonnac, Guillaume de 17, 65, 69
special crossing (crusades) 140, 141, 144
Syria 30–33

T

Templar of Tyre 61, 63–4, 127
Templar Order *see* Templars
Templars: entry to 2, 25, 175, 178, 218; and Louis IX 15–18; history 20–23; organisation 20–23, 125–31; provinces 22–3; rivalry with Hospitallers 34; Chapters 35, 65, 83–4, 88–9, 92, 103; and Mamluks 43–5; testimonies 50; Aragon 63, 74, 83–4, 90–91; sale of property 64; elections to Master 65–70; policy 69–70, 73, 85; leadership 73–4; charitable works 89–90, 124; headquarters 90–91; image 91; reform of 93, 218; Armenia 97; Ruad 103–10; Cyprus 112–36; finances 117–19; ships 117–18, 119; pilgrims 124; maritime policy 125–6; officers 128–31; rumours about 155–7, 158; accusations against 158, 175; arrests 175; interrogations of 175, 182; dissolved 179, 194, 221; defended Order 192; view of JM 214–16

Teutonic Order 7, 20, 32, 70, 113, 146
Thoros 76, 95, 96
Tortosa, isle of *see* Ruad
torture 188
trade 86–7
Tripoli 42–3, 48
Tyre 60

V

Vichiers, Renaud de 17, 34, 50, 65, 69
Villaret, Foulques de *see* Foulques de Villaret

W

'War of Curzola' 75–6
William de la More 121, 136